Johann Jacob Löwenthal

The Chess Player's Magazine

Johann Jacob Löwenthal

The Chess Player's Magazine

ISBN/EAN: 9783337716011

Printed in Europe, USA, Canada, Australia, Japan

Cover: Foto ©Lupo / pixelio.de

More available books at **www.hansebooks.com**

THE

CHESS PLAYER'S

MAGAZINE.

EDITED BY

J. LOWENTHAL.

Vol. II. New Series.

LONDON:
ADAMS & FRANCIS, 59, FLEET STREET.
PARIS: JEAN PRETI, 72, RUE ST. SAUVEUR;
LEIPSIC: VEIT & CO.

1866.

THE Chess Player's Magazine.

REVIEW OF 1865.

THE close of the year imposes upon the Chess journalist the same duty which it brings to the writer of much higher pretensions. We have briefly to review what has been accomplished in the past season, both at home and abroad, to notice any new accessions to the literature of our game, and to consider our prospects for the ensuing year. We shall not need, however, to give more than a very succinct summary of the past, since all events of any consequence in the Chess world have been duly chronicled in our monthly columns.

The Metropolitan Chess Clubs have been well attended during the bygone twelvemonths, and have manifested on several occasions their unabated interest in the game. The two matches played by telegraph between the St. James's and Dublin Clubs excited much interest, and full particulars were given at the time in our pages. The St. George's and London Clubs continue to prosper, while that young and energetic society, the Blackheath Club, is unusually alert in the cause of Chess. In the provinces a tone of healthy activity is equally manifest, and, while the older institutions hold their ground, several new associations have been formed. Among these we may mention the Norfolk Chess Club, and the Mechanics' Institute Chess Class at Nottingham. Capt. H. A. Kennedy has rendered a real service to the cause by the establishment of a West of England Association in connexion with the clubs of Bristol and Bath, while the West Yorkshire Chess Association held a successful meeting at Bradford, in the month of May, under the presidency of Mr. Broughton. A match between

Dundee and Glasgow, a tournament at the Sheffield Athenæum Club, several friendly contests between Bath and Bristol, and a match between Liverpool and Manchester, may also be noted as indications that Chess meets with all due attention throughout the kingdom. The principal event of the year, however, was the Dublin Congress. We have so lately given a full account of that agreeable meeting that we will not here do more than express our approval of the sound judgment and good feeling with which it was conducted. If it had no other good effect than diffusing a knowledge of Chess in Ireland, and promoting a cordial good fellowship between English and Irish amateurs, it must be held to have fully answered the purpose for which it was designed.

Turning to the Continent, we find those excellent players, Anderssen and Paulsen, still in the field. The latter visited Berlin last winter, and contested a series of games with some of the best players of the Prussian capital. Of these he is said to have won thirty-nine, drawing six, and losing only three. This was certainly a remarkable feat, and he was almost equally successful in a brief match with Herr Neumann, of whom he won five games to two. The fine series of games played during the last few months between Anderssen and Neumann confers an especial value on the *Neue Berliner Schachzeitung*, and will give it permanent value as a repertory of Chess. In America the termination of the great civil war renders the prospects of Chess brighter than they have been for some years past, and we are glad to hear that Mr. Morphy seems disposed to re-enter Chess circles, and give fresh proofs of his unrivalled talent. Should he revisit Europe he will be warmly greeted by Chess players of every nation and all degrees of skill. A match is also in course of arrangement between the well-known English amateur, Mr. Mackenzie, and Mr. Perrin of New York. In Australia clubs have been started with success at Melbourne and Sydney.

No very remarkable accession to Chess literature has signalized the past year, always excepting the valuable work of Suhle and Neumann, *Die Neueste Theorie und Praxis des Schachspiels*, which has been elaborately reviewed in our pages. We take this opportunity, however, to notice a book, published in the previous year, which we omitted inadvertently in our review of 1864. It is entitled, *Bibliographie Anecdotique du Jeu des Echecs*. Par Jean Gay. Paris: chez l'editeur, Quai des Augustins, 41. The author gives us in alphabetical order a list of the chief writers on the royal game, ancient and modern, with a brief notice of their works. From Cesolis and Caxton to Dr. Duncan Forbes and Heydebrandt der Laza, most of the names connected with the bibliography of Chess may be found in this compendium, although its limits do not allow more than a short notice to any individual. The writer is evidently honest and impartial as well as industrious, and his book must have cost him many long hours of patient research among the dusty manuscripts of the Royal Library at Paris and the venerable folios of the British Museum. *Le Palamède Francais* is still continued, and a new French magazine, *Le Sphinx*, has appeared on the scene, edited by M. Journoud. Of the unfortunate decision of the problem tournament connected with *Le Palamède*, we will merely say that we have full confidence in the equity of the French character, and we continue to hope that the erroneous award of the committee will yet be reversed.

Germany, like France and England, is blessed with two monthly Chess periodicals. Of our valued contemporary, the *Neue Berliner Schachzeitung*, we have already spoken. Its rival, the *Berliner Schachzeitung*, is also a solid and well-written magazine, edited by Dr. Schmidt and Herr Minckwitz. The retirement, however, of so accomplished a Chess author as Herr Max Lange from the editorship, a few months since, was undoubtedly a serious loss. We are glad to hear that a selection of Anderssen's games, played in 1864-65, will shortly appear, edited and annotated by the indefatigable Herr Neumann. We must here notice a new work by that unwearied writer (*Leitfaden für anfänger im Schachspiel*. Berlin, 1865). It is an introduction to Chess for the use of beginners, arranged on the same plan as the more elaborate work of the same author and Dr. Suhle. Instead of the usual method, by which the openings are successively subjected to a theoretical analysis, the concrete is here substituted for the abstract, and the openings are taught by means of model games, illustrated with appropriate notes. This system has certainly the advantage of being easier and more attractive to the learner than that usually adopted, while in skilful hands it is, perhaps, equally instructive. The games here selected as examples are admirably well chosen, both as specimens of the various *debûts*, and for their intrinsic merit. The book includes a useful selection of end games.

The book of the New York Clipper Problem Tournay was

noticed in our October number. It contains some fine positions, and bears testimony to the ability of Americans in this branch of the art.

The prospects of Chess for the present year are, we think, highly encouraging. In all probability a meeting of the British Chess Association will be held in the course of next summer. No meeting of that important body has been held since 1862, and it is desirable for the interests of Chess that another year should not be suffered to pass away without its being convoked. If its next meeting be (as we hope and expect it will) as successful as the congress of 1862, there will be little more left for us to desiderate. In conclusion, we beg to return our best thanks to our subscribers for the support we have received, and to assure them that no pains will be wanting on our part to render the *Chess Player's Magazine* worthy of their continued approval.

THE NEW SCHEME OF TABULAR CHESS NOTATION.

To the Editor of the "Chess Players' Magazine."

Dublin, 18th December, 1865.

Dear Sir,—Referring to your notice in the October, 1865, number of this magazine of my suggested tabular method of treating the "Chess Openings," I now beg to transmit to you herewith a specimen—the "Evans' Gambit Refused "—illustrative of my scheme.

I must ask your readers not to expect *all* the variations to be in *very great detail*, as my plan professes to be but *a key*, so that, when a student finds by it the position of any variation, he can study it in *greater* detail in other works.

I have called attention in the annexed key to all the principal variations (many of which I have given to a pretty considerable length) that I could find in this magazine and the "Chess World Magazine" from their commencement, in "Staunton's Praxis," "Wormald's Chess Openings," "Lowenthal's Book of the Congress," "Lowenthal's Morphy's Games," "The Era," and Chess periodicals; and one advantage at least there will be in my plan, that many variations of this opening, which hitherto have been scattered throughout various works, papers, and magazines (some being found in one author which do not appear in another), are here for the most part collated together, and can be perused at a glance by the student—being spread out before him in one mass, over which his eye can run without having to turn over a single leaf, and from which mass he will be able almost instantaneously to see, by *direct* comparison of the variations (*they being all visible at the same time*), where they differ the one from the other.

I have given in all between thirty and forty variations in pretty fair detail (independently of those in the notes), and I venture to think there is no *single* English work extant which has so many variations of this opening collected together. I think that the student will, from this tabular plan, not only be able to see the position of any particular key move, the turning point of a variation, with but little trouble or research, but that the impressions left upon his memory will be more lasting than on the old methods of treating the openings.

Many variations being equally sound for adoption, but some strong players preferring one variation, and some another, I have here and there given the names of well-known players of skill, with the variations adopted by them, which will, I think, be of interest to students, who often are heard saying, "Oh! I wonder what Morphy would play here, or Staunton, or Lowenthal!"

In the annexed key the terms first and second player have been used in preference to the usual ones of White and Black, as the adoption of the latter terms has a tendency to make the learner open the game with the White men, thereby often leading him to prefer one colour to another, which should not be the case.

Treatises on the openings have now become so numerous, and the variations in the openings themselves so multitudinous, and treated in such detail by authors, that I think the Chess public will agree with me in saying that an abstract or key to all these analyses is much required by the majority of Chess players, but would be a boon to the young student in particular, who is now sorely puzzled in his efforts to master "the openings;" and I think the tabular form is the clearest, and, at the same time, the very simplest to adopt in the framing of such a key.

This very opening (the "Evans' Gambit Evaded") that I have selected for an example of my suggested tabular system is in itself a good instance to show in how great a degree the analysing of the openings has increased of late years, for, in "Staunton's Handbook," this opening is disposed of in six lines; but, in the "Praxis," subsequently published, it occupies nearly as many pages. Take also the "Evans' Accepted," and other openings, new variations in which are being discovered almost daily, rendering the number of them so great, that I venture to think a tabular form of them has now become almost absolutely indispensable to enable the student to gain a knowledge of their forms and positions without months of research and study.

Feeling that such preliminary key is required to enable the student (by his first acquiring a general knowledge of an opening with comparatively little difficulty) to unlock the portals of many a noble work—English and foreign—on Chess, and to master its *detailed* contents with more ease and celerity than he can at present, I have ventured to introduce to the Chess public my plan, which, if carried out with respect to the "openings" generally, would, I think, greatly facilitate their study in more detailed works, because the student, having had his way thus cleared for him before,—the various bye-paths of departure from the main roads clearly defined for him,—*started* on his tour of investigation with a *general knowledge* of the country beforehand,—would go to the study of more detailed works forearmed, as it were; and, doubtless, in consequence of such increased facility, the number of Chess students would be considerably swelled, a knowledge of "openings" more widely disseminated, and the popularity of the game greatly increased.

With respect to the theory of the "Evans' Gambit Refused,' authorities appear not to agree as to which is the most satisfactory way of evading the Evans, but, as there is no very satisfactory way of accepting it, why the Evans offer may as well be declined as accepted; for, although the latter in theory ought to win for the second player, yet in practice it does not, in the vast majority of cases, the forms of attack on the part of the opening player being so strong, varied, and numerous, and the defences to them being so difficult and non-apparent.

The two forms of refusing the Evans are 4. B. to Q. Kt. third, retreating the attacked Bishop to right wing, and 4. P. to Q. fourth, a counter attack (on the first player's Bishop also) in the centre of the line of battle. For the former move (4. B. to Q. Kt. third) see Game I., with its main variations, A, B, C, D, E, and F, printed in large black type, with their respective subsidiaries printed in Roman letter, where commenced by the first player, and in italics, where initiated by the second player. The words *if* and *then* will also, *in addition* to the difference of type, serve clearly to show when the *subsidiary* variations are *commenced* by the first or second player—the move at which the word *if* occurs indicating the point of departure, or, in other words, the exact place where the subsidiary branches off from its parent or main variation.

For the other move of 4. P. to Q. fourth, see Game II., with its main variations, W, Y, Z, and *their* subsidiary variations, similarly identified as those of Game I.

When in the main variations (largest type) a move is underlined, such move is the key move of that particular variation, marking where such main variation differs *first* from the main one which precedes it.

The following abbreviations, wherever they occur, stand respectively as follows, viz.:—C. P. Mag., for "Chess Players' Magazine;" C. W. Mag., for "Chess World Magazine;" S. Praxis, or Praxis, for "Staunton's Praxis;" S. H., or H., for "Staunton's Handbook;" Wormald, or W. C. O., for "Wormald's Chess Openings;" L. M. G., for "Lowenthal's Morphy's Games;" L. B. Cong., for "Lowenthal's Book of the Congress."

The first way of refusing the Evans—viz., by retreating the Bishop (4. B. to Q. Kt. third)—is preferred by Boden and others; but Staunton and others prefer the counter move of 4. P. to Q. fourth.

The best move on the part of the first player, after 4. B. to Q. Kt. third, appears to be to continue the advance of the Q. Kt. P. (5. P. to Q. Kt. fifth), according to a number of authorities (although not so according to Staunton's Handbook and Praxis), to which the second player has three principal answers (after his King's Pawn is captured by first player at move 6), viz., 6. Q. to K. B. third, or 6. Kt. to K. R. third, or 6. B. to Q. fifth (see Game I., variations C, D, & E respectively), each of which has its advocates. On the whole, however, the weight of authority appears to be against them all, and to prove that there is no satisfactory defence to the first player's move of 5. P. to Q. Kt. fifth, which would consequently tend to show that the first-named form of evasion of the Evans' Gambit (4. B. to Q. Kt. third) has no sound continuation for the second player.

With respect to the second move (4 P. to Q. fourth), no very definite or conclusive opinion has, it appears, been authoritatively pronounced as to whether this is a satisfactory way of avoiding the Evans, excepting Mr. Wormald, who says in his work, p. 131, that it leads to "a tolerably even game." The principal replies for the first player are—5. K. P. takes P. (var. W); 5. K. B. takes P. (var. Y); and 5. B. to Q. Kt. fifth (var. Z); the last mentioned appearing to be the one most recommended.

Altogether the evasion of the Evans (by either of the forms, 4. B. to Q. Kt. third, or 4. P. to Q. fourth), if not altogether satisfactory, leads, however, to interesting positions, and less hazardous ones for the second player than when he *accepts* the Gambit.

In my plan I have given in a great many places the opinion of authorities upon particular moves, variations, and positions, referring the student to the very pages of the works of such authors.

Trusting, then, that my "Key to the Evans Refused," annexed herewith, will enable your readers without much trouble to judge for themselves as to what particular moves or lines of play they would prefer to adopt, and hoping my suggested plan of treating the "openings"—of which the enclosed is an illustration—will meet with their approval,

I remain, my dear Sir,
Yours very truly,
THOS. LONG.

CHESS LITERATURE.

Sociable Chess, an Amusing Game for Winter Evenings, which may be played by any even number of persons, not less than four. By a CAMBRIDGE MAN. Cambridge: Deighton, Bell, & Co.; London: Bell & Daldy.

We have to introduce to our readers a chess novelty invented by an amateur of Cambridge. It was courteously forwarded to us for insertion, in November last, by the author. Extreme pressure upon our space, however, prevented its insertion in the December number. It seems to resemble in some respects the game known as double or four-handed chess, which we have occasionally seen practised at the Strand Divan. We doubt whether it will ever become very popular, but we have much pleasure in giving it a place in our columns.

RULES.

I. As many ordinary chess-boards and sets of chess-men must be provided as half the number of persons who intend to play.

    N.B.—A sufficient number of these might be collected for a large party, by friends lending to each other for the occasion.

II. The first thing to be done is to choose a leader for each side. Each player writes on a small piece of paper the names of two persons, always excepting his own. The two who have the greatest number of votes are elected leaders, one on each side. They are to play together, according to the rules of ordinary Chess.

III. The leader who had the greater number of votes is to choose from among the other players one to be "on his side." Then the leader on the opposite side is to choose an antagonist for the last-chosen player. And this is to be continued until both sides are selected.

IV. The leader who had the greater number of votes is entitled to the choice of colour for his side, and each player on that side is entitled to the first move.

V. In cases where the leaders have an equal number of votes, they are to toss up for those privileges which are otherwise acquired by a majority.

VI. The players will then sit down to as many single combats as there are individuals on each side.

VII. When any single combat is finished, the leader of the winner (after examining the position of his other friends) is entitled to take the winner's men (with the exception of the King), and distribute them among his friends, according to the best of his judgment.

VIII. But no player, by this means, is to have his forces increased to more than their original strength. That is to say, he is not to have more than one Queen, two Castles, two Bishops, two Knights, and eight Pawns.

IX. The last rule, however, is not to prevent a player's Pawns from being promoted according to the rules of ordinary Chess.

X. When a player's men are re-inforced in the manner mentioned in Rule VII., the re-inforcements are to be placed as follows:—Queen on Queen's square; Castle on either Castle's square (one may be placed on each, if possible, and without violation of Rule VIII.); Bishop on either Bishop's square (one may be placed on each, if possible, and without violation of Rule VIII.); Knight on either Knight's square (one may be placed on each, if possible, and without violation of Rule VIII.); and Pawns on the squares of the Pawns. But when any square here mentioned is already occupied, the re-inforcement (so far as regards each piece or pawn which should have been placed on an occupied square) cannot take place.

XI. When any single combat is finished, the leader of the winner is entitled to substitute him for any other player on his own side, if he wishes to do so.

XII. Of course the side which wins the greater number of games is the conqueror. Single combats, in which the result is a drawn game, or stale-mate, are not counted on either side. When an equal number of games is won on each side, the contest is to be decided by a single combat between the leaders who were chosen at the commencement of the game.

XIII. On the defeat of a leader, he is to be succeeded in the office by the player on his own side who was chosen immediately after himself.

XIV. All the laws of ordinary Chess are to be obeyed, except in cases (if there be any) in which they are in opposition to these Rules.

BLACKHEATH CHESS CLUB.—At the weekly meeting of this Society on the 5th ult., which was very well attended, Mr. Sich and Mr. Lowenthal, of the St. James's, were present. A consultation game came off, the President and Mr. Sich consulting together against Mr. Lowenthal, who besides played several other games simultaneously. The interchange of such visits between the members of the London, St. James's, and Blackheath clubs is well calculated to promote a friendly feeling among chess players, and we are glad to see that the same custom prevails to a large extent among our provincial brethren.

GAMES.

A NEW CHESS MATCH.

A match of great interest is now pending between Herr Steinitz and Mr. De Vere, the former gentleman giving the odds of Pawn and move. Two hours are allowed to each player for every twenty-four moves, and the player first scoring seven games is to be the conqueror. The match has been arranged under the auspices of the London Chess Club, for a prize to be presented to the winner by that liberal body. Mr. De Vere is well known in metropolitan chess circles as a player of considerable skill, and it will add largely to the deserved reputation of Herr Steinitz should he be able to render the odds with success. We give below the opening games of the match.

GAME III.

Game the first in the match between Mr. De Vere and Herr Steinitz.

(*Remove Black's K. B. Pawn.*)

White. (Mr. DE VERE.)	Black. (Herr STEINITZ.)
1. P. to K. fourth	1. Q. Kt. to B. third
2. P. to Q. fourth	2. P. to K. fourth
3. P. takes P.	3. Kt. takes P.
4. P. to K. B. fourth	4. Kt. to K. B. second
5. B. to Q. B. fourth	5. K. Kt. to R. third
6. Kt. to K. B. third	6. B. to Q. B. fourth
7. Q. Kt. to B. third	7. Castles
8. Q. to Q. third (*a*)	8. P. to Q. B. third (*b*)
9. B. to Q. second (*c*)	9. P. to Q. fourth
10. B. to Q. Kt. third	10. P. to Q. Kt. fourth
11. Castles (Q. R.) (*d*)	11. P. to Q. R. fourth
12. P. to Q. R. fourth	12. P. to Q. Kt. fifth
13. Kt. takes Q. P. (*e*)	13. P. takes Kt.
14. K. B. takes P.	14. B. to Q. R. third
15. Q. to Q. Kt. third	15. R. to Q. Kt. square
16. Kt. to K. Kt. fifth (*f*)	16. Q. to K. second
17. P. to B. fifth	17. K. to R. square
18. Kt. to K. sixth	18. K. R. to K. square
19. Q. to K. Kt. third	19. R. to K. Kt. square
20. P. to K. R. fourth	20. B. to Q. third
21. Q. to Q. Kt. third	21. K. B. to K. fourth

22. Kt. to K. Kt. fifth	22. K. R. to K. B. square.
23. P. to K. Kt. fourth	23. B. to Q. square
24. Kt. to K. B. third (*g*)	24. Kt. takes Kt. P.
25. B. takes Q. Kt.	25. Kt. to B. seventh
26. Kt. takes B. (*h*)	26. Q. takes Kt.
27. K. R. to K. B. square	27. Kt. takes Q. R.
28. B. to K. B. fourth	28. Q. takes K. P.
29. B. takes Q. R.	29. Kt. to K. sixth
30. R. to K. square	30. B. takes P. (*i*)
31. B. to R. fifth (*k*)	31. R. takes B.
32. R. takes Kt.	32. Q. to R. eighth (check)
33. B. to Q. square	33. R. to Q. square
34. P. to B. fourth	34. Q. takes P.
35. R. to K. second	35. Q. to B. fifth (check)
36. Q. to K. third	36. Q. takes B. P. (check)
37. B. to B. second	37. B. takes B.

And White resigns.

NOTES.

(*a*) K. Kt. to Kt. fifth looks promising, but would not have been so good as the move in the text.

(*b*) This move leads to an interesting and complicated position.

(*c*) B. to K. third would, we believe, have been better play.

(*d*) We should have much preferred taking Pawn with Pawn.

(*e*) To escape more serious loss White is now compelled to sacrifice a piece.

(*f*) White has now three Pawns for the piece, and has not only relieved himself from the pressure of Black's attack, but has moreover turned the tables upon his opponent.

Position after White's 16th move.

BLACK.

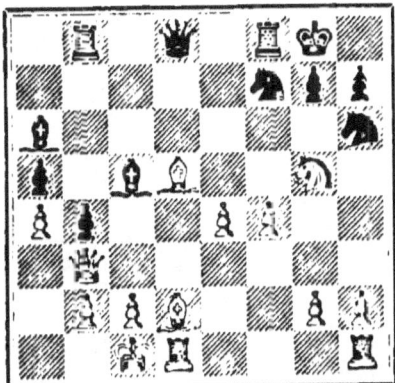

WHITE.

(g) The last series of moves was played by White with equal judgment and ingenuity; the retreat of the Knight, however, was at least premature. He should first have played the Q. R. to K. Kt. square, which would have rendered the move when made afterwards more effective.

(h) The position is very complicated, requiring great nicety of play.

(i) This move ensures a speedy victory.

(k) We see nothing better, for if
31. R. takes Kt. 31. Q. to R. eighth (check)
winning in a few moves; and if 31. Q. to Q. third, Black replies with Q. to Q. B. third, winning easily.

GAME 112.

Game the second in the match between Mr. De Vere and Herr Steinitz.

(*Remove Black's K. B. Pawn.*)

White. (Mr. DE VERE.)	Black. (Herr STEINITZ.)
1. P. to K. fourth	1. P. to K. third
2. P. to Q. fourth	2. P. to Q. fourth
3. P. to K. fifth	3. P. to Q. B. fourth
4. Kt. to K. B. third	4. P. takes P.
5. Kt. takes P.	5. Kt. to Q. B. third
6. Kt. takes Kt.	6. P. takes Kt.
7. B. to Q. third	7. Kt. to K. second
8. Q. B. to K. Kt. fifth	8. Q. to Kt. third
9. P. to Q. Kt. third (*a*)	9. B. to Q. second
10. Castles	10. Castles
11. Kt. to Q. B. third	11. P. to K. R. third
12. Kt. to Q. R. fourth (*b*)	12. Q. to Q. B. second
13. B. to K. third	13. Kt. to K. B. fourth
14. B. takes Kt.	14. P. takes B.
15. Q. to Q. fourth	15. K. to Q. Kt. square
16. P. to K. B. fourth	16. B. to Q. B. square
17. Kt. to Q. B. fifth (*c*)	17. K. to Q. R. square
18. P. to Q. R. fourth	18. B. to K. second (*d*)
19. P. to Q. Kt. fourth	19. K. R. to K. square
20. P. to Q. Kt. fifth	20. Q. to Q. Kt. third
21. P. takes P.	21. B. takes Kt.
22. Q. takes B.	22. Q. takes Q.
23. B. takes Q.	23. B. to R. third
24. K. R. to Q. square	24. Q. R. to B. square
25. R. takes P.	25. R. takes Q. B. P.
26. R. to Q. sixth (*e*)	26. B. to Kt. second
27. R. takes R.	27. B. takes R.
28. B. to Q. sixth	28. K. to Kt. second
29. P. to K. R. fourth	29. R. to K. Kt. square
30. K. to B. second	30. P. to Kt. fourth

31. B. P. takes P.	31. P. takes P.
32. P. to K. R. fifth (*f*)	32. R. to K. R. square
33. R. to K. R. square	33. B. takes R P.
34. P. to R. sixth	34. B. takes P.
35. P. to K. sixth	35. P. to K. B. fifth
36. B. to K. fifth	36. R. to R. second
37. B. to K. Kt. seventh	37. P. to Q. R. fourth
38. P. to K. seventh	38. B. to K. Kt third
39. R. to Q. square	

And Black resigns.

NOTES.

(*a*) The following is the probable result if White had taken the Kt. :—

9. B. takes Kt.	9. B. takes B. (best) (or A)
10. Q. to R. fifth (check)	10. K. to Q. square
11. Kt. to Q. second (best, for if 11. P. to Q. Kt. third, 11. Q. to Q. fifth, wins a piece)	
	11. Q. takes P.
12. Castles	12. P. to Q. B. fourth, &c.

(A)

	9. Q. takes P.
10. B. takes B.	10. R. takes B. (best),
	(for if 10. Q. takes P. (check)
11. B. to K. second	11. Q. takes R.
12. Q. B. to Kt. fourth, with a superior game)	
(Or if	10. Q. takes B.
11. B. takes K. Kt. P.	11. K. R. to Kt. square
12. Q. to R. fifth (check) and wins.	
11. Kt. to Q. second	11. Q. takes P. (check)
12. B. to K. second	12. B. to R. third
13. Q. R. to Kt. square, &c.)	

(*b*) This is a good move, and the Knight becomes an important auxiliary in the coming attack.

Position after White's 32nd move.

BLACK.

WHITE.

(c) White has opened the game well, not only retaining the Pawn given, but having also a fine position.

(d) White's situation is now so very superior that Black's only chance of escape seems to lie in remaining with a Bishop of a different colour to his opponent's. In his place, therefore, we should rather have taken off the Knight at this juncture.

(e) Well played, as Black would lose by taking the Bishop on account of White's superiority of Pawns.

(f) We invite the attention of our readers to this very instructive and interesting end game, which was played by Mr. De Vere with great ability.

GAME 113

Game the third in the match between Mr. De Vere and Herr Steinitz.

(Remove Black's K. B. Pawn.)

White. (Mr. De Vere.)	Black. (Herr Steinitz.)
1. P. to K. fourth	1. P. to K. third
2. P. to Q. fourth	2. P. to Q. fourth
3. P. takes P.	3. P. takes P.
4. B. to Q. third	4. Kt. to K. B. third
5. B. to K. Kt. fifth	5. B. to K. second (a)
6. Kt. to Q. B. third	6. Q. B. to K. Kt. fifth
7. P. to K. B. third	7. B. to K. R. fourth
8. Q. to K. second	8. Castles
9. Castles (Q. R.)	9. P. to Q. B. third
10. Kt. to R. third	10. B. to Q. Kt. fifth
11. Kt. to B. fourth	11. R. to K. square
12. B. takes K. Kt.	12. Q. takes B.
13. Kt. takes B.	13. Q. to R. third (check)
14. Q. to Q. second	14. Q. takes Kt.
15. P. to K. R. fourth	15. Kt. to Q. second
16. Q. to K. Kt. fifth (b)	16. Q. takes Q. (c)
17. P. takes Q.	17. Kt. to K. B. square
18. Kt. to K. second	18. R. to K. sixth
19. P. to Q. R. third	19. B. to Q. third
20. P. to K. B. fourth	20. Q. R. to K. square
21. K. to Q. second	21. P. to Q. Kt. third
22. Q. R. to K. B. square	22. K. R. to K. second
23. P. to K. B. fifth	23. K. R. to B. second
24. P. to K. Kt. fourth	24. B. to K. second
25. P. to K. Kt. sixth (d)	25. P. takes P.
26. P. takes P.	26. B. to Kt. fourth (check)
27. K. to Q. square	27. R. to B. third
28. R. to K. B. fifth	28. R. takes R. (e)
29. P. takes R.	29. Kt. to Q. second

30. P. to Q. Kt. fourth	30. Kt. to K. B. third
31. R. to Kt. square	31. B. to R. third
32. P. to R. fourth	32. K. to B. square
33. R. to Kt. second	33. K. to K. second
34. Kt. to Kt. square	34. K. to Q. third
35. Kt. to B. third	35. B. to K. B. fifth
36. Kt. to Kt. fifth	36. B. takes Kt.
37. R. takes B.	37. P. to Q. B. fourth
38. P. takes P. (check)	38. P. takes P.
39. P. takes P. (check)	39. K. takes P.
40. R. to Kt. second	40. K. to Kt. fifth
41. K. to Q. second (*f*)	41. K. takes P.
42. R. to Kt. square	42. R. to K. second
43. K. to B. third	43. R. to B. second (check)
44. K. to Q. fourth	44. K. to R. sixth
45. R. to Q. R. square (check)	45. K. to Kt. seventh
46. R. to R. sixth (*g*)	46. K. to B. eighth
47. R. takes Kt.	47. P. takes R
48. K. takes P.	48. P. to Q. R. fourth
49. K. to Q. sixth	49. R. to B. square.
50. B. to Q. Kt. fifth.	50. K. takes P.
51. K. to K. seventh, and wins	

NOTES.

(*a*) We prefer B. to Q. third at this point.

(*b*) This move is finely conceived, and had no doubt been previously calculated on by Mr. De Vere.

Position after White's 25th move.

BLACK.

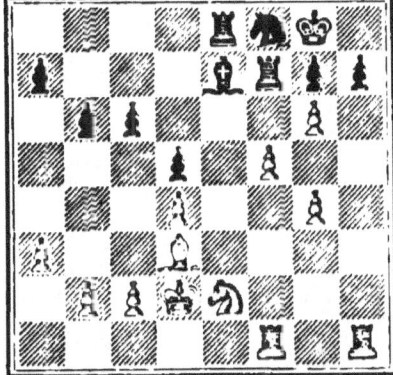

WHITE.

(c) Under the circumstances we should rather have played Q. to K. B. second. White's attack, though still very powerful, would then have been less overwhelming.

(d) From this point the game exhibits some features of remarkable interest.

(e) We see no better move for Black.

(f) A fine *coup de repos*, which would do credit to a first-rate player.

(g) This is decisive, and was evidently foreseen by White when he gave up the Pawn.

The two following games afford a good illustration of an important variant in the Two Knights' Defence.

GAME 114.
(Two Knights' Defence.)

White. (Mr. Wayte.)	Black. (Herr Lowenthal.)
1. P. to K. fourth	1. P. to K. fourth
2. K. Kt. to B. third	2. Q. Kt. to B. third
3. K. B. to Q. B. fourth	3. K. Kt. to B. third
4. K. Kt. to Kt. fifth	4. P. to Q. fourth
5. P. takes P.	5. Kt. to Q. R. fourth
6. B. to Q. Kt. fifth (ch.) (a)	6. P. to Q. B. third
7. P. takes P.	7. P. takes P.
8. B. to K. second (b)	8. P. to K. R. third
9. K. Kt. to B. third	9. P. to K. fifth
10. K. Kt. to K. fifth	10. Q. to Q. fifth
11. K. Kt. to Kt. fourth (c)	11. Q. B. takes Kt.
12. B. takes B.	12. P. to K. sixth (d)
13. B. to K. B. third	13. P. takes P. (check)
14. K. to B. square	14. Castles
15. Q. to K. second	15. B. to Q. B. fourth (e)
16. P. to Q. B. third	16. Q. to Q. R. fifth
17. Q. to Q. R. sixth (ch.) (f)	17. K. to Kt. square
18. P. to Q. fourth	18. K. R. to K. square
19. Q. B. to K. B. fourth (ch.) (g)	19. B. to Q. third
20. B. takes B. (ch.)	20. R. takes B.
21. P. to Q. Kt. third	21. Q. to Q. Kt. fourth (check)
22. Q. takes Q.	22. P. takes Q.
23. K. takes P.	23. Kt. to K. fifth (check) (h)
24. B. takes Kt.	24. R. takes B.
25. Kt. to Q. second	25. Q. R. to K. B. third (check)
26. Kt. to K. B. third	26. P. to Q. Kt. fifth
27. P. takes P.	27. Kt. to Q. B. third
28. K. R. to K. square	28. R. takes Q. P.
29. P. to Q. Kt. fifth.	29. Kt. to Q. Kt. fifth

30. K. to Kt. square	30. R. to Q. second
31. P. to Q. R. fourth	31. Kt. to Q. B. seventh (i)
32. K. R. to K. eighth (check)	32. K. to Kt. second
33. Q. R. to Q. B. square	33. Kt. to Q. Kt. fifth
34. Kt. to K. fifth	34. R. to Q. seventh
35. R. to K. seventh (ch.)	

And Black resigns.

NOTES.

(a) Suhle and Neumann prefer this to the move now in vogue, 6. P. to Q. third. (See p. 322 of our November number.)

(b) Q. to K. B. third may also be played, but fails to equalise the game. (See pp. 298, 861 of our last volume.) 8. B. to Q. R. fourth is still worse. (See p. 363.)

(c) The *Theorie und Praxis* advocates 11. P. to K. B. fourth; the *Handbuch* prefers the move in the text.

(d) The *Theorie und Praxis* (p. 132) pronounces this move only apparently strong; but it may be doubted whether Kt. to Q. B. fifth, the alternative move given in the *Handbuch*, is any better. With the best play, Black must remain a Pawn minus, but, *en revanche*, maintains a greater or less superiority of position.

(e) The correct move: if White now played to win the Kt. he would be mated in a few moves, *e.g.*,

16. Q. to Q. R. sixth (check)	16. K. to Kt. square
17. Q. takes Kt.	17. Q. R. to K. square
(Better than K. R. to K. square, as will appear anon.)	
18. B. to K. second	18. R. takes B.
19. K. takes R.	And Black mates in two moves.

Had the K. R. been played, White could have prolonged the defence by 19. Q. takes Q. R. (check).

Position after Black's 15th move.

BLACK.

WHITE.

(f) If 17. P. to Q. fourth, or P. to Q. Kt. fourth, Black could play with advantage Kt to Q. Kt. sixth. (See a game cleverly won by Mr. Zytogorsky, in the "Chess Praxis," p. 197.)

(g) In the *Chess Players' Magazine* for 1863, p. 151, the following moves are given:—

19. P. to Q. Kt. third	19. Q. to Q. Kt. fourth (check)
20. Q. takes Q. (check)	20. P. takes Q.
21. Q. B. to K. B. fourth (check)	21. K. to B. square
22. Kt. to Q. second, with the better game.	

But by 21. B. to Q. third, Black may arrive at the same position as in the text; and the check of the Bishop at move 19 has this advantage, that if Black in reply move 19. K. to R. square, White may play 20. Q. takes Kt., (mating if the Queen be taken) with a winning advantage.

(h) This seems scarcely so good as 23. K. R. to Q. B. square, a move which retards the development of White's forces, and cramps him for some time longer.

(i) A lost move, after which it is impossible to save the game.

GAME 115.

(*Two Knights' Defence.*)

[Moves 1 to 22 as in the preceding game. See Diagram.]

Situation after the 22nd move of Black.

BLACK.

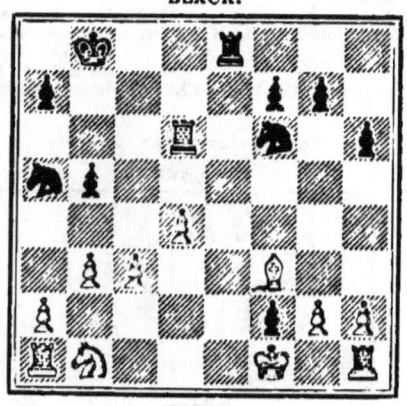

WHITE.

White. (MR. WAYTE.)	*Black.* (MR. RANKEN.)
23. K. takes P. (a)	23. K. R. to Q. B. square (b)
24. K. R. to K. sq.	24. P. to Q. R. third
25. R. to K. third (c)	25. P. to Q. Kt. fifth
26. P. takes P.	26. Kt. to Q. B. third
27. Kt. to Q. second	27. Kt. takes P. at Kt. fifth
28. R. to K. seventh	28. Q. R. to Q. second (d)
29. R. takes R.	29. K. Kt. takes R.
30. Kt. to Q. B. fourth	30. Kt. to K. B. third
31. P. to Q. R. third	31. Q. Kt. to Q. fourth
32. R. to K. square	32. R. to Q. B. second

33. R. to K. fifth	33. R. to Q. second
34. P. to K. R. third	34. Q. Kt. to Q. B. second (e)
35. K. to K. third	35. Q. Kt. to K. third
36. B. to Q. B. sixth	36. R. to Q. square
37. P. to Q. fifth	37. Q. Kt. to Q. B. second
38. P. to Q. sixth	38. Q. Kt. to K. square
39. P. to Q. seventh	39. Q. Kt. to Q. B. second
40. Kt. to Q. sixth	40. K. Kt. takes P.
41. R. to K. seventh	41. K. Kt. to Q. B. fourth
42. Kt. takes K. B. P.	42. R. to Q. sixth (check)
43. K. to K. second	43. R. takes Q. Kt. P.
44. R. to K. third	44. Q. Kt. to K. third
45. R. takes R.	45. K. Kt. takes R.
46. K. to K. third	

And the game was abandoned as drawn.

NOTES.

(a) If Kt. to Q. second, Black can play 23. K. R. to Q. B. square with even more effect; for if then 24 Q. R. to Q. B. square, 24. R. takes Q. P., &c.

(b) The best move, we believe.

(c) The correct move.

(d) Better than R. to Q. B. second.

(e) From this point Black seems sure of recovering his Pawn, and drawing the game.

GAME 116.

(*Evans's Gambit.*)

White. (Mr. Wayte.)	Black. (Mr. Ranken.)
1. P. to K. fourth	1. P. to K. fourth
2. K. Kt. to B. third	2. Q. Kt. to B. third
3. K. B. to Q. B. fourth	3. K. B. to Q. B. fourth
4. P. to Q. Kt. fourth	4. B. takes Q. Kt. P.
5. P. to Q. B. third	5. B. to Q. B. fourth
6. Castles	6. P. to Q. third
7. P. to Q. fourth	7. P. takes P.
8. P. takes P.	8. B. to Q. Kt. third
9. Q. Kt. to B. third	9. Kt. to Q. R. fourth
10. K. B. to Q. third	10. Kt. to K. second
11. P. to Q. fifth	11. Castles
12. Q. B. to Kt. second	12. P. to K. B. fourth (a)
13. Kt. to K. Kt. fifth	13. Q. to K. square (b)

14. Kt. to K. sixth	14. B. takes Kt.
15. P. takes B.	15. P. to K. B. fifth (c)
16. Kt. to Q. fifth	16. P. to K B. sixth (d)
17. P. takes P.	17. Q. to K. Kt. third (check)
18. K. to R. square	18. Q. takes P. at K. third
19. R. to K. Kt. square	19. R. to K. B. second
20. Q. to Q. second	20. P. to Q. B. third
21. Kt. takes Kt. (check)	21. Q. takes Kt. (e)
22. Q. to K. R. sixth	22. K. to R. square (f)
23. R. takes P.	23. R. takes R.
24. B. to K. B. sixth	24. Q. to K. B. second
25. P. to K. fifth	25. K. to Kt. square.
26. K. B. takes R. P. (check) (g)	

And Black resigns.

NOTES.

(a) An analysis of this move, from the *Schachzeitung*, was given at p. 272 of our last volume. The result was favourable to the attack, but Black's moves may apparently be strengthened, as the present game shows.

(b) This is unquestionably better than the move given by the *Schachzeitung*, 13. P. to K. R. third.

(c) Probably the best move. The following variations from this point suggested themselves during an examination of this opening by the present opponents:—

(A)

	15. Q. to K. Kt. third (or B)
16. P. takes P.	16. Kt. takes P.
17. P. to K. Kt. fourth	17. P. to K. R. fourth
18. P. to K. R. third	18. P. takes P.
19. P. takes P.	19. Q. R. to K. square
20. Kt. to K. fourth	(We see no better move.)

Followed by Kt. to K. Kt. third, winning the piece.

(B)

	15. P. takes P.
16. Kt. takes P.	16. Kt. to K. B. fourth

(If 16. Kt. to K. Kt. third, White can play with advantage 17. Q. to K. R. fifth.)

17. Q. to K. Kt. fourth	17. Q. takes Pawn
18. Kt. to K. B sixth (check)	

And White wins the exchange, but Black's two Pawns render the game equal.

(d) This is playing White's game; the opening of the K. Kt's file greatly strengthens the attack. Instead of this, Black should have played—

	16. Kt. to K. Kt. third
17. Q. to K. Kt. fourth	17. Kt. to K. fourth
18. B. takes Kt.	18. P. takes B.

And Black has a good game, White's advanced Pawn being difficult to defend.

(e) R. takes Kt. would have been better play, though White would still have had a very powerful attack by moving Q. to K. Kt. fifth. Black's last move, P. to Q. B. third, was undoubtedly a lost one.

(f) His only move to delay the fatal advance of P. to K. fifth.

(g) The game is played by White with great ability.

Position after White's 15th move.
BLACK.

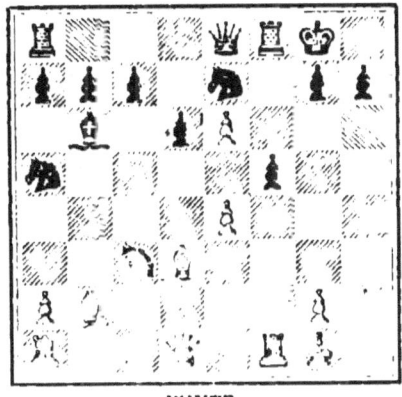

WHITE.

GAME 117.

The following brilliant Game, which we take from *Le Palamède Français*, was played at St. Petersburgh in 1862, between Messrs. Kolisch and Schumoff:—

(*Giuoco Piano.*)

White. (M. Schumoff.)	Black. (M. Kolisch.)
1. P. to K. fourth	1. P. to K. fourth
2. Kt. to K. B. third	2. Kt. to Q. B. third
3. B. to Q. B. fourth	3. B. to Q. B. fourth
4. Castles.	4. Kt. to K. B. third
5. P. to Q. fourth	5. B. takes P.
6. Kt. takes B.	6. Kt. takes Kt.
7. P. to K. B. fourth	7. P. to Q. third
8. P. takes P.	8. P. takes P.
9. B. to K. Kt. fifth	9. Q. to K. second
10. P. to Q. Kt. fourth	10. B. to K. third (*a*)
11. B. takes Kt.	11. P. takes B.
12. B. takes B.	12. P. takes B.
13. Q. to K. R. fifth (check)	13. Q. to K. B. second
14. Q. to K. R. fourth	14. Castles (Q. R.)
15. Kt. to Q. R. third (*b*)	15. P. to K. B. fourth
16. Q. to K. B. second	16. Q. to K. R. fourth
17. Q. R. to K. square (*c*)	17. P. to K. B. fifth

18. P. to Q. B. third	18. Kt. to Q. B. third
19. P. to Q. Kt. fifth	19. Kt. to Q. Kt. square
20. Q. takes Q. R. P.	20. P. to Q. Kt. third (*d*)
21. Q. to Q. R. fourth	21. K. R. to K. Kt. square
22. R. to Q. square	22. R. takes P. (check) (*e*)
23. K. takes R.	23. Q. to K. seventh (check)
24. K. to R. square (*f*)	24. R. to Q. seventh

And White cannot save the game.

NOTES.

(*a*) Black might safely have taken the proffered Pawn.
(*b*) Evidently White dare not take the B. P.
(*c*) To prevent Kt. to K. seventh (check).
(*d*) This shuts out the Queen, and stops the advance of the hostile Pawn.
(*e*) Brilliant and decisive.
(*f*) If K. to R. third, then R. to K. Kt. square—wins.

Position after White's 22nd move,

BLACK.

WHITE.

DUBLIN CHESS CLUB.—At a recent meeting the following gentlemen were elected as officers of the club for the ensuing year:—Rev. G. A. McDonnell, President; Sir John Blunden, Bart., Rev. G. Salmon, D.D., and Coote Carrol, Esq., Vice-Presidents; Committee: Rev. E. J. Cordner, J. Pim, Esq., J. V. Mills, Esq., S. Barry, Esq., G. F. Barry, Esq., and R. D. Barbor, Esq.; Treasurer, R. C. H. Collins, Esq.; Secretary, Peter Jones, jun., Esq.; Librarian, A. Rynd, Esq.

CHESS INTELLIGENCE.

ANNUAL GENERAL MEETING OF THE ST. JAMES'S CHESS CLUB.

The annual general meeting of this club took place at the rooms of the club, in King-street, St. James's, on Saturday, the 9th ult. Present W. G. Ward, Esq. (in the chair), H. T. Young, A. Sich, — Baker, C. Barthes, H. C. Stewart, W. M. Chinnery, and J. Lowenthal, Esqs.

The Hon. Sec. (Mr. H. C. Stewart) having read the minutes of the last meeting, which were duly confirmed, read the following Report for the past year :—

"The committee have much pleasure in presenting to the society their annual report, and although the proceedings of the past year have not been so interesting as in former seasons, still on several occasions specialties have been introduced which have received the warmest approbation from all the members.

"At a meeting of the committee, early in January, the match by telegraph with the Dublin Chess Club was definitively fixed for Wednesday, February 22. It is gratifying to be able to report that after the proposal from the Dublin committee the many arrangements were so speedily completed. The wires were introduced into the club rooms both in Dublin and London, and the presence of nearly all the leading Chess notabilities, in addition to other visitors, was the highest testimony of the success of the evening. The rapidity with which the moves were conveyed to and fro was a source of much astonishment to many who witnessed the telegraphic operations for the first time. In cases where the move was made without delay the reply was frequently received from Dublin in two minutes from the time the move was made in London, and *vice versa*. The number of moves made during the evening was 646, consequently the same number of messages were sent along the wires, exclusive of those necessary for intimations and explanations.

"In April, at a committee meeting, the chairman, Mr. Ward, urged the desirability of making arrangements to excite the general interest among the members of the club in behalf of the then forthcoming Dublin Chess Congress, and it was then unanimously resolved that, apart from a subscription from the funds of the club, that the secretary should be authorised to communicate with the members for their individual co-operation, the result of which was that a handsome subscription was duly forwarded to the Dublin club.

"In July the club tourney, which was commenced in the previous year, was brought to a conclusion, the first and second prizes falling respectively to Mr. H. C. Stewart and Mr. W. Moresby Chinnery.

"During September Mr. Thomas Long, of Dublin, opened a correspondence with the secretary, in which he stated the desire of the Dublin players to manage, if possible, a return telegraphic match during their congress in October with the St. James's Chess Club; and in order to remove any difficulty which otherwise might exist, had himself effected the whole of the details. With so liberal and generous an offer, the committee at once instructed the hon. secretary to comply with Mr. Long's wishes, believing that as the former match had been productive of so much pleasure, an equal interest would be found for its successor. The success of the match was decidedly in favour of the St. James's Club. At the same time they wish it to be recorded that the telegraphic games have been a source of much enjoyment, and have largely contributed to the pleasures of the club meetings

"At the last committee meeting the final conditions were agreed upon in reference to the present handicap tourny.

"In conclusion, the committee are glad that the St. James's Chess Club still continues to receive the visits of the leading players of the three metropolitan chess clubs, namely, the St. George's, the London, and the Blackheath, and among the list of their many visitors they have been pleased to see those of Messrs. Steinitz and Meinertshagen, of Germany ; also Messrs. Medley (of the London), M'Donnell, De Vere, G. Walker, Boden, Blackburn, Bird, M. de Riviere (the French champion), Dr. Kebble (of Brighton), Mr. Peter Jones, Hon. Sec. Dublin Club, &c."

The Chairman (Mr. W. G. Ward) moved the adoption of the report ; Mr. H. T. Young seconded, and it was carried unanimously.

The following resolutions were then passed :—" That the report and the balance sheet be distributed to the members of the club, and to the leading daily and weekly metropolitan papers." "That Mr. H. Mann be elected a member of the committee." "That the Hon. Secretary be authorised to arrange consultation and alternation games for the ensuing season." "That the honorary officers and committee of the club be re-elected."

A vote of thanks to the chairman concluded the proceedings.

THE BRITISH CHESS ASSOCIATION.

It is with much regret that we return to a question that we hoped had been definitively settled by the straightforward letter of Mr. Medley, which we so recently published. As, however, our opponents still persist in their misstatements, we are compelled briefly to revert to them.

In their letters to our contemporary, *The Illustrated London News*, Messrs. Staunton and Wormald virtually contradict Mr. Medley's statement—viz., that at the last general meeting of the British Chess Association (held on July 17th 1862) a resolution was put from the chair, and carried unanimously, that the managing committee continue their labours until the next general meeting. We have, however, been informed by several gentlemen, members of the Association, who were present on the occasion, that they are able to confirm in the strongest manner the entire accuracy of Mr. Medley's statement. It is further corroborated by the memoir of the British Chess Association, prefixed to the "Book of the Congress of 1862," from which we take the following extract (p. lxxiii) :—
"The Rev. G. A. McDonnell, in the absence of the Rev. J. Owen, to whom the resolution had been entrusted, and who had been obliged to leave, moved that the managing committee continue their labours until the next general meeting. He paid a tribute to the exertions of that body, and thanked the members for the efficient way in which the arrangements had been carried out. Mr. Deacon seconded the motion, which was carried unanimously."

The above statement, having been drawn up from the minutes of the meeting taken at the time, is the best possible authority as to what really took place.

Apart from this misrepresentation (which, however, we could not suffer to pass without correction) the writers in our contemporary describe the association as being virtually defunct. No charge can be more unfounded. Several meetings of the managing committee have been held during the last two years, and in all likelihood a general meeting of the Association will be convened during the summer or autumn of 1866. It is true that no general meeting has been held since 1862, but it must be remembered that unusual exertions were made to render this assemblage of chessplayers entirely successful, and to signalise it by adequate results. Those efforts were amply rewarded. Party spirit seemed for the first time among chessplayers to be completely forgotten; the proceedings were characterised by a general unanimity of feeling; a most valuable collection of games and problems was formed; and the meeting was allowed on all sides to be the most agreeable and successful ever held in England. But the labour and expense which it entailed cannot be exacted every year. Some interval of repose was needed, and if an equally satisfactory result attend a congress to be convened for 1866, few amateurs, we think, will be inclined to condemn the officers of the Association for not having sooner summoned a general meeting.

CHESS ASSOCIATION AT REDCAR.

We have much pleasure in giving publicity to the annexed letter. Nothing can be more desirable than that the meeting proposed should be entirely successful. We doubt, however, whether the committee are well-advised in wishing to give their provincial assembly a national character. A general meeting of the British Chess Association will probably be held during next summer, and it is hardly possible to convene the chess public twice in one year without failure. As a provincial gathering the Redcar Association would be almost certain of success, and might become a worthy co-rival of the West Yorkshire Chess Association.

TO THE EDITOR OF THE "CHESS PLAYERS' MAGAZINE."

Sir,—It is intended to hold a grand chess meeting at Redcar in August or September of next year. We should be glad, as far as is possible, to give it a national character; and perhaps you will kindly enable us, through your columns, to invite British chess clubs generally to aid us;. each club favourable to our proposition, and able to help us, choosing at once one member, who shall act upon the committee.

The Earl of Zetland has promised to preside, and we have already a long list of noblemen and gentlemen as vice-presidents. May I also ask secretaries of clubs, and all chess players who desire to be informed of our arrangements, to forward their address, without delay, to "the Secretary," Chess Association, Redcar, Yorkshire. I am, sir, yours obediently,

A. B. SKIPWORTH,
One of the Committee.

Bilsdale, Nov. 28, 1865.

P.S. While we are desirous of being aided by suggestions from the various British chess clubs, and while we promise that every suggestion shall have its due weight and consideration, we feel that it will be necessary for the executive committee, who reside in and near Redcar, to make the final arrangements.

LEICESTER CHESS CLUB.—The winter season of this spirited little society commenced in October, and we are glad to hear that although only in its fifth year it numbers already about fifty members. They meet twice a week, on Tuesday and Thursday. The officers are—President, Mr. Burrows; Vice-President, Mr. Worth; Treasurer, Mr. Hazelgrave; and Secretary, Mr. Green.

[We give the following Problem, hitherto unpublished, by the late Mr. Brewster, a young American composer of great merit, too early lost to us.]

Problem No. 61. By the late E. S. BREWSTER, Esq., of Pittsfield, U.S.

White to play, and mate in five moves.

Problem No. 62. By Herr Kockelkorn, of Cologne.

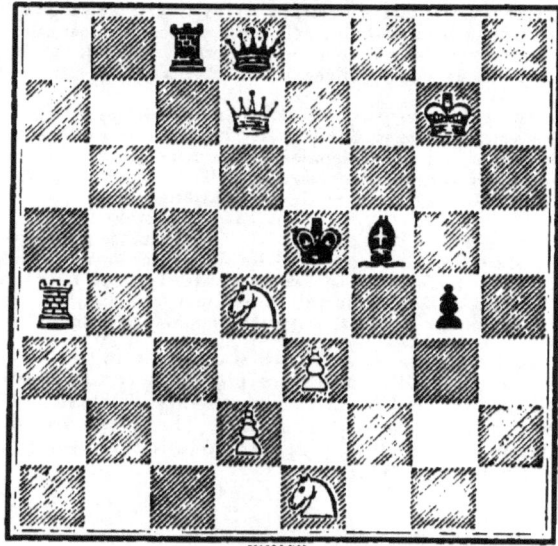

A competing Problem in the late Tourney of *Le Palamède Français*.
No. 63. By T. SMITH, Esq. Motto: "I am here."

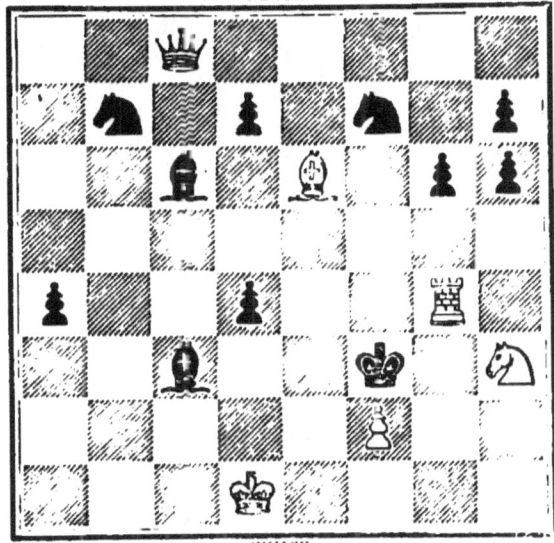

White to play, and mate in four moves.

A competing Problem in the late Tourney of *Le Palamède Français*.
No. 64. By T. SMITH, Esq. Motto: "I am here."

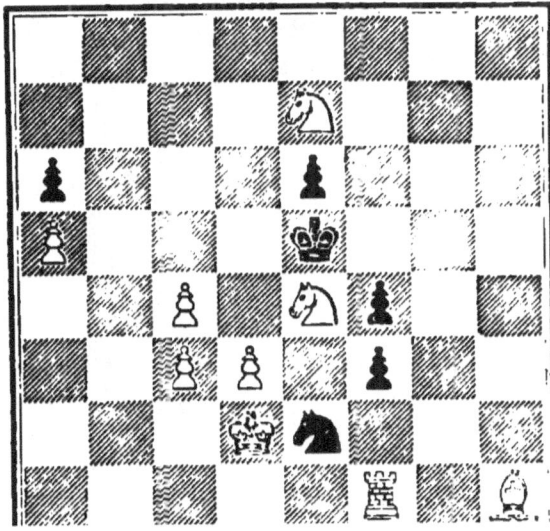

Problem No. 65. By C W., of Sunbury.

White to play, and mate in three moves.

Chess Study No. 11. By Herr Kling.

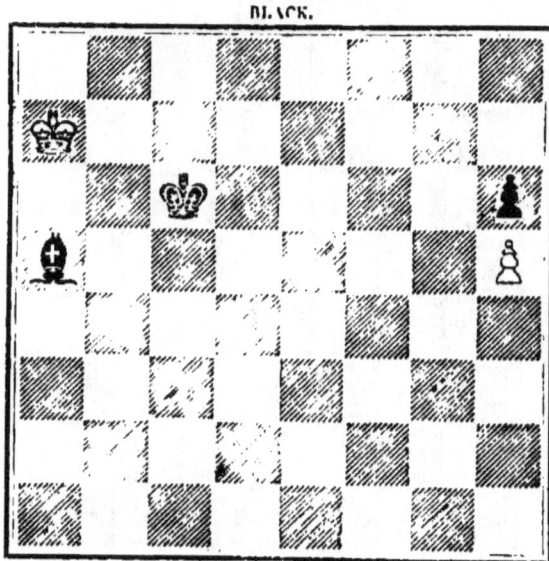

SOLUTIONS TO PROBLEMS.

No. 27.—By Herr Rothmaler.

White.
1. Kt. to K. fifth.
2. R. to K. fourth (check)
3. Kt. to B. fourth (check)
4. R. to K. fifth (mate).

Black.
1. P. to Q. fifth (A)
2. K. to Q. fourth
3. K. takes P.

(A)
1. P. takes Kt. or P. to R. fifth (a)

(If Kt. to K. seventh, White takes B. with Kt., and mates next move.)
2. P. to Kt. third
2. B. takes P. (B)
3. Kt. to K. seventh, and mates next move.

(B)
2. B. takes B. (C)
3. Kt. to Q. sixth, and mates next move.

(C)
2. Kt. to K. seventh
3. Kt. takes B., and mates next move.

No. 28.—Herr Anton Koenig.

White.
1. Kt. to K. sixth
2. R. to Q. sixth
3. Q. or Kt. mates.

Black.
1. B. takes Kt. (at K. sixth)
2. Any move.

No. 29.—By Herr Mayer, of Hanover.

White.
1. B. to Q. B. seventh
2. B. to Q. Kt. eighth
3. P. to K. B fourth
4. B. takes R. P.
5. B. takes Kt. P. (checkmate).

Black.
1. P. moves
2. P. takes P.
3. P. Queens
4. Any move

No. 30.—By Herr Mayer, of Hanover.

White.
1. B. takes P. on Q. third
2. R. to Q. fifth
3. Q. to K. R. fifth (check)
4. Queen mates accordingly

Black.
1. P. takes B.
2. K. takes R. (A)
3. K. moves

(A)
2. K. to B. fifth
3. K. to Kt. fifth

3. Q. takes B.
4. Q. to K. fourth (mate)

(A)

3. K. to B. sixth
4. B. mates

2. R. takes Q.
3. Any move

No. 39.—By F. Healey, Esq.

White.
1. Q. to B. fourth
2. R. to B. sixth
3. R. to Q. B. sixth
4. Mates accordingly.

Black.
1. P. takes Q. (best)
2. B. to Q. B. fourth (best)
3. Any move

No. 40.—By T. Smith, Esq.

White.
1. Q. to K. seventh (check)
2. R. to K. second (check)
3. R. to Q. fourth (check)
4. Q. to Kt. fourth (check)
5. Kt. mates

Black.
1. R. to K. fourth (best)
2. P. takes R. (A)
3. K. takes R. (best)
4. Any move

(A)
2. K. to B. fourth
3. Q. to B. seventh (check), and mates in two moves.

No. 41.—By Herr Kling.

White.
1. K to Q. sq.
2. K. to Q. second
3. B. to Kt. seventh
4. B. takes P. and mates next move.

Black.
1. K. to B. fifth
2. K. to Kt. fourth (A)
3. K. to B. fifth

(A)

3. B. to Q. seventh
4. B. takes P.
5. B. mates.

2. K. to Q. fourth
3. K. to B. fifth
4. K. to Kt. sixth

No. 42.—By J. J. Watts, Esq.

White.
1. B. to Q. fourth (check)
2. Q. to B. seventh
3. Q. or Kt. mates

Black.
1. K. takes B. (best) (A)
2. B. or Kt. moves

(A)

2. Kt. to Kt. sixth
3. B. mates.

1. K. to Q. third
2. Anything

THE
PUBLIC LIBRARY

ASTOR, LENOX AND
TILDEN FOUNDATIONS
R   L

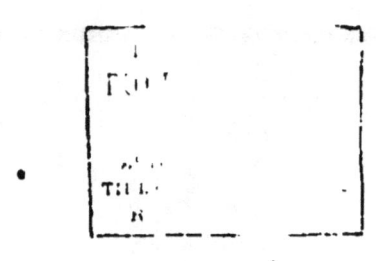

THE Chess Player's Magazine.

THE TWO KNIGHTS' DEFENCE.
(Concluded from our December number.)

GAME VIII.

In this game we shall examine the various probable moves which White may adopt, in lieu of playing 4. Kt. to K. Kt. fifth. These are P. to Q. third, Kt. to Q. B. third, Castles, and P. to Q. fourth.

In the first place—

4. P. to Q. third	4. B. to Q. B. fourth
5. Castles	5. P. to Q, third

and the game is reduced into an ordinary Giuoco Piano.

In the second place—

4. Kt. to Q. B. third	4. B. to Q. Kt. fifth
5. Castles	5. Castles
6. Kt. to Q. fifth, with a good game.	

In the third place—

4. Castles	4. B. to Q. B. fourth
5. P. to Q. third	5. P. to Q. third.

Equal game.

In the fourth place—

4. P. to Q. fourth	4. P. takes P.

The game is now converted into a variation of the Scotch Gambit, of which we have not room to give all the results. The following, however, are some of the most important:—

5. Castles (or A.)	5. Kt. takes P. (best)
6. R. to K. square	6. P. to Q. fourth.
7. B. takes P.	7. Q. takes B.
8. Kt. to Q. B. third	8. Q. to K. R. fourth

9. Kt. takes Kt.	9. B. to K. third (best)
10. B. to K. Kt. fifth	10 B. to Q. Kt. fifth
11. P. to Q. B. third	11. P. takes P.
12. P. takes P.	12. B. to K. second
13. B. takes B.	13. Kt. takes B.
14. Q. Kt. to K. Kt. fifth	14. Castles (K. R.)

and the game is about even. These moves are from a game between Mayet and Der Laza. If Black had played 9. B. to K. second, the reply is 10. B. to K. Kt. fifth.

(A)

5. P. to K. fifth, or (B)	5. P. to Q. fourth.
6. B. to Q. Kt. fifth	6. Kt. to K. fifth
7. Kt. takes P.	7. B to Q. B. fourth
8. P. to Q. B. third	8. Castles
9. B. takes Kt.	9. P. takes B.
10. Castles	

and again the game is reduced into the Giuoco Piano.

(B)

5. Kt. to K. Kt. fifth	5. P. to Q. fourth (best)
6. P. takes P.	6. Kt. to Q. R. fourth
7. B. to Q. Kt. fifth (check)	7. P. to Q. B. third
8. P. takes P.	8. P. takes P.
9. Q. to K. B. third	9. Q. to Q. Kt. third, with a manifest advantage.

We must here close our examination of this interesting opening. It has been shown that the defence, if properly conducted, is, in our opinion, satisfactory against every mode of attack. We do not, however, pretend to have made an exhaustive analysis of the variations, and it is quite possible that some amateur, with more leisure than we can command, may be able to invalidate our conclusions.

CHESS IN INDIA.

LETTER II.

TO THE EDITOR OF THE "CHESS PLAYER'S MAGAZINE."

Sir,— As India is now generally held to have the best claim to be considered the birthplace of Chess, a brief account of the particulars in which the Hindoo game, as played at the present day, differs from our own, may not be without interest. I must premise, however, that considerable diversities of practice appear to exist in various parts of Hindostan. The following rules are those which I found in force among the players of the Deccan:—

1. The King is always placed on the right of the Queen. Hence, of course, the King of one player is always stationed opposite to the Queen of the other.

2. The board is placed with a white or black square to the right hand indifferently.

3. The two royal Pawns and the Rooks' Pawns may advance two squares on their first move, provided the pieces in front of which they are respectively stationed have not been moved. But if any of the said pieces has moved, the Pawn in front of it may only advance one square. The four remaining Pawns may only advance one square on their first move.

4. Taking Pawn with Pawn *en passant* is altogether unknown.

5. Castling is not allowed. Once in the game, however, the King has the privilege of moving like a Knight, provided he has not been checked.

6. When a Pawn arrives at its eighth square it can only be exchanged for the piece on whose file it has been marching, or a piece of the same denomination. Thus, a Bishop's Pawn becomes a Bishop, a Knight's Pawn becomes a Knight, &c. But if a Bishop's Pawn, for example, becomes transferred to the Knight's file, and reaches the eighth square, it then becomes a Knight, and *vice versâ*. This rule cannot, of course, apply to the King's Pawn, which on reaching the eighth square may be exchanged for any piece which the player chooses to demand.

7. If, at the end of the game, either player is left with only one piece, with or without Pawns, the game is drawn; or if only Pawns are left the game is drawn. This rule, however, admits of various modifications. In some cases, if one piece only is left, it becomes endowed with new powers, and renders it difficult for the adversary to escape. But this, I presume, is rather a mode of giving odds than a distinct variety of the game.

8. At the commencement of the game White makes four moves first, of course without crossing his own half of the board. Black, then, under the same limitation, makes four moves in his turn. After that they move alternately, as in the European game. It may be remarked that Mr. Lewis found the same custom (which is probably very ancient) still in force among the villagers of Stroebeck.

The above are the rules commonly followed in the Bombay Presidency, so far as I was able to ascertain them. I must observe, however, that some of the native players, through their intercourse with Europeans, have introduced the practice of castling. Hence I have seen them practice castling in a great variety of strange fashions, and I once observed a player move his King to Bishop's second square, then leap the Rook to King's square over the heads of Bishop and Knight, and finally place his King in the corner, all these evolutions being considered as one move. Most Hindoos, however, seem to maintain the ancient laws of the game, to which castling is unknown.

In the North-west Provinces, where Chess exists more nearly in its primitive form than in the Deccan, none of the Pawns are allowed to advance more than one square for their first move. I believe that I also observed some other points of difference, but my memory will not now serve me with the particulars.

The pieces commonly used in India are of a very rude and ancient type, resembling rather draughts than chessmen. The King and Queen are not much larger than the Pawns, and it is hard to distinguish one piece from another. The Rook is termed the Camel, the Knight is the Horse, and the Bishop is the Elephant. The Queen is called the Wuzeer—*i. e.*, Vizier, or Prime Minister, while the Pawn is the Peon, or Foot Soldier.

One very singular variety of the game should be mentioned as still extant in Western India. In this mode of play, no piece can be taken as long as it is supported by any other piece, but in other respects the rules are similar to those of ordinary Chess. This description of game forms a connecting link between Chess and draughts, to which last it bears in principle a strong resemblance.

I remain, Sir, yours, &c.,

INDUS.

THE NEW SCHEME OF TABULAR CHESS NOTATION.

We are glad to find from numerous communications lately received that the ingenious method of notation brought forward by our esteemed correspondent Mr. Thomas Long meets with very general approval. The specimen of it which we printed last month sufficiently exhibits its advantage over our cumbrous system of ordinary notation, and we quite hope to see it adopted in future works on the theory of the openings.

We have much pleasure in extracting the following eulogium from our popular contemporary, *Bell's Life in London*:—

"In the January number of Löwenthal's *Chess Player's Magazine* we have an interesting article contributed by Thomas Long, Esq., of the Dublin Chess Club, being a variation of the Evans's Gambit, displayed in a huge broadside, with the best moves taken from the chief writers and players on both sides. We only wish Mr. Long had given instead one of the more brilliant variations of our favourite *début*, since declining the Gambit by simply retreating Bishop to Q. Kt. third will rarely be countenanced by those who wish to elicit interesting positions to play."

In justice to Mr. Long we ought to say that he had originally selected the Allgaier Gambit as a specimen of his plan. Finding that, however, too lengthy for our pages, he chose the Evans's Gambit Declined as an opening sufficiently distinct in itself, and admitting of compression into a more moderate compass.

GAMES.

GAME 118.

Game the fourth in the match between Mr. De Vere and Herr Steinitz.

(Remove Black's K. B. Pawn.)

White. (Mr. De Vere.)	Black. (Herr Steinitz.)
1. P. to Q. fourth	1. K. Kt. to B. third
2. Q. Kt. to B. third	2. P. to K. third
3. P. to K. fourth	3. K. B. to Kt. fifth
4. Q. B. to Kt. fifth	4. P. to K. R. third
5. B. takes Kt.	5. Q. takes B.
6. P. to K. fifth	6. Q. to B. second
7. K. B. to Q. third	7. Castles
8. K. Kt. to B. third	8. Q. Kt. to B. third
9. Castles	9. K. B. to K. second (*a*)
10. Kt. to K. fourth	10. P. to Q. Kt. third
11. P. to B. third	11. B. to Kt. second
12. B. to B. second	12. B. to Q. square
13. Q to Q. third	13. P. to Kt. third
14. Q. R. to K. square	14. K. to Kt second
15. Kt. to Kt. third	15. Kt. to K. second (*b*)
16. Kt. to R. fifth (check)	16. K. to R. square
17. Kt. to B. sixth	17. Kt. to B. fourth (*c*)
18. P. to K. Kt. fourth	18. B. takes Kt.
19. P. takes Kt. (*d*)	19. Kt. P. takes P. (*e*)
20. P. takes B.	20. R. to Kt. square (check)
21. K. to R. square	21. Q. to K. fourth
22. B. to Q. square	22. R. to Kt. fifth
23. R. to K. Kt. square	23. Q. R. to K. Kt. square
24. P. to B. fourth	24. B. to K. fifth
25. Q. to K. third	25. Q. R. to Kt. fourth (*f*)
26. Q. takes B. (*g*)	26. P. takes Q.
27. Kt. takes R.	27. R. takes R. (check)
28. R. takes R.	28. Q. to Kt. third
29. P. to B. seventh	29. Q. to K. B. third

30. B. to R. fifth	30. P. takes Kt.
31. R. takes P.	31. Q. takes R. (*h*)
32. P. Queens (check)	32. K. to R. second
33. Q. to B. seventh (check)	33. K. to R. third
34. B. to Q. square	34. Q. to Q. seventh
35. Q. to R. fifth (check)	35. K. to Kt. second
36. Q. to Kt. fourth (check)	36. K. to B. square
37. K. to Kt. second	37. Q. takes Q. P.
38. P. to K. R. fourth	38. Q. takes Q. B. P.
39. P. to K. R. fifth	39. Q. takes Q. R. P.
40. Q. to B. fourth (check)	40. K. to Kt. square
41. Q. to Kt. fifth (check)	41. K. to B. second
42. Q. to Kt. sixth (check)	42. K. to K. second
43. Q. to Kt. seventh (check)	43. Resigns

NOTES.

(*a*) Apprehensive, no doubt, of Kt. to K. R. fourth.
(*b*) Although this masks the King's Bishop, it seems to be the best move.
(*c*) Evidently the best resource.

Position after Black's 18th move.

BLACK.

WHITE.

(*d*) If at this point White had taken the Bishop, the following is the probable result :—

P. takes B.	Kt. to Q. third, or (A)

Kt. to K. R. fourth, with a manifest advantage.

(A)

	R. to K. Kt. square (best)
P. takes Kt.	Kt. P. takes P. (dis. check)
K. to R. square	Q. to K. R. fourth
B. to Q. square	R. to K. Kt. fifth
R. to K. Kt square	Q. R. to K. Kt. square

And the position is the same as in the actual game.

(e) If Black had retreated the Bishop to Queen's square, he would have been involved in almost hopeless difficulties. By the move adopted he obtained a fine attack.

(f) The position here is one of unusual interest, and both attack and defence are conducted with great skill. Black now threatens mate thus:—

	26. Q. takes R. P. (check)
27. K. takes Q.	27. R. to R. fourth (check)
28. Kt. to K. R. fourth	28. K. R. takes Kt. (check)
29. K. to Kt. third	29. P. to K. B. fifth (check)
30. Q. takes P.	30. R. to K. R. sixth (check)
31. K. to Kt. fourth	31. Q. R. to R. fifth, mate.

(g) This is very finely played, and is as sound as it is brilliant.

(h) There was nothing better to do.

Position after White's 26th move.

BLACK.

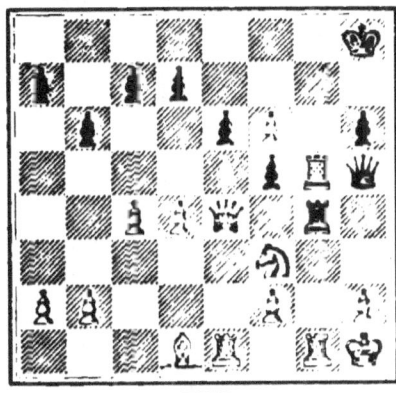

WHITE.

GAME 119

Game the fifth in the match between Mr. De Vere and Herr Steinitz.

(*Remove Black's K. B. Pawn.*)

White. (Mr. DE VERE.)	Black. (Herr STEINITZ.)
1. P. to K. fourth	1. P. to Q. Kt. third
2. P. to Q. fourth	2. B. to Kt. second
3. B. to Q. third	3. Kt. to Q. B. third
4. P. to Q. fifth	4. Kt. to K. fourth
5. P. to K. B. fourth	5. Kt. takes B. (check)
6. Q. takes Kt.	6. P. to K. Kt. third
7. B. to K. third	7. K. B. to Kt. second
8. B. to Q. fourth	8. Kt. to B. third
9. Kt. to Q. B. third	9. Castles

10. B. takes Kt. (*a*)	10. B. takes B.
11. P. to K. fifth	11. B. to Kt. second
12. K. Kt. to K. second	12. P. to Q. third
13. P. to K. sixth	13. P. to Q. B. third
14. Castles (K. R.)	14. P. takes P.
15. Kt. takes P.	15. B. takes Kt. P.
16. Q. R. to Kt. square	16. B. to Kt. second
17. Kt. to K. Kt. third	17. B. takes Kt.
18. Q. takes B.	18. Q. to B. second
19. P. to Q. B. fourth	19. Q. R. to Q. B. square
20. Q. R. to Q. B. square	20. Q. to B. fourth (check) (*b*)
21. K. to R. square	21. Q. takes Q.
22. P. takes Q.	22. R. takes R.
23. R. takes R.	23. R. takes P.
24. R. to Q. B. eighth (check)	24. B. to B. square
25. P. to K. R. third	25. R. to Q. fifth
26. R. to Q. R. eighth	26. R. takes Q. P.
27. R. takes Q. R. P.	27. R. to K. fourth
28. R. to R. sixth	28. R. takes P.
29. R. takes P.	29. R. to K. eighth (check)
30. K. to R. second	30. B. to Kt. second
31. R. to Q. Kt. third	31. B. to K. fourth
32. P. to K. R. fourth	32. R. to Q. R. eighth
33. P. to Q. R. third	33. P. to Q. fourth
34. K. to R. third	34. P. to K. R. fourth, and wins

NOTES.

(*a*) Having parted already with one Bishop we should have preferred retaining the other. K. Kt to K. second seems a good move.

(*b*) Black has now recovered the Pawn given, and, as he is enabled to exchange Queens, the superior position of his Pawns gives him the victory.

GAME 120.

Game the sixth in the match between Mr. De Vere and Herr Steinitz.

(*Remove Black's K. B. Pawn.*)

White. (Mr. DE VERE.)	*Black.* (Herr STEINITZ.)
1. P. to K. fourth	1. P. to Q. Kt. third
2. P. to Q. fourth	2. B. to Q. Kt. second
3. B. to Q. third	3. Kt. to Q. B. third
4. Kt. to K. B. third (*a*)	4. P. to K. third
5. Castles	5. K. Kt. to K. second
6. B. to K. Kt. fifth	6. P. to K. R. third
7. B. to K. third	7. P. to K. Kt. third

8. P. to Q. B. third	8. B. to K. Kt. second
9. Kt. to R. fourth	9. Castles
10. P. to K. fifth	10. P. to K. Kt. fourth
11. Kt. to K. B. third	11. Kt. K. B. fourth
12. Q. Kt. to Q. second	12. P. to K. Kt. fifth
13. Kt. to K. square	13. Q. to R. fifth
14. B. to K. fourth	14. P. to Q. fourth
15. B. takes Kt.	15. R. takes B.
16. P. to K. B. fourth	16. Q. B. to R. third (b)
17. P. to K. Kt. third	17. Q. to her square
18. R. to K. B. second	18. P. to K. R. fourth
19. Kt. to K. Kt. second	19. Kt. to K. second
20. Kt. to K. R. fourth	20. R. to B. second
21. P. to K. R. third	21. Kt. to K. B. fourth
22. Kt. takes Kt.	22. P. takes Kt.
23. P. to K. R. fourth	23. B. to K. B. square
24. Q. to Q. B. second	24. Q. to Q. second
25. P. to Q. R. fourth	25. P. to Q. B. fourth
26. R. to K. square	26. Q. to her B. third
27. Kt. to K. B. square	27. Q. B. to B. square
28. K. R. to Q. second	28. B. to K. third
29. B. to K. B. second	29. P. to Q. B. fifth
30. P. to Q. Kt. third	30. Q. B. P. takes P.
31. Q. takes Q. Kt. P.	31. R. to Q. B. square
32. R. to Q. B. square	32. Q. to Q. B. fifth
33. Q. to Q. square (c)	33. B. to Q. R. sixth
34. Kt. to K. third	34. Q. to R. third
35. R. from Q. B. sq. to Q. B. 2	35. R. to Q. second (d)
36. Q. to her R. square	36. B. to K. B. square
37. Q. to R. second	37. Q. to Q. Kt. second
38. Q. to Q. Kt. third	38. K. R. to Q. B. second
39. R. to Q. square	39. Q. to B. third
40. K. R. to Q. B. square	40. Q. to Q. Kt. second
41. Q. to Q. Kt. fifth	41. K. to B. second (e)
42. Q. to Q. third	42. K. to Kt. third
43. B. to K. square	43. Q. to Q. B. third
44. Q. to Q. Kt. fifth	44. B. to Q. R. sixth
45. R. to Q. R. square	45. Q. takes Q.
46. P. takes Q.	46. B. to K. second
47. R. from B. 2nd to Q. R. 2nd	47. R. to Q. R. square
48. K. to Kt. second	48. R. to Q. second
49. B. to K. B. second	49. K. to B. second
50. P. to Q. B. fourth (f)	50. P. takes P.

51. P. to Q. fifth	51. B. takes P. (check)
52. Kt. takes B.	52. R. takes Kt.
53. R. takes P.	53. R. takes R.
54. R. takes R.	54. R. takes Kt. P.
55. R. to Q. B. seventh	55. R. to Q. Kt. fifth (*g*)
56. R to Q. B. sixth	56. R. to Q. Kt. seventh (*h*)
57. K. to B. square (*i*)	57. P. to Q. Kt. fourth
58. P. to K. sixth (check)	58. K. to Kt. third
59. B. to Q. fourth	59. R. to Q. seventh
60. B. to K. fifth	60. R. to Q. square
61. K. to K. second	61. R. to Q. R. square
62. R. to Q. B. seventh	62. B. to K. B. third
63. R. to Q. Kt. seventh	63. R. to Q. R. seventh (check)
64. K. to Q. square	64. B. takes B.
65. P. takes B.	65. R. to R. third
66. P. to K. seventh	66. R. to K. third (*k*)
67. R. to Kt. sixth	67. K. to B. second
68. R. takes R.	68. And Black resigns.

NOTES.

(*a*) We like this better than pushing the Queen's Pawn, as in the previous game

(*b*) R. to R. fourth would have been bad play; let us suppose

	16. R. to R. fourth
17. P. to K. R. third	17. P. takes P.

18. B. to B. second, winning without difficulty.

(*c*) To exchange Queens would have been imprudent, as the Pawns on Queen's side would soon have been indefensible.

Position after White's 85th move,

BLACK.

WHITE.

(d) Taking the proffered Pawn would have involved the loss of a piece—e. g.,
　　　　　　　　　　　　　　　　35. Q. takes R. P.
36. P. to Q. B. fourth　　　　　36. K. R. to Q. B. second
37. P. takes P.　　　　　　　　37. R. takes R.
38. R. takes R.　　　　　　　　38. R. takes R.
39. Q. takes R.　　　　　　　　39. Q. takes Q.
40. Kt. takes Q., and wins.

(e) This was very well conceived. Had Black made the apparently obvious move, B. to R. sixth, White would have speedily obtained an easy victory, thus:—
　　　　　　　　　　　　　　　41. B. to R. sixth
42. R. to R. square　　　　　　42. R. takes P.
43. R. takes R.　　　　　　　　43. R. takes R.
44. Q. to K. eighth (check), winning a piece.

(f) Premature; White should first have played 50. R. to R. sixth, compelling Black to move R. to Kt. second, and by then playing 51. P. to Q. B. fourth, White's attack becomes irresistible.

(g) Very well played, if
　　　　　　　　　　　　　　　55. R. to Kt. seventh
56. K. to B. square.　　　　　　56. P. to Kt. fourth
57. B. to B. fifth, winning a piece.

(h) Black again selected the best move.

(i) It is obvious that taking the P. with R. would lose White the exchange, at least, by Black's reply B. to B. fourth.

(k) What a mistake to occur in a match game! Throwing away a won game.

GAME 121.

Game the seventh in the match between Mr. De Vere and Herr Steinitz.

(*Remove Black's K. B. Pawn.*)

White. (Mr. DE VERE.)	*Black.* (Herr STEINITZ.)
1. P. to K. fourth	1. P. to Q. Kt. third
2. P. to Q. fourth	2. B. to Q. Kt. second
3. B. to Q. third	3. Kt. to Q. B. third
4. Kt. to K. B. third	4. P. to K. third
5. Castles	5. Kt. to K. R. third
6. Kt. to Q. B. third	6. Kt. to B. second
7. B. to K. B. fourth	7. B. to K. second
8. B. to K. Kt. third	8. Castles
9. P. to Q. R. third	9. R. to Q. B. square
10. P. to Q. fifth	10. P. takes P. (*a*)
11. P. takes P.	11. Q. Kt. to Kt. square
12. Q. Kt. to Kt. fifth	12. Q. Kt. to R. third
13. Kt. takes R. P.	13. R. to R. square
14. Kt. to Q. Kt. fifth	14. K. B. to B. third
15. P. to Q. B. third	15. K. to R. square
16. B. to B. second	16. Q. to K. second
17. P. to Q. Kt. fourth	17. P. to Q. third
18. Q. to Q. third	18. P. to K. Kt. third

19. Q. R. to K. square	19. Q. to Q. second
20. P. to Q. B. fourth	20. Kt. to Kt. square
21. R. to K. sixth	21. Kt. to Q. square
22. R. takes B.	22. R. takes R.
23. Q. to B. third	23. K. to Kt. second
24. B. to K. R. fourth	24. Q. to B. second
25. Kt. to Kt. fifth	25. Q. to B. square
26. Kt. takes B. P.	26. K. to Kt. square (b)
27. Kt. takes R.	27. B. takes Kt.
28. Kt. takes R. P.	28. And Black surrenders.

NOTES.

(a) It would, perhaps, have been better to retreat the Kt. at once to Kt. square.

(b) In order to save the Queen Black is now compelled to submit to the loss of the exchange. His game, however, is past redemption.

GAME 122.

Game the eighth in the match between Mr. De Vere and Herr Steinitz.

(Remove Black's K. B. Pawn.)

White. (Mr. DE VERE.)	*Black.* (Herr STEINITZ.)
1. P. to K. fourth	1. P. to Q. third
2. P. to Q. fourth	2. Kt. to K. B. third
3. Kt. to Q. B. third	3. Kt. to Q. B. third
4. B. to K. Kt. fifth	4. P. to K. third
5. Kt. to K. B. third	5. P. to K. R. third
6. B. takes Kt.	6. Q. takes B.
7. B. to Q. third	7. B. to Q. second
8. P. to Q. R. third	8. Kt. takes P. (a)
9. Kt. takes Kt.	9. Q. takes Kt.
10. Q. to R. fifth (check)	10. K. to Q. square
11. Castles (K. R.)	11. B. to K. second
12. Q. R. to Q. square	12 P. to B. third
13. Q. to K. second	13. K. to B. second
14. B. to B. fourth	14. Q. to B. fourth
15. R. to Q. second	15. Q. R. to Q. square
16. P. to Q. Kt. fourth	16. Q. to K. fourth (b)
17. Q. to K. third	17. P. to K. Kt. fourth
18. B. to K. second	18. K. to Kt. square
19. R. to Kt. square	19. P. to K. R. fourth
20. P. to Q. Kt. fifth	20. P. to Q. B. fourth (c)
21. P. to Kt. sixth	21. P. to R. third
22. P. to Q. R. fourth (d)	22. Q. B. to Q. B. third

23. K. B. to Q. B. fourth	23. P. to K. R. fifth
24. P. to K. R. third	24. P. to K. Kt. fifth (e)
25. Q. to Q. third	25. P. to Q. fourth
26. P. takes P.	26. P. takes P.
27. R. to K. second	27. Q. to K. Kt. fourth
28. B. takes Q. P.	28. B. takes B.
29. Kt. takes B.	29. R. takes Kt.
30. Q. to K. fourth	30. B. to Q. square
31. P. takes P.	31. R. to Q. fifth
32. Q. to K. sixth	32. R. takes P. at K. Kt. fourth
33. Q. to Q. sixth (check)	33. K. to R. square
34. P. to K. B. third	34. R. to Q. fifth, and wins.

NOTES.

(a) White gives up a Pawn designedly, in order to displace Black's King. The sacrifice, however, was hardly judicious.

(b) Black's forces are now well developed. He has recovered his Pawn, and his position is certainly superior to that of White.

(c) Taking the Pawn would evidently be imprudent.

(d) If,

22. B. takes R. P.	22. P. takes B.
23. Q. to K. second	23. Q. B. to B. square
24. P. to Kt. seventh	24. B. takes P.
25. Q. takes Q. R. P.	25. R. to Q. second

With a safe game.

(e) Threatening to win the exchange, and also having an eye to the advance of the Queen's Pawn.

GAME 123.

Game the ninth in the match between Mr. De Vere and Herr Steinitz.

(*Remove Black's K. B. Pawn.*)

White. (Mr. DE VERE.)	Black. (Herr STEINITZ.)
1. P. to K. fourth	1. P. to Q. third
2. P. to Q. fourth	2. Kt. to K. B. third
3. Kt. to Q. B. third	3. Kt. to Q. B. third
4. B. to K. Kt. fifth (a)	4. P. to K. third
5. Kt. to K. B. third	5. P. to K. R. third
6. B. to R. fourth	6. P. to K. Kt. fourth
7. B. to Kt. third	7. B. to Kt. second
8. K. B. to Kt. fifth	8. Castles
9. Castles	9. K. Kt. to R. second
10. P. to K. R. third	10. K. to R. square
11. B. takes Kt.	11. P. takes B.
12. P. to K. fifth	12. Q. to K. second (b)
13. Q. Kt. to K. fourth	13. R. to Q. square
14. Q. to K. second	14. P. to Q. R. fourth

15. Q. to K. third	15. Kt. to B. square
16. Q. to Q. R. third (c)	16. P. to B. fourth
17. P. takes Q. P.	17. B. P. takes P.
18. P. takes B. P.	18. P. takes P.
19. K. Kt. to K. fifth (d)	19. R. to Q. fourth
20. Kt. to Q. third (e)	20. B. to Q. R. third
21. K. R. to K. square	21. B. takes Kt.
22. P. takes B.	22. Q. to Q. Kt. second
23. Q. R. to Kt. square	23. Q. to Kt. fifth
24. K. R. to K. third (f)	24. Kt. to Q. second
25. Kt. to Q. sixth	25. Q. takes Q.
26. P. takes Q.	26. P. to K. fourth
27. Kt. to B. fourth	27. P. to R. fifth (g)
28. Kt. to Kt. sixth	28. R. to Q. Kt. square
29. Kt. takes R.	29. R. takes R. (check)
30. K. to R. second	30. R. to Q. eighth (h)
31. Kt. to K. seventh	31. R. to Q. seventh
32. Kt. to Kt. sixth (check)	32. K. to R. second
33. Kt. takes P.	33. Kt. takes Kt.
34. B. takes Kt.	34. R. takes R. P.
35. B. takes B.	35. K. takes B.
36. R. to K. fifth	36. R. takes R. P.
37. R. takes P.	37. R. takes P.
38. R. to Q. B. sixth	38. P. to R. sixth (i)
39. R. to R. sixth	39. P. to R. fourth
40. P. to Kt. third	40. K. to B. second
41. K. to Kt. second	41. K. to K. second
42. P. to R. fourth	42. P. takes P.
43. P. takes P.	43. K. to B. second
44. P. to B. third	44. R. to Q. seventh (check)
45. K. to Kt. third	45. P. to R. seventh
46. K. to B. fourth	46. R. to K. Kt. seventh
47. K. to B. fifth	47. R. to Q. Kt. seventh
48. R. to R. seventh (check)	48. K. to B. square
49. P. to B. fourth	49. R. to K. Kt. seventh
50. K. to B. sixth	50. K. to Kt. square
51. P. to B. fifth	51. K. to R. square
52. R. to R. eighth (check)	52. K. to R. second
53. R. to R. seventh (check)	53. K. to R. square
54. K. to K. sixth	54. K. to Kt. square
55. P. to B. sixth	55. R. to K. seventh (check)
56. K. to B. fifth	56. R. to K. Kt. seventh

Drawn game.

NOTES.

(*a*) P. to Q. fifth is usually played here, but the move made (to which Mr. De Vere seems partial) is not without its merits.
(*b*) Taking the Pawn would leave Black's Pawns very much broken.
(*c*) At first sight this appears to win a Pawn, but Black's reply prevents any loss.
(*d*) Taking Pawn with either Queen or Knight would be very unwise.
(*e*) Kt. to Q. B. sixth would be very imprudent.
(*f*) This is much better than changing Queens.
(*g*) Correctly played, since White will gain nothing by Kt. to Kt. sixth.
(*h*) R. to Q. Kt. seventh seems a good move.
(*i*) The game, which has been remarkably well contested throughout, now becomes drawn by its nature.

GAME 124.

Game the tenth in the match between Mr. De Vere and Herr Steinitz.

(*Remove Black's K. B. Pawn.*)

White. (Mr. DE VERE.)	Black. (Herr STEINITZ.)
1. P. to K. fourth	1. P. to Q. third
2. P. to Q. fourth	2. Kt. to K. B. third
3. Kt. to Q. B. third	3. Kt. to Q. B. third (*a*)
4. P. to Q. fifth	4. Q. Kt. to K. fourth
5. P. to K. B. fourth	5. Kt. to K. B. second
6. Kt. to K. B. third	6. P. to K. fourth
7. Q. P. takes P. (*en passant*)	7. B. takes P.
8. P. to K. B. fifth (*b*)	8. B. to Q. second
9. B. to Q. B. fourth	9. Q. to K. second (*c*)
10. Castles	10. Castles
11. B. to K. Kt. fifth	11. P. to Q. B. third
12. Q. to Q. fourth	12. P. to Q. Kt. third
13. P. to Q. R. fourth (*d*)	13. K. to Kt. square
14. K. B. takes Kt. (*e*)	14. Q. takes B.
15. P. to Q. R. fifth	15. P. to Q. Kt. fourth
16. P. to K. fifth	16. P. takes P.
17. K. Kt. takes P.	17. Q. to K. second
18. B. to K. third	18. B. to K. square
19. Q. to K. B. fourth	19. Q. to Q. B. second
20. K. R. to K. square (*f*)	20. B. to Q. third
21. B. to K. B. second	21. Q. B. to K. R. fourth
22. Q. to K. third	22. B. takes Kt.
23. Q. takes B.	23. Q. takes Q.
24. R. takes Q.	24. Kt. to Kt. fifth (*g*)

Game drawn.

NOTES.

(a) P. to K. fourth is preferred by some players at this point.
(b) This gives White an excellent attack.
(c) Up to this move the opening is identical with that of a game between Popert and MacDonnell.
(d) White has now an overwhelming superiority of position.
(e) P. to Q. R. fifth would, perhaps, have been equally effective.
(f) Sacrificing the Bishop, though very tempting, is not sound.
(g) We cannot understand why White consented to draw the game, since to us he appears to have obtained an easy winning situation.

GAME 125

Consultation Game played in the St. James's Chess Club: Herr Lowenthal and Mr. Stewart against Messrs. Ranken and Wayte.

(*Evans's Gambit.*)

White. (Messrs. L. & S.)	Black. (Messrs. R. & W.)
1. P. to K. fourth	1. P. to K. fourth
2. K. Kt. to B. third	2. Q. Kt. to B. third
3. K. B. to Q. B. fourth	3. K. B. to Q. B. fourth
4. P. to Q. Kt. fourth	4. B. takes Q. Kt. P.
5. P. to Q. B. third	5. B. to Q. B. fourth
6. P. to Q. fourth	6. P. takes P.
7. Castles	7. P. to Q. third
8. P. takes P.	8. B. to Q. Kt. third
9. Q. Kt. to B. third	9. Kt. to Q. R. fourth
10. B. to Q. third	10. Kt. to K. second
11. P. to Q. fifth	11. Castles
12. B. to Q. Kt. second	12. Kt. to K. Kt. third
13. Q. to Q. second	13. P. to Q. B. fourth
14. Q. Kt. to K. second	14. P. to K. B. third
15. Q. R. to B. square	15. B. to Q. second
16. K. to R. square	16. P. to Q. R. third
17. K. Kt. to K. square	17. B. to Q. Kt. fourth
18. B. takes B. (*a*)	18. P. takes B.
19. P. to K. B. fourth	19. Kt. to Q. B. fifth
20. R. takes Kt. (*b*)	20. P. takes R.
21. P. to Q. R. third	21. B. to Q. R. fourth
22. Q. to K. third	22. P. to Q. Kt. fourth
23. Q. to Q. B. square (*c*)	23. P. to K. B. fourth (*d*)
24. Kt. to K. Kt. third	24. P. takes P.
25. Kt. takes P.	25. R. to K. B. fourth
26. P. to K. Kt. fourth	26. R. takes Q. P.

27. P. to K. B. fifth	27. Kt. to K. fourth
28. P. to K. B. sixth (e)	28. B. takes Kt. (f)
29. Q. to K. Kt. fifth	29. Q. to K. B. square
30. R. takes B.	30. Q. R. to R. second
31. Q. to K. B. fifth	31. Q. to Q. R. square (g)
32. P. takes K. Kt. P. (h)	32. Q. R. to K. B. second
33. Q. to K. sixth	33. R. to Q. eighth

And White resigns.

NOTES.

(a) The same situation occurs, with some transpositions, after the 17th move in a game between Messrs. Kolisch and Paulsen. It is difficult to suggest a good move for White at this point; the move in the text is obviously not the best, as it opens a good square for the adverse Knight on Q. B. fifth. The game just referred to was continued thus :—

18. P. to K. B. fourth	18. P. to Q. B. fifth
19. B. to Q. Kt. square	19. P. to Q. B. sixth.

By sacrificing this Pawn Mr. Paulsen obtained a winning attack. (See the "Games of the Congress," p. 357, where it is remarked that White should rather have played Q. B. to his third, instead of Q. R. to Q. B. square). If White now played 18. Q. B. to B. third, the correct reply is K. Kt. to K. fourth, with the advantage.

(b) White's only chance lies in sacrificing the exchange, and trying to get up an attack. If the Queen is moved, R. takes Q. R. P., with a winning game.

(c) To check the further advance of Black's Pawn.

(d) Hazardous again on the other side. By leaving the position on the King's side undisturbed, and preparing to advance on the Queen's wing, Black must have won without much trouble.

(e) White has now a threatening position, demanding the greatest exactitude in the defence.

Position after White's 28th move.
BLACK.

WHITE.

(f) Gaining time, since White must take with Rook, and the K. B. file is relieved from the attack.

(g) The winning move.

(h) K. to Kt. square would not have led to any better result.

GAME 126.
(Allgaier Gambit.)

White. (Mr. WATYE.)	Black. (Mr. LOWENTHAL.)
1. P. to K. fourth	1. P. to K. fourth
2. P. to K. B. fourth	2. P. takes P.
3. K. Kt. to B. third	3. P. to K. Kt. fourth
4. P. to K. R. fourth	4. P. to K. Kt. fifth
5. Kt. to K. fifth	5. K. Kt. to B. third
6. B. to Q. B. fourth	6. P. to Q. fourth
7. P. takes P.	7. B. to Q. third
8. P. to Q. fourth	8. Q. to K. second
9. Q. B. takes P.	9. K. Kt. to R. fourth
10. P. to K. Kt. third	10. P. to K. B. third
11. Q. to K. second	11. P. takes Kt.
12. P. takes P.	12. Kt. takes B.
13. P. takes Kt.	13. B. to Q. B. fourth
14. Kt. to Q. second	14. B. to K. B. fourth (a)
15. Castles (Q. R.)	15. Kt. to Q. second
16. P. to K. sixth	16. Kt. to Q. Kt. third (b)
17. B. to Q. Kt. fifth (check)	17. K. to Q. square (c)
18. Q. to K. fifth (d)	18. R. to K. B. square
19. Kt. to K. fourth	19. B. to K. sixth (check)
20. K. to Kt. square	20. B. takes Kt.
21. P. to Q. sixth (e)	21. P. takes P.
22. R. takes P. (check)	22. K. to B. square
23. B. to Q. seventh (check)	23. Kt. takes B.
24. R. takes Kt.	24. B. takes Q. B. P. (check)
25. K. takes B.	25. Q. to Q. B. fourth (check)
26. Q. takes Q.	26. B. takes Q.
27. R. takes K. R. P.	27. P. to Q. R. fourth
28. P. to K. seventh	28. K. R. to K. square
29. K. R. to K. square	29. Q. R. to R. third
30. Q. R. to K. Kt. seventh	30. R. to Q. B. third
31. K. to Q. third	31. P. to K. Kt. sixth
32. R. takes P.	32. B. takes P. (f)
33. R. to K. Kt. fourth	33. K. R. to Q. square (check)
34. K. to K. second	34. B. to Q. Kt. fifth
35. K. R. to Q. Kt. square	35. Q. R. to K. third (check)
36. K. to B. square	36. K. R. to Q. seventh
37. P. to Q. R. third	37. B. to Q. B. fourth
38. Q. R. to K. Kt. second	38. R. to Q. sixth
39. Q. R. to Q. B. second	39. R. to Q. B. third
40. R. to Q. B. square	40. R. to Q. fourth

41. P. to Q. Kt. fourth	41. P. takes P.
42. P. takes P.	42. B. takes P.
43. R. takes R. (check)	43. P. takes R.
44. R. takes P. (check)	44. K. to Q. second
45. R. to K. Kt. sixth	

And the game was ultimately drawn.

NOTES.

(a) The opening moves are the best on both sides in this branch of the Allgaier Compare pp. 11, 373 of our last volume.

(b) Kt. to K. B. third is, perhaps, better.

(c) If K. to R. square, White would win a piece by playing Q. to K. fifth.

(d) This move is now useless. White should have played at once Kt. to K. fourth.

(e) The only resource to avoid the loss of a Pawn.

Position after White's 21st move.

BLACK.

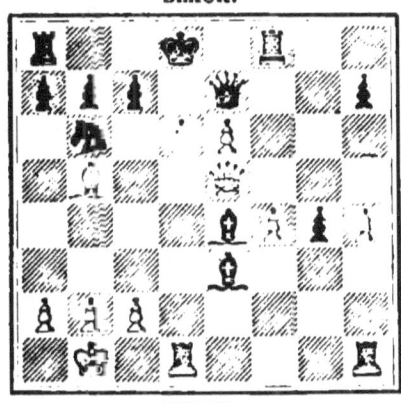

WHITE.

(f) Had he played B. to K. B. seventh, as he must have intended when he advanced the P. to K. Kt. sixth, White would have replied with R. to K. Kt. eighth, and have escaped without loss.

GAME 127.

One of five games played a short time since between Mr. Robey and Herr Steinitz, of which Herr S. won four, and lost the one which we produce to our readers.

(*Evans's Gambit.*)

White. (Mr. ROBEY.)	Black. (Herr STEINITZ.)
1. P. to K. fourth	1. P. to K. fourth
2. Kt. to K. B. third	2. Q. Kt. to B. third
3. B. to Q. B. fourth	3. B. to Q. B. fourth

4. P. to Q. Kt. fourth	4. B. takes Kt. P.
5. P. to Q. B. third	5. B. to B. fourth
6. Castles	6. P. to Q. third
7. P. to Q. fourth	7. P. takes P.
8. P. takes P.	8. B. to Q. Kt. third
9. Q. Kt. to B. third	9. Q. Kt. to R. fourth
10. P. to K. fifth	10. P. takes P.
11. B. takes P. (check)	11. K. to B. square (a)
12. B. to Q. R. third (check)	12. Kt. to K. second
13. Kt. takes K. P.	13. Q. takes P.
14. Q. to K. R. fifth	14. Q. takes Q. Kt.
15. Q. R. to Q. square	15. P. to Q. B. fourth
16. R. to Q. third (b)	16. Q. takes R. (c)
17. Kt. takes Q.	17. P. to K. Kt. third
18. Q. to B. third	18. K. to Kt. second
19. B. to Kt. second (check) (d)	19. K. to R. third

White mates in four moves (see Diagram).

Final position.
BLACK.

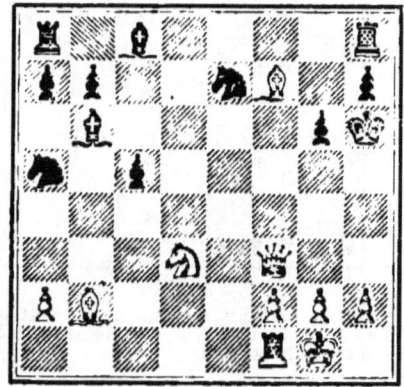

WHITE.
White to play, and mate in four moves.

NOTES.

(a)]
12. Kt. takes K. P., with a fine attacking game.   11. K. takes B.

(b) B. to Q. Kt. third could have been played with equal effect—e. g.,

16. B. to Q. Kt. third, threatening mate   16. P. to K. Kt. third (A)
17. Q. to R. sixth (check)   17. K. to K. square
18. B. to B. seventh (mate)

(A)

                                          16. Kt. to Kt. third
17. Kt. takes Kt. (check)   17. P. takes Kt.
18. Q. takes R. (check), followed by K. R. to K. square (ch.), winning easily.

(c) Compulsory; for if 16. Q. to Q. B. seventh, 18. B. to Q. Kt. third, &c.

(d) Mr. Roboy conducted the game throughout with great dash and spirit.

GAME 128.

We extract the following instructive Game from the *Neue Berliner Schachzeitung*:—

(*Ruy Lopez Knight's Game*).

White. (Herr Neumann.)	*Black.* (Herr Anderssen.)
1. P. to K. fourth	1. P. to K. fourth
2. Kt. to K. B. third	2. Kt. to Q. B. third
3. B. to Q. Kt. fifth	3. P. to Q. third
4. B. takes Kt. (check) (*a*)	4. P. takes B.
5. P. to Q. fourth	5. P. takes P.
6. Kt. takes P.	6. P. to Q. B. fourth
7. Kt. to K. B. third	7. P. to K. Kt. third
8. Castles	8. B. to K. Kt. second
9. Kt. to Q. B. third	9. Kt. to K. second
10. P. to K. fifth	10. Castles (*b*)
11. B. to K. Kt. fifth	11. P. to K. B. third
12. P. takes K. B. P.	12. B. takes P.
13. B. takes B.	13. R. takes B.
14. R. to K. square	14. B. to Q. Kt. second
15. Kt. to K. Kt. fifth	15. Q. to Q. second
16. Q. Kt. to K. fourth	16. R. to K. B. fourth
17. Q. to Q. third	17. Q. R. to K. B. square
18. Q. R. to Q. square	18. Kt. to Q. fourth
19. Q. to K. R. third (*c*)	19. Kt. to K. B. fifth
20. Q. to Q. Kt. third (check)	20. B. to Q. fourth
21. P. to Q. B. fourth	21. B. takes Kt. (*d*)
22. Kt. takes R.	22. Q. to K. Kt. fifth
23. Q. to K. Kt. third	23. Q. takes R.
24. R. takes Q.	24. Kt. to K. seventh (check)
25. K. to R. square	25. Kt. takes Q. (check)
26. K. B. P. takes Kt.	26. B. takes Q. B. P.
27. P. to Q. Kt. third	27. B. to Q. fourth
28. Kt. to K. R. third	28. B. to K. fifth
29. R. to K. square	29. P. to Q. fourth
30. K. to Kt. square	30. R. to K. B. third
31. R. to Q. B. square	31. R. to Q. B. third
32. Kt. to K. Kt. fifth	32. B. to Q. sixth
33. K. to B. second	33. P. to Q. B. fifth
34. K. to K. third	34. P. takes P.

And White resigns.

NOTES.

(*a*) P. to Q. R. third leads to a far more powerful attack. In general it is wrong to take off the Knight early in this opening.

(*b*) This is much better than taking Pawn with Pawn.
(*c*) This is mere loss of time, and enables Black to form an attack too powerful to be long resisted.
(*d*) A fine combination, which leads to a speedy victory.

Position after Black's 21st move.
BLACK.

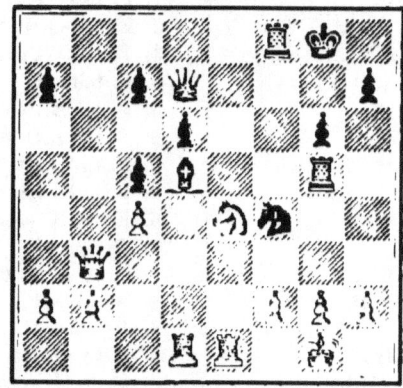

WHITE.

GAME 129.

The following two Games were played in Tournament No. 2 at the late Dublin meeting:—

(*Philidor's Defence.*)

White. (Mr. Bolt.)	Black. (Mr. G. F. Barry.)
1. P. to K. fourth	1. P. to K. fourth
2. Kt. to K. B. third	2. P. to Q. third
3. P. to Q. fourth	3. P. takes P.
4. Q. takes P.	4. Kt. to Q. B. third (*a*)
5. B. to Q. Kt. fifth	5. B. to Q. second
6. B. takes Kt.	6. B. takes B.
7. B. to Kt. fifth	7. P. to K. B. third
8. B. to R. fourth (*b*)	8. Kt. to R. third (*c*)
9. P. to K. R. third	9. B. to K. second
10. Kt. to B. third	10. Kt. to B. second
11. Castles (Q. R.)	11. Castles
12. Q. to B. fourth (*d*)	12. K. to R. square
13. Q. to Kt. third	13. Kt. to K. fourth
14. Kt. to Q. fourth	14. Q. to B. square (*e*)
15. P. to B. fourth	15. Kt. to Kt. third

16. B. to Kt. third	16. B. to Q. second
17. P. to B. fifth	17. Kt. to K. fourth
18. Kt. to Q. fifth	18. B. to Q. square
19. Kt. to B. fourth	19. P. to Q. R. fourth
20. P. to K. R. fourth (*f*)	20. P. to R. fifth (*g*)
21. Q. to Q. B. third	21. P. to B. fourth (*h*)
22. K. Kt. to K. sixth	22. B. to R. fourth
23. Q. to K. third	23. R. to B. second
24. Q. to K. second	24. R. to R. third
25. B. to B. second	25. R. to Kt. third
26. Q. to K. R. fifth	26. B. to K. square
27. Q. R. to Kt. square (*i*)	27. Q. to Q. second
28. Kt. to Kt. sixth (check)	28. K. to Kt. square
29. Kt. takes Kt.	29. Q. P. takes Kt.
30. R. to Q. square	30. Q. to Q. Kt. fourth
31. P. to Q. Kt. third	31. R. to Q. B. third
32. B. to K. square (*k*)	32. P. takes P.
33. R. P. takes P.	33. R. to R. third
34. K. to Kt. second	34. R. to K. second
35. Q. to B. third	35. R. to Q second
36. Q. to Kt. fourth	36. B. to Q Kt. third
37. R. to Q. sixth	37. P. to B. fifth
38. B. to B. third	38. P. takes P.
39. P. takes P.	39. P. to K. R. fourth
40. Q. to Q. square	40. R. takes R.
41. Q. takes R.	41. Q. to K. seventh (check)
42. Q. to Q. second	42. Q. takes K. P.
43. R. to K. B. square	43. B. to Q. B. third
44. R. to K. B. third	44. Q. takes R. P.
45. Q. to Q. sixth	45. Q. to Kt. fifth
46. Q. to B. eighth (check)	46. K. to R. second
47. R. to Q. third	47. Q. takes P. (check)
48. R. to Q. second	48. Q. to Kt. eighth
49. Q. to B. seventh	49. Q. to R. eighth (check)

And mates in four moves.

NOTES.

(*a*) B. to Q. second is now generally preferred.

(*b*) B. to K. third is by some considered better.

(*c*) The correct move here is Kt. to K. second.

(*d*) Mr. Bolt is evidently well versed in the theory of this opening; he conducted the attack most correctly, thereby maintaining the advantage of the first move.

(*e*) Feebly played. Black should have boldly sacrificed a pawn, moving B. to Q. second; for if, in reply, White takes Pawn with Queen, Black retorts with Q. R. to Kt. square, with an attacking position.

(*f*) To the tyro this move would seem insignificant, nay, a loss of time; a close scrutiny, however, will show how cleverly it was designed. White intended to advance this Pawn still further, having in view Kt. to Kt. sixth (check), &c.

(*g*) Well played, at once frustrating the design with which Black was menaced.

(*h*) From this point to the end the game is conducted by Mr. Barry with considerable ability.

Position after Black's 26th move.

BLACK.

WHITE.

(*i*) A lost move, by which Black is enabled to improve his position considerably

(*k*) For the purpose of playing the Rook afterwards to Q. eighth should Black exchange Bishops?

GAME 130.

(*Sicilian Opening.*)

White. (Mr. Jones).	Black. (Mr. Cronhelm.)
1. P. to K. fourth	1. P. to Q. B. fourth
2. B. to Q. B. fourth	2. P. to K. third
3. Kt. to K. second (*a*)	3. P. to Q. fourth
4. B. to Kt. fifth (check)	4. B. to Q. second
5. B. takes B. (check)	5. Q. takes B.
6. P. to K. fifth	6. Kt. to Q. B. third (*b*)
7. P. to K. B. fourth	7. P. to K. B. third (*c*)
8. P. takes P.	8. Kt. takes P.
9. P. to Q. fourth	9. P. takes P.
10. Kt. takes P.	10. B. to Q. B. fourth
11. Kt. to K. B. third	11. Castles (*d*)
12. P. to Q. R. third	12. Q. R. to K. square
13. P. to Q. Kt. fourth	13. B. to Q. Kt. third

14. B. to Q. Kt. second	14. Kt. to K. Kt. fifth
15. R. to K. B. square	15. Kt. to K. sixth
16. Q. to Q. third	16. Kt. takes Kt. P. (check)
17. K. to Q. square	17. Kt. to K. sixth (check)
18. K. to Q. B. square	18. Kt. takes R.
19. Kt. to K. Kt. fifth	19. B. to K. sixth (check)
20. K. to Q. square	20. R. to K. B. fourth
21. Q. takes Kt.	21. B. takes K. B. P.
22. Kt. to K. R. third	22. B. to K. fourth

And White resigns.

NOTES.

(*a*) A bad move, which enables Black to develop his game rapidly. Kt. to Q. B. third is here the correct play.

(*b*) Black has thus early obtained a superior game.

(*c*) Very well played; it not only breaks up White's Pawns, but also brings an important auxiliary into the field.

(*d*) Black's forces are so well disposed, and his position so very superior, as to render victory an easy matter.

GAME 131.

(French Opening.)

White. (Mr. FALKBEER.)	Black. (Mr. LOWENTHAL).
1. P. to K. fourth	1. P. to K. third
2. Kt. to K. B. third	2. P. to Q. fourth
3. P. takes P.	3. P. takes P.
4. P. to Q. fourth	4. Kt. to K. B. third
5. B. to Q. third	5. B. to Q. third
6. B. to K. third	6. Castles.
7. P. to K. R. third	7. Kt. to Q. B. third
8. P. to Q. B. third	8. P. to K. R. third
9. Q. Kt. to Q. second	9. B. to K. third
10. P. to K. Kt. fourth	10. Q. to Q. second
11. Q. to Q. B. second	11. Kt. to K. square.
12. Kt. to K. R. fourth	12. Q. Kt. to K. second
13. Kt. to K. B. fifth	13. B. takes Kt.
14. P. takes B.	14. Kt. to K. B. third
15. Castles (Q. R.)	15. P. to Q. Kt. third
16. Q. R. to K. Kt. square.	16. K. to R. square
17. Kt. to K. B. third	17. P. to Q. B. fourth
18. Kt. to K. fifth	18. Q. to B. second
19. Kt. to K. Kt. fourth	19. Q. Kt. to K. Kt. square
20. Kt. takes Kt. (*a*)	20. Kt. takes Kt.

21. Q. to Q. second	21. R. to K. Kt. square
22. K. to Q. Kt. square (b)	22. K. to R. second
23. R. to Kt. fourth	23. Q. R. to K. square (c)
24. R. to K. R. fourth	24. B. to K. B. square
25. Q. B. to K. B. fourth	25. Q. to K. second
26. P. to K. B. third (d)	26. P. to Q. B. fifth (e)
27. B. to Q. B. second	27. Q. to K. seventh
28. Q. takes Q. (f)	28. R. takes Q.
29. R. to K. Kt. square	29. R. to K. square
30. B. to K. fifth	30. B. to K. second
31. P. to Q. R. fourth	31. B. to Q. square
32. P. to Q. Kt. third	32. P. to Q. R. third (g)
33. P. takes B. P.	33. P. takes P.
34. B. takes Kt.	34. B. takes B.
35. R. to K. fourth	35. P. to Q. Kt. fourth.
36. P. takes P.	36. P. takes P.
37. R. takes R.	37. R. takes R.
38. B. to K. fourth	38. K. to Kt. square
39. K. to B. second	39. R. to Q. Kt. square (h)
40. R. to Q. R. square	40. P. to Q. Kt. fifth
41. R. to Q. R. eighth	41. R. takes R.
42. B. takes R.	42. P. takes P.
43. K. takes P.	43. K. to B. square
44. K. takes P.	44. B. to K. second
45. K. to Kt. fifth	45. B. to R. sixth
46. K. to B. sixth.	46. K. to K. second

Drawn game.

Position after Black's 23rd move.

BLACK.

WHITE.

NOTES.

(a) White has conducted the opening with great judgment, and has now obtained a most formidable attack. Q. to Q. second would perhaps, however, have been still stronger here.

(b) Threatening to take R. P. with Bishop.

(c) Winning the exchange would have been very dangerous.

(d) B. to K. fifth seems to us stronger.

(e) If Kt. to K. fifth White wins easily by P. to K. B. sixth.

(f) Q. to Q. B. square seems also promising.

(g) If
33. P. to K. B. sixth
34. R. takes R.
35. B. to K. B. fourth, and wins.

32. Kt to K. fifth
33. P. takes B. P.
34. R. takes R., or (a).

Position after White's 32nd move.

BLACK.

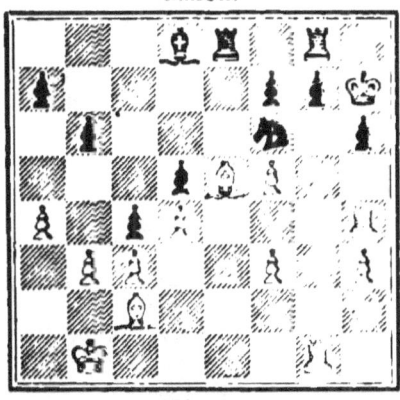

WHITE.
(a)

35. P. takes Kt.
36. R. to K. Kt. fourth (check)
37. P. takes Q. P., with the advantage.

34. K. takes R.
35. P. takes B.
36. K. moves.

(h) Black has a most arduous task to defend himself throughout this game, and his difficulties are not over even yet.

TERMINATION OF THE MATCH BETWEEN MR. DE VERE AND HERR STEINITZ.—This interesting contest was brought to a conclusion on Wednesday, the 10th inst., by the English player winning his seventh game. The final score: Mr. De V., 7; Herr S., 3; drawn, 3. The skill and brilliancy displayed on so many occasions could not prevail against so excellent a player as Mr. De Vere, fortified as he was by receiving the odds of a Pawn and move. We congratulate Mr. De Vere; he has clearly demonstrated that no player can hereafter yield him these odds, and he may fairly claim henceforth a place in the rank of first-class Chess-players.

Problem No. 66. By the late E. S. Brewster, Esq., of Pittsfield, U.S.

White to play, and mate in four moves.

A competing Problem in the Tourney of *Le Palamède Français*.
No. 67. By T. Smith, Esq. Motto: "I am here."

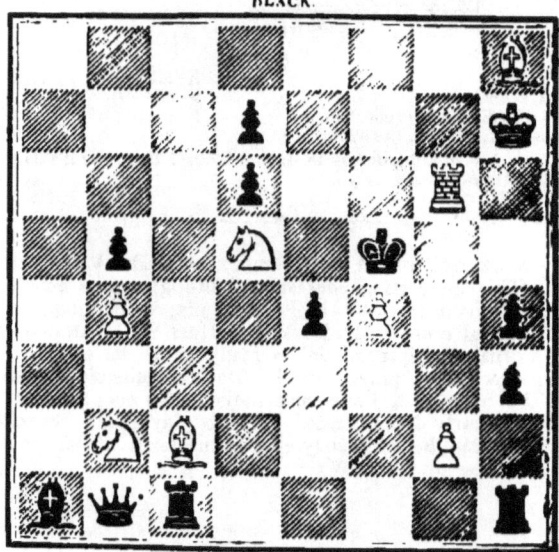

White to play, and mate in five moves.

A competing Problem in the late French Tourney.
No. 68. By C W., of Sunbury.

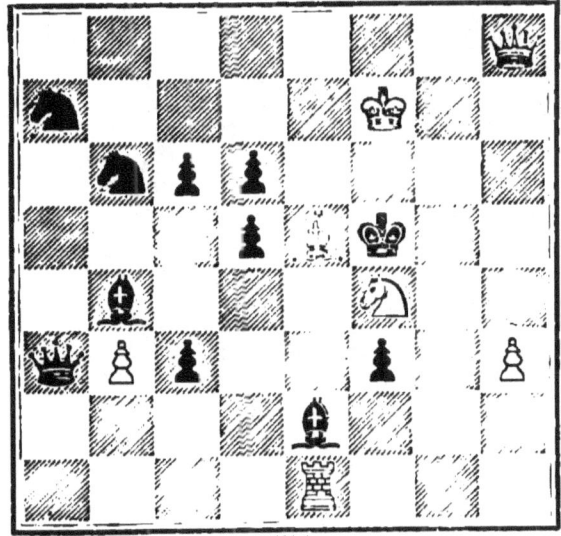

White to play, and mate in four moves.

A competing Problem in the late French Tourney.
No. 69. By C. W., of Sunbury.

White to play, and mate in three moves.

Chess Study No. 12. By G. F. RAINGER, Esq., of Norwich.

Black, even without the move, wins.

Suicidal Problem No. 8. By the Rev. W. WAYTE.
[This Problem has been previously published in an incorrect form. The author has favoured us with a corrected version.]

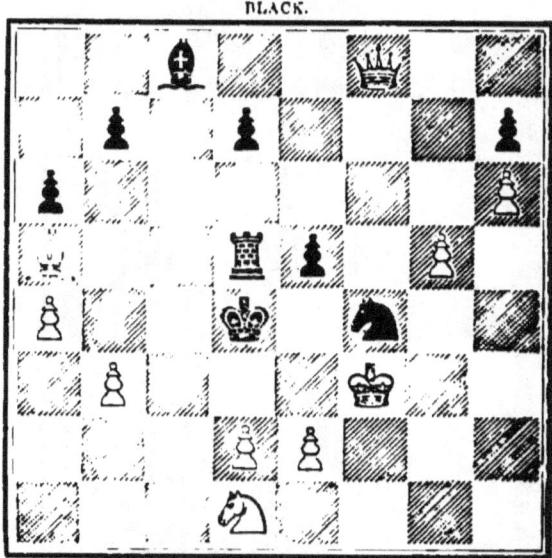

White to play, compels Black to mate him in six moves.

CHESS INTELLIGENCE.

(From the Era.)

BIRMINGHAM AND EDGBASTON CHESS CLUB.

For some years past the members of this Club have been in the habit of holding a Tournament amongst themselves, to decide who was to be the holder of the Champion's Board and Ivory Men. Any player who could keep the lists for a *second year* against all the members of the Club was to retain this prize as his own property. In this manner this much-coveted reward had passed through the hands of nearly all the leading members of the Club, and no Knight of the chequered Board had been able to make it his own. Under these circumstances the Committee determined that two Tournaments should take place this year; the winner in the first to be entitled to the first prize, together with possession for twelve months of the Champion's Board and Men; and the second prize to be given to the victor in the second Tournay, the combatants in the latter affair being only those gentlemen who should be so unfortunate as to be vanquished in the first and second rounds of the chief Tournament. In both contests eight weeks were allowed for each round, and the Committee decided that four games in each round should be played, exclusive of drawn ones. The players were all paired by lot. The following is the score in the chief Tournament, just concluded:—

FIRST ROUND, COMMENCED 6TH APRIL, 1865.

	Wins	Draws		Wins	Draws
Mr. Balden	3	0	Mr. Fry (President)	4	0
Mr. Haselden	4	...	Mr. Stone	1	...
Mr. Best (Secretary)	4	1	Mr. Halford (ex-Chm.)	0	0
Mr. H. Hill	2	...	Mr. F. Hill	4	...
Mr. Buncher	0	1	Mr. Kempson	4	0
Mr. Warren	4	...	Mr. Smith	2	...
Rev. S. W. Earnshaw	1	0	Dr. Lloyd	0	0
Mr. Sutton resigned	0	...	Mr. Saunders resigned	0	...

SECOND ROUND, COMMENCED 5TH JUNE, 1865.

Mr. Fry	3	0	Mr. F. Hill	4	1
Mr. Best	4	...	Mr. Warren	2	...
Rev. S. W. Earnshaw	4	1	Mr. Kempson	3	0
Mr. Haselden	1	...	Dr. Lloyd	4	0

THIRD ROUND, COMMENCED 7TH AUGUST, 1865.

Rev. S. W. Earnshaw	4	0	Dr. Lloyd	2	0
Mr. F. Hill	0	...	Mr. Best	4	..

FOURTH ROUND, COMMENCED 5TH OCTOBER, 1865.

Rev. S. W. Earnshaw	1	2	
Mr. Best	0	...	and Mr. Best resigned the match.

ERRATA.—In Problem No. 62 a Black Rook should be placed at Black's K. B. eighth. In Problem No. 65 a Black Knight should be substituted for a White Knight.

SOLUTIONS TO PROBLEMS.

No. 61.—By the late E. S. Brewster, Esq.

White.
1. Q. to Kt. eighth (check)
2. Kt. to B. third (check)
3. B. to K. sixth
4. Q. takes R.
5. Mates

Black.
1. K. takes P. (best)
2. K. to K. fifth
3. B. to Kt. third (a)
4. Anything

(a) Black has a variety of moves equally good, but none that can defer the mate more than two moves.

No. 62.—By Herr Kockelkorn.

White.
1. Kt. from Q. fourth to K. B. third (ch.)
2. Kt. to Q. third (check)
3. R. to K. fourth (check)
4. mates accordingly.

Black.
1. R. takes Kt.
2. B. takes Kt.
3. B. takes R., or K. moves

No. 63.—By T. Smith, Esq.

White.
1. Q. to Q. Kt. eighth
2. Q. to K. Kt. eighth
3. B. to K. B. fifth
4. R. mates.

Black.
1. P. to Q. third (A)
2. B. to K. square
3. any move

(A)
1. Q. Kt. to Q third
2. Q. to Q. Kt. square, and mates in two moves.

ANSWERS TO CORRESPONDENTS.

*** We have to apologise for the delay which has taken place in replying to some of our correspondents; it has been caused by a more than usual demand upon our space for other contributions.

T. Smith, Esq.—In response to a request made to us by the Chess editor of the *New York Clipper*, we beg "to forward his compliments for your very interesting stratagem (suicidal Problem), which he has repeated for the gratification of American amateurs; and he would be very proud to receive some original contributions from your fertile and ingenious laboratory."

T. M. B.—We have sent the number containing your position. Further contributions will be esteemed a favour.

S. R.—If you will let us know by what channel we can send you the missing numbers we will duly forward them.

S. H. (Nottingham).—The position shall be published shortly.

G. F. R.—We have examined your position, and found it so interesting as to publish it in this number.

I. O. T.—Many thanks for your polite communication.

J. W. (Huddersfield).—After re-examination the position has been found correct. It shall be published as an Enigma.

Dr. C. B., Herr H. (Prussia), W. W., T. S., I. T. W., J. J. W., Herr K., H. A. K. (Bath), C. W. (of Sunbury), Ch. T., P. J. (Paris), J. P. (Paris).—Accept our best thanks for your continued favours.

B. R.—An analysis of the variation you refer to was given in the "Book of the Congress," p. 117.

C. R. H.—You omitted to notice one variation—viz., Kt. to B. sixth. The result accruing from this move will entirely change the aspect of the game.

THE Chess Player's Magazine.

THEORY AND PRACTICE.

WHETHER the unknown but immortal composer of the Indian problem acquired his early knowledge of the game from a handbook of the period, or whether he had nothing to enlighten him as to the theory of Chess but the oral communications of other learned pundits, it may perhaps be bootless to inquire; but how far the immensely voluminous and carefully elaborated treatises of more modern Chessplayers have influenced the progress of the noble game may be a question not unworthy of consideration at the present moment. The end of the fifteenth and the commencement of the sixteenth century witnessed the earliest attempts of the Western nations to construct a literature devoted exclusively to Chess. Vicenza, Lucena, and Damisno in their treatises, however, attempted little beyond giving certain interesting positions, accompanied by a few outlines, or mere skeletons of openings. To Ruy Lopez the honour is due of being the first author who attempted to introduce philosophy into Chess, and deduce from certain given moves in the early part of the game certain inevitable conclusions, but, in spite of the value of his well-known contributions to the science of the game, he can hardly be said to have founded a school, nor did his mantle fall upon shoulders capable of wearing the magnificent garment with proper dignity.

It was in 1572 that the first great Chess match on record took place, in the presence of Philip the Second. Encompassed by the atmosphere of punctilious etiquette which so eminently characterised the Spanish Court, his soul enchained by vast projects for the restoration of the supremacy of the Roman Catholic Church, the shrieks of the victims of the fatal eve of St. Bartholomew yet ringing in his ears, the ruler of Spain and the Indies yet found time and attention to preside at the great trial of skill between Ruy Lopez and "Il Puttino," an Italian player of at least equal prowess over the board, although his pen has left no record of his solitary studies. Not till the year 1625 do we hear any more of Chess matches. In that year the celebrated Greco, with whose sparkling and beautiful games all Chessplayers are or should be familiar, distinguished himself greatly in Paris, playing several matches and winning the round sum of five hundred scudi, a sum which—to the shame of the Chess world be it said—it would be extremely difficult for any player, however talented, to amass during one season in the present day.

About the middle of the next century we find the theory of the game once more seriously taken in hand by Ercole del Rio and the other great masters of the Italian School in the south, and in France by Philidor, the great representative of the north. The different, and, indeed, in many respects utterly opposite systems advocated by these great authorities, caused rapid strides to be made towards evolving a more complete theory of the game than had yet been dreamt of.

The attempt of Philidor, relying on his favourite theory of centre Pawns, to supersede the established Italian defence to the attack of the King's Knight, has occasioned a controversy lasting even unto this day, when in the opinion of many of our best players the question still remains undecided. There is nothing like controversy for introducing vigour into any subject, and of all others Chess has the most to gain by the differences of its doctors. Not only is public attention drawn to the matter, but dormant energies are aroused; those who have let their knowledge of the game become rusty for want of use and all the army of pococuranti have some symptoms of life infused into them. Better still, the rival systems can be brought into actual collision, and the rival professors matched together, to the great and incalculable advancement of Chess science. In Chess, as in most other things, theory is silvern, but practice is golden.

Without for one moment attempting to depreciate the labours of the patient and skilful analysts, whose painfully elaborated works almost persuade the tyro that if he can only master *them* he will be difficult to beat, who will attempt to compare the progress effected by all previous analysts with that effected by the great matches between La Bourdonnais and Macdonnell? These great masters brought the disputed moves and the vexed questions to issue in their wonderful series of matches, and over the board itself stamped their genius upon openings and variations now treasured as classical.

The immense success of the tournaments of 1851 and 1862, in bringing together the brightest luminaries of the Chess universe, has won for their projectors the gratitude of every man who owes to the absorbing influence of Caissa an hour's release from the ordinary everyday soul-wearing cares of life. But one solitary objection could be urged against these two grand gatherings. They were too far apart. Like every other sport under the sun, Chess is very subject to severe attacks of languor, and is especially apt to die of inanition unless the game be kept alive. The British Chess Association is, therefore, most anxious to carry out the scheme of a Chess Congress. It has been suggested that every alternate year a great Chess meeting be held in London, and that a variety of prizes should be presented as rewards of proficiency in the various departments of Chess.

The addition of challenge cups, to be held till " our next merry meeting," has also been hinted at; and we need scarcely add that no portion of the scheme enlists our sympathies more heartily than this. A grand challenge cup, investing its holder with the same distinction in the realms of Chess that the diamond sculls confer in the rowing world, would afford indeed a glorious stimulus to every aspirant for honours in the chequered field. This would be, indeed, a glorious prize for the gradually improving player to strive for, something to cheer his spirits and lighten his heart while ascending each successive step of the Chess-ladder, while wrestling his way from the odds of Rook to Knight, and even while wandering in the desert of the Pawn and two! At present there is no such incentive to exertion, and every Chessplayer who loves the game should do his best to forward so admirable a project. But it must not be forgotten that London alone is unequal to this effort, and, while doing her best, cannot dispense with the aid of the provinces, who send her the players she delights to honour. Nothing but a spirited effort on the part of the whole country will suffice to bring about so great a result as a biennial Congress, and to such an effort we trust that Chess players will not be found unequal.

TELEGRAPH MATCH BETWEEN DUBLIN AND LONDON.

DUBLIN CHESS CLUB,
Athenæum, 33, Anglesea-street,
January 1, 1866.

To the Editor of the " Chess Players' Magazine."

Dear Sir,—In consequence of the statement in the annual report of the "St. James's Chess Club," published in your valuable journal, that the advantage in the recent match by telegraph with this club is claimed for the St. James's Club, there has been a meeting of our committee, under the presidency of the Rev. G. A. Macdonnell, president of our club, for the purpose of examining the unfinished positions; and, taking same into careful examination, and in connection with the games actually finished by wire, this club claims the decided advantage in the match, as per particulars at foot.

Your kindly publishing this letter will be esteemed a favour.

Yours faithfully,

PETER JONES, Hon. Sec.

Claimed for Dublin.
Mr. Buckley's Game .... 1 | Mr. Hunt's Game............ 1
Mr. Collins' Game .... 1 | Mr. Jones' Game............ 1

Adjudged to London.
Mr. Dick's Game............. 1 | Mr. Stewart's Game 1

Drawn Games.
The Consultation............ 1 | Messrs. Barry & Goodwin. 1
Mr. Macdonnell 1

Annulled by mutual consent 3

[*** We have been specially requested to publish the foregoing letter, and we do so with pleasure, as an act of justice. Our Dublin friends must, however, perceive that as only two games were played out, each side winning one, opinions may very naturally be divided as to the probable result of the ten unfinished games. The St. James's Club adhere, we understand, to their belief that the issue of the contest would have been in their favour.]

BRITISH CHESS ASSOCIATION.

At a meeting of the Committee of Management, held at the St. George's Chess Club, on Saturday, January 27th, the scheme for placing the Association on a more permanent basis was fully discussed, and after careful deliberation the report, which we proceed to publish, was approved by the Committee, and it was then decided to lay it before a General Meeting of the Association. There were present at the meeting of the Committee Lord Cremorne (in the chair), Lord Walden, Mr. Strode, Mr. H. Waite, Mr. Mongredien, Captain H. A. Kennedy, Mr. Hampton, Mr. Medley, and Mr. Lowenthal.

Report of the Managing Committee to be laid before a General Meeting to be held at the St. George's Chess Club, 20, King Street, St. James's, London, on Tuesday, March 6th, 1866, at eight p.m.

TO THE MEMBERS OF THE BRITISH CHESS ASSOCIATION.

In accordance with resolutions passed at general meetings held in Bristol and in London, the Managing Committee have consulted as to the steps to be taken to place the Association on a permanent basis.

But, before entering into the detail of the propositions which they are prepared to make, they deem it useful to touch lightly on a few points connected with its formation and history. It will be recollected that the Yorkshire Chess Association originally sprang from a local gathering held a quarter of a century ago. Fourteen years after its first meeting in Leeds it expanded into the Northern and Midland Counties Association, which, subsequently dropping its local prefix, and holding meetings in places outside these limits, styled itself the British Chess Association, and now counts among its members players from all parts of the kingdom. The object of the promoters of the early meetings was to enable the members of the Yorkshire clubs to enjoy a day's play, but as time rolled on, and the cultivation of the game extended, increasing interest was excited, and so short a period was found insufficient for play and for the discussion of matters connected with the laws and other important points. The meetings, therefore, soon began to occupy several days, and in 1862, the year of the London Congress, the proceedings absorbed several months. Until then the gatherings had all been held in the provinces, and so long as the proceedings were confined to one day, their organisation involved but little exertion on the part of the local committees, but, as the business increased in amount and importance, there was a corresponding increase in the labour, and it has of late become a matter of great difficulty to put the machinery in motion. It was with the view of obviating this difficulty that the managing committee of 1862 have been retained in office.

With the foregoing preliminary remarks the Committee proceed to give a sketch of their plan.

In the various discussions which have taken place all parties have recognised the necessity of establishing head quarters, and of constituting a permanent and efficient staff; they therefore propose—

First. That London be the head-quarters of the association.

Second. That the staff be constituted as follows:—

A President, and six or more Vice-Presidents, who shall hold office permanently. A Treasurer, an Honorary Secretary, a Manager, and an Auditor; to hold their offices for two years, but to be re-eligible. A General Committee, to consist of not less than thirty, nor more than fifty members, one-third to go out of office in rotation every two years, but to be re-eligible. A Managing Committee, to consist of the President, Vice-Presidents, the Treasurer, the Honorary Secretary, the Manager, and ten other members chosen from the General Committee; four to form quorum, and the Chairman to have the casting vote.

In addition to these officers, all of whom shall be elected by general meetings, the committee propose that all secretaries of provincial clubs who may be willing to act in the capacity be constituted local secretaries to the association.

Passing on to the plan of action which in their opinion should be followed, they recommend—

First. That a Meeting or Congress be held every alternate year in London, during which various contests shall take place, prizes being given to successful competitors in tournaments, problem tournays, and to authors of discoveries in openings and end games, and of meritorious additions to chess literature. With regard to the form in which the prizes should be given, the committee recommend that they should not always be in money, but should sometimes take other shapes, especially that of challenge or presentation cups, which, judging from the interest which their introduction into other pursuits has excited, would contribute greatly to promote emulation, and to extend the scientific cultivation of the game.

Second. That in those years in which no congress is held in London the managing committee be empowered to assist, by funds for prizes or otherwise, any provincial meetings with which they may deem it desirable to co-operate.

Third. That a "Book of Transactions" be issued to the members on such terms and at such intervals of time as may appear advisable, and that an alphabetical list of the names and addresses of clubs and players be opened and kept up, with a view, when sufficiently complete, to be published as a "Chess Directory."

To raise funds for these purposes the committee recommend—First That each member shall pay to the general fund an annual minimum subscription of five shillings. Second. That the treasurer be empowered to receive any additional voluntary subscriptions to the said fund. Third. That members shall be at liberty to contribute special subscriptions towards any of the objects mentioned in the preceding paragraph, all sums thus subscribed to be applied in accordance with the wishes of the donors.

Such, briefly stated, is the plan which the committee recommend for adoption. If carried out, the association, without supplanting or competing with Chess clubs, will be a representative of them all, and be an organisation ready when occasion arises for the general body of players to act in common. But if, as it is hoped, it is to form one of our permanent institutions, it must be remembered that this position will involve duties and responsibilities. Its members must not be content with merely watching with complacency the struggles of contending players, and of rewarding the victors, as if there were nothing of loftier aim connected with Chess. Bearing in mind that for the most part social improvement works from the higher to the lower classes, and that Chess has something of a refining and elevating power, they should endeavour to carry it into regions which it has not hitherto penetrated—into the working man's club, into the barrack, and into the man-of-war. The association would then occupy higher ground than has yet been taken, and thus, it is to be hoped, contribute something, if but a little, to our advancing civilisation.

GEO. W. MEDLEY, Hon. Sec.

London, 14th February, 1866.

GAMES.

GAME 132.

Game the eleventh in the match between Mr. De Vere and Herr Steinitz.

(*Remove Black's K. B. Pawn.*)

White. (Mr. DE VERE.)	Black. (Herr STEINITZ.)
1. P. to K. fourth	1. P. to Q. third
2. P. to Q. fourth	2. Kt. to K. B. third
3. Q. Kt. to B. third	3. P. to K. third (*a*)
4. B. to Q. third	4. Q. Kt. to B. third
5. K. Kt. to B. third	5. B. to K. second
6. Q. Kt. to K. second	6. Castles
7. P. to Q. B. third	7. Q. to K. square
8. Q. Kt. to Kt. third	8. P. to K. fourth
9. P. to Q. fifth	9. Q. Kt. to Q. square
10. P. to K. R. third	10. Q. Kt. to B. second
11. B. to K. third	11. Q. Kt. to K. R. square
12. Q. to Q. Kt. third	12. Q. Kt. to Kt. third
13. Castles (Q. R.)	13. P. to Q. R. fourth
14. Kt. to B. fifth	14. B. to Q. square (*b*)
15. P. to K. Kt. fourth	15. Q. Kt. to K. second (*c*)
16. Q. R. to Kt. square	16. K. to R. square
17. Kt. to K. Kt. fifth	17. P. to K. Kt. third (*d*)
18. Kt. to R. sixth	18. K. Kt. to Kt. square
19. B. to Q. Kt. fifth (*e*)	19. P. to Q. B. third
20. P. takes P.	20. P. takes P.
21. Q. Kt. to B. seventh (ch.)	21. K. to Kt. second
22. Q. Kt. takes P.	22. Q. to Q. second
23. Kt. takes B.	23. Q. takes Kt.
24. Kt. to K. sixth (check)	24. K. to B. second
25. Kt. takes B. (dis. check)	25. K. to K. square
26. Kt. to K. sixth	

And Black resigns.

NOTES.

(a) P. to K. fourth is here generally considered preferable; for if then—

    4. P. takes P.   4. P. takes P.

and if White exchanges Queens he has no advantage in position, while Black has an open game; and if 4. P. to Q. fifth, Black can at once break up the centre Pawns by 4. P. to Q. B. third.

(b) Black's situation, owing mainly to his third move, is much cramped; but the move made is not calculated to improve it. We should much have preferred P. to Q. R. fifth.

(c) In the first fifteen moves this Knight has already changed his quarters six times, and these useless manœuvres involve of necessity a serious loss of time.

(d) Very injudicious, driving the Knight into a still stronger position.

(e) This is very well played, and leaves Black no good reply; for if—

                                    19. B. to Q. second

    20. B. takes B.   20. Q. takes B.

    21. Q. Kt. to K. B. seventh (check)   21. K. to Kt. second

    22. Kt. takes B.   22. K. R. or Q. R. takes Kt.

    23. Kt. to K. sixth (check) winning the exchange.

Position after White's 19th move.

BLACK.

WHITE.

GAME 133.

Game the twelfth in the match between Mr. De Vere and Herr Steinitz.

(*Remove Black's K. B. Pawn.*)

White. (Mr. DE VERE.)	Black. (Herr STEINITZ.)
1. P. to K. fourth	1. P. to Q. third
2. P. to Q. fourth	2. Kt. to K. B. third
3. Kt. to Q. B. third	3. P. to K. third
4. Kt. to K. B. third	4. Kt. to Q. B. third

5. B. to Q. Kt. fifth	5. P. to Q. R. third
6. B. takes Kt. (check)	6. P. takes B.
7. Castles	7. B. to K. second
8. Q. to Q. third	8. Castles
9. Q. Kt. to K. second	9. P. to Q. R. fourth
10. Kt. to K. Kt. third	10. B. to R. third
11. P. to Q. B. fourth	11. P. to Q. fourth
12. P. to Q. Kt. third	12. P. to Q. B. fourth
13. K. P. takes P. (a)	13. K. P. takes P.
14. Q. to K. third	14. Q. P. takes P.
15. Kt. to K. B. fifth (b)	15. R. to K. B. second
16. R. to K. square	16. Kt. to Q. fourth
17. Q. to K. sixth	17. B. to B. third
18. Kt. to K. fifth	18. B. takes Kt.
19. R. takes B.	19. Kt. to Q. Kt. fifth
20. Kt. to K. R. sixth (check)	20. P. takes Kt.
21. B. takes P.	21. Q. to K. B. third
22. R. to K. Kt. fifth (check)	22. Q. takes R.
23. B. takes Q.	

And after a few more moves Black resigned the game and the match.

NOTES.

(a) Kt. to K. Kt. fifth leads to some interesting variations.

(b) The key move of a fine combination.

(c) This brief game is admirably played by Mr. De Vere, and forms a fitting termination to a very interesting contest. In looking over these games we have been especially struck with the originality and inventive power displayed by the winner, and we predict for him a high place among the very best English players.

Position after Black's 19th move.

BLACK.

WHITE.

GAME 134.

For the following game we are indebted to our distinguished friend M. Arnous de Rivière. It is one of the series, played some years ago by him against Mr. Paul Morphy during the sojourn of the latter gentleman in the French capital, and will well repay close examination. For another game of the series, vide our last volume, p. 165.

(*King's Knight's Gambit.*)

White. (Mr. P. MORPHY.)	Black. (M. A. de RIVIERE.)
1. P. to K. fourth	1. P. to K. fourth
2. P. to K. B. fourth	2. P. takes P.
3. Kt. to K. B. third	3. P. to K. Kt. fourth
4. B. to Q. B. fourth	4. B. to Kt. second
5. Castles	5. P. to K. R. third
6. P. to Q. B. third	6. K. Kt. to K. second
7. P. to Q. fourth	7. P. to Q. third
8. P. to K. R. fourth (*a*)	8. K. Kt. to Kt. third
9. P. to R. fifth	9. Kt. to K. second
10. P. to K. Kt. third	10. B. to K. Kt. fifth
11. P. takes P.	11. B. takes R. P.
12. P. takes P.	12. Q. to Q. second
13. Kt. to K. fifth	13. Q. to R. sixth
14. Q. to Q. third (*b*)	14. Q. takes Q.
15. Kt. takes Q.	15. P. takes P.
16. Q. Kt. to R. third	16. P. to Q. B. third
17. Q. B. takes P.	17. B. takes Q. P. (ch.) (*c*)
18. P. takes B.	18. R. to K. Kt. sq.
19. R. to B. sixth	19. R. takes B. (ch.)
20. K. to B. second	20. Q. Kt. to Q. second (*d*)
21. R. takes Q. P.	21. Castles
22. Q. R. to K. Kt. sq.	22. R. takes R.
23. K. takes R.	23. K. to B. second
24. R. to R. sixth	24. B. to Kt. third
25. Kt. to K. B. fourth (*e*)	25. B. takes P.
26. B. takes K. B. P.	26. B. to K. B. fourth
27. B. to K. sixth	27. Kt. to K. B. sq.
28. P. to Q. fifth	28. Kt. takes B.
29. Kt. takes Kt. (ch.)	29. B. takes Kt.
30. P. takes B.	30. R. to Q. fifth
31. K. to B. second	31. P. to Kt. fourth
32. K. to B. third	32. R. to Q. seventh
33. Kt. to Kt sq.	33. R. takes P.
34. Kt to B. third	34. K. to Q. third
35. K. to B. fourth	35. Kt. to Q. fourth (check)

36. Kt. takes Kt.	36. P. takes Kt.
37. P. to K. seventh (dis. ch.)	37. K. takes P.
38. R. to Q. R. sixth	38. R. to K. seventh
39. P. to R. third	39. K. to Q. second
40. R. takes P. (ch.)	40. K. to B. third
41. K. to B. third	41. R. to K. fifth
42. R. to R. eighth	42. R. to Q. R. fifth
43. R. to Q. B. eighth (ch.)	43. K. to Q. third
44. R. to Q. B. third	44. P. to Q fifth (*f*)
45. R. to Q. Kt. third	45. K to B. fourth
46. K. to K. fourth	46. R. to R. sq.
47. K. to Q. third	47. R. to K. R. sq.
48. K. to Q. second	48. R. to R. seventh (ch.)
49. K. to B. sq.	49. K. to B. fifth
50. R. to K. Kt. third (*g*)	50. P. to Q. sixth
51. R. to K. Kt. eighth	51. R. to Q. R. seventh
52. R to Q. B. eighth (ch.)	52. K. to Kt. sixth
53. R. to Q. Kt. eighth	53. R. to Q. B. seventh (ch.)
54. K. to Q. sq.	54. R. to Q. B. fourth
55. K. to Q. second	55. K. takes P.
56. K. takes P.	56. P. to Kt. fifth

And Black won the game.

NOTES.

(*a*) Some suggest here P. to K. Kt. third, to which Black's best reply would be probably Kt. to K. Kt. third.

Position after White's 14th move.

BLACK.

WHITE.

(b) At the first glance it would seem as if Mr. Morphy would have done better by taking B. with Q., but the following variation will show that the move would have been disadvantageous:—

14. Q. takes R.
15. K. moves.

14. Q. to K. Kt. sixth (check)
15. P. takes P., winning the Queen.

(c) This is very well conceived..

(d) Black prefers giving up the Q. P. to submitting to the dangerous attack which White would acquire if he were to play P. to Q. fourth.

(e) This is decidedly better than defending the K. P.

(f) We commend this instructive ending to the careful study of our readers' M. de Riviere's play is unexceptionable from this point to the conclusion.

Position after White's 44th move.

BLACK.

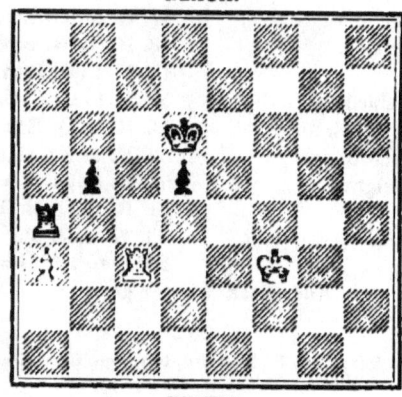

WHITE.

(g) R. to Q. Kt. fourth (check) is at once fatal—e. g.,

51. R. to Kt. fourth (check)
52. K. to Q. square, or (A)

51. K. to Q. B. 6th, threatening mate
52. P. to Q. sixth, winning easily

(A)

52. K. to Kt. square
53. R. takes P.
54. R. to Q. fifth

52. P. to Q. sixth
53. P. to Q. seventh
54. R. to R. eighth (ch.), and wins.

GAME 135.

Another of the match games played in the Tournament at Birmingham in 1858.

(*Ruy Lopez Knight's Game.*)

White. (Mr. LOWENTHAL).
1. P. to K. fourth
2. Kt. to K. B. third
3. B. to Q. Kt. fifth.

Black. (Mr. FALKBEER.)
1. P. to K. fourth
2. Kt. to Q. B. third
3. P. to K. B. fourth

4. Q. to K. second	4. P. takes P.
5. B. takes Kt.	5. Q. P. takes B.
6. Q. takes P.	6. B. to Q. third
7. Kt. takes P.	7. Kt. to K. B. third
8. Q. to K. second	8. Castles
9. P. to Q. fourth	9. K. to R. square
10. Castles	10. P. to Q. B. fourth
11. P. to Q. B. third	11. P. takes P.
12. P. takes P.	12. B. to K. B. fourth (a)
13. Kt. to Q. B. fourth (b)	13. Kt. to K. Kt. fifth (c)
14. P. to K. B. fourth	14. R. to K. square
15. Kt. to K. fifth	15. B. takes Kt.
16. Q. P. takes B.	16. Q. to Q. fifth (ch)
17. K. to R. square	17. B. to Q. sixth
18. Q. to Q. second	18. Q. R. to Q. square
19. P. to K. R. third (d)	19. B. takes R.
20. Q. takes Q.	20. R. takes Q.
21. P. takes Kt.	21. B. to K. seventh (e)
22. Kt. to Q. B. third	22. B. takes P.
23. B. to K. third	23. R. to Q. sixth
24. R. to K. square	24. B. to B. fourth
25. K. to Kt. square	25. K. to Kt. square
26. K. to B. second	26. P. to K. R. fourth
27. P. to K. Kt. third	27. P. to Q. Kt. third (f)
28. Kt. to Q. Kt. fifth	28. P. to Q. B. fourth
29. Kt. to Q. sixth	29. R. to K. B. square
30. K. to B. third (g)	30. P. to K. Kt. third
31. R. to Q. B. square	31. B. to Kt. fifth (check)
32. K. to K. fourth	32. R. to Q. eighth
33. R. takes R.	33. B. takes R.
34. P. to K. sixth (h)	34. B. to Q. R. fifth
35. P. to K. seventh	35. R. to Q. R. square
36. K. to K. fifth	36. K. to Kt. second
37. K. to K. sixth (i)	37. B. to K. square
38. B. to Q. second	38. P. to Q. Kt. fourth
39. B. to B. third (check)	39. K. to Kt. square
40. Kt. to K. fourth	40. B. to B. second (check)
41. K. to Q. seventh (k)	41. B. to K. square (check)
42. K. to K. sixth	42. B. to B. second (check)

Drawn game.

NOTES.

(a) Black has obtained a promising attack in return for the Pawn which he sacrificed.

(b) An error, which ought to have lost White the game. He should have played Kt. to Q. B. third.

(c) Black would have gained a fine attack by sacrificing his Bishop at this point, but the move made is probably sounder play.

(d) He has no better resource.

(e) R. to Q. eighth seems to us stronger.

(f) By this move Black has thrown away a won game. He should have played P. to Q. R. third.

(g) Threatening to take B. with Kt., and then advance K. to K. fourth.

(h) The only move to draw the game.

Position after White's 34th move.

BLACK.

WHITE.

(i) The advance of the King renders it impossible for Black to win.

(k) K. to Q. sixth would be very hazardous. White must rest satisfied with a drawn game.

GAME 136.

The following game occurred in a pool at Chess, played some years ago at the Philidorian Chess Rooms :—

(*Ruy Lopez Knight's Game.*)

White. (Mr. CAMPBELL.)	Black. (Herr FALKBEER.)
1. P. to K. fourth	1. P. to K. fourth
2. K. Kt. to B. third	2. Q. Kt. to B. third
3. B. to Q. Kt. fifth	3. P. to K. B. fourth (a)
4. P. to Q. third	4. B. to Q. B. fourth
5. Kt. to Q. B. third	5. Kt. to K. B. third
6. Castles	6. P. takes P.
7. Kt. takes P. (b)	7. Kt. takes Kt.

8. P. takes Kt.	8. Q. to K. B. third
9. Q. to Q. fifth	9. B. to Q. third
10. B. to K. third	10. P. to K. R. third
11. Q. R. to Q. square	11. P. to K. Kt. fourth
12. P. to K. R. third	12. P. to Q. R. third
13. B. to Q. R. fourth	13. P. to Q. Kt fourth
14. B. to Q. Kt. third	14. B. to Q. Kt. second
15. Q. to Q. second	15. Kt. to K. second
16. Q. to Q. third	16. Kt to K. Kt. third
17. B. to Q. fifth	17. B. takes B.
18. Q. takes B.	18. K. to K. second
19. Kt. to Q. second	19. Kt. to K. B. fifth
20. B. takes Kt.	20. Kt. P. takes B.
21. P. to Q. B. fourth (c)	21. P. takes P.
22. Kt. takes P.	22. Q. R. to K. Kt. square
23. Q. R. to Q. third	23. Q. R. to K. Kt. third
24. P. to K. Kt. third (d)	24. K. R. to K. Kt. square
25. K. to Kt. second	25. P. to K. R. fourth (e)
26. K. R. to Q. square	26. P. to K. R. fifth
27. P. to K. Kt. fourth	27. P. to B. sixth (check)
28. K. to R. square (f)	28. Q. to K. B. fifth
29. Kt. to K. third (g)	29. R. to Q. Kt. square
30. Kt. to B. fifth (check)	30. K. to Q. square
31. R. to Q. Kt. third (h)	31. R. to Q. B. square
32. Q. to K. B. seventh	32. Q. to K. Kt. fourth
33. Kt. takes B.	

And Black resigns.

NOTES.

(a) A very unsound defence.
(b) P. takes P. would also give White a fine game.
(c) The advance of this Pawn is well timed.
(d) This we think was imprudent, as exposing the King to attack.
(e) Black should have played as follows:—

	P. takes P.
P. takes P.	R. takes P. (check)
R. takes R.	R. takes R. (check)
K. takes R.	Q. takes R.

and Black has gained a Pawn.

(f) If
28. R. takes P.	28. R. takes P. (check)
29. P. takes R.	29. R. takes P. (check)
30. R. to Kt. third (best)	30. P. takes R., &c.

(g) The winning move.
(h) A remarkably elegant termination.

GAME 137.

We give two more games of the match between Herr Lowe and the late Mr. Hannah.

(Sicilian Opening.)

White. (Mr. HANNAH.)	Black. (Herr LOWE.)
1. P. to K. fourth	1. P. to Q. B. fourth
2. Kt. to K. B. third	2. Kt. to Q. B. third
3. P. to Q. fourth	3. P. takes P.
4. Kt. takes P.	4. Kt. to K. B. third
5. Kt. to Q. B. third	5. P. to K. fourth
6. K. Kt. to Q. Kt. fifth	6. P. to Q. R. third (*a*)
7. Kt. to Q. sixth (check)	7. B. takes Kt.
8. Q. takes B.	8. P. to K. R. third
9. B. to K. third	9. Q. to K. second
10. B. to Q. B. fifth	10. P. to Q. Kt. fourth
11. Kt. to Q. fifth	11. Kt. takes Kt.
12. P. takes Kt.	12. Q. takes Q.
13. B. takes Q.	13. Kt. to Q. fifth
14. Castles	14. P. to K. B. third
15. P. to K. B. fourth	15. Kt. to K. B. fourth (*b*)
16. P. takes P.	16. B. to Q. Kt. second
17. B. to Q. third	17. Kt. takes B.
18. P. takes Kt.	18. Castles (Q. R.)
19. B. to K. Kt. sixth	19. P. to K. R. fourth
20. K. R. to K. square	20. R. to K. R. third
21. B. to K. B. fifth	21. P. to K. Kt. third
22. B. to Q. third	22. P. to K. B. fourth
23. P. to K. R. fourth	23. K. R. to R. square
24. R. to K. fifth	24. Q. R. to K. square
25. Q. R. to K. square	25. K. to Q. square
26. K. to Q. second	26. R. takes R.
27. R. takes R.	27. R. to K. B. square
28. P. to Q. Kt. third	28. P. to Q. Kt. fifth
29. K. to K. third	29. R. to K. B. third
30. K. to Q. fourth	30. R. takes P.
31. K. to Q. B. fifth	31. K. to Q. B. second
32. B. to Q. B. fourth	32. R. to K. B. third
33. K. takes P.	33. K. to Q. third
34. R. to K. second	34. P. to K. B. fifth (*c*)
35. K. to Q. B. third	35. P. to Q. R. fourth
36. P. to Q. Kt. fourth	36. P. takes P. (check)
37. K. takes P.	37. R. to K. B. fourth

38. B. to Q. third	38. P. to K. B. sixth
39. P. takes P.	39. R. takes B. P.
40. B. takes P.	40. B. takes P.
41. R. to Q. second	41. R. to K. B. fifth (check)
42. K. to Kt. fifth	42. K. to K. fourth
43. B. takes P. (d)	43. R. takes P.

The game was prolonged for some time, and finally drawn.

NOTES.

(a) An inferior move. P. to Q. third is much better.

(b) Although this loses a Pawn we do not see any better line of play for Black.

(c) All this part of the contest is ably conducted on both sides.

(d) From this point we think that Black, with the best play, could always draw the game.

Position after Black's 38th move.

BLACK.

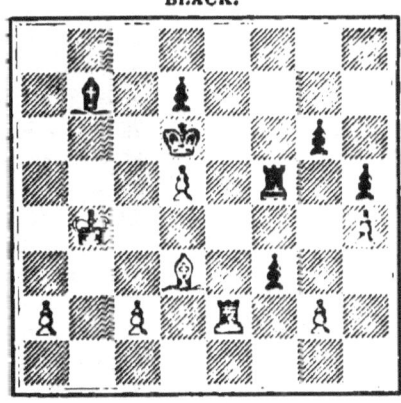

WHITE.

GAME 138.
(French Opening.)

White. (Herr Lowe.)	*Black.* (Mr. Hannah.)
1. P. to K. fourth	1. P. to K. third
2. P. to Q. fourth	2. P. to Q. fourth
3. P. takes P.	3. P. takes P.
4. Kt. to K. B. third	4. Kt. to K. B. third
5. B. to K. third	5. B. to K. third
6. Q. Kt. to Q. second	6. B. to Q. third
7. B. to Q. third	7. Castles

8. Castles	8. P. to K. R. third
9. P. to Q. B. third	9. Kt. to Q. B. third
10. Q. to Q. B. second	10. Kt. to K. square
11. B. to K. B. fifth (a)	11. Q. to K. B. third
12. B. to Q. third	12. Kt. to K. second
13. K. R. to K. square	13. B. to K. Kt. fifth
14. P. to K. R. third	14. B. to K. R. fourth
15. Kt. to K. fifth	15. B. takes Kt.
16. P. takes B.	16. Q. to K. third
17. P. to K. B. fourth	17. P. to K. B. fourth
18. P. to Q. B. fourth (b)	18. P. to Q. Kt. third
19. Q. B. P. takes P.	19. Kt. takes P.
20. B. to Q. B. fourth	20. P. to Q. B. fourth
21. Kt. to Q. Kt. third	21. K. Kt. to Q. B. second
22. K. to R. second	22. K. to R. square
23. Q. to K. B. second	23. Q. to Q. B. third
24. B. to Q. second	24. Q. R. to Q. square
25. B. to K. second (c)	25. B. to K. B. second
26. K. R. to Q. B. square	26. Kt. to K. third
27. Kt. to Q. fourth	27. Kt. takes Kt.
28. Q. takes Kt.	28. Kt. to Q. B. second
29. Q. to Q. B. third	29. B. to Q. fourth
30. R. to K. Kt. square	30. Kt. to K. third
31. B. to K. third	31. B. to K. fifth (d)
32. Q. R. to Q. square	32. R. takes R.
33. B. takes R.	33. R. to Q. square
34. B. to Q. Kt. third	34. Kt. to Q. B. second
35. Q. to Q. B. fourth	35. Kt. to Q. fourth
36. B. to Q. second	36. P. to Q. Kt. fourth
37. Q. to Q. B. square	37. P. to Q. B. fifth
38. B. to Q. B. second	38. Kt. to K. second
39. B. to K. third	39. P. to Q. R. third
40. Q. to Q. Kt square	40. B. takes B.
41. Q. takes B.	41. R. to Q. sixth
42. B. to Q. second	42. Q. to K. fifth
43. Q. to Q. B. square	43. Q. to K. seventh (e)
44. B. to Q. B. third	

Black mates in three moves.

NOTES.

(a) Lost time. White should rather have brought one of the Rooks to K. square.
(b) P. takes P. *en passant* would have been stronger.
(c) We should have preferred R. to K. Kt. square.

(d) From this point the game, which has been extremely well contested, turns in favour of Black.

(e) The *coup de grace*, play as White may.

Position after White's 44th move.

BLACK.

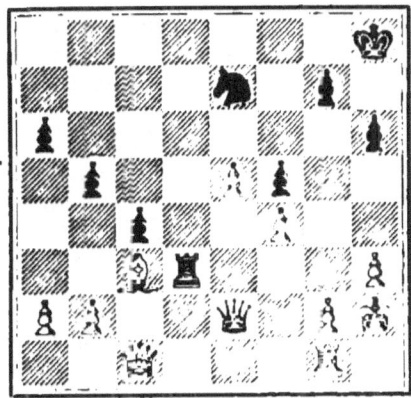

WHITE.

Black to play, and mate in three moves.

GAME 139.

We have much pleasure in laying before our readers a couple of games recently played by correspondence between the clubs of Cambridge University and Dublin. They show that such skilful amateurs as Messrs. Wayte, Skipworth, and Bower have left at their university no unworthy successors.

(*Petroff's Defence.*)

White. (CAMBRIDGE.)	Black. (DUBLIN.)
1. P. to K. fourth	1. P. to K. fourth
2. Kt. to K. B. third	2. Kt. to K. B. third
3. Kt. takes P.	3. P. to Q. third
4. Kt. to K. B. third	4. Kt. takes P.
5. P. to Q. fourth	5. P. to Q. fourth
6. B. to Q. third	6. B. to K. second
7. Castles	7. Kt. to Q. B. third
8. R. to K. square	8. Kt. to Q. third (a)
9. P. to Q. B. third	9. Castles
10. B. to K. B. fourth	10. B. to K. B. third
11. Q. Kt. to Q. second	11. Kt. to K. second

12. B. to K. fifth	12. Kt. to Kt. third
13. Q. to Q. B. second	13. P. to Q. Kt. third
14. P. to Q. Kt. fourth	14. B. to K. second (*b*)
15. Kt. to K. B. square	15. B. to K. Kt. fifth
16. K. Kt. to Q. second	16. Q. to Q. second
17. Kt. to K. third	17. B. to K. third
18. P. to K. Kt. third	18. P. to K. B. fourth
19. Kt. to K. B. third (*c*)	19. Kt. to K. fifth
20. P. to Q. Kt. fifth	20. Q. R. to K. square
21. P. to Q. B. fourth	21. P. takes P.
22. K. B. takes P.	22. B. takes B.
23. Q. takes B. (check)	23. K. to R. square
24. Q. to Q. B. sixth	24. Kt. takes B.
25. Kt. takes Kt.	25. Q. takes P. (*d*)
26. Kt. to Q. seventh	26. R. to K. Kt. square
27. R. to K. B. square	27. Kt. takes K. B. P.
28. Kt. takes K. B. P.	28. Q. to Q. Kt. seventh
29. Q. R. to Q. Kt. square	29. Kt. to R. sixth (check)
30. K. to R. square	30. Q. to Q. seventh
31. Kt. to K. fifth	31. Kt. to Kt. fourth
32. Q. R. to K. square (*e*)	32. K. R. to B. square
33. Kt. takes B.	33. R. takes R. (check)
34. R. takes R.	34. Q. to Q. square
35. Q. to Q. seventh	35. Q. to Q. R. square (check)
36. Kt. from K. fifth to Q. B. sixth	36. Kt. to K. fifth
37. Kt. to K. B. fifth	37. R. to K. Kt. square
38. Kt. to K. R. sixth	

And Black resigns.

NOTES.

(*a*) Thus far the defence has been conducted in accordance with the best authorities. White, however, always obtains the better opening.

(*b*) This looks to us like loss of time.

(*c*) White play throughout with great judgment, never allowing their adversaries to escape from their confined position.

(*d*) The capture of this Pawn loses Black the game.

(*e*) White's attack is now quite irresistible.

GAME 140.

(*Philidor's Defence.*)

White. (DUBLIN.)	Black. (CAMBRIDGE.)
1. P. to K. fourth	1. P. to K. fourth
2. Kt. to K. B. third	2. P. to Q. third
3. P. to Q. fourth	3. P. to K. B. fourth

4. B. to Q. B. fourth (a)	4. Kt. to Q. B. third
5. Kt. to K. Kt. fifth	5. Kt. to K. R. third
6. B. to Q. Kt. fifth	6. P. takes Q. P.
7. B. takes Kt. (check)	7. P. takes B.
8. Q. takes P.	8. P. takes P.
9. Q. takes P. (check)	9. Q. to K. second
10. Castles	10. Q. takes Q.
11. Kt. takes Q.	11. Kt. to K. B. fourth
12. R. to K. square	12. B. to K. second
13. B. to Kt. fifth	13. P. to K. R. third
14. B. takes B.	14. K. takes B.
15. Kt. to Kt. third (dis. check)	15. K. to B. second
16. Kt. takes Kt.	16. B. takes Kt.
17. Kt. to Q. second	17. K. R. to K. square
18. P. to Q. B. third	18. P. to Q. R. fourth
19. P. to K. B. fourth	19. R. takes R.
20. R. takes R.	20. P. to Q. R. fifth (b)
21. R. to K. third	21. R. to Q. Kt. square
22. P. to Q. Kt. third	22. P. takes P.
23. P. takes P.	23. R. to Q. R. square
24. K. to K. B. second	24. R. to Q. R. seventh
25. K. to K. second	25. B. to Kt. fifth (check)
26. K. to K. square	26. R. to Q. R. eighth (check)
27. K. to B. second	27. R. to Q. R. seventh (c)
28. K. to K. square	28. R. to Q. R. eighth (check)
29. K. to B. second	

And the Game was relinquished as drawn.

NOTES.

(a) Q. P. takes P. is the correct move.
(b) The contest already begins to assume the appearance of a drawn battle.
(c) Having won the first game, Cambridge, of course, is satisfied to draw this one.

GAME 141.

We have been favoured by Mr. Charles Tomlinson, the popular writer on Chess, with the following game, recently played by him against a young amateur of considerable promise. It is gratifying to us to find that our esteemed correspondent has not altogether abandoned the practice of Chess:—

(*Hampe's Opening.*)

White. (Mr. E. S.)	Black. (Mr. C. Tomlinson.)
1. P. to K. fourth	1. P. to K. fourth
2. Kt. to Q. B. third	2. P. to Q. third (a)

3. P. to Q. fourth	3. P. takes P.
4. Q. takes P.	4. Kt. to Q. B. third
5. B. to Q. Kt. fifth	5. B. to Q. second
6. B. takes Kt.	6. B. takes B.
7. P. to K. B. fourth	7. Kt. to K. B. third
8. Kt. to R. third	8. B. to K. second
9. B. to K. third	9. Castles
10. Castles (K R.)	10. Kt. to K. Kt. fifth
11. P. to K. B. fifth	11. B. to K. B. third
12. Q. to Q. third	12. B. takes Kt.
13. P. takes B.	13. Kt. takes B.
14. Q. takes Kt.	14. R. to K. square
15. P. to B. sixth	15. P. takes P.
16. Q. to R sixth	16. B. takes P. (*b*)
17. R. takes P.	17. B. to Kt. third
18. Q. R. to K. B. square	18. R. to K. third
19. R. takes R.	19. P. takes R.
20. Kt. to B. fourth	20. Q. to K. square
21. R. to B. third	21. Q. to B. second
22. Q. to Kt. fifth	22. Q. to B. fourth
23. Q. to K. seventh	23. Q. to Q. B. fourth (check)
24. K. to R. square	24. R. to K. square
25. Q. takes P. (check) (*c*)	25. R. takes Q.
26. Kt. takes R.	26. Q. to K. B. fourth
27. R. takes Q.	27. B. takes R.
28. Kt. takes Q. B. P.	28. B. takes Q. B. P.
29. Kt. to Kt. fifth	29. P. to Q. fourth
30. Kt. takes R. P., and wins.	

NOTES.

(*a*) The correct move here is K. Kt. to B. third.
(*b*) R. takes P. seems stronger.
(*c*) An unexpected and very ingenious combination.

GAME 142.

Consultation Game played at the Glasgow Chess Club by Messrs. Moffatt and Williams against Messrs. Weaver and E———N.:—

(*French Opening.*)

White. (Messrs. MOFFATT and WILLIAMS.)	Black. (Messrs. WEAVER, and E———N.)
1. P. to K. fourth	1. P. to K. third
2. K. Kt. to B. third	2. P. to Q. fourth

3. P. takes P.	3. P. takes P.
4. P. to Q. fourth	4. K. B. to Q. third
5. B. to Q. third	5. K. Kt. to B. third
6. Castles	6. Castles
7. B. to K. Kt. fifth	7. B. to K. Kt. fifth
8. Q. Kt. to Q. second	8. Q. Kt. to Q. second
9. P. to Q. B. third	9. P. to Q. B. third
10. Q. to Q. B. second	10. P. to K. R. third
11. B. takes Kt. (a)	11. Kt. takes B.
12. Q. R. to K. square	12. Kt. to K. R. fourth
13. P. to K. R. third	13. B. to K. third
14. K. Kt. to K. fifth	14. Kt. to B. fifth
15. R. to K. third	15. P. to Q. B. fourth (b)
16. Q. to Q. square	16. B. takes Kt.
17. P. takes B.	17. Q. to K. Kt. fourth
18. R. to Kt. third	18. Q. takes P.
19. K. R. to K. square	19. Q. to K. B. third
20. B. to Q. Kt. square	20. Q. R. to K. square
21. K. to B. square	21. P. to Q. B. fifth
22. K. R. to K. third	22. P. to K. R. fourth
23. Q. to Q. B. second	23. Kt. to Q. sixth
24. Kt. to K. B. third	24. P. to K. R. fifth
25. Q. R. to K. Kt. fifth	25. P. to K. Kt. third
26. R. takes Kt.	26. P. takes R.
27. Q. takes P.	27. R. to K. second
28. R. to K. R. fifth (c)	28. B. to K. B. fourth
29. R. takes B.	29. Q. takes R.
30. Q. takes Q.	30. P. takes Q.
31. B. takes P.	31. K. R. to K. sq. (d) and wins

NOTES.

(a) Better to have retreated the Bishop.
(b) A good move, giving Black the attack.
(c) Q. to Q. second gives White more resource.
(d) Black plays very well throughout this game.

GAME 143.

The two games which follow were played some time since between Signor Dubois and Mr. A. Kempe, the former giving Pawn and move.

(Remove Black's K. B. P. from the board.)

White. (Mr. KEMPE.)	Black. (Sig. DUBOIS.)
1. P. to K. fourth	1. Kt. to Q. B. third
2. P. to Q. fourth	2. P. to Q. fourth

3. P. to K. fifth	3. B. to K. B. fourth
4. Kt. to K. B. third	4. P. to K. third
5. B. to Q. third	5. B. to K. Kt. fifth
6. Castles (*a*)	6. Kt. takes Q. P.
7. B. takes K. R. P.	7. Kt. takes Kt. (check)
8. P. takes Kt.	8. R. takes B.
9. P. takes B.	9. Q. to K. R. fifth
10. B. to K. B. fourth	10. Kt. to K. R. third
11. P. to K. B. third	11. B. to Q. B. fourth (check)
12. K. to R. square	12. P. to K. Kt. fourth
13. B. to K. Kt. third	13. Q. takes B. (*b*)
14. P. takes Q.	14. Black mates in two moves.

NOTES.

(*a*) Badly played. It was necessary to defend the Q. P.
(*b*) Both this skirmish and its companion are cleverly played by Sig. Dubois.

GAME 144

(Remove Black's K. B. P. from the board.)

White. (Mr. KEMPE.)	*Black.* (Sig. DUBOIS.)
1. P. to K. fourth	1. P. to K. third
2. P. to Q. fourth	2. P. to K. Kt. third
3. P. to K. B. fourth	3. P. to Q. fourth
4. P. to K. fifth	4. P. to Q. B. fourth
5. B. to Q. Kt. fifth (ch.) (*a*)	5. Kt. to Q. B. third
6. Kt. to K. B. third	6. P. takes P.
7. Q. takes P.	7. Kt. to K. second
8. Castles	8. Kt. to K. B. fourth
9. Q. to Q. R. fourth	9. Q. to Q. Kt. third (check)
10. K. to R. square	10. P. to K. R. fourth
11. P. to Q. B. fourth	11. P. to K. R. fifth
12. Kt. to K. Kt. fifth	12. B. to Q. second
13. P. takes Q. P.	13. P. takes P.
14. P. to K. sixth	14. Kt. to Kt. sixth (ch.) (*b*)
15. P. takes Kt.	15. P. takes P. (dis. check)
16. Kt. to K. R. third	16. Q. B. takes P.
17. P. to K. B. fifth	17. B. takes K. B. P.
18. R. to K. square (check)	18. K. to B. second
19. B. to K. third	19. B. to Q. B. fourth
20. Q. to Q. Kt. third	20. B. to K. fifth
21. K. to Kt. square	21. R. takes Kt.
22. P. takes R.	22. Kt. to Q. fifth

23. R. to K. B. square (check)	23. K. to Kt. square
24. Q. to Q. square	24. Kt. to K. seventh (check)
25. Q. takes Kt.	25. B. takes B. (check)
26. R. to K. B. second	26. B. takes R. (check)
27. K. to B. square	27. P. mates.

NOTES.

(a) This only weakens White's game.
(b) The sacrifice here is quite sound, and leads to a speedy termination of the contest.

GAME 145.
(Ruy Lopez Knight's Game.)

White. (HERR NEUMANN.)	Black. (HERR ANDERSSEN.)
1. P. to K. fourth	1. P. to K. fourth
2. Kt. to K. B. third	2. Kt. to Q. B. third
3. B. to Q. Kt. fifth	3. Kt. to K. B. third
4. Castles	4. Kt. takes P.
5. P. to Q. fourth	5. B. to K. second
6. Q. to K. second	6. Kt. to Q. third
7. B. takes Kt.	7. Q. Kt. P. takes B.
8. P. takes P.	8. Kt. to Q. Kt. second
9. B. to K. third	9. Castles
10. R. to Q. square	10. Q. to K. square
11. Kt. to Q. B. third	11. Kt. to Q. square
12. Kt. to Q. fourth	12. P. to K. B. fourth
13. P. to K. B. fourth	13. Q. to K. Kt. third
14. Kt. to K. B. third	14. Kt. to K. third
15. Q. to K. B. second	15. P. to K. R. third
16. Kt. to Q. R. fourth	16. P. to Q. R. fourth
17. P. to Q. B. fourth	17. P. to Q. third
18. Q. R. to Q. B. square (a)	18. P. to Q. B. fourth
19. Kt. to Q. B. third	19. R. to K. B. second
20. Kt. to Q. fifth	20. B. to K. B. square
21. R. to Q. second	21. R. to Q. Kt. square
22. P. to Q. Kt. third	22. P. to Q. R. fifth
23. P. takes R. P. (b)	23. Q. to K. R. fourth
24. Kt. to Q. B. third	24. R. to Q. Kt. fifth
25. Kt. to K. second	25. P. to K. Kt. fourth (c)
26. P. to Q. R. fifth	26. B. to Q. R. third
27. K. R. to Q. B. second	27. P. takes K. B. P.
28. B. takes P.	28. P. to Q. fourth (d)

And Black won the game.

NOTES.

(*a*) Up to this point the moves are almost identical with those of a game between the same players, published at p. 304 of our October number. In that game, however, Mr. Neumann advanced the Pawn to Queen's Bishop's fifth before moving his Queen's Rook. This we think was the preferable course, as Black is now enabled to stop the advance of the Pawn.

(*b*) It to Q. Kt. second seems preferable.

(*c*) Bringing forward this Pawn for the attack was a fine stroke of Chess generalship.

(*d*) The advance of this Pawn leaves White without resource.

Position after Black's 25th move.
BLACK.

WHITE.

GAME 146.

We place before our readers an unpublished game played several years ago, in which Mr. Staunton gave the odds of the Pawn and two moves to "Gamma," well known in Chess circles as one of the leading Scotch amateurs.

(*Remove Black's K. B. Pawn.*)

White. ("GAMMA.")	Black. (Mr. STAUNTON.)
1. P. to K. fourth	1.
2. P. to Q. fourth	2. P. to K. third
3. B. to Q. third	3. P. to Q. B. fourth
4. P. to K. fifth	4. K. Kt. to K. second
5. P. to K. B. fourth	5. P. takes P.
6. K. Kt. to B. third	6. Q. Kt. to B. third
7. Castles	7. P. to K. Kt. third
8. Q. Kt. to Q. R. third	8. B. to K. Kt second
9. Q. Kt. to Q. B. fourth	9. Castles

10. Q. Kt. to Q. sixth	10. K. Kt. to Q. fourth
11. K. Kt. to Kt. fifth (a)	11. Q. Kt. to K. second
12. R. to K. B. third	12. K. Kt. to K. sixth (b)
13. Q. to K. second	13. Q. Kt. to Q. fourth
14. P. to K. Kt. third	14. K. Kt. to K. B. fourth (c)
15. K. Kt. to. K. fourth	15. K. Kt. to K. second
16. B. to Q. second	16. P. to Q. Kt. third
17. Q. R. to K. B. sq.	17. Q. R. to Q. Kt. square
18. P. to K. Kt. fourth	18. B. to Q. Kt. second
19. Kt. takes B.	19. R. takes Kt.
20. P. to K. Kt. fifth (d)	20. K. Kt. to K. B. fourth
21. Kt. to B. sixth (check)	21. B. takes Kt.
22. K. P. takes B.	22. R. to Q. B. second
23. B. takes Kt.	23. K. P. takes B.
24. Q. to Q. third	24. Q. to Q. R. sq.
25. K. to Kt. second (e)	25. K. R. to Q. B. sq.
26. R. to Q. B. sq.	26. R. to K. sq.
27. K. to B. second	27. R. to K. fifth
28. P. to Q. R. third	28. Q. to Q. B. third
29. Q. to Q. Kt. third	29. K. to K. B. sq.
30. P. to Q. B. fourth	30. Kt. to K. sixth
31. B. takes Kt.	31. P. takes B. (check)
32. K. to Kt. third	32. Q. to Q. third
33. R. to Q. sq.	33. P. to K. seventh
34. R. takes Q.	34. P. Queens (ch.) & wins (f).

Position after Black's 24th move.

BLACK.

WHITE.

NOTES.

(*a*) Threatening to take R. P. with Kt., and then check with Q.
(*b*) This leads to no advantage, since the Knight must retreat ultimately.
(*c*) The manœuvring of the Knights renders this part of the game very interesting.
(*d*) P. to Q. B. fourth is perhaps more forcible.
(*e*) A fatal blunder, throwing away a won game. White up to this point conducted the attack with great skill, and took full advantage of the odds given. Instead of K. to Kt. second, however, he should have played thus:—

Q. takes Q. P.   R. takes P.
R. to Q. third, winning without much trouble.

(*f*) This is conclusive, for if

35. K. to R. third (best)	35. Q. to K. Kt. eighth
36. R. to K. Kt. third	36. Q. to K. B. eighth (check)
37. R. to K. Kt. second	37. R. takes K. B. P.
38. R. to Q. third (best)	38. Q. R. takes P., and wins.

CHESS INTELLIGENCE.

THE SHEFFIELD ATHENÆUM CHESS CLUB.

We have been requested by the honorary secretary of the Sheffield Athenæum Chess Club to publish the following extract:—

The annual general meeting of this club was held on Tuesday, at the Athenæum. The report having been read and adopted, the President, G. S. Taylor, Esq., gave an account of the correspondence which had passed between this and the Huddersfield Chess Club, relative to the challenge which that club had received from the Sheffield Athenæum Club to play a return match. It appeared that in consequence of having lost two or three of its members, and of the disinclination of those remaining to play in matches, the Huddersfield Club had declined to accept the Sheffield challenge. Much disappointment was felt by the Sheffield players at not having been afforded the chance of retrieving their defeat of last year, and there was a very general expression of regret that chess at the Huddersfield Club had "fallen to so low an ebb." Dr. J. C. Hall tendered to the members present a set of Staunton chess men to be played for in a handicap tournament; his offer was thankfully accepted. The following gentlemen were appointed officers—viz.: G. S. Taylor, Esq., president; J. Greening, Esq., vice-president; Mr. J. J. Champion, secretary (elected in place of Mr. G. B. Cocking, who had held the post for twelve years, and whose resignation was accepted amid manifestations of great regret); Messrs. Cockayne, Latham, Mort, and Rowbotham as members of the council.—*Sheffield and Rotherham Independent*, Feb. 1, 1866.

MATCH BETWEEN MESSRS. ANDERSSEN AND STEINITZ.—We are enabled to state that Professor Anderssen has accepted the challenge of Mr. Steinitz to play a match at Chess in the course of next summer. The details will be arranged in due course, and we shall not fail to acquaint our readers with them.

ST. JAMES'S CHESS CLUB.—A match has been arranged between Mr. A. Sich and Mr. Lowenthal, the latter giving the odds of Pawn and two moves, the winner of the first seven games to be the conqueror.

THE BATH AND BRISTOL CHESS CLUBS.—Under the presidency of Captain Kennedy these societies have made arrangements for a meeting to be held at Bristol on Monday, March 10th, when it is expected that many of the Bath amateurs will be present. A telegraphic match between these clubs and the St. George's Club, London, will take place on Wednesday, March 14th, commencing early in the afternoon, so as to allow, if possible, of the conclusion of the games the same evening. On Thursday, March 15th, a meeting will commence at Bath, when many members of the Bristol Club will, it is hoped, return the friendly visit of their neighbours. A soiree at the Assembly Rooms, on Saturday, will wind up the proceedings. Mr. Lowenthal has been invited to be present during the week, and will superintend the arrangements of the telegraphic match.

NEW YORK CHESS CLUB.—A tourney has been commenced at this club on a somewhat novel plan, in which eighteen players have entered the lists. They were divided into three classes, according to their strength, the antagonists for the first round in each class being determined by lot. One game decides the fate of each pair, and lots are again drawn, until only one player in each class remains. A system of odds is then agreed upon between the different classes, and the contest proceeds to its conclusion. The following were the entries:—First class: Capt. Mackenzie v. C. H. Stanley, Dr. Burnett v. H. T. Worrall, Thompson v. Zerega, Johnson v. Belcher. Second class: De Trovriand v. Dill, Graves v. Martinez, Graham v. Ward. Third class: Arietta v. Gilbert, Schultz v. Young. Since writing the above we learn that Messrs. Mackenzie, Thompson, Belcher, Dill, Ward, and Arietta have respectively defeated their opponents.

No. 70.   By T. SMITH, Esq.

White to play, and mate in five moves.

No. 71. By Dr. Conrad Bayer.

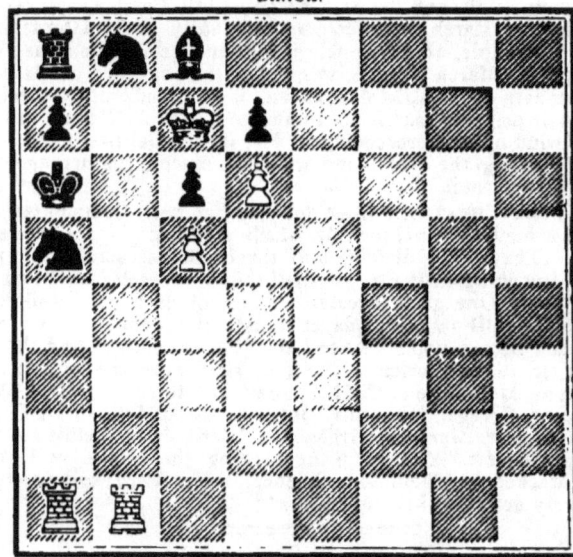

White to play, and mate in eight moves.

No. 72. By Dr. Conrad Bayer.

No. 73. By Mr. J. A. Graves, of Brooklyn.

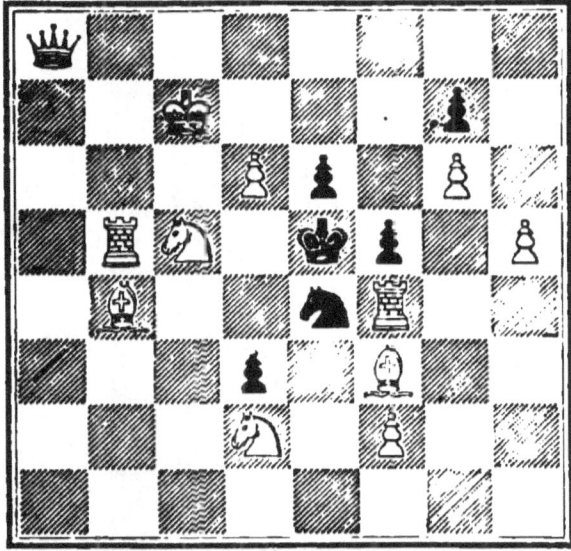

White to play, and mate in two moves.

Chess Study No. 13, "The Whirligig." By W. T. Pierce, Esq.

Chess Study No. 14. By Herr Kling.

White, playing first, can draw.

ANSWERS TO CORRESPONDENTS.

J. W. (Huddersfield).—Your communication has been received, and the enclosed letter forwarded to its destination.

J. J. W. (City of London Chess Club).—We feel ourselves perfectly satisfied with your explanation.

Dr. F.—We are extremely grateful for your kind promise.

J. P. (Paris).—A private letter has been forwarded.

C. W. (of Sunbury).—A few more of your compositions would be acceptable.

F. R. D. (Malvern).—Many thanks for the game, which will receive our best attention. We are glad to hear you have some prospect of forming a club.

W. W. (Eton).—Our grateful acknowledgments for your continued favours. The games shall appear in our next impression.

F. T. (Secretary of the "Pesti Sakk-kor").—We are gratified by your communication, and intend writing to you privately at an early date.

T. L. (Dublin).—Delayed only, but not forgotten.

G. (Sheffield).—Many thanks for the corrected copy. As to your query—five minutes per move.

E. T. (Bath).—We look forward with pleasure to your promised contributions.

W. C. G.—Many thanks for your contribution.

F. W. (Howard College).—We have severally answered your various questions by private letter.

Mr. Healey's Problems.—This long-expected volume has just been published. We have not time or space to review it in our present number, but we hope to do it full justice in our impression for April. The genius of such a composer demands no slight or hasty recognition at our hands.

THE Chess Player's Magazine.

"BLACKWOOD" ON CHESS.

CHESS labours under a greater disadvantage than any other pastime—the disadvantage of not being generally understood. Even that brilliant creature, the novelist of modern days, who is supposed to comprehend all things from Divinity to the Derby, seems incapable of grasping the mystery of the chequered field. Worse still, when the novelist philosophises, and delivers himself of his opinions on that great and comprehensive subject, "Things in General," his incisive wit and keen powers of observation avail him but little when levelled against the Game of Games.

The brilliant essayist of *Blackwood's Magazine*, who once revelled in what may most fitly be designated the "rollicking" school of fiction—who told a good story, and told it well; whose hero comes down to morning parade with the soot of last night's Othello still adhering to his manly countenance; whose bright examplar's brightest deeds consist in riding wild Irish steeplechasers over impossible stone walls or equally impracticable water jumps—has lately taken it into his head to make a horse, foot, and artillery attack on Chess and Chess players.

With an amount of modesty marvellously rare—and therefore most highly to be commended in an Irishman—the essayist admits that he does not "even seek to make converts," and in almost the next sentence concedes that the "false idols" *he* "bowls over" are very likely to be set up again. All this is very kind and good humoured of the essayist, but it does not say much for his bowling. After denouncing, as merely possessing a "mock air of intellectuality," all players of games, he proceeds to make a most wonderful exception.

We are informed, to our utter amazement, that "Whist is a specialty, and it would be as impossible for a first-rate whister not to be a man of more than average ability, as for a first-rate swimmer not to be endowed with strength and symmetry.

"Next to whist comes picquet, but after a long interval. As for Chess, I hold skill in it very cheaply. Much has been said of the superiority Chess possesses in the absence of all element of chance. It is a trial of skill on such perfectly equal grounds. No question of luck, no disturbing incident of fortune interferes.

"Now, it is exactly in this very positiveness I declare Chess to be inferior to whist. It is the 'possible,' the unknown something of whist that imparts the highest interest to the game, and exercises the most subtle powers of the player."

Verily this is a new doctrine. Henceforth bid adieu ye abject exact sciences to the proud position ye hold in the minds of men. It is the lucky guesser, the man who succeeds by a "fluke," who should be honoured in his generation. The clear and accurate reasoner, he who deduces certain positive results from certain given facts, shall henceforth hide his diminished head.

The "unknown something," the "possible," may be an attraction from a sensational and gambling point of view, but can scarcely be considered as a desirable addition to an intellectual pastime. Moreover, our experience of whist teaches us that its votaries cling quite as closely to tradition as Chess players, and that the troublesome addition of a partner prevents any of those brilliant outbreaks of originality which so frequently illumine the world of Chess. Again — "There are dealers who have all their wares in the shop-windows; such are the players of games. Whatever they possess of readiness, memory, or address, is at hand, and they display their gifts to the world with all the alacrity and all the insistance of the pedlar. Test any of these people, however, by the rude stern proof of success in some career, and what a sorry figure they cut!

"Who ever met a great Chess player great in any other relationship in life? They are as insignificant as the pianists, if there be anything can vie with these creatures of chords and pedals. Your Chess player is rarely a conversationalist; he is either morosely silent and repelling, or he is of a mulish obstinacy of temperament, self-opinionated, and reliant on the miserable pre-eminence his skill in his game has bestowed upon him."

It is really wonderful what conclusions the most highly-cultivated men can arrive at when dealing with subjects of which they know nothing!

Innumerable great men have played Chess from Tamerlane to Napoleon. The conquerors and rulers of the earth have revelled in the mimic war. Franklin, the old man of Ferney, and Jean Jacques Rousseau have shown the attraction Chess possesses for minds of the highest order.

But a very short time has elapsed since the world of letters and the world of Chess wept the loss of one subtle brain, merciless in logic, indefatigable in application, calm, studious, patient, and bold —Henry Buckle. Who wrote the *Handbuch?* The acknowledged Chess king of Europe, Heydebrand von der Lasa, the Prussian ambassador at the Court of Denmark. Who beat the best players of Europe at the two great tournaments held in London but Anderssen, Professor of Mathematics at the University of Breslau.

It is not difficult to comprehend why those men who have filled a large space in the world's history have almost invariably played Chess indifferently. It is not that the game is in itself dull, plodding, and humdrum, but that, from the very variety and beauty of its combinations, it requires more time and more singleness of thought than great soldiers can afford to bestow upon it.

If Napoleon I. had been occupied in mastering the difficulties of Chess he would not have had time to conquer Europe, nor could Frederick the Great have seized Silesia by the help of the Muzio Gambit. All this does not in anywise invalidate the claim of Chess to be considered the queen of all games.

The essayist, to the contrary notwithstanding, it is the very elimination of what he is pleased to designate the "grand element of chance," which constitutes the great attraction of Chess for many minds of the highest order. But it is not enough to denounce the game; its wretched and deluded followers are also held up to derision. They are either "morosely silent and repelling" or "mulishly obstinate." The essayist has been truly unfortunate in not meeting any of the many *good* Chess players who are not only men of far more than average intellectual attainments, but right cheerful and joyous companions.

But all his ill-humour is easily explained. He cannot play. He has tried to learn; and has found himself stopped, like another famous person, by the elements. He has found himself beaten hollow by persons immeasurably his inferiors in wit, imagination, and conversational brilliancy, and pours forth his vial of wrath upon them accordingly, entirely omitting to do justice to the positive mathematical order of mind necessary to make a good Chess player.

This is grossly unfair, and it is too much to expect Chess players to listen tamely to a scolding from a clever and amusing novelist, who is angry with Chess because he has never been able to get over the odds of the Rook.

CHESS IN INDIA.
LETTER III.
TO THE EDITOR OF THE "CHESS PLAYER'S MAGAZINE."

Sir,—I remarked in a former letter, which you did me the honour to publish in your periodical, that I was not fortunate enough, during a residence of some years in India, to meet with more than two Chessplayers of first-rate ability. Of the Bareilly champion, Lek Raj, I have already given a brief notice; permit me to follow it with a short account of Hurri Ramchunder, the best player of Poona.

Hurri Ramchunder is employed at a small salary under Government as teacher in a school. Though a Brahmin by caste, he is almost wholly ignorant of English—a fatal disqualification in the present day for rising in the world to any native servant of Government. He has, nevertheless, a very high reputation as a mathematician, and I have heard him rated by an excellent judge as one of the best astronomers in the Bombay Presidency. That a close relation of some sort exists between mathematics and Chess is indeed well known, and probably no player ever contested a game with a Cambridge wrangler without being convinced that his opponent was at least possessed of great natural aptitude for Chess.

For some time past Hurri Ramchunder, now about forty-five years of age, has been generally esteemed the most skilful Chessplayer of Western India. This distinction he owes in some degree to his having defeated a famous player of Baroda; but his excellence in the game he himself ascribes mainly to his teacher, a venerable Brahmin of Poonah, recently deceased at an advanced age.

I had the pleasure of contesting a long series of games with Hurri Ramchunder, both at odds and upon even terms. When giving me the heavy odds of Pawn and two moves he made about even games. Giving me Pawn and move, he won about four to one, and he gained (as might be expected) a still larger majority upon even terms. I cannot better conclude this letter than by subjoining the following specimens of his skill:—

Remove Black's K. B. P. from the board.

White. (INDUS.)	*Black.* (HURRI RAMCHUNDER.)
1. P. to K. fourth	1. P. to K. third
2. P. to Q. fourth	2. P. to Q. B. fourth
3. B. to Q. B. fourth	3. P. takes P.
4. Kt. to K. B. third	4. B. checks
5. P. to Q. B. third	5. P. takes P.
6. Kt. takes P.	6. B. takes Kt. (check)
7. P. takes B.	7. Q. to Q. B. second
8. Q. to Q. third	8. Kt. to Q. B. third
9. Castles	9. K. Kt. to K. second
10. B. to Q. R. third	10. Castles
11. Q. R. to Q. square	11. R. to K. square
12. B. to Q. Kt. third	12. Q. to K. B. fifth
13. B. to Q. B. second	13. Kt. to K. Kt. third
14. Q. B. to his square	14. Q. to K. Kt. fifth
15. P. to K. R. third	15. Q. to K. R. fourth
16. Kt. to K. R. second	16. Q. Kt. to K. second
17. P. to K. B. fourth	17. P. to Q. fourth
18. P. to K. fifth (*a*)	18. Kt. to K. B. square
19. P. to K. Kt. fourth	19. Q. to K. B. second
20. Kt. to K. B. third	20. P. to K. R. third
21. Kt. to K. R. fourth	21. P. to Q. R. fourth (*b*)
22. P. to K. B. fifth	22. P. takes P.
23. P. takes P.	23. Kt. to Q. B. third
24. P. to K. sixth	24. Q. to K. R. fourth
25. P. to K. B. sixth (*c*)	25. P. takes P.
26. R. takes P.	26. R. takes P.
27. R. takes Kt. (check)	27. K. takes R.
28. R. to K. B. square (check)	28. K. to his square
29. Q. to K. R. seventh	29. Kt. to K. second
30. B. to Q. R. fourth (check)	30. K. moves
31. Q. to K. R. eighth (ch.) (*d*)	31. K. moves
32. B. to K. B. fourth (check)	32. K. to Kt. third
33. R. to Q. Kt. square (check)	33. K. to R. second

34. Q. to Q. fourth (check)	34. P. to Q. Kt. third
35. B. to Q. B. seventh	35. R. to Q. Kt. square (e)
36. B. takes R. (check)	36. K. takes B.
37. R. takes P. (check)	37. K to R. square
38. R. to Q. Kt. fifth (f)	38. R. to K. eighth (check)
39. K. to R. second	39. Q. to K. fourth (check)
40. Q. takes Q.	40. R. takes Q.
41. R. takes P. (check)	41. K. to Kt. square
42. Kt. to K. B. third	42. R. to K. seventh (check) (g)
43. K. to Kt. third	43. R. takes P.
44. R. to Q. Kt. fifth (check)	44. K. to B. second
45. B. to Q. Kt. third	45. R. to Q. Kt. seventh
46. Kt. to Q. fourth	46. R. to Q. seventh
47. B. takes P.	47. Kt. takes B.
48. R. takes Kt.	48. R. to Q. sixth (check)
49. K. to B. fourth	49. R. takes K. R. P.

Drawn game.

NOTES.

(a) Q. to Q. Kt. fifth is also a good move.
(b) The best move on the board, opening a square for the Q. R.
(c) This is perhaps premature, yet it certainly looks like a winning line of play.
(d) This is much better than checking with Rook.
(e) Checking with Queen would be inferior.
(f) Better than exchanging Rooks.
(g) This game abounds throughout with critical and perplexing situations for either player.

Remove Black's K. B. P. from the board.

White. (INDUS.)	Black. (HURRI RAMCHUNDER.)
1. P. to K. fourth	1. P. to K. third
2. Kt. to Q. B. third	2. Kt. to Q. B. third
3. P. to Q. fourth	3. Q. to K. B. third (a)
4. P. to K. fifth	4. Q. to K. B. second
5. P. to K. B. fourth	5. B. to Q. Kt. fifth
6. Kt. to K. B. third	6. B. takes Kt. (check)
7. P. takes B.	7. P. to K. R. third
8. B. to Q. third	8. K. Kt. to K. second
9. P. to Q. B. fourth	9. P. to Q. Kt. third
10. B. to K. fourth	10. B. to Q. Kt. second
11. Castles	11. Castles (Q. R.)
12. P. to Q. fifth (b)	12. Q. Kt. to his square
13. B. to Q. R. third	13. P. takes P.
14. Q. B. takes Kt.	14. P. takes B.
15. B. takes R.	15. P. takes Kt.
16. B. to K. R. fourth	16. Q. takes K. B. P.
17. B. to K. Kt. third	17. Q. to K. sixth (check)

18. R. to K. B. second	18. P. takes P.
19. Q. to Q. third	19. Q. to Q. B. fourth
20. R. to Q. square (c)	20. R. to K. square
21. Q. to K. Kt. sixth	21. R. to K. second
22. B. to K. R. fourth	22. R. takes P.
23. Q. takes K. Kt. P.	23. B. to Q. B. third
24. Q. takes R. P.	24. K. to Kt. second
25. B. to K. B. sixth.	25. R. to K. seventh
26. Q. to K. B. fourth	26. R. to K. fifth
27. Q. to Q. second	27. R. takes P.
28. P. to Q. B. third	28. P. to Q. third
29. B. to Q. fourth	29. Q. to K. R. fourth
30. Q. to Q. third	30. R. to Q. R. fifth
31. R. to K. square	31. Kt. to Q. second
32. Q. to K. second	32. Q. to K. R. fifth
33. Q. to K. seventh	33. R. takes B. (d)
34. P. takes R.	34. Q. takes Q. P.
35. Q. to K. third	35. Q. to K. R. fifth
36. Q. to K. B. fourth	36. Q. to K. R. fourth
37. Q. to K. B. fifth	37. Q. to K. R. fifth
38. Q. to K. B. fourth	38. Q. to K. R. sixth
39. Q. to K. third	39. Q. to K. R. fourth
40. Q. to K. second	40. Q. to K. R. fifth
41. Q. to K. seventh	41. Q. to Q. Kt. fifth
42. P. to K. R. fourth	42. Q. to K. Kt. fifth
43. Q. to K. Kt. fifth	43. Q. to K. R. sixth
44. R. takes P.	44. Kt. to K. fourth
45. R. takes Kt.	45. P. takes R.
46. Q. to K. Kt. third	46. Q. to K. B. fourth
47. Q. to K. Kt. fifth	47. Q. to Q. Kt. eighth (check)
48. K. to R. second	48. B. takes R.
49. Q. takes B. (check)	49. P. to K. fifth
50. P. to K. R. fifth	50. P. to Q. B. third
51. P. to K. R. sixth	51. P. to K. sixth
52. Q. to K. Kt. seventh (ch.)	52. K. to R. third
53. P. to K. R. seventh	53. P. to K. seventh
54. P. Queens	54. P. Queens
55. Q. to Q. B. eighth (check)	55. K. to Kt. fourth
56. Q. to K. Kt. fifth (check)	56. P. to Q. B. fourth
57. Q. to Q. seventh (check)	57. K. to R. third
58. Q. to Q. B. eighth (check)	58. K. to R. fourth
59. Q. to K. Kt. second (f)	59. Q. to K. R. fifth (check)
60. Second Q. covers	60. Q. takes Q. (check)
61. K. takes Q.	61. Q. to K. R. 2nd (ch.) & wins.

NOTES.

(a) Though rarely adopted at these odds, this move affords the defence considerable resource.

(*b*) This combination wins the exchange, but at the expense of two valuable Pawns.

(*c*) This confines the Knight, and is much stronger than R. to K. square.

(*d*) An excellent stroke of play. By giving up a second exchange Black is enabled to win the game.

(*e*) From this point Black seems to have a forced won game.

(*f*) It very seldom occurs in actual play that there are four Queens (as here) on the board at the same time.

I remain, Sir, yours, &c..

London, March 22, 1866.   INDUS.

HUDDERSFIELD CHESS CLUB,
March 6th, 1866.

TO THE EDITOR OF "THE CHESS PLAYER'S MAGAZINE."

Dear Sir,—It is with some reluctance that I trespass on your valuable space, but as the statement put forward in your last number by the Sheffield Athenæum Chess Club respecting the Huddersfield Club is not altogether correct, perhaps you will allow me briefly to lay the facts of the case before your readers.

In the winter of 1864 the Huddersfield Chess Club received a challenge from the Sheffield Club to contest a friendly home-and-home match. The distance between the two towns—some thirty miles—and the corresponding expense, in addition to the inability of the Sheffield Club to play the match on a Saturday, which day is in this neighbourhood a half-holiday, were all felt to be serious obstacles in the way, but we waived them all, played the match, and won by a large majority.

Some few months ago we received another challenge to play a return match on similar conditions to the former. We replied that we should be very glad to play them again, with some modification of the terms. In the first match we were enabled to enter the field with as many as twelve players. Owing to losses which the club had sustained, and other causes, we were now unable to muster so strongly, but we offered to play the *same number of games* as in the previous match, by the six best players of each club, meeting at both towns, the total number of games to be added together.

The Sheffield Club, as they had a perfect right to do, refused to accept this modification of the terms, and so the match fell to the ground; and I leave it to your readers to decide whether the Sheffield Club is justified in now saying unreservedly, and without any explanation, that "the Huddersfield Club had declined to accept their challenge."

The rule we have always acted upon in club matches has been for the club of the smaller town to fix the number of players, and, I ask, is it reasonable to expect the club of a small town like Huddersfield to be able at all times to rival in point of numbers the club of a town four or five times its size.

Since 1856 the Huddersfield Chess Club has contested no less than twelve matches with the clubs of Bradford, Holmfirth, Leeds, Sheffield, and Wakefield, and has been successful in winning eight and drawing one. I believe I am correct when I further state that during this time none of these clubs have ever entered the lists against each other, or in other words, whenever any of these clubs have been engaged in a match, Huddersfield has been one of the contending parties. The now flourishing West Yorkshire Chess Association, too, was originated at a meeting of the Huddersfield Club in 1856. From these facts, and others I might name, I think it will appear that we have done our share at Huddersfield in keeping up the "sacred fire" of Chess; and, although we have recently lost several of our experienced players, we have the satisfaction of knowing that they have allied themselves with other clubs, and are doing good service to the cause of Chess in other parts of the country.

We have lately had accessions of young and very promising players to our ranks, and I trust, Mr. Editor, you have not yet heard the last of the Huddersfield Chess Club.

I remain, dear Sir, yours very truly,
JOHN WATKINSON.

THE CHESS CONGRESS OF 1866.

OUR readers will learn with satisfaction from the account of the meeting of the British Chess Association, which we publish at p. 107, that a congress of Chess players will be held in London on the 18th of June next. It remains for all amateurs throughout the kingdom, and especially the secretaries of provincial clubs, to do their part in rendering the meeting of the present year as successful as that of 1862.

After what we have urged in former pages it will not be needful for us to say much on the importance of placing the Association on a more permanent basis. This is indeed generally conceded. The organisation, originally designed for a local gathering, was felt in 1862 to be inadequate to the enlarged requirements of a national association. The four years which have since elapsed, while bringing with them a considerable addition to the Chess community, bear manifest witness to the need which exists for an institution which, without supplanting or competing with Chess clubs, will be a representative of them all, a sort of parliament wherein the general body of players can, when occasion arises, act in concert, and carry out their designs for the common benefit. This point was well handled by Lord Lyttelton, in his address to the recent meeting. "The time," he said, "seemed to have arrived when the meetings of the Association, hitherto only held at uncertain intervals, should be definitively fixed to take place at stated periods. The plan," he went on to say, "which he submitted to the meeting, would manifestly tend not only to render the Association a permanent centre of Chess, but also to diffuse the influence of the game more widely throughout the country, in every class of the community." It may indeed be hoped that the Association will in time become a truly national institution.

Nothing, we believe, could contribute more to ensure the stability of the Association than the resolution passed by the late meeting, that a congress should be held in London every alternate year, and that a general meeting for the transaction of business should be held in London every year. The first enactment secures a contest of skill between some of our finest proficients at least once in two years, while the second provides for the due representation of public opinion, and makes it imperative that the business of the society be transacted with method and regularity. The next resolution places beyond all doubt the anxious wish of the meeting to give all possible consideration to the country players. It declares that in each year in which no congress is held in London a congress shall be held in some provincial town where there is a local Chess club, if in the opinion of the managing committee for the year the state of the finances and condition of the Association render it desirable. To have resolved absolutely on holding a meeting every other year in the provinces would clearly have been imprudent, as so much must depend on the funds at the disposal of the committee. But we are certain that whenever circumstances enable them to do so they will gladly avail themselves of the opportunity. The impartiality, moreover, of the managing committee is guaranteed by the fact that more than half the gentlemen composing it are influential members of provincial clubs.

A noteworthy feature in the approaching congress is the intended presentation of challenge cups. Those who reflect how much similar honorary distinctions have done for nearly all our national amusements must agree with the committee that they will greatly tend to promote the cultivation and enlarge the popularity of the game.

We may be pardoned if we remember with pleasure that we were the first to call public attention to this mode of giving a new interest to our friendly contests. In addition to the cups, the committee intend, we believe, to offer handsome prizes in money to the successful players.

Nor have our ingenious friends, the problematists, been forgotten. A problem tournament, with liberal prizes, forms part of the programme. The great merit of the positions sent in for competition in 1862 has been universally acknowledged. May the present season be equally auspicious.

It has also been agreed that a "Book of Transactions" shall be published, under the sanction of the committee. It will include a full account of the proceedings of all the meetings of the Association, together with all games played and problems sent in at the same. It will further contain a "Chess Directory," whereby the address of any player, English or foreign, who will kindly forward it to the committee, may be at once ascertained.

We cannot refrain from expressing our satisfaction that the "Book of the Congress" (containing as it does that code of laws and that report of the proceedings of the congress which have been so bitterly and unfairly attacked by some of our contemporaries) has received at length the emphatic approval and sanction of the British Chess Association.

BRITISH CHESS ASSOCIATION.
GENERAL MEETING.

A most influential and important meeting of the members of the British Chess Association took place at the rooms of the St. George's Club, on Tuesday, the 6th March. There were present Lord Lyttelton (in the chair), Lord Cremorne, Lord Walden, Sir John Trelawney, Bart., Sir Theophilas Metcalfe; the Revs. G. A. MacDonnell, W. Wayte, Salter, and Skipworth; Messrs. Baker, Barber, Bourne, Chinnery, Coffey; Captain Cunningham, S. J. Green, Gover, Greenaway, T. J. Hampton, H. S. Kennedy, Harris, A. Jones, Jackson, Lowenthal, Mongredien, H. Mann, Medley, Mongredien, jun., Sich, Slous, Stewart, N. Strode, Taylor, Young, &c. A letter was received from Captain H. A. Kennedy, expressing his regret at being unable to attend.

Lord Lyttelton opened the proceedings by reading the minutes of the last General Meeting, which were then confirmed. He then made some remarks on the important objects which had led to the propositions which he was about to lay before the meeting, in doing which, he said, he could not help observing that the proceedings of the Association had been commented on in some quarters, and by writers sometimes giving their names, sometimes not, with a degree of bitterness and personality which he was wholly unable to account for. The time, he said, seemed to have arrived when the meetings of the Association, hitherto only held at uncertain intervals, should be definitively fixed to take place at stated periods. Frequent meetings had been held by the Managing Committee, and a scheme had been carefully prepared by them with a view to placing the Association on a more permanent basis. It might, perhaps, have been desirable to hold a meeting of the Association between their last meeting in 1862 and the present date, but circumstances had, no doubt, rendered it inconvenient. He had himself been requested to take part in a meeting proposed to be held at Redcar during the ensuing summer. It appeared to him, however, that the proposed meeting at Redcar would be likely (though, of course, undesignedly) to interfere with the organisation of the Chess Association, and he had, therefore, declined. The Redcar amateurs, when they drew up their programme, were doubtless ignorant of the intended meeting of the Association. He was about to submit to the meeting a plan which, if they should approve it, would manifestly tend not only to render the Association a permanent centre of Chess, but also to diffuse the influence of the game more widely throughout the country in every class of the community. Before, however, he laid this before them, he would ask them to give their sanction to "The Book of the Chess Congress of 1862." In that work were embodied not only all the Games and Problems resulting from that Congress, but also a full report of all the proceedings of the Congress, together with the code of laws adopted at the last general meeting of the Association.

It was then unanimously resolved that "The Book of the Chess Congress of 1862" is fully sanctioned and approved by the meeting.

The Chairman then read the proposals of the Managing Committee for the reorganisation of the Association as follows:—

(1) "That London be the head-quarters of the Association."—Carried unanimously.

(2) "That the staff be constituted as follows:—A President, and six or more Vice-Presidents, who shall hold office permanently. A Treasurer, an Honorary Secretary, a Manager, and an Auditor; to hold their offices for two years, but to be re-eligible. A General Committee, to consist of not less than thirty, nor more than fifty members, one-third to go out of office in rotation every two years, but to be re-eligible. A Managing Committee, to consist of the President, Vice-Presidents, the Treasurer, the Honorary Secretary, the Manager, and ten other members chosen from the General Committee; four to be a quorum, and the Chairman to have a casting vote."

Upon the resolution respecting the Vice-Presidents,

Mr. Young moved as an amendment—"That the word 'six' be struck out, and the word 'three' substituted."—Carried.

Mr. Young then proposed, and Mr. Harris seconded—"That all the officers of the Association should be appointed for two years only, but shall be re-eligible."—This amendment was also carried.

Lord Cremorne proposed, and Mr. Mongredien seconded, a resolution—"That a General Meeting (for the transaction of business) should be held every year in London, and that a Congress should be held in London every alternate year."—This was agreed to.

A long conversation then took place as to the advisability of holding a meeting of the Association in the provinces (for the purpose of play) in those years when no Congress would take place in London.

Mr. Skipworth took the opportunity of explaining a misapprehension which had arisen in regard to the intended meeting at Redcar. It had at first, he said, been contemplated to invite the members of the Association to Redcar, but when it was found that this might interfere with the arrangements of the Association, the Redcar committee, of course, abandoned their design, confining their plan to a provincial gathering. Ultimately, on the suggestion of Lord Lyttelton, the following resolution was passed:—

"That in each year in which no Congress is held in London a Congress be held in some provincial town, where there is a local Chess Club, if, in the opinion of the Managing Committee for the year, the state of the finances and condition of the Association render it desirable."

The other resolutions embodied in the report of the Managing Committee were passed without opposition.

Lord Cremorne then moved that Lord Lyttelton be chosen President of the Association. He paid a high tribute of respect to the ability and energy previously manifested by Lord Lyttelton in that capacity, and the great interest he had ever taken in the welfare of the Society. The proposal was seconded by Lord Walden, and carried by acclamation.

Lord Lyttelton briefly returned thanks, and expressed his intention to do all in his power to promote the benefit of the Society.

The following gentlemen were then elected Vice-Presidents;—Lord Cremorne, Lord Walden, Sir John Blunden, Bart., Capt. H. A. Kennedy, Mr. A. Mongredien; and the following were chosen as officers:—Hon. Secretary, Mr. G. W. Medley; Hon. Treasurer, Mr. T. J. Hampton; Auditor, Mr. H. C. Stewart; Manager, Mr. J. Lowenthal.

The following gentlemen were then elected to serve on the General Committee:—Sir A. H. Elton, Bart., Sir J. Trelawny, Bart., Sir C. Rowley, Bart., Sir C. Marshall, J. M. Gaskell, Esq., M.P., M. Wyvill, jun., Esq., M.P., Revs. J. Donaldson, T. Gordon, G. A. M'Donnell, J. Owen, C. E. Ranken, D. Salter, G. Salmon, W. Wayte, Capt. J. Hamilton, Dr. J. Freeman, Messrs. T. Avery, T. W. Barnes, S. S. Boden, H. G. Cattley, D. B. Chapman, J. Duncan, M.A., W. J. Evelyn, A. Fonblanque, R. T.

Forster, G. B. Fraser, J. F. Gillam, W. S. Gover, F. E. Greenaway, J. W. Hampton, J. M. Heathcote, A. Jones, S. Newham, H. T. Prinsep, A. G. Puller, J. Rhodes, G. Samuel, M. Sparke, H. Staunton, H. C. Sturt, F. L. Slous, N. W. I. Strode, C. R. M. Talbot, E. Thorold, W. G. Ward, H. Waite, G. Walker, J. W. R. Wilson, T. H. Worrall, and H. T. Young.

The following gentlemen were then chosen to serve on the Managing Committee (in addition, of course, to the *ex officio* members:—Rev. W· Wayte, Rev. G. A. M'Donnell, Messrs. N. Strode, H. Waite, Rimington Wilson, A. G. Puller, R. T. Forster, J. W. Hampton, John Baker, and S. Boden.

It was then unanimously agreed that a Congress be held in London, to commence on June 18th, 1866.

Mr. Medley explained that, so far as the matter had been considered by the late Committee, it would be desirable to give a Challenge Cup on that occasion, to be played for by English players only, as the prize of British championship. The cup, of the value of from £30 to £50, in which will be placed the entrance fees of the combatants, in addition to a money prize from the Association. The winner in 1866 to receive the cash, but the cup not to become his property except it be won by him for the second time at the Congress to be held in London in 1868, he, in the meantime, to hold the cup as a trophy, on giving the usual securities. Players intending to compete, to signify the same to the Managing Committee on or before Friday, 1st June, and to pay an entrance fee of £3 3s. The number of games to be played will be fixed by the Committee when they shall have ascertained the number of the combatants.*

Mr. Mongredien then moved a vote of thanks to Mr. Medley and Mr. Lowenthal for their labours in editing "The Book of the Congress of 1862." He highly eulogised the judgment, tact, and impartiality which they had shown in their difficult and laborious task.

Lord Cremorne, in seconding the motion, said that while he fully endorsed Mr. Mongredien's remarks, he could not but add his own warm appreciation of the patience and industry manifested by the gentlemen referred to.

Lord Lyttelton, in supporting the motion, which was carried unanimously, said he himself intended to propose a vote of thanks to the editors of "The Book of the Congress," if he had not been

---

* The Committee will be happy to receive from members special subscriptions towards the cup. Subscriptions received by T. I. Hampton, Esq., Treasurer, St. George's Club, 20, King Street, St. James's; and G. W. Medley, Esq., Hon. Secretary, London Chess Club, Pursell's, Cornhill. Cheques to be crossed London and Westminster Bank. Letters containing remittances to be sent to T. I. Hampton, Esq., as above; all other communications to be addressed to the British Chess Association, Pursell's, Cornhill, London, E.C.

anticipated by Mr. Mongredien. It gave him very great pleasure to support the motion.

A vote of thanks to the noble chairman was then proposed by Mr. Hampton, and carried by acclamation. After which the meeting separated.

GAMES.

GAME 146

(*Queen's Bishop's Pawn Opening.*)

White. (Mr. RANKEN.)	Black. (Mr. WAYTE.)
1. P. to K. fourth	1. P. to K. fourth
2. K. Kt. to B. third	2. Q. Kt. to B. third
3. P. to Q. B. third	3. K. Kt. to B. third
4. P. to Q. fourth	4. Kt. takes K. P.
5. P. to Q. fifth	5. K. B. to Q. B. fourth
6. P. takes Kt.	6. K. B. takes P. (check)
7. K. to K. second	7. P. to Q. fourth
8. P. takes P.	8. Q. B. takes P.
9. Q. to Q. R. fourth (check)	9. P. to Q. B. third
10. Q. Kt. to Q. second	10. P. to K. B. fourth
11. Kt. takes Kt.	11 K. B. P. takes Kt.
12. K. takes B.	12. Castles (*a*)
13. Q. B. to K. third	13. P. takes Kt.
14. P. to K. Kt. third	14. P. to Q. R. fourth
15. Q. R. to Q. square	15. Q. to Q. third
16. K. B. to Q. third	16. P. to Q. B. fourth (*b*)
17. K. B. to Q. B. fourth (*c*)	17. K. to R. square
18. Q. to Q. R. third (*d*)	18. Q. to K. third (*e*)
19. Q. B. takes P.	19. P. takes K. B.
20. B. takes R.	20. Q. to K. R. sixth
21. B. takes P. (check)	21. K. to Kt. square
22. Q. R. to K. Kt. square	22. R. to Q. square
23. Q. to K. seventh (*f*)	23. R. to Q. seventh (check)
24. K. to K. square	24. R. to K. seventh (check)
25. K. to Q. square	25. Q. to K. B. fourth
26. Q. to K. B. eighth (ch.) (*g*)	26. Q. takes Q.
27. B. takes Q.	27. K. takes B.
28. Q. R. to K. square	28. R. takes Q. Kt. P.
29. K. R. to B. square	29. P. to K. fifth
30. P. to Q. R. third	30. K. to Kt. second

31. P. to K. R. third	31. R. to Q. R. seventh
32. K. to Q. B. square	32. P. to K. B. seventh
33. Q. R. to Q. square	33. P. to K. sixth
34. R. to Q. seventh (check)	34. K. to Kt. third
35. R. takes B. (*h*)	35. R. to Q. R. eighth (check)

And White resigns.

NOTES.

(*a*) The German *Handbuch* and Staunton's *Praxis* here dismiss the game as favourable for Black. (See, however, some remarks on this point at p. 326 of our last volume.) At his last move White could also, perhaps more advantageously, play 12. Kt. takes P. The following moves, which occurred lately in a game between Mr. Wayte and an eminent player, throw some light on this variation:—

White. (Mr. ———.)	Black. (Mr. W.)
12. Kt. takes K. P.	12. Q. to Q. Kt. third
13. Kt. to K. Kt. fourth	13. Castles
14. Q. to Q. Kt. third	14. Q. B. to B. square
(The only move to avoid the exchange of Queens.)	
15. P. to K. R. third	15. B. takes Kt. (check)
16. P. takes B.	16. Q. to Q. B. fourth
17. R. to K. R. third	
(Fatal K. to Q. square was the proper play.)	
	17. Q. R. to Kt. square
18. Q. to Q. R. fourth	18. B. to K. Kt. eighth

and White cannot save the game.

Position after Black's 11th move.

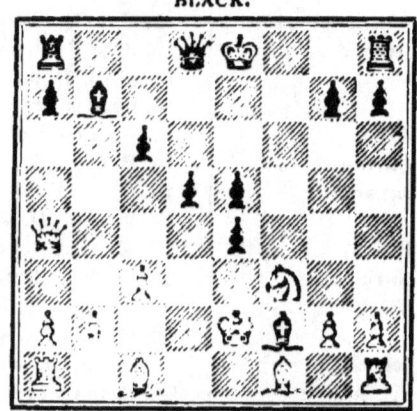

BLACK.

WHITE.

(*b*) This looks somewhat hazardous, as it exposes the Queen's Pawn to attack.

(*c*) Before making this move White should have played Q. to K. R. fourth, threatening mate. The Bishop could then be played to Q. B. fourth with greater effect.

(*d*) By this move White gains a Pawn, but at the same time puts his Queen out of play, and affords his opponent an opportunity of attack, of which he is not slow to avail himself. Had he played instead 18. B. takes Q. P. and 19. P. to Q. B. fourth, Black could have escaped by 19. Q. to Q. B. third, challenging an exchange of Queens.

Position after Black's 18th move.

BLACK.

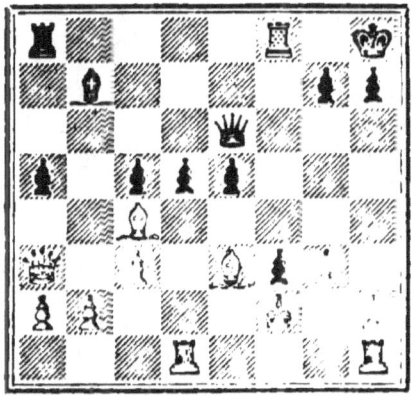

WHITE.

(e) The key-move of an interesting combination.

(f) The only move to prevent Black checking with Queen at move 25, which would have forced the mate.

(g) This also was compulsory. Black is now *minus* the exchanges, but he has a won game, through the strength of his advanced Pawns and the confinement of his adversary's pieces.

(h) R. to Q. sixth (check) would evidently have been useless.

GAME 147.

Game played recently at the Brighton Chess Club, by Mr. H. C. Stewart, of the St. James's Club, against one of the leading members.

(Evans's Gambit.)

White. (Mr. STEWART.)	Black. (Mr. ———.)
1. P. to K. fourth	1. P. to K. fourth
2. Kt. to K. B. third	2. Kt. to Q. B. third
3. B. to Q. B. fourth	3. B. to Q. B. fourth
4. P. to Q. Kt. fourth	4. B. takes P.
5. P. to Q. B. third	5. B. to Q. B. fourth
6. P. to Q. fourth	6. P. takes P.
7. P. takes P.	7. B. to Q. Kt. third
8. Castles	8. Kt. to Q. R. fourth (a)
9. B. to Q. third	9. P. to Q. third
10. B. to Q. Kt. second	10. B. to Q. second
11. P. to Q. fifth	11. P. to K. B. third (b)
12. P. to K. R. third (c)	12. Kt. to K. second

13. Kt. to Q. B. third	13. Kt. to K. Kt. third
14. Kt. to K. second	14. Castles
15. P. to K. Kt. fourth	15. P. to Q. B. fourth
16. R. to Q. B. square	16. Kt. to K. fourth
17. Kt. takes Kt.	17. B. P. takes Kt.
18. K. to Kt. second	18. Q. to K. R. fifth
19. P. to K. B. fourth	19. P. to Q. B. fifth
20. B. to Q. B. second	20. B. to K. sixth
21. P. to K. B. fifth	21. P. to K. R. fourth
22. Q. to K. square	22. Q. to K. Kt. fourth (d)
23. Q. takes Kt.	23. P. takes P.
24. P. takes P.	24. Q. takes P. (check)
25. Kt. to K. Kt. third	25. R. to K. B. third
26. Q. R. to K. square	26. B. to K. B. fifth
27. Q. to Q. B. third	27. R. to K. R. third
28. R. to K. R. square (e)	28. K. to B. second
29. R. takes R.	29. P. takes R.
30. B. to Q. square	30. Q. to K. Kt. fourth
31. B. to K. R. fifth (check)	31. K. to B. third
32. B. to Q. B. square	32. R. to K. Kt. square
33. B. takes B.	33. Q. takes B.
34. Q. to K. B. third	34. R. to K. Kt. fourth
35. K. to B. second	35. P. to Q. B. sixth
36. B. to K. Kt. sixth	36. Q. to Q. seventh (check)
37. Kt. to K. second	37. P. to Q. B. seventh
38. Q. to Q. B. third	38. Q. to Q. eighth
39. Q. to Q. B. seventh	39. R. to K. Kt. seventh (ch.)
40. K. takes R.	40. Q. takes R.

White mates in four moves.

NOTES.

(a) We prefer P. to Q. third at this point.

(b) This defence is tame, and cannot be pronounced satisfactory.

(c) This is not sufficiently attacking; Kt. to K. R. fourth would be stronger.

(d) An unsound sacrifice; by exchanging Queens Black would have had the better game.

(e) White plays the remainder of the game extremely well.

A match by correspondence is now in progress between the Chess Clubs of New York and Kingston. The games have proceeded far enough to determine the character of each opening, four moves having been played on each side. In the first two games Kingston opened with the Giuoco Piano and the King's Gambit, and the players of New York adopted the Queen's Knight's opening.

GAME 148.

The following game has been forwarded to us as a contribution to the theory of the Two Knights' Defence :—

(*Two Knights' Defence.*)

White. (Mr. RANKEN.)	Black. (Mr. WAYTE.)
1. P. to K. fourth	1. P. to K. fourth
2. K. Kt. to B. third	2. Q. Kt. to B. third
3. K. B. to Q. B. fourth	3. K. Kt. to B. third
4. Kt. to K. Kt. fifth	4. P. to Q. fourth
5. P. takes P.	5. Kt. to Q. R. fourth
6. B. to Q. Kt. fifth (check)	6. P. to Q. B. third
7. P. takes P.	7. P. takes P.
8. B. to K. second	8. P. to K. R. third
9. Kt. to K. B. third	9. P. to K. fifth
10. Kt. to K. fifth	10. Q. to Q. fifth
11. Kt. to K. Kt. fourth	11. B. takes Kt.
12. B. takes B.	12. P. to K. sixth
13. B. to K. B. third	13. P. takes P. (check)
14. K. to B. square	14. Castles
15. Q. to K. second	15. B. to Q. B. fourth
16. P. to Q. B. third	16. Q. to Q. sixth (*a*)
17. Q. takes Q. (*b*)	17. R. takes Q.
18. P. to Q. Kt. fourth	18. K. R. to K. square
19. B. to K. second	19. Q. R. to Q. third
20. P. takes B. (*c*)	20. Q. R. to K. third
21. B. to Q. R. sixth (check)	21. K. to B. second
22. K. takes P.	22. Kt. to K. fifth (check)
23. K. to Kt. square	23. Kt. takes P. at B. fourth
24. B. to K. B. square	24. Q. R. to K. eighth
25. Kt. to Q. R. third (*d*)	25. Kt. to Q. sixth
26. B. to Q. Kt. second (*e*)	26. Kt. takes B.
27. R. takes R.	27. R. takes R.
28. K. to B. second (*f*)	28. R. to Q. R. eighth
29. Kt. to Q. B. second	29. R. takes P.
30. B. to K. second	30. Kt. from Kt. 7th to B. fifth

And White resigns.

NOTES.

(*a*) The usual move at this point has been Q. to Q. R. fifth (see p. 16 of our January number, and the notes there). In that case, however, White by playing 17. Q. to Q. R. sixth (check), and 18. P. to Q. fourth, can maintain the advantage of a Pawn, with scarcely any inferiority of position. The counter move in the text has probably hitherto been rejected by analysts, as for the moment it loses a piece; but we believe that Black is sure of recovering more than an equivalent both in force and position, and that the first player's game is already irretrievably compromised.

(*b*) This is obviously compelled, in the face of Black's threatened move, K. R. to K. square.

Position after Black's 18th move.

BLACK.

WHITE.

(*c*) P. to Q. fourth, an apparently good move, would not be so in reality; Black would reply with Q. R. to K. third, with a winning game.

(*d*) At this point he may also play 25. B. to Q. R. third, with the following result:—

25. B. to Q. R. third	25. Kt. to Q. sixth
26. P. to K. Kt. third	26. K. R. to K. seventh, and wins

(*e*) Kt. to Q. B. second would have been preferable—*e. g.*,

26. Kt. to Q. B. second	26. R. takes B.
27. R. takes R.	27. Kt. takes R.
28. K. to B. second	28. Kt. takes R. P.
29. B. to K. second	29. Kt. to Q. third

30. Kt. to Q. fourth, and Black will have great difficulty in extricating his Kt

(*f*) If Kt. to Q. B. second, Black plays 28. R. to Q. eighth, &c., White's game is lost in its nature—his pieces are so helpless that the Pawns must be cut off in detail.

GAME 149.

An Evans' Gambit between the same players. This game is remarkable for the energy and correctness of the defence:—

(*Evans' Gambit.*)

White. (Mr. WAYTE.)	Black. (Mr. RANKEN.)
1. P. to K. fourth	1. P. to K. fourth
2. K. Kt. to B. third	2. Q. Kt. to B. third
3. K. B. to Q. B. fourth	3. K. B. to Q. B. fourth
4. P. to Q. Kt. fourth	4. B. takes Q. Kt. P.

5. P. to Q. B. third	5. B. to Q. B. fourth
6. Castles	6. P. to Q. third
7. P. to Q. fourth	7. P. takes P.
8. P. takes P.	8. B. to Q. Kt. third
9. P. to Q. fifth	9. Kt. to Q. R. fourth
10. B. to Q. Kt. second	10. Kt. to K. second
11. B. to Q. third	11. Castles
12. Q. Kt. to B. third	12. Kt. to K. Kt. third
13. Q. Kt. to K. second	13. P. to Q. B. fourth
14. Q. to Q. second	14. P. to K. B. third
15. K. to R. square	15. B. to Q. second
16. K. Kt. to K. square	16. Kt. to K. fourth (a)
17. Q. R. to Q. B. square (b)	17. P. to Q. R. third
18. P. to K. B. fourth	18. Kt. takes B.
19. Kt. takes Kt.	19. Q. B. to Q. Kt. fourth
20. P. to K. B. fifth	20. Kt. to Q. B. fifth (c)
21. Q. to K. square	21. Kt. takes B.
22. Kt. takes Kt.	22. K. B. to Q. R. fourth
23. Q. to K. B. second	23. R. to K. square
24. Q. to K. B. third	24. Q. to K. second
25. Kt. to Q. B. fourth	25. B. takes Kt.
26. R. takes B.	26. P. to Q. Kt. fourth

And White resigns.

NOTES.

(a) This is a critical moment of the defence, and Black selected, in our opinion, the best move, though P. to Q. R. third might also have been played without danger. Compare p. 271 of our last volume, where the following moves occurred between Professor Anderssen (White) and Herr Neumann (Black):—

	16. P. to Q. R. third
17. P. to K. B. fourth	17. Q. B. to Kt. fourth
18. Q. R. to Q. B. square	18. Q. R. to Q. B. square.

This last move of Herr Neumann's involved an error which, slight as it seems, ultimately lost him the game. His correct play was 18. P. to Q. R. fifth, and 19. P. to Q. B. sixth, the position being the same as in p. 45 of our February number, note (a).

(b) If 17. P. to K. B. fourth, Black equally succeeds in the two main objects of the defence in this and similar positions, viz., bringing the Q. Kt. into play and preventing his opponent from establishing a Kt. at K. sixth. The following moves occurred in another game between the same players:—

17. P. to K. B. fourth	17. Q. Kt. to B. fifth
18. Q. to Q. B. square	18. Q. Kt. takes B.
19. Q. takes Kt.	19. Kt. takes B.
20. Kt. takes Kt.	20. Q. to K. square
21. Kt. to K. Kt. third	21. B. to Q. Kt. fourth
22. R. to K. B. third (best)	

and Black maintains his Pawn, with a good position.

(c) All this series of moves is admirably timed, and exactly in the right order. White is now unable to avert the loss of a second Pawn, and his attack is exhausted.

CHESS INTELLIGENCE.

MEETING OF THE BRISTOL AND BATH CHESS CLUBS.

An important meeting of the above societies was held at Bristol on Monday, March 12th. Mr. Lowenthal was present by special invitation, and there was a numerous attendance of amateurs from the surrounding district, besides nearly all the principal players of Bath and Bristol. Many ladies also graced the meeting with their presence. Capt. H. A. Kennedy, the President of the Bristol Chess Club, was prevented by a severe cold, much to the regret of all who knew him, from being present on the occasion. Play was carried on in the large lecture-hall of the Athenæum till a late hour on Monday evening. On Tuesday twenty games were contested simultaneously by Mr. Lowenthal, who was fortunate enough to win eighteen, drawing one, and losing one. The chief interest, however, of the meeting centred on Wednesday, that being the date fixed for a telegraphic match with the St. George's Club, London. Play commenced about half-past four, Mr. Medley acting as umpire in London, and Mr. Lowenthal at Bristol. The adversaries were arranged thus:—

St. George's.	*Bristol.*
1. Mr. De Vere	1. Mr Thorold
2. Mr. Chinnery	2. Mr. Isaacs, jun.
3. Sir J. T. Metcalfe	3. Mr. Fedden
4. Mr. Sich	4. Mr. Holloway
5. Mr. Baker	5. Mr. Franklin
6. Mr. Salter	6. Mr. Fenton
7. Mr. Young	7. Mr. Meeker
8. Mr. Shaw	8. Mr. Gamman
9. Mr. Hampton Mr. Medley Mr. Stewart { consulting against }	9. Rev. Mr. Rowley Mr. Vines Mr. Phillips

Two games only were decided, when it became necessary to break off the contest, Mr. Franklin and Mr. Fedden having won their games, while the rest were given up at midnight as drawn. So far, therefore, the match was in favour of the Bristol representatives, whom we must congratulate on their success against such formidable opponents. We hope to publish next month some of the games. There was a full attendance at the rooms of the St. George's Club, and there were present, among others, Lord Cremorne, Sir Charles Marshall, Sir Theophilus Metcalfe, Mr. Wyvill, M.P., Mr. Strode, Mr. Fonblanque, Capt. Hamilton, Mr. Forster, Mr. Turner, and Mr. Young. The telegraphic communication was very skilfully managed, and no interruption occurred throughout. We ought to add, that the general success of the arrangements was mainly due to the exertions of Mr. Stewart, in London, and Mr. Berry, at Bristol.

On Saturday evening, the 17th ult., a *soirée* of the Bath Chess Association was held at the assembly rooms, and was attended by a large and selected number of ladies and gentlemen. On Thursday and Friday, the 15th and 16th ult., Mr. Lowenthal played a number of games at the Literary Institution and at the Bath Chess Club against the members. On the Saturday Mr. Lowenthal conducted twenty-eight games simultaneously against as many amateurs, and succeeded in winning twenty-four, losing only two. On the same evening three gentlemen of Bath, Messrs. Biggs, Cooper, and Fenton, engaged three members of the Bristol club, Messrs. Berry, Meeker, and Selkirk, in a consultation game. The Bristolians adopted the Evans' gambit attack, but were defeated after an interesting contest.

We take this opportunity of stating that the first meeting of the West of England Chess Association will be held next year in Bristol. Owing to the zealous aid of the amateurs of Bath and Bristol, headed by that staunch patron of Chess, Capt. Kennedy, the association promises to become a highly successful institution. With regard to the meeting just held, we will merely add that, as the meeting at Bristol in 1861 was the precursor, and, indeed, in a large degree the author, of the congress 1862, so we hope and believe the recent most agreeable réunion in the West is the herald of an equally successful assemblage of Chess players in London in the ensuing summer.

BRITISH CHESS ASSOCIATION.—MEETING OF THE MANAGING COMMITTEE.—On Saturday, the 17th inst., a Committee Meeting of this Association took place at the rooms of the St. George's Chess Club, 20, King Street, St. James's. Present: Lord Cremorne (in the chair), Messrs. Forster, Hampton, Medley, Mongredien, Waite, and the Revs. Messrs. MacDonnell and Wayte. The minutes of the last meeting having been read and confirmed, Mr. Medley, the Hon. Sec., laid before the meeting the preliminary address and programme for the coming Congress in June. After some discussion both of these were agreed to, and ordered to be printed and circulated amongst the members. The manager of the Association was requested to commence the compilation of a Chess Directory. The meeting was then adjourned to Saturday, the 7th of April next. When the above-named papers shall have been distributed amongst, and perused by, Chess amateurs, they will be enabled to judge of the energy, impartiality, and candour with which the members of this Committee have been actuated in their endeavours to promote the interests of the British Chess Association, which we feel certain they will now be of opinion has been rendered a permanent institution. We are glad to perceive in the programme that a suggestion which we made last year, that a Challenge Cup be offered for competition by British amateurs, has been adopted by the Committee. Biennial meetings of Chess players in the provinces will be encouraged and supported by this Association. We hope, therefore, that our provincial friends will heartily co-operate, and support the London meeting in June.

NORFOLK CHESS ASSOCIATION.—The first annual meeting of this Association will take place, we understand, in May next, in Norwich. The Committee are making great exertions to render their first réunion a pleasant and interesting one.

CITY OF LONDON CHESS CLUB.—The annual soirée of this well-conducted club was held at their new room, in Mouflet's Hotel, Newgate Street, on Tuesday, the 6th ult. About forty members and their friends were present. H. F. Down, Esq., President of the club, in the chair. Various toasts having been proposed and responded to, in the course of which the chairman spoke at some length of the advance of the club, and impressed upon the meeting the desirability of continuing in active operation for the still further developing its influence. A handicap tournament was arranged. A handsome cup was presented to Mr. Comber, the proprietor of the tavern in which the club used to assemble, as an acknowledgement of the courtesy and attention the members had received from him. The City of London Chess Club is now in the eighth year of its existence, and, from what we learn of the zeal and activity displayed by its members, we are disposed to believe that it will continue to be an agreeable metropolitan *réunion*.

A problem tourney, open to all competitors, is in contemplation, which shall be arranged to take place at the approaching London Chess Congress. Problem composers will, therefore, do well to be prepared with their productions, so that they may be able to compete for the prizes which will then be offered.

From New York we learn that the Chess Club tournament has been brought to a close; Capt. Mackenzie, of London, was the victor. The following is the score: First section, Mackenzie won three, Stanley one, drawn two. Second section, Mackenzie won three, Bennett none, drawn one. Third section, Mackenzie won three, Thompson none.

MATCH FOR THE CHAMPIONSHIP OF THE UNITED STATES.—It is with great pleasure that we announce to our readers that a match has been definitely arranged by the New York and Philadelphia Chess Clubs, between their respective champions, Mr. G. H. Mackenzie and Mr. G. Reichelm. A proposition to that effect was received here last week, but we refrained from mentioning it, as it was the desire of the parties concerned that no publicity should be given to the affair until its consummation. The proposal of the Philadelphia Club was received with great favour, and the contest being once determined upon, but little trouble was experienced in arranging the preliminaries. It has been agreed that the victory shall consist in the winning of seven games; that neither player is to consume more than an hour upon twelve moves, and that there shall be two sittings each day until the conclusion of the match. This contest promises to be of itself the most interesting that has taken place in this country for years, and will derive additional importance from the fact that it may be looked upon as a trial of arms for the championship of the United States. The proposed match is one in which New Yorkers find themselves possessed, like the unhappy Desdemona, of "a divided duty." Mr. Mackenzie is an Englishman, and, by virtue of a two years' residence, a New Yorker, while Mr. Reichelm is the champion of a city which has often measured swords with our own, but is an American. The contest is, therefore, in some sort, an international affair, Mr. Mackenzie being one of the best of English players, and Mr. Reichelm occupying the first place among American practitioners of the game.—*New York Leader*.

CHESS IN HUNGARY.—We have received the gratifying intelligence that a Chess Club has been re-established in Pesth, the metropolis of Hungary, the city whose amateurs distinguished themselves many years back in a match by correspondence against Paris.

ERRATA.—In the last number, page 68, *read* Mr. Sich's game instead of Mr. Dick's game.

Problem No. 74. By T. Smith, Esq.

White to play, and mate in five moves.

Problem No. 75. By Dr. Alexander.

Problem No. 76.   By J. J. Watts, Esq.

White to play, and mate in five moves.

Problem No. 77.   By Herr Kockelkorn, of Cologne.

Chess Study No. 15.

The following interesting position occurred in a game between Mr. W. G. WARD and Mr. LOWENTHAL.

White, having the move, wins.

Chess Study No. 16. By W. T. PIERCE, Esq.

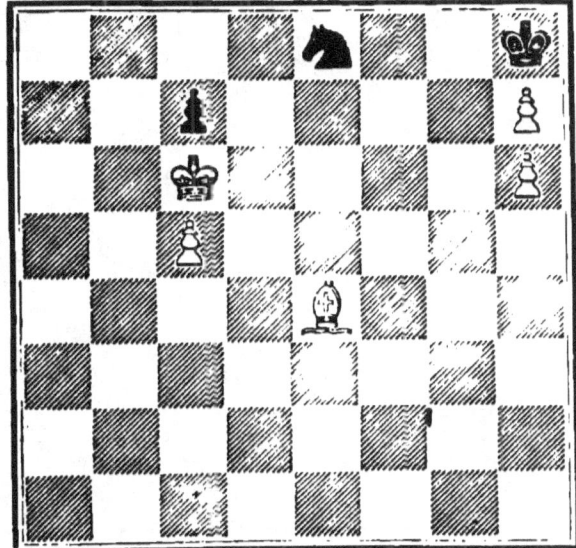

Chess Study No. 17.
Position occurring in play to Mr. WATKINSON.

White to move, and win.

Suicidal Problem No. 9. By the Rev. W. WAYTE.

SOLUTIONS TO PROBLEMS.

No. 64.—By T. Smith, Esq.

White.   *Black.*
1. R. to Q. B. square
2. P. to Q. fourth (check)
3. P. takes Kt. (check)
4. Kt. mates.

1. P. to B. seventh (A)
2. Kt. takes P.
3. K. takes P.

(A)
1. Kt. to Kt. sixth
2. P. to Q. fourth (check)   2. K. takes Kt.
3. R. to K. square (check)   3. Kt. to K. seventh
4. R. takes Kt., mate

No. 65.—By C. W. (of Sunbury).

White.   *Black.*
1. R. to K. R. third
2. Q. to K. fifth (check)
3. Q. or R. mates.

1. K. takes B. (A)
2. any move

(A)
1. P. to K. B. sixth
2. K. to K. sixth, and mates next move.

No. 66.—By the late E. S. Brewster, Esq.

White.   *Black.*
1. R. to K. Kt. seventh (check)
2. R. to K. third (check)
3. Kt. to K. B. sixth (check)
4. R. to K. Kt. fourth mate

1. R. to Q. fourth (best)
2. P. takes R.
3. B. takes Kt. (A)

(A)
3. K. to B fifth
4. P. to Kt. third mate

No. 67.—By T. Smith, Esq.

White.   *Black.*
1. B. to Q. fourth
2. B. to K. third
3. Kt. to Q. B. fourth
4. B. to Q. R. fourth
5. B. mates.

1. Q. R. to K. eighth (best)
2. R. takes B.
3. P. takes Kt.
4. Any move

No. 68.—By C. W., of Sunbury.

White.   *Black.*
1. B. to Q. fourth
2. Q. to K. R. seventh (check)
3. Q. to Q. third (check)
4. Mates.

1. K. to K. fifth (best)
2. K. takes B. (best)
3. Any move

No. 69.—By C. W., of Sunbury.

White.   *Black.*
1. Q. to Q. B. sixth
2. Q. to Q. R. eighth
3. Mates.

1. Kt. P. takes P.
2. Any move

No. 70.—By T. Smith, Esq.

White.
1. Kt. to K. fourth
2. R. to K. R. second
3. B. to K. Kt. sixth
4. R. to K. R. seventh, and mates next move.

Black.
1. Kt. to Q. sixth (A)
2. B. to Q. B. sixth, or any move
3. P. takes B.

(A)
1. Kt. to Q. R. fifth
2. P. takes Kt.
3. Kt. to Q. sixth
4. B. takes P. (check)
5. Kt. mates.

2. B. to Q. fifth
3. P. to K. fifth
4. K. moves

No. 71.—By Dr. C. Bayer.

White.
1. K. to Q. eighth
2. K. to K. seventh
3. K. to B. sixth
4. K. to K. fifth
5. K. to Q. fourth
6. K. to B. third
7. K. to Kt. fourth
8. K. takes Kt. or R. takes Kt. (mate).

Black.
1. B. to Kt. second
2. B. to B. square
3. B. to Kt. second
4. B. to B. square
5. B. to Kt. second
6. B. to B. square
7. K. or B. moves

No. 72.—By Dr. C. Bayer.

White.
1. R. to K. third (check)
2. Kt. to Kt. third (check)
3. B. to K. fifth (check)
4. Q. to Kt. second
5. Q. takes P. or to Q. fourth (mate)

Black.
1. K. to Q. fifth
2. P. takes Kt.
3. K. takes R. (A)
4. Any move

(A)

4. R. to B. third (check)
5. Q. takes P. (mate)

3. K. to B. fourth
4. K. anywhere

No. 73.—By Mr. J. A. Graves, of Brooklyn.

White.
1. Q. to Q. R. fourth
2. Mates accordingly.

Black.
1. Any move

CHESS STUDY.

No. 11.—By Herr Kling.

White.
1. K. to Kt. fourth
2. B. to Kt. third
3. K. to B. third
4. B. to B. seventh
5. K. to Q. fourth
6. K. to K. fourth
7. K. to K. B. fourth
8. B. to R. second, and wins.

Black.
1. K. to Kt. seventh
2. K. to B. eighth
3. K. to Kt. eighth
4. K. to R. eighth
5. K. to Kt. seventh
6. K. to K. B. sixth
7. K. to Q. fifth (A)

(A)

8. K. to Kt. fifth	7. K. to Kt. fifth
9. K. takes P.	8. K. to B. fourth
10. K. to Kt. fifth, and wins.	9. K. to Q. third

No. 12.—By G. F. RAINGER, Esq., of Norwich.

White.	Black.
1. R. to K. sixth	1. B. to K. B. fifth
2. K. to K. square (best)	2. B. to Q. B. second
3. R. to B. sixth (check)	3. K. to Kt. fifth
4. R. to K. sixth, or (A)	4. B. to Q. R. fourth (check)
5. K. moves	5. K. to K. B. fifth
6. R. to K. eighth	6. B. to Q. Kt. fifth
7. R. to K. sixth	7. K. to B. sixth
8. R. to K. B. sixth (check)	8. K. to K. fifth
9. R. to K. sixth (check)	9. K. to B. fifth, and wins.

For if R. checks at B. sixth, K. to K. fourth, and, if R. to K. eighth, K. to B. sixth, &c.

(A)

4. R. to K. Kt. sixth (check)	4. K. to K. B. fourth
5. R. to K. Kt. second	5. B. to Q. R. fourth (check)
6. K. to K. B. square (B)	6. B. to Q. seventh
7. R. to R. second	7. K. to Kt. fifth
8. R. to Kt. second (check)	8. K. to B. sixth
9. R. to B. second (check)	9. K. to K. fifth
10. R. to R. second	10. K. to Q. fifth
11. R. to R. fourth (check)	11. K. to B. sixth
12. R. to R. second	12. K. to B. seventh
13. R. to Kt. second	13. K. to Q. eighth, and wins

(B)

6. K. to Q. square	6. K. to K. fifth
7. R. to K. R. second	7. K. to B. sixth
8. R. to B. third (check)	8. K. to B. seventh
9. R. to R. second (check)	9. K. to B. eighth
10 B. to R. square (check)	10. K. to Kt. seventh, and wins.

No. 13, "The Whirligig."—By W. T. PIERCE. Esq.

White.	Black.
1. R. to K. eighth (check)	1. R. takes R. (best)
2. R. to R. sixth (check)	2. R. takes R., or (A.)

3. Q. takes R. (check), and draws by perpetually checking on Q. Kt. fifth, K. second, K. R. fifth, and K. eighth.

(A)

2. K. to Q. fourth
3. B. to Q. sixth (dis. check)   3. K. to K. fifth (best)
   (If 3. K. to K. third, White plays B. to K. fifth, as before),
4. Q. to K. second (check)   4 K. to B. fourth
   (If 4. K. to to Q. fourth, White checks again at K. R. fifth),
5. Q. to R. fifth (check)   5. K. to K. third
6. B. to K. fifth (dis. check), and the position is the same as at the 2nd move.

No. 14.—By Herr KLING.

White.	Black.
1. R. to K. R. fourth	1. Q. to Q. B sixth (A)
2. R. to K. B. fourth	2. Q. takes R.
3. R. to K. B. second (check) and draws	

(A) If K. play, then R. to Q. R. fourth and draws.

SUICIDAL PROBLEM.

No. 8.—By the Rev. W. WAYTE.

White.	Black.
1. B. to Q. Kt. sixth (check)	1. R. to Q. B. fourth
2. Q. to Q. sixth (check)	2. Kt. to Q. fourth
3. P. to Q. R. fifth	3. P. to K. fifth (check)
4. K. to Kt. fourth	4. P. to K. sixth
5. K. to B. fifth	5. P. takes Q. P.
6. Q. takes Q. P.	6. B. takes Q. (mate)

ANSWERS TO CORRESPONDENTS.

D. F.—The game has come to hand. Many thanks.

W. G. (Halifax).—Your version of Problem No. 72 is quite correct. We shall communicate with the author. The position you forwarded is excellent, and shall be used.

G. B. C.—The game was published in the *Era* of the 25th ult.

DE R.—Many thanks for your courteous consideration.

C. R. D.—You cannot do better than procure the "Book of the Chess Congress," published by Bohn. It contains the code of laws, as revised by the committee of the British Chess Association, and adopted at a general meeting of the members in 1862.

C. R.—The Chess library for sale by an American amateur has, we hear, been purchased by an English gentleman for £120. It contained, among other valuable works, a complete file of the *Era* Chess column since its commencement.

A. M.—The American Congress picture is, we regret to say, out of print, and cannot be procured.

C. R. (Sheffield).—The move you mention occurred in a game between Boden and Morphy (see "Morphy's Games," Bohn's edition, page 292).

T. S.—Our grateful acknowledgments.

J. W.—We shall with pleasure accede to your request.

W. T. P.—They shall all appear in due course.

S. D.—You shall hear from us privately.

BARON R.—Your budget has come to hand. We shall give you our opinion in a private letter.

NEUE BERLINER SCHACHZEITUNG.—Die Angabe in der *Era*, sich auf Herren Neumann und L. Paulsen beziehend (*Era*, Jan. 7th, 1866), haben wir aus authentischen Quellen—so glaubten wir wenigstens zur zeit—geschöepft. Sollte diese Angabe irgend einer Berichtigung bedürfen, so bitten wir uns selbe einzusenden.

W. P. (Colchester).—Your solutions of Nos. 71 and 73 are both correct.

The Chess Player's Magazine.

THE LIMITATION OF TIME.

Economy in the use of time has ever been regarded as a great and indispensible virtue, and, moreover, a valuable element in the achievement of all success. This maxim, we opine, holds equally true with respect to a pastime as well as any other object upon which it is exercised. And, taking that view of the value of time, we will endeavour to show that it bears a direct and important relation to the game of Chess, to its more extensive cultivation, and to a wider interest being taken in its development and success.

Chess may be defined as a game which, more than any other calls forth into exercise the analytical power of the mind. The forethought, deliberation, and study which it involves render it an invaluable agent in developing and maturing the mental faculties; and this duty it discharges by exhibiting the difference of time which two individuals occupy at the same operations, technically termed *moves*. We will simply content ourselves with showing that this is clearly demonstrated in a contest in which genius and talent are opposed in friendly rivalry. Many persons regard genius and talent as mere synonyms, and assert that no real distinction characterises the two terms. However, there does exist a very wide difference, and the true definition, as we believe, consists in regarding genius as innate, while talent is acquired. A poet is a genius: *poeta nascitur non fit*. Study, plodding habit, and determination to succeed, on the other hand, develope talent, but can never result in producing poetry out of an unpoetic nature. Each person, the one a man of genius, the other possessed of talent, may show an equal aptitude for the game of Chess, but there cannot be a shadow of doubt that there is an essential and an important difference in their method of conducting its operations. The man of genius will master the key of his position with facility, rapidly adopt his line of attack or defence, and abide by his decision, be it right or wrong. The man of talent, however will waste considerable time in study and contemplation; suspecting dangers where none exist, and speculating on hazardous means of improving his ground; and he in his conclusions more often proves erroneous than correct. Nay, we will go further, and say that a profound thinker, as a rule, is a worse player than he who after a casual but penetrative survey of the battle-field, at the critical moment, resolves on his policy in the engagement.

But to give our remarks a closer application we maintain that, in the interest of Chess players in general, it is highly desirable that no unnecessary delays should take place in a game; and when a player has no choice or alternative, and only a single move left, it is an absolute want of courtesy to his adversary to speculate about future combinations, when he is fully aware that an unavoidable move is his only resource.

It is alleged, and very erroneously, that some minds require more time for making their calculations, but this is refuted by the fact that slow thinking in the game of Chess, from the results arrived at, generally ends in the defeat of those who resort to the practice. After all, what is slow thinking but a mere habit; and if the mind is only tutored to a course of training, enabling it to concentrate its ideas at any given moment, without allowing the imagination to wander at random, the whole evil could easily be obviated. This can be brought into operation without much difficulty or discussion, inasmuch as of late years, in the various Chess clubs in England, the playing of simultaneous games has become a fashion, and the player has, in several instances, some twenty boards or more to go over, without having even a quarter of a minute to determine on his move. And yet, under these circumstances, he is naturally compelled to make his combinations of attack and defence as rapidly, and with almost the same perfection, as if he were sitting over a single board.

It is highly important that our remarks should be clearly understood, and in no way misconstrued. A simple desire to promote the development of Chess has actuated us in making them, and we believe that our observations bear most materially on the interests of a game which we all so cherish and admire. It is the want of some uniform and universally binding rule, deciding a limit as to the duration of time in the consideration of moves and of games, which has materially tended to diminish and retard its cultivation among the masses. And this seems to us a very opportune moment for reviving the discussion on the subject, as the British Chess Congress will hold its meeting in the metropolis next month, when it can be thoroughly ventilated and finally decided. It is not an innovation, but simply a reform, likely to be more beneficial to the cause than other measures which have lately agitated the Chess-playing world. A rule of a similar nature has been in operation since 1862 in the London Chess Club, dating from the International Chess Congress held in that year, and, in the private matches played under its auspices, it has been found to work admirably. The games possessed more features of interest to the bystanders, many of whom were tyros in the theory of the pastime; and the contests themselves were of a far higher character than the former matches, in which long and indefinite deliberation was allowed.

Those who have pondered well over this question cannot fail to have been surprised at the slow progress which this queenly and philosophical recreation has made in winning its way to general approval in literary, scientific, and mechanic institutions. In this practical age time is regarded of equal value as money; and it cannot, if impartially viewed, seem strange that, as has often been the case, when more than an hour has been expended on a single move, a learner or a mere bystander, uninitiated in its mysteries, lost all interest in the game, and was inspired with a feeling bordering on disgust at the tediousness and unnecessary protraction of a contest. It is generally admitted that a happy medium should exist in all things; and we are at a loss to know why the same observation does not hold good with regard to the limit assigned to deliberation in a game of Chess.

THE NORFOLK CHESS ASSOCIATION.—The first annual general meeting of this Association will be held in Norwich, on Tuesday and Wednesday, the 8th and 9th of May, 1866. We shall give a detailed report of the proceedings in our June number.

NEW VARIATION IN THE TWO KNIGHTS' DEFENCE.

An interesting novelty has lately been discovered in this opening by the Rev. W. Wayte, to which we desire to call our readers' attention. By the sacrifice of a piece Black appears to obtain the advantage against the best play on the part of White. We give a diagram of the position after Black's 16th move.

BLACK.

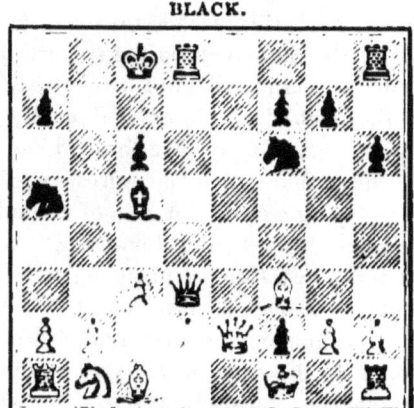

WHITE.
White to move.

The previous moves will be found in a game played by Mr. Wayte, given at p. 115 of our last number. Black's 16th move, Q. to Q.'s 6th, on which the variation turns, is the invention of Mr. Wayte, and does great credit to his ingenuity. The game now proceeds as follows:—

17. Q. takes Q.   17. R. takes Q.
18. P. to Q. Kt. fourth   18. K. R. to K. square
19. B. to K. second   19. R. to Q. third.

The above are certainly the best moves on either side. White's 18th and 19th moves may, however, be transposed without affecting the result.

20. P. to Q. fourth.

This, we think, is better than 20. P. takes B., which was adopted in the game referred to.

                                          20. Q. R. to K. third (best)

[If, instead, Black take Q. P. with R., the following is the result:—
                        20. R. takes Q. P.

21. P. takes R. (best)   21. B. takes Q. P.
22. P. takes Kt.   22. B. takes R.
23. K. takes P.   23. B. to Q. fifth (check)
24. K. to B. third, and wins]

21. B. to Q. R. sixth (check)	21. K. to Q. second (best)
22. K. takes P. (best)	22. Kt. to K. fifth (ch.)(best)
For if he take either piece Kt. to K. Kt. fifth wins.	If he check at Kt. fifth, K. goes to Kt. third, &c.
23. K. to Kt. square (best), or (A.)	23. B. to Q. Kt. 3rd (best)
24. P. takes Kt.	24. B. takes P., and Black

has more than an equivalent in position for the piece given up. Instead of taking the Knight on his last move White might do better, perhaps, to bring out a piece, but Black's game would still be superior:—*ex. gra.*

24. B. to K. B. fourth	24. P. to K. Kt. fourth
25. B. to K. Kt. third	25. Kt. takes B.
26. P. takes Kt.	26. R. to K. eighth (ch.)
27. K. to R. second (best)	27. R. takes R. (check)
28. K. takes R.	28. R. to K. eighth (check)
29. K. to R. second	29. B. to Q. B. second
30. P. takes Kt.	30. P to K. R. fourth, and wins.

White's moves in this variation are not forced but Black, we believe, can always obtain the advantage

A.

23. K. to K. square. The result is similar, if White play K. to K. third, or K. to K. second.

	23. Kt. to K. Kt. 6th (dis. ch.)
24. K. to Q. second	24. Kt. takes R.
25. Q. P. takes B. (or B.)	25. Kt. to Q. Kt. second
26. B. takes Kt.	26. Q. R. to K. seventh (ch.)
27. K. to Q. third	27. K. R. to K. fifth
28. B. to K. third (to save mate)	28. Q. R. takes B. (check, and wins).

B.

25. P. takes Kt.	25. B. to Q. third
26. P. to K. Kt. third	26. R. to K. B. third, with the advantage.

The above variations certainly tend to show the soundness of Mr. Wayte's clever move. If, however, we have overlooked any line of play by which White may escape from his difficulties, practice will doubtless soon supply the omission.

CHESS LITERATURE.

A Collection of Two Hundred Chess Problems. Composed by F. HEALEY, Esq. Longman and Co., Paternoster Row.

Mr. Healey, long known to the Chess world as one of the most skilful living problematists, has at length complied with a very general desire that his best compositions should appear in a collected form. This handsome volume includes the Problems to which the prizes were awarded by the committees of *The Era*, the Manchester, the Birmingham, and the Bristol Problem Tournaments. It is appropriately dedicated to Mr. Henry Waite, a gentleman well known for the interest he takes in this important branch of Chess, in which he is himself eminently proficient. It is unnecessary for us to dwell on the conspicuous merits of Mr. Healey's compositions; they are familiar to all who study this interesting department of our art. Nor is it too much to say that they combine the subtilty of D'Orville with the depth of Bolton, while they possess a grace of their own scarcely to be found in either of those eminent artists' productions. Great judgment, we think, has been shown by Mr. Healey in not including in this collection any Problem of more than five moves; it has therefore the especial value of being useful to the practical player as well as to the student of recondite checkmates. The book is introduced by a well-written preface, from which we extract the following passage:—"Turning for a brief moment to the history of Problems, it cannot but strike the student with some surprise to discover how few names, comparatively speaking, are inscribed on the honourable roll of inventors. From the illustrious Damiano downwards the following brief register includes I believe most of the celebrities to our own day:—Lolli, Ponziani, Stamma, D'Orville, Kuper, Mendheim, Kieseritzky, and Silberschmidt. In our own time we have indeed a brilliant constellation of genius, in which Anderssen, Kling, Bayer, Horwitz, and Grosdemange, among our continental brethren, Angas, Bolton, Bone, R. A. Browne, J. B. of Bridport, Campbell, MacArthur, Grimshaw, T. Smith, C. W. of Sunbury, and Turton, among ourselves, with Theodore Brown, S. Lloyd, and E. B. Cook, in America, shine pre-eminent.

"Coming now to compare the ancient with the modern school of Problems, I feel much diffidence in attempting so delicate a task. It has been justly observed by a clever Spanish writer that there is as much difference between the styles of two skilful Problem composers as between the paintings of Raphael and Titian, the one excelling in expression, the other in colour. Similarly, one Problematist is known for his originality and brilliancy of conception, while another excels in giving that artistic finish which really constitutes the **perfect** problem. In truth, the beauty of Problems does not consist so much in the intricacy of the theme as in the manner in which the idea is treated or woven in by the composer. The finest end games have often a very simple solution, but it is so hidden among numerous other modes of play, which mislead the solver, that it is very difficult to discover."

We proceed to notice in detail some of the most ingenious of these Problems. The leading idea in No. 1 is the succession of two *coups de repos*, by which mate is effected in three moves. The position is extremely elegant. No. 2, though a conception of remarkable talent, is marred by an unfortunate flaw, since mate cannot be given under five moves. The author, however, has utilized the same idea with better success in No. 178, a very fine composition. No. 3 is very difficult, as the *coup* with the Rook, on which it turns, is especially hard to discover. No. 4 is a clever conception, happily worked out, the black King being forced to move to the square on which he is finally mated by discovery. No. 6 is one of the best in the collection, every move is a separate enigma, and the manner in which Black is compelled, by a series of forced captures, to block up all the squares open to his King is eminently skilful. No. 8 is constructed on a similar principle, though free from any too great similarity. No. 7 was one of the successful Problems at the Manchester tourney. Here the Queen is brought unexpectedly to a square from which she is enabled to pin the adverse Bishop, and thus execute the design.

Notwithstanding the care which has evidently been taken in the preparation of the work, we regret to see that some few errors have crept in, which we think it right to notice, with a view to their being corrected in a second edition. The fault in No. 2 we have already stated.

No. 14 admits of a second solution, viz. :—

    1. Q. to Q. second (check)   1. Kt. covers
    2. P. to Q. B. fourth (check)   2. K. moves

and White mates in two moves accordingly.

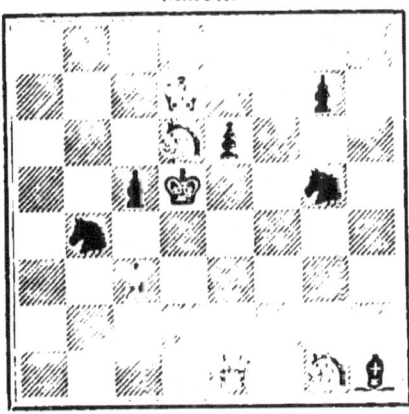

WHITE.
White to play, and mate in four moves.

No. 30 may be solved thus:—
  1. Q. to Q. B. sixth and mates next move.

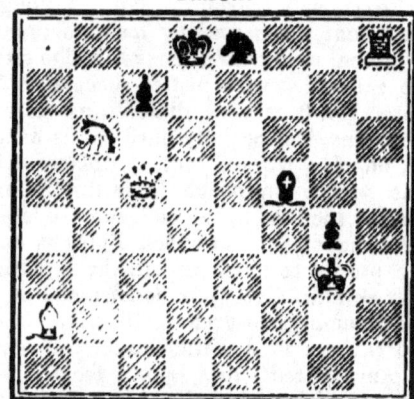

WHITE.
White to play, and mate in two moves.

No. 31 may be solved thus:—
  1. Q. to Kt. square (check)   1. K. moves
  2. Q. to K. Kt. fifth (mate).

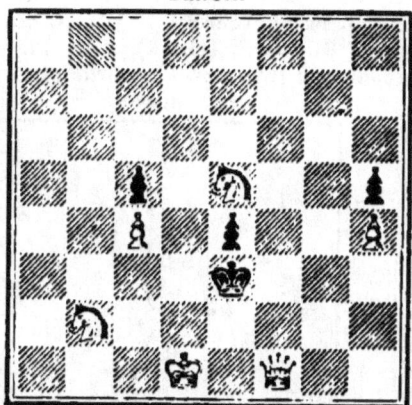

WHITE.
White to play, and mate in two moves.

No. 180 also admits of a double solution:—
  1. B. to K. B. third   1. P. moves
  2. B. to Q. fifth   2. P. moves

3. B. to K. sixth   3. P. moves (or *a*)
4. Kt. to Kt. second (check) 4. K. moves
5. P. mates.

(*a*)

                             3. K. moves
4. Kt. to Kt. second   4. P. moves
5. P. mates.

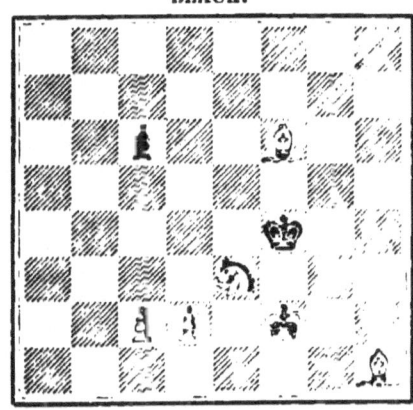

BLACK.

WHITE.
White to move, and mate in five moves.

No. 185 may be solved in three moves:—
1. Kt. from B. 2 to Kt. 4th (ch.) 1. P. takes Kt.
2. Kt. takes P. (check)   2. K. moves
3. R. mates.

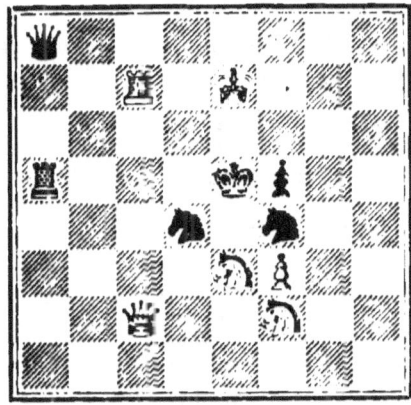

BLACK.

WHITE.
White to play, and mate in three moves.

We are glad to observe that Mr. George Walker, who as an authority on every department of Chess is second to no living Englishman, has expressed a decided opinion that this is the best English collection of Problems which has yet appeared. We shall return to the subject, if our space permits, in a future number. Here we will only add that we cordially endorse Mr. Walker's judgment.

PROBLEM TOURNAMENT OF THE BRITISH CHESS ASSOCIATION.

A meeting of the managing committee of the Association was held at the St. George's Club on Saturday, the 7th ult., Mr. A. Mongredien in the chair. The Hon. Secretary reported that the subscriptions already received, since the prospectus of the Congress was issued, gave every promise of a successful meeting. The committee then proceeded to make arrangements for holding a problem tournament on a handsome scale, when Mr. Mongredien and Mr. Henry Waite liberally volunteered their assistance to make the prizes equal to those given in 1861. It was accordingly resolved that prizes should be awarded in a problem tournament open to the world : The first of £20, the others of £10, £5, and £2 10s. respectively. In addition to these a separate prize of £10 will be given to English composers only. The following gentlemen were nominated as a committee of award for the adjudication of the prizes :—Rev. W. Wayte, Rev. C. E. Ranken, Messrs. Slous, Medley, H. Waite, Alfred Jones, Young, and Lowenthal. We trust that our problematists will set to work without delay, and that the handsome prizes offered may educe as fine a collection of positions as those sent in at the Congress of 1862. We feel sure that the spirit evinced by the managing committee cannot fail to meet with cordial acceptance and support from chessplayers throughout the country. We are pleased to state that several gentlemen have already promised to enter their names in the contest for the Challenge Cup. To all young and ambitious players this trophy must surely offer a strong inducement to enter the lists.

The competition for prizes will take place on the following conditions :—

The Tournay to be open to the world.

Each competitor to send in a set of six ordinary Problems, neither more nor less ; each Problem to be free from conditions and to require for its solution not less than three, nor more than five moves, and to be an original composition not previously published. The Problems to become the property of the Association, and not to be published or given for publication without the consent of the managing committee.

The problems to be sent in on or before the 1st January, 1867.

Each competitor to send in two sealed enclosures, one containing his Problems, each position to be printed or written plainly on a diagram, to be accompanied by its solution, and to be marked by a distinguishing motto. The other enclosure to be marked on the outside by a corresponding distinguishing motto, and to contain within the name and address of the competitor.

All letters to be post-paid and to be addressed "British Chess Association, Purssell's, Cornhill, London."

Non-compliance with the foregoing conditions will entail on competitors a forfeiture of their chances.

GAMES.

GAMES 150 & 151.

The two following slight skirmishes are offered in support of the thesis that there exists a perfectly satisfactory defence to the Ruy Lopez Knight's Game:—

I.

White. (Mr. Skipworth.)	Black. (Mr. Wayte.)
1. P. to K. fourth	1. P. to K. fourth
2. K. Kt. to B. third	2. Q. Kt. to B. third
3. K. B. to Q. Kt. fifth	3. P. to Q. R. third
4. B. to Q. R. fourth	4. K. Kt. to B. third
5. Castles	5. B. to K. second
6. P. to Q. third (*a*)	6. P. to Q. Kt. fourth
7. B. to Q. Kt. third	7. P. to Q. third
8. B. to K. Kt. fifth (*b*)	8. Kt. to Q. R. fourth (*c*)
9. B. takes Kt.	9. B. takes B.
10. P. to Q. B. third	10. Kt. takes B.
11. P. takes Kt.	11. Castles
12. Q. Kt. to Q. second	12. B. to K. second
13. K. Kt. to K. square	13. P. to K. B. fourth (*d*)
14. P. to K. B. third (*e*)	14. P. to K. B. fifth
15. Q. to K. second	15. R. to B. third
16. K. to R. square (*f*)	16. R. to K. R. third
17. K. Kt. to Q. B. second	17. B. to K. R. fifth
18. K. to Kt. square	18. B. to K. Kt. sixth (*g*)
19. P. to K. R. third	19. Q. B. takes K. R. P.
20. P. takes B.	20. R. takes P.
21. Q. to K. Kt. second	21. Q. to K. R. fifth

And White resigns.

NOTES.

(*a*) P. to Q. fourth, or Q. Kt. to B. third, is usually recommended; but the move in the text (a favourite one of Mr. Paulsen's in this opening), is perhaps equally good.

(*b*) We doubt the policy of this move and of the subsequent capture of the K. Kt.

(*c*) In this opening Black should always endeavour to get rid of the adverse K. B. If this move were not made now the Bishop would be played to Q. fifth, and Black would be compelled to lose time.

(*d*) At this point we already prefer Black's game. He has two Bishops against two Knights, and his K. B. P. will get first into the field.

(*e*) This Pawn should have been advanced two steps. White's game now becomes completely locked, and his opponent has ample time to mature his attack.

(*f*) White appears to have anticipated 16. P. to Q. fourth, followed by a check at Q. B. fourth. This loss of time, however, mattered little, as White has no good move on the board.

(*g*) If this Bishop is taken Black simply retakes with Pawn, and mate is inevitable.

Position after Black's 18th move.

BLACK.

WHITE.

II.
(*Ruy Lopez Knight's Game*).

White. (Mr. SKIPWORTH.)	Black. (Mr. WAYTE.)
1. P. to K. fourth	1. P. to K. fourth
2. K. Kt. to B. third	2. Q. Kt. to B. third
3. K. B. to Q. Kt. fifth	3. P. to Q. R. third
4. B. to Q. R. fourth	4. K. Kt. to B. third
5. Castles	5. B. to K. second
6. P. to Q. fourth	6. P. takes P.
7. P. to K. fifth	7. Kt. to K. fifth
8. R. to K. square	8. Kt. to Q. B. fourth
9. B. to Q. Kt. third (*a*)	9. Kt. takes B. (*b*)

10. R. P. takes Kt.	10. Castles
11. Kt. takes P.	11. Kt. takes Kt.
12. Q. takes Kt.	12. P. to Q. fourth
13. Kt. to Q. B. third	13. B. to K. third
14. P. to Q. Kt. fourth	14. Q. to Q. second
15. Kt. to K. second	15. P. to Q. B. third
16. P. to Q. B. third	16. P. to K. B. third (c)
17. Kt. to K. B. fourth	17. Q. R. to K. square
18. Kt. takes B. (d)	18. Q. takes Kt.
19. B. to K. B. fourth	19. B. to Q. third
20. R. to K. third (e)	20. P. takes P.

Winning a piece and the game.

NOTES.

(a) The "Handbuch" gives
    9. B. takes Kt.   9. Q. P. takes B.
   10. Kt. takes P.   10. Castles,
with an even game. The move in the text is also noticed, but is inferior.

(b) By 9. Kt. to K. third, followed by B. to Q. B. fourth, Black might have retained the Pawn. By giving it up, however, he obtains a free well-opened game, every way equal to his opponent's.

(c) Ensuring a fine opening for his Rooks.

(d) This loses a Pawn.

(e) This was, of course, an error, but the game was already much in Black's favour

---

GAME 152.

(Pawn and two moves.)

White. (Mr. A. Sich.)	*Black.* (Mr. Lowenthal).
1. P. to K. fourth	
2. P. to Q. fourth	2. P. to Q. third
3. Kt. to K. B. third	3. B. to K. Kt. fifth
4. K. B. to B. fourth	4. P. to K. third
5. Kt. to B. third	5. P. to Q. B. third
6. Kt. to K. second	6. B. takes Kt.
7. P. takes B.	7. P. to Q. fourth
8. B. to Q. third	8. B. to Q. third
9. P. to K. fifth	9. B. to B. second
10. B. to K. third	10. Kt. to Q. second
11. Q. to Q. second	11. Kt. to K. B. square (a)
12. P. to K. B. fourth	12. P. to K. Kt. third
13. P. to K. R. fourth	13. Kt. to R. third
14. P. to B. fifth	14. Kt. takes P.
15. B. to K Kt. fifth	15. Q. to Q. second
16. Kt. to K. B. fourth	16. Q. to K. B. second

17. Q. to Q. Kt. fourth	17. B. to Q. Kt. third
18. P. to Q. B. third	18. Q. to Q. B. second
19. B. takes Kt.	19. K. P. takes B.
20. P. to R. fifth	20. R. to K. Kt. square
21. P. takes P.	21. P. takes P.
22. Castles (Q. R.)	22. Q. to K. Kt. second
23. P. to K. sixth (b)	23. Kt. to R. second
24. R. takes Kt.	24. Q. takes R.
25. Kt. takes Q. P. (c)	25. P. takes Kt.
26. Q. to Kt. fifth (check)	26. K. to B. square
27. P. to K. seventh (check)	27. K. to Kt. second
28. Q. takes Q. P.	28. Q. to K. R. fourth
29. B. to K. B. fourth	29. K. R. to K. square
30. B. to K. fifth (check)	30. K. to R. third
31. R. to R. square	31. R. takes P.
32. R. takes Q. (check)	32. K. takes R.
33. Q. to R. square (check)	

And Black resigns.

NOTES.

(a) This cramps Black's game, and gives his adversary too much time.
(b) Well-conceived and admirably followed up.
(c) The termination is very cleverly played by Mr. Sich.

GAME 153.

Played at Houghton-le-Spring, March 31st, 1866, Mr. John Watkinson giving the odds of the Q. Kt. to Mr. G. H. Taylor.
Remove White's Queen's Knight.

(*Petroff's Defence.*)

White. (Mr. WATKINSON.)	Black. (Mr. TAYLOR.)
1. P. to K. fourth	1. P. to K. fourth
2. Kt. to K. B. third	2. Kt. to K. B. third
3. P. to Q. fourth	3. P. to Q. fourth
4. Kt. takes P.	4. Kt. takes P.
5. B. to Q. third	5. Kt. to K. B. third
6. Castles	6. B. to K. second
7. P. to Q. B. third	7. Castles
8. P. to K. B. fourth	8. Kt. to K. fifth
9. P. to K. B. fifth	9. P. to K. B. third
10. Kt. to K. Kt. fourth	10. P. to Q. B. fourth
11. B. to K. third	11. Kt. to Q. B. third
12. P. to Q. R. third	12. P. to Q. B. fifth (a)

13. B. to Q. B. second	13. Q. to K. square
14. K. to R. square	14. P. to K. R. fourth (b)
15. B. takes Kt.	15. P. takes B.
16. P. to Q. fifth (c)	16. P. takes Kt. (d)
17. P. takes Kt.	17. P. takes P.
18. Q. takes P.	18. B. to Q. third
19. Q. R. to Q. square	19. Q. to K. second
20. B. to K. R. sixth	20. R. to K. B. second
21. Q. R. to Q. fourth	21. Q. to Q. B. second
22. Q. R. takes K. P.	22. B. to Q. Kt. second
23. Q. to K. Kt. sixth	23. P. to Q. B. fourth
24. Q. R. to K. R. fourth	24. B. to K. fourth
25. B. to K. B. fourth	25. B. takes B.
26. K. R. takes B.	26. Q. R. to Q. square
27. R. to K. B. square	27. R. to Q. seventh
28. Q. to K. R. seventh (ch.) (e)	28. K. to B. square
29. Q. to K. R. eighth (check)	29. K. to K. second
30. R. to K. square (check)	30. K. to Q. third
31. R. to K. sixth (check)	31. K. to Q. fourth
32. Q. to K. R. fifth	32. R. to Q. sixth
33. Q. to K. second (f)	33. Q. to K. fourth
34. Q. takes R. (check)	34. P. takes Q.
35. P. to Q. B. fourth (mate).	

NOTES.

(a) P. takes P. is better in this position.

(b) Black plays throughout in a style much superior to that of an ordinary Knight player.

(c) Well conceived, as leading to a very tenacious attack.

(d) If Kt. to K. fourth, White may exchange Knights, and then advance the Q. P.

(e) Mr. Watkinson has now a forced won game. His play is admirable throughout.

(f) If Q. to K. Kt. fourth, Black replies with Q. to K. B. fifth.

GAME 154.

Game at Board C. in the late Telegraphic Match between London and Bristol, played March 14, 1866.

(*King's Bishop's Opening.*)

BRISTOL.	LONDON.
White. (Mr. N. FEDDEN.)	*Black.* (Sir T. METCALFE.)
1. P. to K. fourth	1. P. to K. fourth
2. B. to Q. B. fourth	2. B. to Q. B. fourth
3. P. to Q. Kt. fourth	3. B. to Q. Kt. third

4. K. Kt. to B. third	4. P. to Q. third
5. P. to K. R. third	5. P. to K. R. third
6. P. to Q. B. third	6. Q. B. to K. third
7. Q. to Q. Kt. third	7. B. takes B.
8. Q. takes B.	8. K. Kt. to B. third
9. P. to Q. third	9. Q. Kt. to B. third (a)
10. Castles	10. Castles
11. P. to Q. R. fourth	11. P. to Q. R. third
12. Q. Kt. to R. third	12. K. to K. R. square
13. Q. Kt. to B. second	13. P. to Q. fourth
14. P. takes P.	14. Kt. takes P.
15. Q. Kt. to K. third	15. Kt. to K. B. fifth
16. P. to Q. fourth	16. P. to K. fifth
17. K. Kt. to K. fifth	17. Kt. takes Kt.
18. P. takes Kt.	18. Q. to Q. sixth (b)
19. Q. takes Q.	19. P. takes Q.
20. K. to R. second	20. Q. R. to Q. square
21. Kt. to Q. B. fourth	21. Kt. to K. seventh
22. B. to Q. second	22. B. to R. second
23. P. to K. B. fourth	23. B. to Kt. square
24. R. to B. third	24. P. to Q. Kt. fourth
25. Kt. to Kt. second	25. R. to Q. second
26. P. takes P.	26. P. takes P.
27. Q. R. to R. eighth (c)	27. Kt. to Q. B. eight
28. B. takes Kt.	28. P. to Q. seventh
29. B. takes P.	29. R. takes B.
30. Kt. to Q. third	30. P. to Q. B. third
31. Kt. to Q. B. fifth	31. B. to Q. third
32. R. takes R. (check)	32. B. takes R.
33. R. to Q. third	

And White scored the game, Sir T. Metcalfe being obliged to leave.

NOTES.

(a) The opening is now resolved into an ordinary Giuoco Piano, neither party having any advantage.

(b) This is too hazardous, as the advanced Pawn will be very hard to defend.

(c) White plays the termination very skilfully.

WEST YORKSHIRE CHESS ASSOCIATION, President, John Rhodes, Esq.; Vice-President, Robert Cadman, Esq.—The eleventh annual meeting of the West Yorkshire Chess Association will be held at the Victoria Hotel, Leeds, on Saturday, the 26th May, 1866. The usual arrangements will be made on the day of play for the formation of matches, and one-game Tournays.

GAME 155.

Consultation game played at the late meeting at Bath, between Messrs. Meeker, Berry, and Selkirk, against Messrs. Fenton, Briggs, and Cooper.

Bristol—MEEKER, BERRY, and SELKIRK.
Bath—FENTON, BRIGGS, and COOPER.

(*Evans' Gambit.*)

White. (Bristol.)	Black. (Bath.)
1. P. to K. fourth	1. P. to K. fourth
2. Kt. to K. B. third	2. Kt. to Q. B. third
3. B. to Q. B. fourth	3. B. to Q. B. fourth
4. P. to Q. Kt. fourth	4. B. takes P.
5. P. to Q. B. third	5. B. to K. R. fourth
6. P. to Q. fourth	6. P. takes P.
7. Castles	7. Kt. to K. B. third (*a*)
8. P. to K. fifth (*b*)	8. P. to Q. fourth
9. P. takes Kt.	9. P. takes B.
10. R. to K. square (check)	10. B. to K. third
11. P. takes K. Kt. P.	11. R. to K. Kt. square
12. Kt. takes K. Kt. fifth	12. Q. to Q. second
13. Kt. takes B.	13. P. takes Kt.
14. Q. to K. R. fifth (check)	14. K. to Q. square
15. B. to K. Kt. fifth (check)	15. K. to Q. B. square
16. B. to K. B. sixth (*c*)	16. P. to Q. Kt. third
17. Q. takes K. R. P.	17. K. to Q. Kt. second
18. Q. to K. fourth	18. P. to K. fourth
19. P. to K. Kt. fourth	19. Q. R. to K. square
20. P. to K. R. fourth	20. K. to Q. Kt. square
21. P. to K. R. fifth	21. Q. to K. B. second
22. Q. to K. B. fifth	22. R. to K. third
23. P. to K. Kt. fifth	23. R. takes Kt. P.
24. K. to K. B. square	24. R. takes Kt. P.
25. Q. takes R.	25. R. takes B.
26. R. to K. second	26. P. to K. fifth (*d*)
27. P. takes P.	27. Kt. takes P.

And White resigned.

NOTES.

(*a*) This move ought to lose the game. P. to Q. third should be played instead.

(*b*) B. to Q. R. third is the correct play, and leaves Black almost helpless. See Morphy's Games.

(*c*) The Bristol amateurs were afterwards of opinion, and we believe rightly, that they would have done better by taking R. P. with Queen at once.

(*d*) Black deserve great commendation for the care and steadiness of their defence.

GAME 156.

(Remove Black's K. B. Pawn.)

White. (Mr. Sicn.)	Black. (Mr. Lowenthal).
1. P. to K. fourth	
2. P. to Q. fourth	2. P. to Q. third
3. Kt. to K. B. third	3. Kt. to K. B. third
4. Kt. to B. third	4. P. to K. third
5. B. to Q. third	5. B. to K. second
6. Castles	6. Castles
7. P. to K. fifth	7. Kt. to K. square
8. Kt. to K. Kt. fifth (a)	8. B. takes Kt.
9. Q. to R. fifth	9. B. to R. third (b)
10. B. takes B.	10. P. takes B.
11. Q. takes P.	11. Q. to K. second
12. Kt. to K. fourth	12. Q. to Kt. second
13. Q. to R. fourth	13. Q. Kt. to B. third
14. Kt. to Kt. fifth (c)	14. P. to K. R. third
15. Kt. to K. fourth	15. Kt. takes Q. P.
16. Kt. to B. sixth (check)	16. Kt. takes Kt.
17. Q. takes Q. Kt.	17. Kt. to K. square
18. P. to K. B. fourth	18. B. to Q. second
19. R. to B. third	19. P. takes P.
20. Q. to Q. B. fourth	20. P. to Q. Kt. fourth (d)
21. Q. to Q. B. fifth	21. P. takes P.
22. Q. R. to K. B. square	22. Q. to K. Kt. fourth
23. Q. to Q. fourth	23. B. to Q. B. third
24. K. R. to B. second	24. Q. R. to Q. square
25. Q. to K. third (e)	25. P. to K. fourth
26. Q. to Q. B. fifth	26. R. to Q. third
27. R. to K. square	27. P. to K. fifth
28. Q. takes Q.	28. P. takes Q.
29. B. takes K. P.	29. B. takes B.
30. R. takes B.	30. R. to Q. eighth (check)
31. R. to B. square	31. R. takes R. (check)
32. K. takes R.	32. Kt. to Q. third
33. R. to K. fifth	33. R. to B. fourth
34. R. to K. seventh	34. R. to B. second
35. R. to K. fifth	35. R. to K. Kt. second
36. P. to Q. R. fourth	36. P. to Q. R. third
37. P. takes P.	37. P. takes P.
38. P. to Q. Kt. third	38. K. to B. second
39. R. to Q. B. fifth	39. K. to K. third

40. P. to Q. B. fourth	40. P. takes P.
41. P. takes P.	41. R. to K. second
42. R. to Q. B. sixth	42. K. to K. fourth
43. R. to B. fifth (check)	43. K. to Q. fifth
44. R. takes K. Kt. P.	44. Kt. takes P.
45. P. to K. R. fourth	45. P. to Q. B. fourth
46. R. to R. fifth	46. K. to K. sixth
47. R. to R. eighth	47. Kt. to K. fourth
48. P. to R. fifth	48. R. to Q. R. second
49. P. to Kt. fourth	49. P. to B. sixth
50. K. to Kt. square	50. R. to R. eighth (check)

And Black wins.

NOTES.

(*a*) An over-bold venture, to which the ultimate loss of the game may be ascribed.

(*b*) P. to K. R. third would be dangerous. White would reply P. to K. B. fourth, and then play Q. to K. Kt. sixth, with an irresistible attack.

(*c*) This loses an important Pawn. P. to Q. B. third should have been played.

(*d*) To enable Black to capture the K. B. P. advantageously, and still further improve his position.

(*e*) Ingenious, but of no avail. Of course, if Black had taken the Queen in reply, he would have been mated in two moves.

Position after White's 25th move.

BLACK.

WHITE.

CHESS IN NEW YORK.

We give two games in the match between Capt. Mackenzie and Mr. Reichhelm, which terminated in favour of the former. Final score: Capt. M., 5; Mr. R., 0; drawn, 1.

GAME 157.
(Ruy Lopez Knight's Game.)

White. (Capt. MACKENZIE.)	Black. (Mr. REICHHELM.)
1. P. to K. fourth	1. P. to K. fourth
2. K. Kt. to B. third	2. Q. Kt. to B. third
3. B. to Kt. fifth	3. P. to Q. R. third
4. B. to R. fourth	4. K. Kt. to B. third
5. Castles	5. B. to K. second
6. Kt. to Q. B. third	6. P. to Q. Kt. fourth
7. B. to Kt. third	7. Castles
8. P. to Q. third	8. P. to K. R. third
9. Kt. to Q. fifth	9. P. to Q. third
10. P. to K. R. third	10. Kt. to Q. R. fourth
11. Kt. takes B. (check)	11. Q. takes Kt.
12. Kt. to R. second	12. Kt. takes B.
13. R. P. takes Kt.	13. Kt. to R. second
14. P. to K. B. fourth	14. P. to K. B. fourth
15. P. takes K. P.	15. Q. P. takes P.
16. P. takes P.	16. B. takes P.
17. B. to K. third	17. Q. to K. third
18. Q. to Q. second	18. Kt. to B. third
19. Q. R. to K. square	19. P. to K. fifth (*a*)
20. B. to B. fifth	20. R. to B. second
21. P. to Q. Kt. fourth	21. Q. to Q. fourth
22. Q. to B. second	22. B. to R. second
23. P. to Q. fourth	23. Q. R. to K. square
24. Q. to Kt. third	24. Q. to K. third
25. Kt. to B. third	25. Kt. to Q. second (*b*)
26. Kt. to K. fifth (*c*)	26. Kt. takes Kt.
27. P. takes Kt.	27. Q. takes P.
28. Q. takes Q.	28. R. takes Q.
29. R. takes R.	29. K. takes R.
30. B. to Q. fourth	30. R. to Q. fourth
31. P. to Q. B. third	31. P. to K. R. fourth (*d*)
32. R. to Q. third	32. B. to B. fourth
33. R. to Kt. third	33. P. to K. Kt. third
34. R. to K. third	34. R. to Q. square
35. R. to K. square	35. R. to Q. R. square
36. R. to Q. R. square	36. K. to K. third

K. to B. second	37. K. to Q. fourth
K. to K. third	38. B. to Q. second
39. R. to Q. R. third	39. K. to Q. second
40. P. to Kt. third	40. B. to B. fourth
41. R. to R. second	41. R. to K. B. square
42. K. to K. second	42. B. to Q. B. square
43. K. to K. third	43. K. to K. third
44. R. to Q. second	44. R. to B. eighth
45. K. takes P.	45. B. to Kt. second (check)
46. K. to Q. third	46. K. to Q. second

And the game was drawn by mutual consent.

NOTES.

(a) This is well timed, and tends to improve Black's position.
(b) Black plays throughout with care and judgment.
(c) Although this loses a Pawn, White can reckon confidently on drawing the game, as the Bishops are on different colours.
(d) The game is now drawn by its nature.

GAME 158.
(*Evans' Gambit.*)

White. (REICHHELM.)	Black. (MACKENZIE.)
1. P. to K. fourth	1. P. to K. fourth
2. K. Kt. to B. third	2. Q. Kt. to B. third
3. B. to B. fourth	3. B. to B. fourth
4. P. to Q. Kt. fourth	4. B. takes P.
5. P. to B. third	5. B. to B. fourth
6. Castles	6. P. to Q. third
7. P. to Q. fourth	7. P. takes P.
8. P. takes P.	8. B. to Kt. third
9. B. to Kt second	9. Kt. to R. fourth
10. B. to Q. third	10. Kt. to K. second
11. Kt. to Kt. fifth (*a*)	11. P. to R. third
12. Q. to R. fifth	12. Castles
13. P. to K. fifth	13. B. to B. fourth
14. B. takes B.	14. Kt. takes B.
15. Kt. to K. B. third	15. Q. to Q. second
16. Q. Kt. to Q. second	16. P. to Q. fourth
17. P. to K. Kt. fourth	17. P. to K. Kt. third
18. P. to K sixth (*b*)	18. P. takes Q.
19. P. takes Q.	19. P. takes P.
20. Kt. to K. fifth	20. B. takes Q. P.
21. B. takes B.	21. Kt. takes B.

22. Kt. takes Kt. P.	22. K. to Kt. second
23. K. to R. square	23. Q. R. to Q. square
24. R. to K. Kt. square	24. Kt. to K. seventh
25. R. to Kt. second	25. Kt. to K. B. fifth
26. R. to Kt. third	26. Kt. to Kt. third
27. P. to K. B. fourth (c)	27. Kt. takes P.
28. R. to K. B. square	28. Kt. to Kt. third
29. Kt. to B. sixth	29. Kt. to B. third
30. P. to K. R. fourth	30. K. to R. square
31. Q. R. to K. Kt. square	31. P. to K. R. fourth
32. R. to Kt. fifth	32. Q. Kt. to K. fourth
33. R. takes P. (check)	33. K. to Kt. second
34. Kt. to K. eighth (check)	34. K. R. takes Kt.
35. P. takes R. (Queens)	35. R. takes Q.
36. R. to B. fifth	36. R. to K. R. square
37. P. to R. fifth	37. P. to K. B. third
38. R. takes Q. Kt. (d)	38. P. takes R.
39. R. takes Kt. (check)	39. K. to B. second, and wins.

NOTES.

(*a*) This leads to a fine attack, requiring very careful play from the defence.

(*b*) We would rather have played thus:—
18. Q. to K. R. third   18. Kt. to K. Kt. second (best)
19. P. to K. sixth, with a fine game.

(*c*) An ingenious combination, but Black has too great a superiority of Pawns to be successfully resisted.

(*d*) There is nothing better. Black's Pawns must now advance to victory.

GAME 159.

(*Bishop's Gambit*).

White. (Mr. LOWENTHAL).	Black. (Mr. WAYTE.)
1. P. to K. fourth	1. P. to K. fourth
2. P. to K. B. fourth	2. P. takes P.
3. K. B. to Q. B. fourth	3. K. Kt. to B. third (a)
4. Q. Kt. to B. third	4. Q. Kt. to B. third
5. K. Kt. to B. third	5. B. to Q. Kt. fifth
6. Castles	6. P. to Q. third
7. Q. Kt. to Q. fifth	7. Castles (b)
8. P. to Q. B. third	8. B. to Q. R. fourth
9. Kt. takes Kt. (check)	9. Q. takes Kt.
10. P. to Q. fourth	10. B. to K. Kt. fifth
11. Q. to Q. third	11. B. to Q. Kt. third

12. K. to R. square	12. Kt. to K. second
13. Kt. to K. Kt. square	13. Kt. to K. Kt. third
14. P. to K. Kt. third	14. Q. R. to K. square
15. Q. B. takes P.	15. Q. to K. second
16. Q. R. to K. square	16. Q. to Q. second
17. B. to Q. second	17. K. to R. square
18. B. to Q. Kt. third	18. P. to K. B. fourth (c)
19. P. takes P.	19. R. takes R.
20. B. takes R. (d)	20. Q. B. takes P.
21. Q. to K. second	21. B. to K. fifth (check)
22. Kt. to K. B. third	22. Q. to K. B. fourth
23. K. to Kt. second (e)	23. B. to Q. sixth
24. Q. to K. B. second	24. B. takes R. (check)
25. Q. takes B.	25. Q. to K. Kt. fifth (f)
26. B. to Q. square	26. R. takes Kt.
27. Q. to Q. B. fourth	27. Kt. to K. R. fifth (check)
28. K. to Kt. square	28. Q. to K. fifth

And White resigns.

NOTES.

(a) A favourite move of Mr. Morphy's in defending the Bishop's Gambit. See "Morphy's Games," pp.

(b) The opening moves are the best on both sides. See the "Games of the Congress," p. 99.

(c) The advance of this Pawn is well-timed. White, however, ought still to have made an even game.

(d) This loses the exchange. R. takes R. was the proper play.

(e) B. to Q. square would have been better.

(f) Black must now gain, at the least, two pieces for his Rook.

CHESS DIRECTORY.

We wish to call the attention of Chess players to the new publication which the managing committee of the British Chess Association purpose issuing under the above title. Its object is to register the address of every Chess player, whether English or foreign. Such a Directory would prove we think of real value to the public. It would greatly tend to facilitate friendly intercourse between players of distant countries, to which in these days of steam packets and electric telegraphs ignorance of the precise address of an individual is often the principal hindrance. Mr. Lowenthal has special advantages for editing such a work, from his intimate acquaintance with the leading players both of Europe and America. It is hoped that the secretaries of provincial and foreign clubs will kindly co-operate with the managing committee, by forwarding the address of the chief players of their respective societies.

CHESS INTELLIGENCE.

MATCH BETWEEN THE BIRMINGHAM AND WORCESTER CHESS CLUBS.

On Easter Monday last, on the invitation of the Worcester players, several members of the Birmingham Chess Club, visited Worcester to contest a short match with the champions of that ancient city. The antagonists were arranged by lot, and only three games were to be played at each board. Play commenced at 3.30 P.M., and was carried on, with only a short interval for refreshment, until 9 P.M.

The following was the result of the contest:—

Wins.	Birmingham Players.		Worcester Players.	Wins	Draws
2	Mr. Warren.........	v.	Lord Lyttelton	1	0
2	Dr. Freeman	v.	Rev. Sir G. F. Lewis, Bart.	1	0
1	Mr. J. Halford......	v.	Mr. Zachary..................	2	0
0	Mr. Kempson	v.	Mr. Parrott	2	0
2	Mr. S H. Hill......	v.	Rev. F. G. Eld...............	0	0
0	Rev. S. W. Ernshaw	v.	Mr. Hooper	2	1
2	Mr. Th. Avery ...	v.	Mr. Wood.....	0	0
9				8	1

Majority for Birmingham............ 1 game.

We hear that the return match will be played in Birmingham next Whit Monday.

SHEFFIELD ATHENÆUM CHESS CLUB.

Having last month printed a letter from the Hon. Secretary of the Huddersfield Chess Club, we think it right to comply with the request of the Hon. Sec. of the Sheffield Club in publishing the following letter. We cannot, however, publish any further correspondence on the subject, and we hope that both clubs will contrive to settle in a friendly manner any little differences which may have arisen between them.

April 11, 1866.

TO THE EDITOR OF THE "CHESS PLAYER'S MAGAZINE."

Sir,—I trust you will be kind enough to insert these few lines in reply to the letter of the Secretary of the Huddersfield Chess Club, which appeared in your last number. I should not have troubled you with this communication had not the letter above referred to contained, by implication, a charge that the report of the meeting of the Sheffield Athenæum Chess Club, which was inserted in your number for March, in stating that "the Huddersfield Club had declined the Sheffield challenge"—was incorrect. I feel compelled to assert that inasmuch as we challenged that club to play a *return* match on the same terms and conditions as regulated the match which was played between the two clubs, which challenge the Huddersfield Club declined, the report in question was strictly correct. As to the modifications mentioned in Mr. Watkinson's letter, I consider that as of the six players Mr. Watkinson would be one, and would in all probability win his six games, we were indeed justified in rejecting them: we wished to play a *return* match.

Respecting his assumption that, because his club is in a town of only 40,000 inhabitants, and the Sheffield Club is in one containing 200,000, his club should choose the number of players, I can only repeat that which has been previously explained to him—viz., that in consequence of persons being unable to join our Chess club except they are members of an expensive institution (the Athenæum), our club does not get that proportion of the towns population which one on the footing of the Huddersfield club receives; and I am sure that the Huddersfield club could at the time the match was played, and can now, boast of a larger number of members than can the Sheffield club—consequently, I cannot admit the justness of his assumption.

The club I represent is quite prepared to give full credit to Mr. Watkinson and the Huddersfield club for their exertions in the cause of Chess. I am, Sir, yours faithfully,

J. J. CHAMPION, *Hon. Sec.*

BLACKHEATH CHESS CLUB.

The annual general meeting of the Blackheath Chess Club was held at the Club Rooms, Blackheath, on Tuesday evening, April 10th.

The following members were present:—Messrs. W. Sutton Gover (president), in the chair, George Barber (treasurer), W. Moresby (secretary). E. Middleton, C. D. Philpot, J. B. Spencer, W. Symons, W. C. Taylor, J. Terry, and R. Theobald.

The minutes of the last general meeting (Feb., 1865) having been read and confirmed, the honorary secretary read the report of the committee as follows:—" In presenting their annual report with the accounts for 1865, the committee have much pleasure in again announcing that after the payment of all expenses, there remains a balance in hand, which, although not large, shews the affairs of the club to be in an healthy condition.

The most important event in connection with the club which occurred during the past year was the *soireé* held in April last at the Alexandra Rooms. Mr. Mongredeen, president of the London Chess Club, kindly presided, and nearly all the leading Chess players of the metropolis were present. The proceedings included a highly entertaining and instructive lecture on Chess, which was delivered by Mr. Lowenthal, and an exhibition by Mr. Blackburne of his extraordinary power of blindfold Chess-play. Several consultation games were played during the evening between the celebrities present. On the whole, the meeting may be considered as most successsessful, although the club did not gain as many new members from it, as were desired and anticipated.

The ordinary meetings have been well attended throughout the year by the members and their friends, and the club has been occasionally visited by members of the London and St. James's Chess Clubs, and also by several players of distinction. The hon. secretary having read the accounts for the past year, it was resolved that the report and accounts, now read, be and are hereby adopted, and they shall be printed for circulation.

The officers and the committee were re-elected, namely, W. Sutton Gover, Esq., president; George Barber, Esq., treasurer; W. Moresby Chinery, Esq., hon. secretary. Messrs. W. J. Franklin, R. Hewetson, W. G. Lemon, C. Dawson Philpot, J. B. Spencer and W. Colledge Taylor, committee.

Votes of thanks were passed to the president, treasurer, and the hon. secretary, for their management of the affairs of the club.

It was resolved, that the committee be and are hereby requested to make the necessary arrangements for a *soirée* to be held at Blackheath, similar to that of 1865, and to which all leading Chess players are to be invited.

It was resolved, that this club approves most thoroughly the British Chess Association as at present constituted, and will assist its operations as much as possible. (COMMUNICATED).

RETIREMENT OF MR. LOWENTHAL FROM THE "ERA" NEWSPAPER.

After a connection of twelve consecutive years with the *Era* newspaper, Mr. Lowenthal has been obliged by a concurrence of circumstances, with which we need not trouble our readers, to discontinue the editorship of the Chess column in that journal. He takes this opportunity of tendering his grateful acknowledgments for the kind consideration and support which during that period have always been evinced towards him by the Chess public, both individually and collectively. From the Chess societies of this country, as well as from those of foreign nations, he has ever received cordial encouragement. Mr. Lowenthal feels that his thanks are also due to Mr. F. Ledger, the proprietor and editor of the *Era*, for the space which he has so long kindly accorded to Chess in the columns of that newspaper.

MEETING OF THE NORTH YORKSHIRE AND DURHAM CHESS ASSOCIATION.

We have received the programme of this meeting, which is to take place on Monday, August 6th, under the presidency of the Earl of Zetland. It contains the names of so many highly influential gentlemen as vice-presidents and members of its general committee, that the meeting can scarcely fail to be a great success. The following arrangements are the chief items:—

Prizes will be offered for competition in four classes.

Class 1.—Open to all British amateurs. The first prize of the value of £10 at least.

Class 2.—Open to North Yorkshire and Durham specially; but other amateurs may be admitted (on application) into this class, by consent of the members of the executive committee. The first prize of the value of £10 at least.

Class 3. Open to amateurs who have never made a study of the game, or who have not frequently played with strong players.

Class 4.—Open to ladies only.

A.—As Mr. Staunton and Mr. Lowenthal, and many distinguished provincial players have promised, all being well, to be present, and as Herr Anderssen and Herr Steinitz have been invited, an appeal is made to Chess players generally to aid this Association to offer a prize for competition, in consultation games, English *versus* Foreign Players.

B.—It is intended there shall be an exhibition of blindfold play. Amateurs making special donations for prizes in these games may have an opportunity of playing against the blindfold player.

It is intended that the prizes shall not be given in money; but in books, plate, or anything that a winner may select.

For any further information, application may be made to

J. H. BENNETT, M.D., } *Hon. Secs.*
G. F. BODINGTON,
W. GRIMSHAW, Whitby, or
A. B. SKIPWORTH, B.A., Bilsdale, Northallerton.

Redcar, Yorkshire, April 16th, 1866.

HUDDERSFIELD CHESS CLUB.—The concluding meeting for the season of the Huddersfield Chess Club was held on Saturday last, at the rooms of the Literary and Scientific Society, Queen Street. The club room was opened for chess play at four o'clock in the afternoon, and among the company present were David Marsden, Esq. (the president of the club), Mr. John Watkinson (the honorary secretary), and Messrs. J. R. Robinson, D. A. Cooper, J. H. Finlinson, T. Ruddock, G. Tindall, W. Senior, E. Dyson, F. Curzon, &c. Holmfirth was represented by Mr. Thomas Arkwright (the secretary of the club) and Mr. J. Moorhouse. At six o'clock a cessation of hostilities took place, and an excellent knife-and-fork tea, provided at the rooms by Mr. Cardno, New-street, was partaken of, after which Mr. Watkinson gratified the members by contesting six games simultaneously against Messrs. D. A. Cooper, J. H. Finlinson, J. Moorhouse, W. Senior, E. Dyson, and T. Ruddock. The result of this compound contest was that Mr. Watkinson won all the six games in less than an hour. Other games were engaged in between the members present, and the gathering broke up at a late hour.—From the *Huddersfield Examiner*, March 31st, 1866.

THE CHESS MEETING AT REDCAR.—There will be a problem tournament in connection with this meeting (which is to be held in August next), open to all British amateurs. Prizes will be awarded to the best sets of two original and hitherto unpublished problems, with unconditional mates of two, three, or four moves. Competitors, who are non-members, or who are subscribing members of less than £1 1s. of the North Yorkshire and Durham Chess Association, must pay 10s. to the prize fund. The problems may be sent in at any time until June 2, 1866, addressed, *The Secretary, Chess Association, Redcar, Yorkshire.* Before the award of the prizes, the correctness of the problems will be tested by publication. All problems sent for this tournament must be considered the property of the association. The number and value of the prizes must necessarily depend upon the number of competitors and the amount of the funds at the disposal of the committee. J. H. BENNETT, M.D., G. F. BODINGTON, Hon. secretaries.—Post-office orders may be made payable at the Redcar post-office, to the Rev. B. N. R. Batty, Redcar, the treasurer of the association.

CARDIFF CHESS CLUB. The annual soirée in connexion with the Cardiff Chess Club was held on Tuesday, April 12, at the commodious rooms at Winstone's Hotel. Play commenced at 4 P.M., and was continued with much spirit during the whole evening. Shortly after nine o'clock there was a suspension of operations, and the party sat down to an excellent supper, the chair being occupied by Mr. Langley and the vice-chair by Mr. Fedden. Amongst the visitors were Mr. Thorold and Mr. Fenton, from Bath; Mr. Berry and Mr. Gamman, from Bristol; and some others from the more immediate neighbourhood. A variety of animated encounters came off during the evening, and the gentlemen of the Cardiff Club have every reason to be satisfied with the way in which their réunion was celebrated. There was an unusual display of good chessmen and boards, and no pains had been spared to ensure the comfort and enjoyment of the visitors. Mr. Fedden, the honorary secretary, besides being a strong player himself, is well known as one of the most enthusiastic promoters of the game; and to this fact much of the success of the recent gathering is undoubtedly due. Although Chess cannot be considered to thrive particularly amongst the Welsh, yet it is pleasing to find, as here, exceptional districts in which a genuine devotion to the game is very plainly visible.

MATCH BETWEEN ANDERSSEN AND STEINITZ. Our readers will learn with satisfaction that all the preliminaries for the match between those gentlemen, which is to take place in London, have been definitively settled. Mr. Anderssen is expected to arrive here in June, and the match will then immediately commence.

Problem No. 78. By Dr. CONRAD BAYER.
BLACK.

WHITE.

Problem No. 79. By T. Smith, Esq.

BLACK.

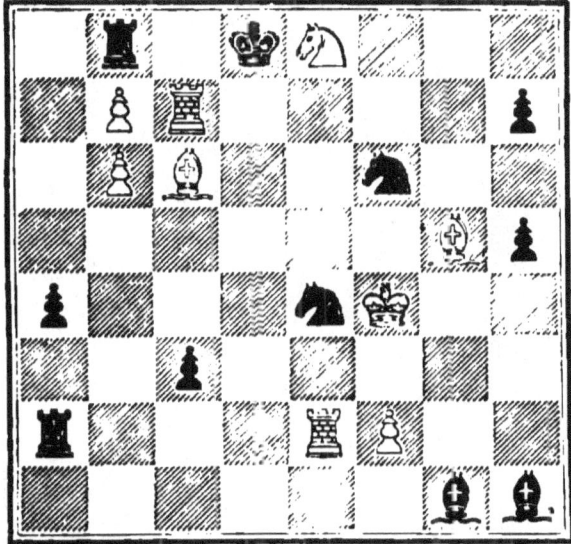

WHITE.

White to play, and mate in five moves.

Problem No. 80. By T. Smith, Esq.

BLACK.

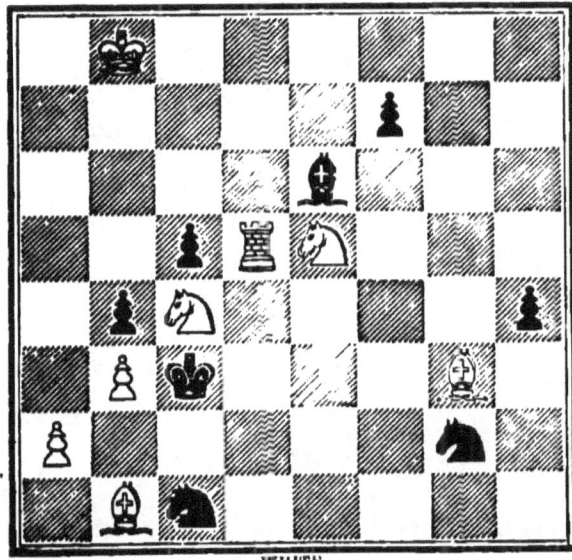

WHITE.

Problem No. 81. By J. J. Watts, Esq.

White to play, and mate in three moves.

Chess Study No. 18. By Herr Kling.

Chess Study No. 19. By W. T. Pierce, Esq.

White to move, and win.

SOLUTIONS TO PROBLEMS.

No. 74.—By T. Smith, Esq.

White.	Black.
1. P. to B. fourth (check)	1. K. to K. fourth
2. P. to Q. fourth (check)	2. B. takes P.
3. B. to R. third	3. B. takes R. or (A)
4. Kt. to Q. third (check)	4. Kt. takes Kt.
5. B. mates.	

(A)

	3. B. to K. fifth
4. R. takes B. (check)	4. Kt. takes R.
5. Kt. mates.	

No. 75.—By Dr. Alexander).

White.	Black.
1. Q. to K. B. sixth	1. R. to Kt. second or (A)
2. Q. to K. R. fourth (check)	2. P. to K. fifth (best)
3. Q. to B. sixth (check), and mates next move.	

(A)

	1. Kt. to Q. B. third
2. Q. takes Kt.	2. P. takes Kt. (best)
3. Q. to Q. B. fifth (check)	3. Kt. takes Q.
4. B. takes Kt. mate.	

No. 76.—By J. J. Watts, Esq.

White.
1. R. to Q. B. third (check)
2. P. to Q. fourth (check)
3. Q. to Q. B. sixth (check)
4. Kt. to K. Kt. fifth
5. Kt. mates accordingly.

Black.
1. P. takes R. (best)
2. Kt. takes P.
3. Kt. takes Q.
4. either Kt. moves

No. 77.—By Herr Kockelkorn, of Cologne.

White.
1. Q. to Q. B. second
2. R. to Q. Kt. third
3. Kt. takes P. (mate).

Black.
1. Q. takes Q.
2. Q. takes R.

CHESS STUDY.

No. 15.—Mr. O. G. Ward and Mr. Lowenthal.

White.
1. Q. to B. fourth
2. Q. to K. fourth (check)
3. Q. to K. B. third
4. Q. to K. Kt. fourth (check)
5. Q. to Q. square
6. P. to Q. R. sixth, and wins.

Black.
1. K. to K. seventh (best) or (A)
2. K. to B. eighth
3. K. to Kt. eighth (best)
4. K. to R. seventh
5. K. to Kt. sixth

(A)
1. K. to B. eighth
2. Q. to Q. B. fourth, and wins as above.

No. 16.—By W. T. Pierce, Esq.

White.
1. B. to K. B. third.
(The only move, excepting B. to Kt. second and R. square, to prevent Black succeeding in giving up his Kt. for White's Q. B. P., and so ensuring a drawn game)

Black.

2. K. takes P.
3. K. to Kt. sixth
4. B. to K. fourth
5. P. to B. sixth
6. B. to B. third
7. B. to Kt. fourth
8. K. to B. fifth (the only move)
9. K. to Q. sixth, and wins.

1. Kt. to Q. third (best)
2. Kt. to Kt. fourth (check) or (A)
3. Kt. to Q. fifth
4. Kt. to K. third, or Kt. fourth
5. Kt. to B. second
6. Kt. to K. third
7. Kt. to B. fifth (best)
8. Kt. to Q. sixth (check)
(8. Kt. to Kt. third is no better)

(A)
2. Kt. to K. B. fourth
3. Kt. to Q. fifth
4. Kt. to Kt. fourth
5. Kt. to B. second
6. Kt. to Kt. fourth
7. Kt. to R. second
8. K. takes P.
9. K. takes P.
10. K. to Kt. second
11. K. to B. second

3. K. to Q. seventh
4. B. to K. fourth
5. P. to B. sixth
6. B. to B. third
7. B. to K. second
8. P. to B. seventh
9. B. to R. sixth
10. K. to Q. sixth
11. K. to B. fifth
12. K. to Kt. sixth, and wins.

THE Chess Player's Magazine.

THE BRITISH CHESS ASSOCIATION.

FEW associations, taking into consideration the short time it has been in existence, have proved more successful than the British Chess Association. When first started it stood alone. Those enthusiastic lovers of the art who inaugurated the idea of such an institution could scarcely have anticipated the prosperous issue which has rewarded their maiden efforts. The most valuable aid has been rendered towards the development of the game by its establishment, inasmuch as by the means used, direct and indirect, under its auspices the association has disseminated far and wide the knowledge and practice of its details, by giving the strongest encouragement to the formation of kindred organizations in the provinces. The recent foundation of the society upon a permanent basis will still more enlarge its opportunities of promoting the culture and development of a pastime which in every respect has the highest claim to public support, not only on account of its intrinsic value, but also the genial recreation which it affords. We trust that the future of the British Chess Association may prove as brilliant as its antecedents lead us to anticipate, and as bright as its most sanguine supporters can desire. It is by such means that the theory of the game of Chess and interest in it can be satisfactorily diffused among the various classes of society; and we sincerely hope that at the forthcoming Congress some initiatory steps may be taken for the general formation of branch associations of a similar character. And in throwing out this suggestion we cannot but impress on every Chess amateur the absolute necessity of cordial co-operation with the managing committee, who are straining every nerve to effect the object. The names and reputation of its members guarantee the sincerity of their motives in advocating the interests of the British Chess Association; and we have no hesitation in predicting that at not a very distant period every individual who lays claim to the title of a Chess player in Great Britain will feel proud to be enrolled in its ranks. We will go even further, and assert that every player is in duty bound to belong to the Association. The real importance and value of the movement can hardly at present be duly or fully appreciated. But they who have carefully examined the prospectus, and observed the objects which are aimed at, cannot fail to have seen what valuable assistance it is calculated to confer on Chess in every respect. Amongst the many advantages which it affords, the following may be adduced as a proof of its utility:—The encouragement of native talent, the organization of clubs and Associations, and the completion of the necessary arrangements for provincial meetings.

The British Chess Association, as we have before said, was the first institution formed of its kind, but from the success which has crowned the labours of its founders, some foreign countries have been led to adopt the plan, and have been equally rewarded. This additional bond which unites the Chess playing world will prove greatly instrumental in bringing together players from various parts. And to carry this out in a satisfactory manner, we are glad that it has been determined to publish a Chess directory which will embrace in itself a perfect guide to Chess associations, and be of great advantage to any amateur visiting the provinces or the Continent, inasmuch as at a glance he will be able to discover who are the resident Chess players; and the bond of freemasonry which exists among the brotherhood requires no further passport or introduction. We hope that all provincial secretaries and others who are lovers of the art will, without delay, afford the editor (Mr. Lowenthal) the amplest information at their command, and render the work as full and complete as possible. Its want is much felt, and every one who cares about the development of Chess should support it.

The managing committee of the British Chess Association have great schemes in contemplation. They propose to take prompt action in endeavouring to introduce the game in every possible way. And very wisely they have resolved to initiate the rising generation in its mysteries, by asking the co-operation of the principals and masters of educational institutions and schools. They intend also making an effort in the direction of popularizing the game as much as possible in mechanic's institutes and working men's clubs. They desire, also, that Chess should become familiar in the Army and Navy, and we fervently trust that in this latter point they may be successful. Barrack life is at the best wearisome and monotonous, and the introduction of this excellent and noble recreation into soldier's quarters and into our fleets would eradicate much vice and dissipation, and give a healthy moral tone to a state of existence which is naturally surrounded with temptation.

And if these are some of the features which distinguish the objects of the British Association every one should feel proud to have any share in the good work which it has in hand. The terms of the annual subscription are by no means extravagant. The payment of five shillings per annum constitutes the title to membership; and this trifling subscription assuredly places it within the reach of all amateur players. The Congress which will be held on the 18th inst. will doubtless draw together the *elite* of the Chess playing world, and as considerable interest attaches to it from the various subjects which will then be discussed, the exciting contests which are anticipated, and the meeting of competitors to contest the Grand Challenge Cup, we hope that the occasion will tend to swell the number of members in a large proportion.

The Book of the Congress, which recorded the remarkable proceedings of the meeting of 1862, contains a full and faithful report of its deliberations, and will be handed down to posterity as a lasting memento of the glorious and untiring efforts which the British Chess Association made to render its success complete Future generations will admire the ingenuity and perseverance by which this triumphant result accrued, and it will attribute the glorious victory which was achieved to the fact that the Congress was held under the auspices of the Association. That magnificent result, we venture to believe, will tend to make the forthcoming

Congress more interesting than its predecessor, and will inaugurate a new era in the annals of the game.

MATCH BETWEEN ANDERSSEN AND STEINITZ.
"Coming events cast their shadows before."

In the Congress of 1862 last but not least in the list of conquerors was the name of Herr Steinitz. The difficulties which that gentleman surmounted were of a varied and formidable character. An entire stranger to the metropolis and London Chess circles, unacquainted with the different players and their respective styles, and not even speaking the English language, the success which he achieved proved a greater triumph than the Chess playing public had been led to anticipate under the peculiar circumstances of the case. The subsequent success of the youthful Vienna champion has, however, raised him to the foremost rank, he having contended with players of European renown, such as Signor Seraphino Dubois, and Mr. Blackburn, the well-known blind-fold amateur; and lastly, at Dublin, the victory which he achieved over the redoubtable Rev. G. A. McDonnel has entitled him to the highest honours in the Chess world. In fact, he is the coming man of the day; for at present there is no other competitor in the field to dispute the laurel crown with him. Under these circumstances it will be highly interesting to witness the contest between Herr Steinitz and the veteran Professor Anderssen. It seems almost a struggle between two different generations; for there is, we believe, a difference of nearly a quarter of a century between their respective ages. When the professor first entered the field there existed the well-known constellation of "The Seven Stars" in the Berlin Chess heaven, most of whom have since shone on different horizons. We are well acquainted with the glorious play of the Breslau "hermit; and although Herr Steinitz has never yet engaged first-rate players in any series of matches, his brilliant style, intuitive power, dash, and spirit exhibited in the contests in which he has engaged *entitle* him to be ranked as one of the chiefest players. He had not arrived in London when the brilliant American meteor passed through our clouded heavens, and it is, moreover, true, that he once came in contact with his present opponent Professor Anderssen, and with the widely celebrated L. Paulsen, but on these occasions he suffered defeat for the reasons above stated. The progress which he has, however, since made, his youth and untiring energy render the issue of the forthcoming struggle very uncertain, and preclude our pronouncing judgment in favour of our veteran opponent, or presuming to foretel what victories may be in store for Mr. Steinitz in the future.

THE RELATIVE VALUE OF THE CHESS PIECES.

We have abridged the following article from our valued contemporary the *Berliner Schachzeitung*:—

As the King is not, like the other pieces, liable to capture, no comparison can properly be drawn between him and them. We may, however, state his aggressive power, which is generally considered greater than that of the Knight or Bishop, and less than that of the Rook. The King commands or attacks eight squares, except when placed on the eighth line, when he commands only five, or on a corner square, when he commands but three squares. He can attack all the pieces excepting the Queen, who remains always out of his reach.

The Queen, combining the action of the Rook and Bishop, commands no less than 27 squares when placed on one of the four central squares, 14 of them belonging to her action as a Rook, and 13 to her action as a Bishop; on the eighth line she commands 21, on the seventh 23, on the sixth 25 squares. The Rook commands 14 squares wherever he may be placed. The Bishop, when placed on one of the four central squares, commands 13, on the eighth line only 7, on the seventh 9, and on the sixth line 11 squares. The Knight commands 8 squares when placed in the centre, but only 2 in the corner of the board. The Pawn can at the most only threaten 2 squares; yet positions may arise when a Pawn is more valuable than even the Queen, as in the annexed example.

BLACK.

WHITE.

Black moves and wins; but if a Pawn is substituted for the Queen the game is drawn.

Having thus briefly stated the power and activity of the pieces, it will be easier for us to estimate their relative value. Taking, then, the Pawn as 1, let us see in what proportion he stands to the Knight. The Pawn commands only 2 squares, but the operation of the Knight extends from 2 only up to 3, 4, 6, and finally 8 squares. Upon the average, therefore, the Knight is in this respect hardly equal to three Pawns. It is true the Pawn cannot retrograde, but then he can become a Queen. Most writers, in estimating the value of the pieces by the standard of Pawns, have not paid due regard to practical play, from which it appears that in end-games three Pawns are more valuable than a Knight or even a Bishop, while three pawns with one minor piece will almost invariably win against two minor pieces. The Italian writers, Lolli, Ponziani, and others, greatly underrated the value of Pawns; but this may be accounted for, partly by the Italian mode of castling, which rendered the attack more fierce, and the Pawns less valuable at the beginning of the game, partly by the defective knowledge of openings and end-games at the time, which may be seen from the games that are left us, terminated as they almost invariably are by a brilliant combination. Most modern Chess writers have agreed to fix the value of a Knight at the rate of three Pawns. Certainly three Pawns may be given up for a Knight, and even with advantage, early in the game; but, as the value of Pawns rises as the number of pieces is diminished, it is doubtful whether it would be advisable to exchange three Pawns for a Knight towards the close of the game. The Bishop has greater scope in the command of squares than the Knight; he can move from one end of the board to the other, and can threaten at a distance; the only disadvantage he labours under is that he cannot change his colour, but once upon a white or black square, he must always remain upon the same. But the Knight also labours under a disability peculiar to himself, since he never can gain a move; hence it is that the two Knights alone cannot give checkmate. Another evil to which the Knight is exposed is that in certain positions he cannot escape like the other pieces, but falls an easy prey—*ex. gra.*, if the Knight has retreated to a corner square the King can from the middle of the board stop his egress, and capture him in three moves. The inability of the Knight to gain a move has even been overlooked in the well-known comparison by Carrera, where he shows in juxta-position the different qualities of Knight and Bishop. Since the end-games were more fully examined most players have preferred the Bishop to the Knight; and one of the greatest players of the day—Herr L. Paulsen—opines that the Bishop is decidedly the superior piece. If we, therefore, value the Knight at three Pawns we may safely estimate the Bishop at three-and-a-half. The exchange of a Bishop for a Knight is only advisable, therefore, to avert a loss or to obtain some advantage, as, for example, not less than doubling a Pawn. It is admitted on all sides that two Bishops are stronger than two Knights, and even that a Bishop and Knight are stronger than two Knights. Two Bishops and a Knight are considered stronger than two Knights and a Bishop; the former are considered equivalent to two Rooks, while the latter are held to be inferior to two Rooks. We may fairly conclude that a Bishop is somewhat stronger than a Knight.

The Rook, commanding in every position 14 squares, is evidently superior both to the Knight and the Bishop, who in many positions do not even between them command that number of squares. It has been a matter of dispute at what the actual superiority of the Rook to the Bishop or Knight should be estimated, but the doctors greatly differ on this point. Some contend that a Rook is equal to two Pawns and a minor piece, while others consider one Pawn and a minor piece a fair equivalent. Most Chess writers, however, agree that two minor pieces are equal to a Rook and two Pawns. Major Jaenisch, while admitting this with regard to the two Bishops, believes that the two Knights are decidedly weaker than Rook and two Pawns. In practical play it will be found that a Knight and one Pawn are decidedly inferior to a Rook, to which Knight and two Pawns are a fair equivalent. A Bishop and one Pawn are sometimes equal to a Rook, but mostly inferior, while with a Bishop and two Pawns the contrary is the case. A Rook may, therefore, be rated as equal in number of Pawns to from four-and-a-quarter to four-and-a-half.

The Queen has been generally considered as equal to two Rooks, or three minor pieces, or nine Pawns; of course, in the last case, the exchange is impossible, there being only eight Pawns on the board; but, as a minor piece is considered equal to about three Pawns, the Queen may be exchanged for six Pawns and a minor piece, or for three Pawns and two minor pieces, or for a Rook and five Pawns, at least theoretically, since in practice such an exchange hardly ever occurs. Indeed, a player who at the begining of a game would give up his Queen for a Rook and five Pawns, would probably succumb to the attack of his opponent's Queen, while towards the end a Rook and five Pawns would be more than a match for the Queen. Two Rooks will evidently draw against Queen, if there are no Pawns left; but, when there are several Pawns on each side, the Queen mostly has the advantage. The Queen in most cases draws against two Rooks and Pawn, but should lose against Rook and two Bishops. The Queen draws against Bishop and two Knights, and also against Rook and two Knights. The four minor pieces win against the Queen, as also two Rooks and a Knight. Major Jaenisch agrees with the Italian writers that the Queen may be valued at two Rooks and a Pawn, or to three minor pieces and a Pawn.

The valuation of the pieces by a certain number of Pawns is very uncertain, as the worth of a Pawn varies with its position. Thus, with the progress of the game the value of the Pawns rises considerably. United Pawns are preferable to separated, the more advanced to the less advanced, and the central to the wing Pawns. Two isolated doubled Pawns are weaker than two isolated Pawns on different files. Then again, the fluctuations in the activity and power of the minor pieces render their valuation in Pawns still more difficult. Lolli thus estimates the value of the pieces in the opening and middle game:—

1. A Bishop equal to a Knight.
2. Two minor pieces equal to a Rook and two Pawns.
3. A Rook equal to a minor piece and two Pawns.
4. A Queen equal to two Rooks and a Pawn.

According to this* a minor piece is equal to four Pawns, and a Rook to six Pawns, and a Queen therefore to thirteen Pawns. Lolli here (it is plain), greatly underrates the value of the Pawns.

Ponziani fixes the value of a Knight or Bishop at three-and-a-half Pawns. Major Jaenisch, however, holds that by Ponziani's scale a minor piece is overrated, as according to that a minor piece and two Pawns would outweigh the Rook, and three minor pieces would be stronger than the two Rooks. We on the other hand, are of opinion that a Bishop and two Pawns (but not a Knight and two Pawns) are stronger than a Rook, and that two Bishops and a Knight are stronger than two Rooks, though not two Knights and a Bishop.

Mr. Pratt, in his studies on Chess,† gives the following scale:—Pawn 1, Knight 3¼, Bishop 3½, Rook 5½, Queen 10. The Rook is here evidently overrated, though we rather agree with his relative estimation of the Knight and Bishop. "Bilguer's Handbuch" (4th Ed.) reckons the Knight or Bishop as equal to 3½ Pawns, the Rook to 5½, the Queen 10. With this judgment we cannot agree at all, as in that case two Rooks would be preferable to a Queen, three minor pieces would be weaker than two Rooks, and two minor pieces would be inferior to a Rook and two Pawns. We think the following scale would come nearer the mark:—

Pawn	1	Isolated corner Pawn	¾
Knight	3	Two Knights	6¾
Bishop	3¼	Two Bishops	6¾
Rook	4¾	Two Rooks	9¾
Queen	9½		
King	4 (aggressive value)		

[* This statement is by no means clear. Surely Lolli did not value the Knight or Bishop at four Pawns. Ed. C. P. M.]
[† The writer probably alludes to an edition of Philidor, published by Mr. Pratt, an English amateur, about forty years ago. Ed. C. P. M.]

According to our scale two Bishops would be slightly stronger than a Rook and two Pawns, and two Knights slightly weaker. Again, two Bishops and a Knight would be a little better than two Rooks, and two Knights and a Bishop equal to two Rooks.

It must, however, be well understood that we have spoken only of the relative value of the pieces in general, and not of that value which depends on the position of the game, when a Knight, or Bishop, or even a Pawn may be more valuable than a Queen.

NORFOLK CHESS ASSOCIATION.

We abridge the following from the *Norfolk News*, May 12, 1866:—

"This association held its first annual meeting at the Royal Hotel, Norwich, on Tuesday and Wednesday, the 8th and 9th May. Nearly all the best players in the county were present, and took part in the proceedings.

"Play commenced on Tuesday at twelve o'clock, when a number of friendly games were contested between Norwich and Norfolk players.

"Mr. Blackburne, the celebrated blindfold player, who is unrivalled among Englishmen in this department of Chess, entered the room about two o'clock, and shortly engaged the Rev. W. D. Beard (one of the strongest players in the Norwich club) in a light skirmish, before commencing the arduous task which was the chief attraction of the programme. Mr. Blackburne defeated his antagonist after a gallant contest. A very excellent game was at the same time played by Mr. W. G. Crook (Norwich) and the Rev. G. R. Bell (Great Snoring), which resulted in a draw.

"The players then took up their posts for the grand encounter, Mr. Blackburne quietly seating himself by the fireside. Mr. Rainger announced the moves. The blindfold player began by (1) P. to K. fourth at every board, and in about two hours one of his antagonists succumbed. Other defeats rapidly followed. Mr. Blackburne, after four hours, offered Mr. Knight (who had played very steadily) a draw which was accepted gladly. Mr. Crook, who had lost a piece in the early part of the game, recovered himself, so that Mr. Blackburne agreed to draw. Mr. Blackburne defeated Mr. Howard Taylor after five hours and a half's play in magnificent style, sacrificing first the exchange and then his queen. The conclusion of this game excited the admiration of the members, and it would have done credit to any player over the board. Two opponents still remained, the Rev. W. D. Beard and Mr. W. T. Palmer. The first was shortly afterwards mated in very pretty style, and the latter, being a piece minus, after a gallant contest of nearly six hours, resigned. Mr. Blackburne won eight games and drew two, not having made a single miscalculation throughout.

"The following is the score with the openings:—
1. Mr. G. C. L. Knight, Wymondham (Philidor's defence) ...Drawn.
2. The Rev. W. D. Beard, Norwich (Scotch gambit) ....Lost.
3. Dr. Gardiner, Diss (Irregular) ....Lost.
4. Mr. W. T. Palmer, Norwich (Evan's gambit) ....Lost.
5. Mr. A. H. Thurgar, Norwich (Queen's gambit) ....Lost.

6. Rev. G. R. Bell, Great Snoring (Allgaier gambit) ....Lost.
7. Mr. E. Vince, Barton Bendish (Philidor's defence)............Lost.
8. Mr. Sallett, Norfolk (Damiano's gambit) ....Lost.
9. Mr. I. O. Howard Taylor, Norwich (Sicilian defence).........Lost.
10. Mr. W. G. Crook, Norwich (King's gambit declined)......Drawn.

"On the following day play again commenced at twelve, when some friendly games were contested.

"Mr. Lowenthal arrived about two o'clock. He engaged the Rev. W. D. Beard at the odds of Queen's knight, each party winning a game. He then played a brief game with Mr. I. O. Howard Taylor, to show the true defence of Evan's Gambit, which he won in half an hour.

"Mr. Lowenthal then delivered an address upon Chess, which we regret not being able to report.

"The simultaneous match then came off, Mr. Lowenthal playing against fourteen antagonists.

The following is the score with openings and results:—

1. Mr. G. Rainger, Norwich (Sicillian defence) ....Unfinished
2. Mr. T. Garwood, jun., Wells (French opening)............Lost.
3. Mr. J. A. Miles, Fakenham (Allgaier gambit) ....Lost.
4. Mr. A. H. Thurgar, Norwich (Ruy Lopez)...................Lost.
5. Mr. Tillyard, Norwich (Scotch gambit) ....Lost.
6. Mr. R. H. Household, Lynn (Irregular).....................Lost.
7. Mr. I. O. Howard Taylor, Norwich (Sicilian defence) ...Drawn.
8. Rev. W. D. Beard, Norwich (French opening) ....Lost.
9. Mr. G. Vince, Barton Bendish (Two knight's defence ...Lost.
10. Mr. Massey, Norwich (Irregular Queen's gambit) ......Lost.
11. Rev. G. R. Bell, Great Snoring (King's gambit declined)Lost.
12. Mr. W. G Crook, Norwich (Centre gambit) ....Drawn.
13. Mr. G. C. L. Knight, Wymondham (Philidor's defence)...Won
14. Mr. Sallett, Norfolk (Queen's gambit)........................Lost.

Thus it will be seen that out of thirteen games (one being left unfinished through Mr. Rainger being compelled to leave) Mr. Lowenthal won ten, lost one (through an oversight), and drew two.

"After the conclusion of this match (fatigue preventing players joining in a consultation against Mr. Lowenthal), he offered to play Mr. I. O. Howard Taylor, giving the odds of Queen's Rook in exchange for King's Knight. A game was accordingly played between them, and after a severe contest of two hours and a half, was won by the Norwich player.

"This concluded the meeting, which, as regards the play was very interesting. Among the visitors present during the contest were Canon Heaviside, W. L. Jex-Blake, F. E. Watson, and J. C. Copeman, Esqs., &c., &c.

"The success of the meeting was greatly due to the indefatigable exertions of Mr. Rainger, the secretary, who made all the arrangements."

WEST YORKSHIRE CHESS ASSOCIATION.—This excellent society held its eleventh annual meeting at the Victoria Hotel, Leeds, on Saturday, the 26th ult., under the presidency of John Rhodes, Esq., who has ever been a most liberal patron of this association. The programme consisted of club matches and one or more game tourneys.

THE BRITISH CHESS ASSOCIATION.

The following letter, issued by the managing committee of the British Chess Association, has been distributed among the Chess clubs of Great Britain and Ireland. In laying it before our readers we believe that they will feel convinced that the Association is most willing and anxious to afford its aid to any provincial Chess society which feels disposed to make arrangements for a meeting to be held in its locality in 1867:—

"Purssell's, Cornhill, London.
"21 April, 1866.

"Dear Sir,—

"With reference to the following resolution passed at the general meeting held on the 6th March, 'That in each year in which no Congress is held in London, a Congress be held in some provincial town where there is a local Chess club, if, in the opinion of the managing committee for the year, the state of the funds and condition of the Association make it advisable,' I am directed by the Managing Committee to solicit your aid and advice to enable them efficiently to carry out this expressed desire of the Association. From a circular lately issued you have learned that a Congress will be held in London in June next; consequently no meeting will take place in the country this year. In 1867, however, it is the earnest wish of the Committee that a congress should be held in some provincial town which shall partake of the varied character of those meetings which have proved on many occasions so interesting and instructive. The question then arises, in what town shall the congress of 1867 be held? On this point the Committee cannot of themselves decide, but must look for guidance to the wishes of members, in the various districts—to the support to be locally given—and to other general considerations.

"The committee, therefore, request that you will be good enough to take such steps as may appear to you advisable to ascertain the views of Chessplayers as grouped in the clubs and other local associations of your neighbourhood, and to communicate the result to them.

"I am, dear Sir,
"Your obedient servant,
"GEO. W. MEDLEY, Hon. Sec."

CHESS LITERATURE.

A Collection of Two Hundred Chess Problems. Composed by F. HEALEY, Esq. Longman and Co., Paternoster Row.

We resume this month the review of Mr. Healey's book of Problems, and in so doing cannot but pay a tribute of admiration to the genius of the author, whose productions in this volume have elicited the applause of every problem connoisseur. Nothing, however, is perfect in this sublunary sphere—not even in the literary world; and we may, therefore, be permitted to point out that a few more defects, not to say errors, have been discovered in the work by that highly distinguished problem solver and supporter of Chess, Mr. H. Waite. In mentioning this we have no desire to detract from Mr. Healey's well-merited fame, and we only do so in order to draw the attention of the author to them, so that in future editions the mistakes may be corrected.

This unparalleled and splendid collection of problems has, we sincerely trust, a chance of being augmented by Mr. Healey co-operating with the Congress at the forthcoming problem Tournay, in which every English composer, in fact, should feel in duty bound to enter the lists. The shining talent of Mr. T. Smith, Mr. Grimshaw, Turton, Kidson, Pavitt, Watts and others will, we trust, prevent the prizes from passing out of the limits of Albion—a fact which we feel sure would afford great pleasure to the liberal patron of native genius, who has never failed to give a helping hand to develope rising talent.

The following are the problems referred to in our last number as being incorrect :—

No. 85.

BLACK.

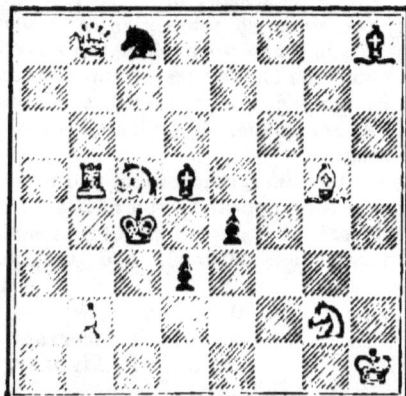

WHITE.

White to play, and mate in three moves.

This can be solved in a different way to that described by the author—viz.,

1. R. to Kt. fourth (check)   1. K. takes Kt.
2. B. to K. seventh (check)   2. K. moves or Kt. takes B.
3. Mates accordingly.

No. 87.

BLACK.

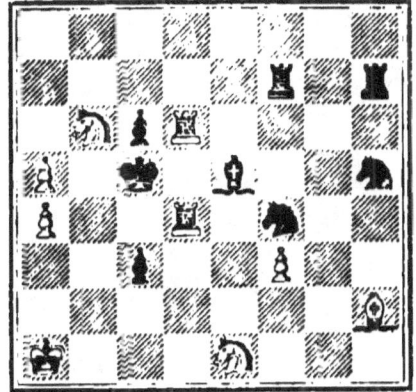

WHITE.

White to play, and mate in three moves.

In this problem mate cannot be effected in the number of moves propounded by the author; for if

1. R. to K. sixth   1. P. to Q. B. seventh

and mate is impossible.

No. 89.

BLACK.

WHITE.

White to play, and mate in three moves.

This is also impossible to be solved. By Black's defence, 1. to K. Kt. fifth,

No. 90
BLACK.

WHITE.

White to play, and mate in three moves.

Is capable of solution in two moves instead of three.

No. 116.
BLACK.

WHITE.

White to play, and mate in four moves.

Two first moves may be made leading to the same result—namely, 1. B. to Kt. sixth, or 1. B. to R. seventh.

No. 126

BLACK.

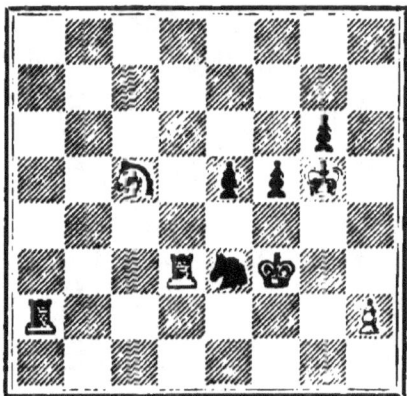

WHITE.

White to play, and mate in four moves.

Admits of a second solution—viz., 1. R. from Q. third to R. third, or 1. R. from R. second to Q. second.

No. 129

BLACK.

WHITE.

White to play, and mate in four moves.

Has also a second solution:—

1. Kt. takes P. (check) 1. P. takes Kt.
2. Q. to K. R. square, &c.

No. 139.
BLACK.

WHITE.
White to play, and mate in four moves.

There is to this also a second solution, in which the White Queen is not required :—

1. Kt. to K. fifth (check) 1. K. to K. second
2. R. to K. B. sixth 2. Any move
3. K. to Kt. 6th or B. 6th accordingly, and mates next move.

No. 142
BLACK.

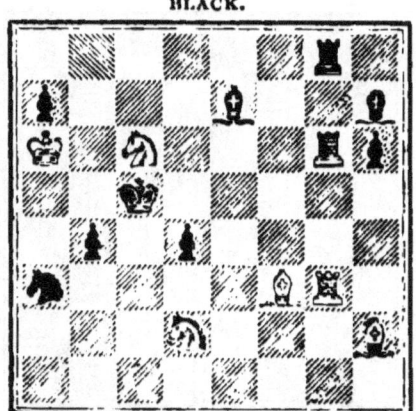

WHITE.
White to play, and mate in four moves.

Admits of a second solution, namely :—

1. Kt. to Kt. (check) 1. K. moves
2. B. to K. fourth 2. P. to Q. sixth
3. R. takes Q. P., and mates next move.

No. 151
BLACK.

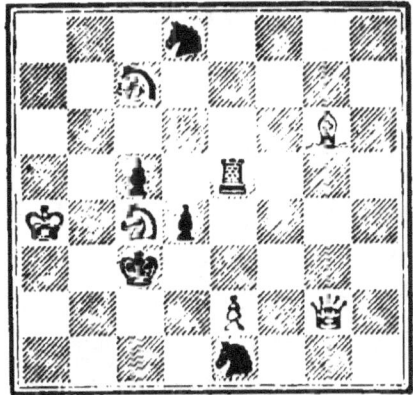

WHITE.
White to play, and mate in four moves.

Admits of a second solution, namely:—

1. Q. to Kt. third (check)	1. Kt. to B. sixth (A)
2. Q. takes Kt. (check)	2. R. covers
3. B. to Q. third	3. Anything
4. Kt. or Q. mates.	

(A)

	1. R. to K. sixth
2. Q. takes Kt. (check)	2. K. takes Kt.
3. Q. to Q. B. square (ch.)	3. R. covers
4. B. to Q. B. third (mate).	

No. 180
BLACK.

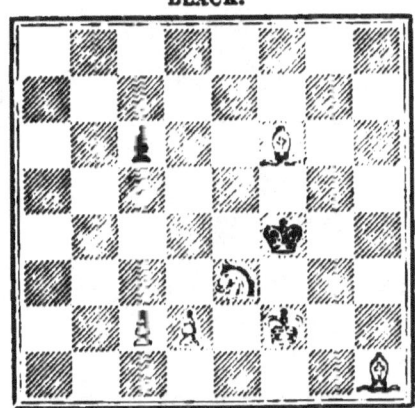

WHITE.
White to play, and mate in five moves.

Admits of a second solution, namely:—

1. B. to B. third	1. P. to B. fourth

3. B. to K. sixth
4. Kt. to Kt. second
5. P. mates.

3. P. moves (A)
4. K. moves

(A)

4. Kt. to Kt. second
5. P. mates.

3. K. to K. fifth
4. P. moves

No. 181.
BLACK.

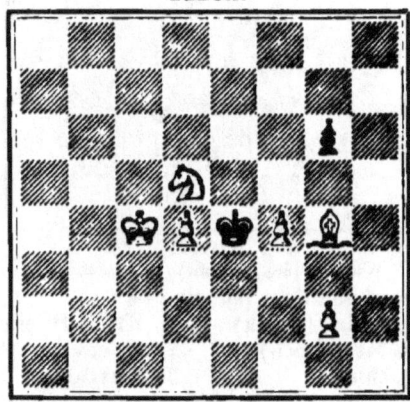

WHITE.
White to play, and mate in five moves.

In this problem the white Bishop can be moved to K. sixth, Q. seventh, B. eighth, or R. third, all leading to the same result.

No. 185.
BLACK.

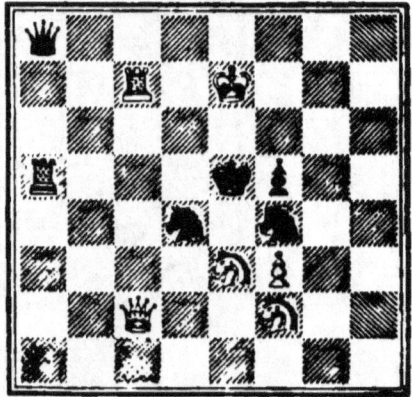

WHITE.
White to play, and mate in five moves.

Can be solved in three moves, namely :—

1. Kt. from B. 2 to Kt. 4 (ch.)
2. Kt. takes P. (check)

1. P. takes Kt.
2. K. moves

GAMES.

THE REV. W. WAYTE AND CAPT. H. A. KENNEDY.—Several weeks since Mr. Wayte visited Bath, and attended the Bath Chess Club, where he played some highly interesting games with Capt. H. A. Kennedy and Mr. Thorold, which are here offered to our readers as being worthy of their close attention. The termination of the second game will specially repay examination.

GAME 160.
(Queen's Gambit refused.)

White. (Capt. KENNEDY.)	Black. (Mr. WAYTE.)
1. P. to Q. fourth	1. P. to Q. fourth
2. P. to Q. B. fourth	2. P. to K. third
3. Q. Kt. to B. third	3. K. Kt. to B. third
4. P. to K. third	4. P. to Q. B. fourth
5. K. Kt. to B. third	5. Q. Kt. to B. third
6. B. to K. second (a)	6. P. to Q. R. third
7. Castles	7. Q. P. takes P.
8. B. takes P.	8. P. to Q. Kt. fourth
9. B. to K. second	9. P. to Q. Kt. fifth
10. Kt. to Q. R. fourth (b)	10. P. takes P.
11. P. takes P.	11. B. to Q. third
12. B. to K. third	12. Castles
13. Q. R. to B. square	13. B. to Q. Kt. second
14. P. to Q. Kt. third	14. Q. R. to Q. B. square
15. K. Kt. to K. square	15. B. to Q. Kt. square
16. B. to K. B. third	16. Q. to her third
17. P. to K. Kt. third	17. B. to Q. R. second
18. K. Kt. to Q. B. second	18. K. Kt. to Q. fourth (c)
19. Q. Kt. to Q. B. fifth	19. Kt. takes B.
20. Kt. takes B.	20. Q. to K. second
21. P. takes Kt.	21. Q. takes Kt.
22. Q. to Q. second	22. P. to Q. R. fourth
23. B. to K. fourth (d)	23. P. to K. B. fourth
24. B. takes Kt.	24. R. takes B.
25. P. to Q. fifth (e)	25. R. to Q. third
26. Kt. to Q. fourth	26. Q. takes Q. P.
27. K. R. to Q. square (f)	27. P. to K. fourth
28. Q. R. to Q. B. seventh (g)	28. B. to Q. Kt. third

And Black wins.

NOTES.

(*a*) P. to Q. R. third is a better move.

(*b*) This Knight is not well placed; the error of White's sixth move is now apparent.

(*c*) Better than 18. K. R. to Q. square, to which the answer would equally have been 19. Kt. to Q. B. fifth.

(*d*) Thinking, perhaps, that Black's position would be weakened by P. to K. B. fourth.

(*e*) This is an error which costs a Pawn.

(*f*) In attempting to avert the loss of a second Pawn White loses a piece. The game, however, was not to be retrieved, play how he might.

(*g*) If Kt. to K. B. third, Black evidently wins a piece by exchanging Queens.

GAME 161.
(*Queen's Gambit.*)

White. (Capt. H. A. Kennedy.)	Black. (Rev. W. Wayte.)
1. P. to Q. fourth	1. P. to Q. fourth
2. P. to Q. B. fourth	2. P. to K. third
3. P. to K. third	3. Kt. to K. B. third
4. Kt. to K. B. third	4. P. to Q. B. fourth
5. Kt. to Q. B. third	5. Kt. to Q. B. third
6. P. to Q. R. third	6. P. to Q. R. third (*a*)
7. P. takes Q. B. P. (*b*)	7. B. takes P.
8. P. to Q. Kt. fourth	8. B. to Q. Kt. third
9. P. to Q. B. fifth	9. B. to Q. B. second
10. B. to Q. third	10. Castles
11. Castles	11. P. to K. fourth
12. P. to K. fourth	12. P. to Q. fifth
13. Q. Kt. to K. second	13. Kt. to K. R. fourth
14. P. to K. R. third	14. P. to K. B. fourth
15. Q. to Q. Kt. third (check)	15. K. to R. square
16. Q. Kt. to K. Kt. third	16. P. takes P.
17. B. takes K. P.	17. Kt. takes Kt.
18. P. takes Kt.	18. Q. to K. square
19. Q. B. to Q. second	19. Q. B. to K. third
20. Q. to Q. third	20. P. to K. R. third
21. Kt. to K. R. fourth	21. B. to K. B. second
22. B. takes K. R. P. (*c*)	22. P. takes B.
23. R. to K. B. sixth	23. K. to Kt. second (*d*)
24. Q. R. to K. B. square	24. Kt. to K. second
25. Q. to Q. second	25. Kt. to K. Kt. square
26. R. takes K. R. P. (*e*)	26. Kt. takes R. (*f*)
27. Q. to K. Kt. fifth (check)	27. B. to Kt. third
28. R. takes R.	28. K. takes R.

29. Q. takes Kt. (check)	29. K to K. second
30. Kt. takes B. (check)	30. K. to Q. second
31. B. takes Q. Kt. P.	31. R. to R. second
32. P. to Q. B. sixth (check)	32. K. to K. third
33. Kt. to K. B. fourth (dis. ch.)	33. K. to K. second
34. Kt. to Q. fifth (check)	

And Black resigns.

NOTES.

(*a*) In this instance it would have been more advantageous to exchange the Pawns.

(*b*) The correct move, by which White is enabled rapidly to develope his game.

(*c*) We invite the attention of our readers to this interesting position, and especially to the skilful manner in which the attack is carried on by White.

Position after White's 22nd move.

BLACK.

WHITE.

(*d*) Had Black played the King to Kt. square White would have won the Queen, at least, by taking Bishop with Kt.

(*e*) All this is finely conceived; the sacrifice is as ingenious as it is sound.

(*f*) The only move to save the mate.

THE REV. MR. WAYTE AND MR. THOROLD.—The following are two of a series of games played as above stated at the Bath Chess Club between these gentlemen.

GAME 162.
(*Evans' Gambit.*)

White. (Mr. WAYTE.)	*Black.* (Mr. THOROLD.)
1. P. to K. fourth	1. P. to K. fourth
2. K. Kt. to B. third	2. Q. Kt. to B. third

3. B. to Q. B. fourth	3. B. to Q. B. fourth
4. P. to Q. Kt. fourth	4. B. takes P.
5. P. to Q. B. third	5. B. to B. fourth
6. Castles	6. P. to Q. third
7. P. to Q. fourth	7. P. takes P.
8. P. takes P.	8. B. to Kt. third
9. P. to Q. fifth	9. Kt. to Q. R. fourth
10. B. to Kt. second	10. K. Kt. to K. second
11. B. to Q. third	11. Castles
12. Q. Kt. to B. third	12. P. to Q. B. fourth
13. Q. Kt. to K. second	13. P. to Q. R. third
14. K. to R. square	14. B. to Q. B. second
15. Q. to Q. second	15. P. to K. B. third
16. Kt. to K. square	16. P. to Q. Kt. fourth
17. P. to K. B. fourth	17. Kt. to Q. Kt. second
18. P. to K. B. fifth	18. P. to Q. B. fifth
19. B. to Q. B. second	19. Kt. to Q. B. fourth
20. Kt. to K. B. fourth	20. R. to Q. Kt. square
21. Kt. to K. sixth (a)	21. B. takes Kt.
22. Q. P. takes B.	22. B. to Q. R. fourth
23. Q. to K. third	23. B. to Q. Kt. third
24. B. to Q. fourth	24. K. Kt. to Q. B. third
25. Kt. to K. B. third	25. Kt. to Kt. fifth (b)
26. Q. to Q. second	26. Kt. takes B.
27. Q. takes Kt.	27. Kt. to Q. sixth
28. B. takes B.	28. Q. takes B.
29. Kt. to K. square	29. Kt. to Q. Kt. fifth
30. Q. to Q. second	30. P. to Q. R. fourth
31. P. to Q. R. third (c)	31. Kt. to B. third
32. Q. takes Q. P.	32. K. R. to Q. square
33. Q. to K. B. fourth	33. P. to Q. Kt. fifth
34. P. takes P.	34. P. takes P.
35. Kt. to K. B. third	35. P. to Q. B. sixth
36. Q. to Q. B. square	36. Kt. to Q. fifth (d)
37. Kt. takes Kt.	37. Q. takes Kt.
38. R. to Q. Kt. square	38. Q. takes P.
39. R. to K. B. fourth	39. Q. to Q. sixth
40. P. to K. R. third (e)	40. P. to Q. Kt. sixth
41. R. to K. B. third	41. P. to Q. Kt. seventh
42. Q. to K. square	42. Q. takes Q. R.
43. Q. takes Q.	43. P. to Q. B. seventh & wins.

NOTES.

(a) This seems to us premature, as it not only loses time, but also enables Black to prepare the eventual advance of the Pawns on his right wing, which, as the result of the game will show, becomes irresistible. B. to Q. B. third would have been the correct move.

(b) A good move, and far more effective than Kt. to K. fourth.

Position after Black's 25th move.

BLACK.

WHITE.

c) It is questionable whether White should not have boldly advanced this Pawn to R. fourth, as it would have broken up the strength of Black's united Pawns. It is true that the move in the text secures the gain of a Pawn, but it affords Black the means of driving the Queen to a square where she seems completely out of play, and Black can then make an easy onward movement with his advanced Pawns.

(d) Well timed; White is now compelled to exchange Knights, and unable to check the progress of the Black Pawns.

(e) Under the circumstances R. to K. B. third would perhaps have been better.

GAME 163.
(*Allgaier Gambit.*)

White. (Mr. WAYTE.)	Black. (Mr. THOROLD.)
1. P. to K. fourth	1. P. to K. fourth
2. P. to K. B. fourth	2. P. takes P.
3. K. Kt. to B. third	3. P. to K. Kt. fourth
4. P. to K. R. fourth	4. P. to K. Kt. fifth
5. Kt. to K. fifth	5. B. to K. Kt. second
6. P. to Q. fourth	6. P. to Q. third (a)
7. Kt. takes K. Kt. P.	7. P. to K. R. fourth
8. Kt. to K. B. second	8. Q. to K. B. third
9. P. to Q. B. third	9. Kt. to K. second
10. B. to K. second	10. Kt. to K. Kt. third
11. K. Kt. to Q. third	11. Kt. takes K. R. P.
12. Kt. takes K. B. P.	12. B. to K. R. third

13. Castles	13. R. to K. Kt. square
14. B. takes K. R. P. (b)	14. Kt. to Q. B. third (c)
15. Kt. to K. Kt. sixth (d)	15. Q. takes R. (check)
16. Q. takes Q.	16. P. takes Kt.
17. Q. B. takes B.	17. P. takes K. B.
18. Q. to K. B. sixth	18. K. Kt. takes P.
19. B. to K. Kt. fifth	19. Kt. to K. R. fifth
20. Kt. to Q. second	20. B. to K. R. sixth
21. P. to Q. fifth	21. R. to K. Kt. third (e)
22. Q. to K. R. eighth (check)	22. K. to B. second
23. Q. takes R.	23. Kt. to K. fourth
24. K. to R. second (f)	

And White wins.

NOTES.

(a) K. Kt. to B. third is here stronger. Still, the position is every way in favour of the second player, after Paulsen's excellent defensive move 5. B. to K. Kt. second.

(b) The situation is now extremely critical for both players.

(c) Ingenious, and would have been satisfactory against any other move than that actually adopted. B. takes Kt. is preferable, and leads to some highly interesting situations.

Position after Black's 14th move.

BLACK.

WHITE.

(d) The effect of this move was not foreseen by Black. He must now give up his Q. or lose a piece. Had White played instead Kt. to Q. fifth, then

	15. R. takes P. (check)
16. K. to R. square	16. Q. to K. Kt. second

Threatening mate in two moves, which White must provide against, and can neither take K. B. P. with R. nor Q. B. P. with Kt. (check).

(e) If

22. Q. to K. Kt. seventh	21. R. to K. B. square
23. Q. to K. R. eighth (check)	22. R. to K. B. second

and Black must equally lose a piece.

(f) White plays the game throughout with his usual skill and ability.

THE REV. J. OWEN AND MR. LOWENTHAL.—The Rev. Mr. Owen recently visited London, and during his stay frequently attended at the St. George's Chess Club, where he engaged in play with some of the leading members. In the series played between him and Mr. Lowenthal the latter won three games; the others were drawn. The following is a game played some months ago between Mr. Owen and Mr. Lowenthal, in which the former was victorious, and which is here offered as a good specimen of Mr. Owen's skill.

GAME 164.
(Fianchetto.)

White. (Mr. LOWENTHAL.)	Black. (Mr. OWEN.)
1. P. to K. fourth	1. P. to Q. Kt. third
2. P. to Q. fourth	2. B. to Q. Kt. second
3. B. to Q. third	3. P. to K. third
4. B. to K. third	4. Kt. to K. B. third
5. Kt. to Q. B. third (*a*)	5. B. to Q. Kt. fifth
6. P. to K. B. third	6. Castles
7. K. Kt. to K. second	7. P. to Q. B. fourth
8. P. takes P.	8. P. takes P.
9. Castles	9. B. takes Kt.
10. Kt. takes B.	10. Q. to Q. R. fourth
11. P. to K. fifth	11. Kt. to Q. fourth
12. B. to Q. second	12. Kt. takes Kt.
13. B. takes Kt.	13. Q. to Q. B. second
14. Q. to K. second	14. Kt. to Q. B. third
15. Q. R. to Q. square	15. P. to K. B. fourth
16. P. takes P. (*en pass.*) (*b*)	16. P. takes P.
17. Q. to K. third	17. Kt. to K. second
18. Q. to K. R. sixth	18. R. to K. B. second
19. Q. B. takes P.	19. P. to Q. B. fifth
20. Q. to Kt. fifth (ch.) (*c*)	20. K. to K. B. square
21. B. to K. second (*d*)	21. Kt. to K. B. fourth
22. B. to Q. B. third	22. P. to Q. R. fourth
23. P. to K. Kt. fourth	23. P. to K. fourth (*e*)
24. R. to K. B. second	24. R. to Q. R. third
25. Q. R. to K. B. square	25. R. to K. Kt. third
26. Q. to Q. second	26. Kt. to K. R. fifth
27. B. takes Q. R. P.	27. Q. to Q. B. third
28. P. to R. third	28. P. to R. fourth
29. B. to Q. B. third	29. P. takes P.
30. R. P. takes P.	30. R. takes P. (ch.) (*f*)

And White resigns.

NOTES.

(*a*) Kt. to Q. second is a better move here.

(*b*) Taking Pawn with Pawn in passing gives White a fine attack.

(*c*) If 20 B. takes R. P. (ch.)   20. R. takes B.
21. Q. to Kt. fifth (ch.)   21. K. to B. square.
with a piece ahead.

(*d*) White, we believe, might have maintained his advantage by taking off the Knight at this point.

(*e*) An ingenious conception, by which Black is enabled to turn the tables in his favour.

(*f*) A pretty termination.

Position after White's 24th move.

BLACK.

WHITE.

GAME 165.

MR. THOROLD AND MR. FEDDEN.—An interesting match was commenced on May 12th between these gentlemen, the conditions being that the one who first scored seven games should be declared victor; the games to be played at the Bristol Chess Club. The following is one of the games played in this match, and is a good example of the legitimate defence in the Evans' Gambit. We have been promised all the other games in this interesting contest, and shall select the best for publication.

(*Evans' Gambit.*)

White. (Mr. FEDDEN.)	Black. (Mr. THOROLD.)
1. P. to K. fourth	1. P. to K. fourth
2. Kt. to K. B. third	2. Kt. to Q. B. third
3. B. to B. fourth	3. B. to B. fourth

4. P. to Q. Kt. fourth	4. B. takes P.
5. P. to Q. B. third	5. B. to B. fourth
6. P. to Q. fourth	6. P. takes P.
7. P. takes P.	7. B. to Q. Kt. third
8. B. to Q. Kt. second	8. Kt. to Q. R. fourth
9. B. to Q. third	9. P. to Q. third
10. P. to K. fifth	10. Kt. to K. second
11. Kt. to K. Kt. fifth.	11. P. to K. R. third
12. Kt. to K. fourth	12. P. to Q. fourth
13. Kt. to K. Kt. third	13. Q. B. to K. third (a)
14. P. to K. B. fourth	14. P. to K. Kt. third
15. Q. Kt. to Q. second	15. Q. to Q. second
16. Q. R. to Q. B. square	16. Castles (Q. R.)
17. Castles (b)	17. P. to K. R. fourth
18. P. to K. R. fourth	18. Kt. to K. B. fourth
19. B. takes Kt. (c)	19. B. takes B.
20. Kt. to K. B. third	20. Kt. to Q. B. fifth
21. Q. Q. Kt. third	21. B. to K. Kt. fifth
22. R. to Q. B. second	22. B. takes Kt.
23. R. takes. B.	23. Q. to K. Kt. fifth
24. P. to Q. R. fourth	24. Q. takes R. P.
25. B. to Q. B. third	25. P. to Q. R. fourth
26. Kt. to K. B. square	26. K. to Kt. square
27. B. to Q. Kt. second	27. K. R. to K. square
28. Kt. to K. third (d)	28. Q. to K. eighth (check)
29. K. to R. second	29. Kt. to Q. seventh
30. R. takes Kt.	30. Q. takes R.
31. Kt. takes P.	31. B. takes P.
32. B. takes B.	32. Q. takes B.
33. R. to Q. third	33. Q. to Q. B. fourth
34. Kt. to K. B. sixth	34. R. takes R.
35. Q. takes R.	35. Q. to K. second
36. Q. to Q. Kt. fifth (e)	36. R. to Q. square
37. Q. takes R. P.	37. R. to Q. fifth
38. Q. to Q. Kt. fifth	38. P. to Q. B. third

And Black must win the game.

NOTES.

(a) Black selected here the best move, adopting effectual means to prevent the eventual advance of the K. B. Pawn.

(b) We should rather have played Q. to Q. B. second at this point.

(c) Taking Kt. with Kt. would have been preferable.

(d) There was no sufficient reason for giving up the exchange. R. to K. second would have enabled White to play Kt. to K. third without loss.

(e) Taking the Rook would not lead to any better result, as Black's superiority of Pawns must prove decisive.

Problem No. 82. By T. SMITH, Esq.

White to play, and mate in four moves.

Problem No. 83. By S. LOYD, Esq., of New York.

White to play, and mate in five moves.

Problem No. 84. By E. B. C., of Hobocken.

BLACK.

WHITE.

White to play, and mate in three moves.

Problem No. 85. By Herr LANDESMAN, of Vienna.

BLACK.

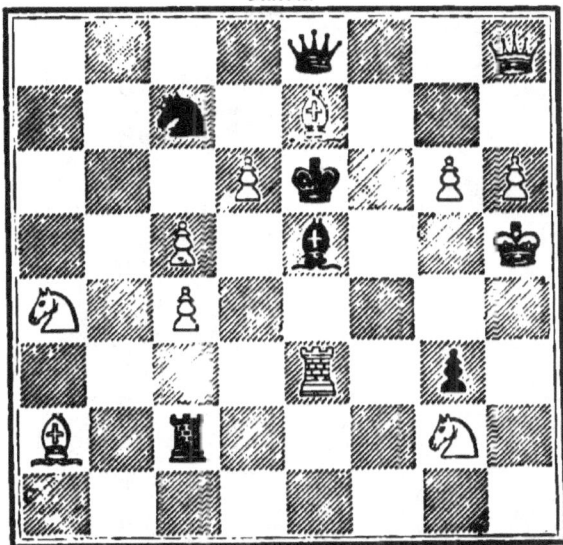

WHITE.

Chess Study No. 20. By W. T. Pierce, Esq.

White to play, and obtain a position in three moves clearly leading to a drawn game.

Chess Study No. 21. By T. Smith, Esq.

CHESS INTELLIGENCE.

MATCH BETWEEN THE GLASGOW AND DUNDEE CHESS CLUBS.

On 25th April a match was played simultaneously in Dundee and Glasgow between these well known clubs, in which ten members on each side took part. Five of the Dundee players repaired to Glasgow to meet their opponents in that city; while the remainder fought out the contest at home, their Glasgow adversaries having come over to Dundee.

We subjoin the particulars of the match, from which it will be seen that in the whole number of games played the Glasgow Club proved victorious by a majority of four:—

AT GLASGOW.

Dundee Club.	Won	Lost	Dr.	Won	Lost	Drawn	Glasgow Club.	
1. G. B. Fraser...	2	0	0	0	2	0	Rev. J. Donaldson	1
2. P. Scott.........	2	1	0	1	2	0	{ W. W. Mitchell and A. Ross...	2
3. D. Lindsay ...	0	2	1					
4. P. Sandeman...	1	2	0	2	0	1	R. S. Moffatt	3
5. G. A. Pattullo.	1	2	0	2	1	0	J. R. Duguid......	4
				2	1	0	J. Roberton	5
	6	7	1	7	6	1		

AT DUNDEE.

Dundee Club.	Won	Lost	Dr.	Won	Lost	Drawn	Glasgow Club.	
1. C. R. Baxter...	1	2	0	2	1	0	B. Eekhout	1
2. J. A. Gloag ...	2	1	0	1	2	0	W. F. Murray ...	2
3. D. Lyall.........	1	2	0	2	1	0	D. Dunlop.........	3
4. D. Sime.........	1	1	1	1	1	0	A. Ross	4
5. T. W. Thoms .	0	2	1	2	0	1	J. Duncan, Jun...	5
	5	8	2	8	5	2		

Glasgow...... 15   Dundee...... 11   Drawn...... 3

Our readers may recollect that in the match which took place last year between these clubs at Edinburgh the Dundee club was fortunate enough to win every game, and its unfavourable position on the present occasion is partly attributable to the absence of several of their best players, who withdrew at the last moment from the contest, so that substitutes of far inferior calibre had to supply their places. Besides this, Glasgow, from its more extensive population admits of a wider range of selection when so many players are required.

Perhaps the best and most stubbornly contested games of the match were those between the Rev. John Donaldson, of Dumfries ("Delta") and Mr. G. B. Fraser. The first game is a very good specimen of the French opening, and Mr. Fraser won it after a struggle of four hours. The second, a Scotch Gambit, opened by Mr. Donaldson, was also scored by his opponent, but the third had to be abandoned for want of time. We hear, however, that at its close the position was much in favour of the Dundee amateur. It is to be hoped that these gentlemen will soon have another opportunity of encountering each other. No doubt dissatisfied with the result of their correspondence match, it is rumoured that the Edinburgh players intend once more to challenge the Dundee Club. With so many able players in Scotland, we are surprised that the supporters and lovers of Chess do not organise a Scottish Chess

Association, the meetings of which might be held annually in the principal towns. We trust that this idea may not be lost sight of, as it would, if carried out, give a very strong impetus to the development of Chess in Scotland.

A CHESS CLUB has recently been formed at Eastbourne, under the presidentship of the Rev. T. Pitman, the vicar, which has already attracted to itself considerable support, and musters a good many members.

DISTINGUISHED VISITORS IN LONDON.—Herr Hirschfeld and Chevalier de St. Bon, both well known in Chess circles, have arrived here, and have already paid several visits to the leading metropolitan clubs.

THE FORTHCOMING MEETING AT REDCAR.—There is every prospect of this meeting, which is to take place in August, being very successful. We hear that already many distinguished amateurs have signified their intention of being present, and that Professor Anderssen and Herr Steinitz have received special invitations. In the problem tourney the competitors should send in their contributions not later than the 2nd of July.

BRITISH CHESS ASSOCIATION.—By this time (June 1st) the names of the competitors for the Challenge Cup must have been sent in, and it is to be hoped in the interests of Chess that all the leading players will have come forward to compete for the first Challenge Cup given to decide the championship of the United Kingdom. We should like to see contending for this prize all the distinguished and well-known British and Irish celebrities, including Boden, Barnes, Bird, De Vere, MacDonnel, Capt. Kennedy, Owen, Staunton, Wyvill, &c. We hear that it has been decided that the Challenge Cup shall be of the value of fifty guineas, and that a prize in money will also be awarded to the fortunate victor.

ANSWERS TO CORRESPONDENTS.

_{*} We are requested by Mr. Wayte to mention that the ingenious move which was analysed in pp. 132, 133, of our last number is the invention of Herr Steinitz. It was never Mr. Wayte's wish to claim the credit of inventing it.

C. T.—The fourth edition of Heydebrandt's Handbuch is procurable through Messrs. Williams & Norgate.

B. R.—Mr. Hampton is the hon. secretary to the St. George's Chess Club. He will, no doubt, with his usual courtesy, furnish you, upon application, with the information you require.

B. W.—The problem tourney in connection with the British Chess Association is open to all comers. Programmes have been prepared and sent to all parts of the globe.

A. M. S.—The playing of several games simultaneously is not so easy as some would imagine. Morphy, with his peculiar genius, was enabled to exhibit his usual skill and ingenuity even whilst playing simultaneously against five of the best European players. Games of this sort are only possible to quicksighted players. Slow thinkers, who sometimes take half an hour over a move, are unable to engage in them.

L. H.—A similar game to that you suggest was proposed in 1820 by Ciccolins. This game consisted of a Chess-board having a hundred squares. We need hardly say that his proposal was unfavourably received.

W. W.—Among the crowned heads noted for their love of Chess were the Emperor Joseph II., who encouraged his officers to study the game. He himself played often. Frederick the Great frequently occupied his leisure hours with Chess. In Rheinsberg he played against General Fouquet successfully. Charles XII., whilst in self-banishment at Bender, amused himself with Chess. Prince Conde used to say that "One who studies for completeness in military tactics should acquire Chess as a preliminary accomplishment.

W. G.—Problem No. 75 cannot be solved in the way you propose, for if the Knight is captured, Black simply replies with B. takes P. and mate is impossible.

HONORARY SECRETARIES OF CHESS CLUBS.—Abingdon, Birmingham, Cardiff, Dundee, Huddersfield, King's Lynn, Norfolk and Norwich, Penzance, Reading and Berkshire, Sheffield, Stamford, Glasgow, Worcester, Leamington, Cardiff. Our grateful acknowledgments.

THE Chess Player's Magazine.

SHAKESPEARE'S SILENCE ABOUT CHESS.

There has been some discussion lately in that very useful periodical "Notes and Queries" touching the complete silence of Shakespeare in regard to tobacco, which is doubtless somewhat of a noteworthy circumstance. We can understand, indeed, why his latter plays should contain at least nothing in favour of the nicotian herb, in respect of the vehement antipathy entertained to it by the British Solomon, gentle King Jamie, as expressed in his famous "Counterblast." No such objection, however, existed in the time of Elizabeth, in whose reign tobacco was first introduced by Raleigh, when its use at once spread rapidly amongst all classes, and the

"Little tube of mighty power"

became, and has ever since continued, an English institution.

There is another subject also totally ignored by Shakespeare, which, to my thinking, is not less difficult to account for than his non-mention of tobacco. I refer to Chess; and I do not consider the solitary instance in "The Tempest,"* where the game is incidentally named, to be any exception, because there is nothing said about it in the text that would not equally apply to any other game that is played between two persons. In the scene alluded to, Ferdinand and Miranda are discovered engaged at Chess:—

Mir. Sweet lord, you play me false.
Fer. No, my dearest love,
I would not for the world.
Mir. Yes, for a score of kingdoms you should wrangle,
And I would call it fair play.

* Act V. Scene I.

The commentator Stevens, remarking on the above passage, says, "Shakespeare might not have ventured to engage his hero and heroine at this game, had he not found Huon de Bourdeaux and a princess employed in the same manner."*

The game of Chess, with its suggestive nomenclature and endless versatility, the intellectual and moral qualities it brings into exercise, the joys and anxieties, triumphs and depressions, which accompany its ever-changing fortunes, has a resemblance to the greater game of human life so striking and unmistakeable, that the analogy has escaped the notice of few imaginative writers either of present or former times. How comes it, then, that Shakespeare, the greatest of all writers, should have neglected to avail himself of a theme affording such abundant scope for happy illustration? It may, perhaps, be said in reply, that Shakespeare was not himself a Chess-player, which is possible; but even the most superficial acquaintance with the game, not extending beyond the names of the pieces, and a slight knowledge of the principles, would have enabled him to use it in his own unapproachable manner as a vehicle for metaphor and comparison.

It must be borne in mind that when Shakespeare lived, Chess was extensively cultivated in England. We can easily imagine, indeed, that in the absence of newspapers and periodicals to wile away their spare time, nearly a total dearth of popular literature, and with few objects of intellectual interest, our ancestors must have resorted to Chess as an occupation for the mind, as well as an agreeable indoor recreation. Accordingly we find in the inventories of old houses which are still extant, a Chess equipage or two almost invariably recorded. The then head of the realm, Queen Elizabeth, was herself an amateur of Chess, and, if we may judge from the vigour and general capacity of her mind, that wise princess was probably no mean proficient in the subtleties of the regal pastime. It is stated in the life of her tutor, Roger Ascham, prefixed to the quarto edition of his works, that after his royal pupil mounted the throne, she still retained him to assist in her private studies, and that she sometimes played with him at Chess and draughts. In a speech of James I., animadverting on some books written by Cowel and Blackwood which were sup-

* Romance of Huon, chap. 53. ed. 1601.

posed to be subversive of the constitution, he says, "The power of kings is in the hands of the Lord. They can exalt low things, and abase high things, making the subjects like men at Chess, a Pawn to take a Bishop or a Knight." Thus we see that Shakespeare's two royal patrons were both conversant with Chess.

Although Shakespeare makes no mention of Chess in his works, it is not so with his fellow dramatists and other writers, who were contemporaneous, or nearly so, with him. There are various allusions to the game in the works of Skelton, who was Poet Laurate to Henry VIII. about 1540. He says in one place:—

> "For ye play so at the chesse
> As they suppose and gesse,
> That some of you but late
> Hath played so checkmate
> With lords of high estate."

and again—

> "Oure dayes be datyed
> To be check matyd."

Many other poets and poetasters of that age drew similes and figures of speech from the Chessboard, including Spencer, Cowley, Denham, Beaumont and Fletcher, quaint Arthur Saul, and glorious John Dryden at a somewhat later period. Nicholas Breton, a minor poet of Elizabeth's reign, and the author of a few pastorals in which some happy thoughts and imagery may be found, wrote a poem descriptive of Chess play, of which the following is a specimen:—

THE QUEENE.

> "The Queene is quaint and quick conceit,
> Which makes hir walke which way she list,
> And roots them up that lie in wait,
> To work hir treason, ere she wist;
> Hir force is such against her foes,
> That whom she meetes she overthrows."

The chivalrous and ill-fated Earl of Surrey, whose poetry is so remarkable for its flowing melody, purity of expression, and melancholy pathos, indited some graceful lines called "The lady that scorned her lover," which turn upon the similarity between the game of Chess and the game of life. Of all the victims of the injustice of Henry VIII. methinks there is no one whose untimely death excites more grief and pity, and is more deserving of execration, than that of this high-born son of genius.

In the beginning of the seventeenth century, about the year 1610, according to Twiss, the well-known dramatic author,

Thomas Middleton, published a comedy, entitled "A Game at Chess," in the shape of a small quarto of sixty-eight pages, in prose, rhyme, and blank verse. It was brought on the stage, and had a run of nine successive days at Shakespeare's own theatre, the Globe, so it is not impossible that the mighty dramatist may himself have witnessed its performance. It has little or no plot, and contains some bitter satire on the Church of Rome. One of the characters is a certain fat bishop, the original of whom was said to have been Antonio de Dominis, Master of the Savoy and Dean of Windsor. Middleton had no reason to plume himself on this production, for the Spanish faction at the court of James I. took in such dudgeon the hits it made at their religion, that by the influence of his Queen, Anne of Denmark, the unlucky author was sent to cool his heels in prison, where he remained for some time, and was only released after sending the following petition to the King, which, we may suppose, touched the fancy of that learned sovereign :—

"A harmless game, coin'd only for delight,
Was play'd twixt the Black house and the White,
The White house won; yet still the Black doth brag,
They had the power to put me in the bag.
Use but your royal hand! 'twill set me free,
'Tis but removing of a man—that's me."

Enough has been said, I think, to show that the omission by Shakespeare of all mention of Chess in his writings is at least a matter of curiosity.

H. A. KENNEDY.

BRITISH CHESS ASSOCIATION. CONGRESS, 1866.

(FROM A SPECIAL CORRESPONDENT.)

The British Chess Association has to congratulate itself upon several very important and interesting meetings of their society, Among others we may enumerate the Congress held at Bristol, and the ever-memorable Chess Congress held in 1862, but no previous meeting had ever the same significance and importance as the Congress of the Association which has just commenced holding its meetings in London; for, apart from the fact that it is the first meeting which has taken place since the reorganisation of the British Chess Association on a permanent basis, there is one feature connected with this meeting which will render the Congress of 1866 the most glorious, successful, and brilliant of events. That feature will stamp it in the historical records of the science, and, without doubt, every Chess amateur will ever look back with deep and fervent gratitude to the original promoters of the scheme. It was a very happy idea to offer a Challenge Cup of the value of £50 to be competed for, and the rules which guide the competition have been admirably framed. The beauty of the prize excited general admiration, and we trust that the successful recipient will treasure it as an heirloom. The great meeting to which we refer was inaugurated on the 19th ult. at the St. George's Chess Club, and was continued for three successive days at St. James's Hall. The great interest taken in the Congress, both by amateurs in the metropolis and provinces, was amply indicated by the presence at the meeting of the most influential players from all parts of Great Britain—a fact sufficient to prove to dispassionate men how heartily they supported the exertions and untiring efforts of the managing committee to render the gathering a thorough success, and that they in every particular endorsed the policy of administration which the society had seen fit to adopt.

It is of course at the present time very difficult to speculate on the result of the contest for the Challenge Cup Tourney, or that of the Handicap Tournament. As far as the contest has as yet proceeded, we have been surprised at some of the failings which players of European repute have made in play; but this may be attributable to the nervous excitement which the extraordinary circumstances attaching to this special case may have helped to contribute. It may be urged that a larger number of competitors ought to have entered the lists for so desirable a prize, but when we recollect that Mr. Staunton and Mr. Boden are prevented by their other avocations from engaging in Chess contests, and that several other distinguished amateurs, from various causes, are likewise debarred, the public may well be satisfied with the catalogue of names who are contending for "the blue riband" of the chequered board.

In accordance with the arrangements of the managing committee, the Congress commenced with a general meeting held at the St. George's Chess Club, 20, King Street, St. James's, on Tuesday, the 19th of June, under the presidency of Lord Lyttelton, who took the chair at 8 o'clock p.m. There was a large attendance of members, among whom were: Lord Cremorne, Sir John Trelawny, Bart., Capt. H. A. Kennedy, the Revs. W. Wayte and G. MacDonnell, Messrs. Alexander, Barber, Chinnery, De Vere, Forster, Gover, Green, Greenaway, Hampton, T. J., Hampton, W., Hewitt, Hunt, Medley, Minchin, Mongredien, Mongredien, jun., Slous, Tripp, and Lowenthal. After the confirmation of the previous minutes his lordship adverted to the labours of the managing committee, who, by their perseverance and energy, had succeeded in satisfactorily completing the arrangements for the Congress, which, thus so well inaugurated, promised to be a great success. His lordship then stated that communications had been entered into with the provincial clubs throughout the kingdom for the purpose of ascertaining their views as to holding a meeting under the auspices of this Association at some provincial town, and that several replies had already been returned; the committee would deal with this matter in due course. After making some general remarks the noble chairman called upon the honorary secretary, Mr. Medley, to read the report:—

REPORT OF THE MANAGING COMMITTEE AND PROGRAMME OF THE CONGRESS, 1866.

Since the general meeting held in March, the committee have been engaged in carrying out the resolutions passed thereat with reference to the various objects of the association.

Their attention has been chiefly directed to making arrangements for the approaching Congress, and they have much pleasure in stating that in the important matter of funds they have to report a successful result to the canvass made, £150 having been subscribed up to this date, with the certainty of this sum being increased before the close of the meeting. It is with satisfaction, therefore, that they have to announce the institution of a Grand Challenge Cup, as the guerdon of British Championship in Chess, the contest for which on this occasion, from the eminent names which have been sent in, will form the most interesting and important feature of the Congress. Without further preface the committee propose that the following arrangements shall form the

PROGRAMME.

A Preliminary General Meeting will be held at the St. George's Chess Club, 20, King Street, St. James's, on Tuesday, 19th June, at eight, p.m., Lord Lyttelton, president, in the chair. Players intending to compete in the tournaments should be present for the purpose of being paired, and of learning the regulations of the managing committee.

Play will commence on Wednesday, 20th June, at the London, and St. George's Clubs, and at the Divan, 102, Strand; and on Friday 22nd, Saturday, 23rd, and Monday, 25th, members and players will meet at St. James's Hall, Piccadilly, which has been engaged for those three days.

Grand Challenge Cup, open to British players only. A Cup,

of the value of £50, in which will be placed the entrance fees of the combatants, £3 3s. each, in addition to a money prize of £10 10s. The winner to receive the cash, but the cup not to become his property except it be won by him for the second time, at the Congress to be held in London in 1868; he in the meantime to hold the cup as a trophy, on giving the usual securities. The number of games to be played will be fixed by the committee when they shall have ascertained the number of the combatants. Names of intending competitors will be received up to the evening of 19th June. Sir John Trelawny, Bart., Messrs. Bird, Burden, De Vere, Minchin, and the Rev. G. MacDonnell have already entered the lists, and others are expected to follow. The cup will be exhibited at the preliminary meeting.

A Handicap Tournament, open to all comers—to consist of eight, twelve, sixteen, or a greater convenient number of players, who will contend according to a scale of odds to be devised by a handicap committee, consisting of Messrs. W. Hampton, J. Lowenthal, Rev. G. MacDonnell, G. Medley, and F. Slous. Should the number of players be sixteen, the prizes will be as follows:—First, £20; second, £10; third, £5; fourth, £2 10s. Entrance, £1 1s. Names of intending competitors will be received up to the evening of 19th June.

Problem Tourney. The conditions of this competition are published on a separate sheet, and may be obtained on application to the manager or hon. secretary. They contain a special clause in favour of British composers. Problems will be received up to 1st January, 1867. The prizes, with the aid of two special subscriptions, amount to £47 10s.

Club, consultation, and other matches will be arranged during the congress, as opportunity may offer.

A Match between Anderssen and Steinitz for £100 a side, the stakes being contributed by personal friends of the players, has been arranged, and will commence on the arrival of Herr Anderssen, who is expected early in July. The match will be played at the London and St. George's Clubs, to which members of the Association will be admitted on presentation of their tickets.

A banquet will take place at such time during the Congress as may be agreed upon.

The adoption of the above report having been proposed, seconded, and unanimously carried, his lordship announced that the following gentlemen had entered the lists for the Challenge Cup, the arrangement being that every player should encounter every other competitor, the winner of the first three games to be the victor in the single contests, and the championship to be awarded to the winner of the greatest number of games:—

Mr. Bird,	Rev. G. MacDonnell,
„ Burden,*	Mr. Minchin.
„ De Vere,	Sir J. Trelawny, Bart.

HANDICAP TOURNAMENT.

The names of the competitors in this tournament were announced by the chairman and handicapped by the committee, consisting of the Revs. W. Wayte and G. Macdonnell, and Messrs. Hampton, Medley, and Slous. The terms of the contest were that the victory in each round should depend on the winning of the first two games, and that the successful competitors remaining after the second round should contend for the four prizes. The following were the arrangements:—

CLASS I.

To give the first move to Class II.; Pawn and move to Class III.; Pawn and two moves to Class IV.; and Rook to Class V. — Messrs. De Vere, MacDonnell, and Steinitz.

CLASS II.

To give the move to Class III.; Pawn and move to Class IV.; Pawn and two moves to Class V. — Mr. E. Thorold.

CLASS III.

To give the move to Class IV.; and Pawn and move to Class V. — Messrs. Chinnery, Gover, V. Green, Minchin, and Mocatta.

CLASS IV.

To give Pawn and two moves to Class V. — Lord Lyttelton, Sir J. Trelawny, Bart., Mr. S. J. Green, and Mr. H. Mann.

CLASS V.

Messrs. Barber, Burne, and Mongredien, jun.

The competitors were then paired off as follows:—

Lord Lyttelton .... v. Mr. Chinnery.
Mr. Burne............... v. „ Minchin.
„ Mann .... v. „ Mocatta.
„ Mongredien, jun., v. Sir J. Trelawny, Bart.
„ Thorold .... v. Rev. G. MacDonnell.
„ De Vere............ v. Herr Steinitz.
„ Barber .... v. Mr. S. J. Green.
„ Gover................ v. „ V. Green.

---

* This gentleman has since been called to Ireland, and was consequently obliged to send in his resignation.

The chairman announced that the above matches would be commenced the next day at the London and St. George's Chess Clubs, and be continued at St. James's Hall on the Friday, Saturday, and Monday following. A vote of thanks concluded the proceedings of Tuesday evening.

The result of Wednesday and Thursday's play was:—
De Vere v. Steinitz—Drawn game.
Sir J. Trelawny v. Minchin—The latter won two games.
Handicap Tourney—Burne v. Minchin—The latter won one game.

THE MEETING AT ST. JAMES'S HALL.

This meeting was opened on Friday, and was numerously attended by members and visitors. The most interesting features of the day were the match between Mr. De Vere and the Rev. G. MacDonnell (which the former won), and a Consultation Match between Capt. H. A. Kennedy, the Rev. C. E. Ranken, and Mr. Lowenthal on one side, and Herr Steinitz, Mr. T. J. Hampton, and Mr. G. W. Medley on the other. The Consultation Match was opened by White, Herr Steinitz and his allies, with the King's Gambit, the attack of which was evaded by their opponents playing B. to Q. B. fourth. When the game was adjourned on Friday evening the position seemed in favour of Black. When on Saturday the game was resumed, a hasty move gave White such an advantage as to render Black's chance almost hopeless. By a skilfully-planned manœuvre, however, Black not only succeeded in retrieving their position, but the game was eventually drawn.

The following are the matches which have been played at the Hall:—

Sir J. Trelawny v. Mongredien, jun.
Score—Sir J. Trelawny won 1; Mr. Mongredien won 2.
Mr. Mann and Mr. Mocatta drew their game.

On Monday two other Consultation games were played—one between Herr Steinitz, Rev. C. E. Ranken, and Messrs. Medley and Balnieff, against Messrs. Hewitt, De Vere, and Lowenthal; and the other between Messrs. Stewart, Sich, Franklyn, and Thompson, against the Rev. W. Wayte, Herr Meyer, Mr. Young, and an amateur. Both these games were continued to a late hour, and were then abandoned as drawn.

The Challenge Cup, a very handsome piece of plate, value £60, was exhibited at the Hall, and was very much admired.

PRESENT SCORE.
Challenge Cup Tourney.
Mr. De Vere won two games of Mr. Minchin.
Mr. Minchin won two games of Mr. Bird.

Mr. De Vere won one game of Mr. MacDonnell.
Mr. Minchin won two games of Sir John Trelawny, Bart.

Handicap Tourney.

	Won.		Won.	Drawn.
Lord Lyttelton	0	Mr. Chinnery	2	0
Mr. Minchin	2	Mr. Burne	0	0
Mr. Mocatta	2	Mr. Mann	0	1
Sir J. Trelawny, Bart.	1	Mr. Mongredien, jun.	2	0
Herr Steinitz	1	Mr. De Vere	0	1
Mr. S. J. Green	1	Mr. Barber	0	1
Mr. W. S. Gover resigned		Mr. V. Green	2	0

THE TWO KNIGHTS' DEFENCE.

The following interesting variations bearing upon the branch of the Two Knights' Defence (given in our May number, page 133) have been forwarded to us for publication by the Rev. W. C. Green, one of the best players in the University of Cambridge:—

Variation on Black's 23rd move in the Two Knights' Defence. See "Chess Players' Magazine," May, page 133.

Position after White's 23rd move.
BLACK.

WHITE.

At the 23rd move, instead of B. to Q. Kt. third let Black play
23. Kt. takes Q. B. P.
[If White now take Black's Kt. with Pawn, mate is forced in five moves. If White take Kt. with Kt., then:—
24. B. takes Q. P. (check)
25. Q. B. to K. third   25. R. takes B.

26. K. to B. square (best)	26. B. takes Kt.
27. R. to Q. square (check)	27. K. to Q. B. second
28. K. to B. second	28. B. takes Q. Kt. P. with a winning game.]

Therefore White plays

24. Q. P. takes B.	24. Kt. to K. seventh (check)

This seems somewhat stronger than R. to K. eight (check); the latter, however, leads to interesting variations, and requires great nicety of play on White's side to avoid loss.

25. B. takes Kt.
[If K. moves then R. to B. third (check), &c.]

	25. R. takes B.
26. P. takes Kt. (A, B, C)	26. R. to K. eight (check)
27. K. to B. second	27. R. takes R.
28. B. to Q. second (C, D)	28. R. to Q. Kt. square
29. B. to K. square	29. R. to Q. Kt. seventh (check)
30. Kt. to Q. second	30. R. takes Kt. (ch.) and wins.

To facilitate the examination of the following variations we give a Diagram of the position as a starting point:—

Position after Black's 25th move.
BLACK.

WHITE.

A.

Beginning at White's 26th move.

26. B. to Q. second	26. Kt. to Q. B. fifth
27. K. to K. B. square	

This seems his best, for if White move B. to Q. B. third, Kt. to K. sixth would be immediately fatal.

	27. Kt. takes B. (check)
28. Kt. takes Kt.	28. R. takes Kt.

Black should win, for he threatens K. R. to K. seventh, winning the Pawns. If, *ex. gra.* :—

29. Q. R. to K. square	29. R. takes R.
30. K. takes R.	30. R. takes Q. R. P.
31. R. to K. B. square	31. R. to R. eighth (check)
32. K. moves	32. R. takes R.
33. K. takes R.	33. K. to K. third, &c., winning.

B.

Beginning at White's 26th move.

26. Kt. to Q. second	26. R. to K. eighth (check)
27. Kt. to K. B. square	27. Kt. to Q. B. fifth
28. K. to B. second	

[If White move K. R. P. or K. Kt. P. Black may move Kt. to Q. seventh or K. sixth and must gain something.]

If

	28. K. R. to K. seventh (check)
29. K. to K. B. third	29. Kt. to K. fourth (check)
30. K. to Kt. third	30. Kt. to Q. sixth, regaining the piece with a winning position.

If

29. K. to Kt. third	29. R. to Q. eighth (best)

And White apparently cannot prevent 30. K. R. to K. eight and loss consequently. Or Black might advance his Pawns on the King's flank at move 29, secure of gaining in the end, White being helpless. If

	29. R. to Q. B. seventh
30. B. to Q. Kt. second	30. Q. R. to K. seventh
31. B. to Q. fourth	31. R. takes K. Kt. P. (check)
32. K. to R. third	

and White may get out though rather in a bad position.

C.

Beginning at White's 26th move.

26. P. to K. R. third	26. R. to K. eight (check)
27. K. to R. second	27. R. takes R. (check)
28. K. takes R.	28. K. R. to K. eight (check)
29. K. to R. second	29. R. takes B.
30. P. takes Kt.	30. K. to K. third
31. K. to Kt. third	31. K. to Q. fourth
32. K. to B. third	32. K. takes P.*
33. K. to K. third	33. P. to K. B. fourth
34. K. to Q. second	34. R. to K. Kt. eight
35. K. to Q. B. second	35. K. to Q. fifth
36. P. to Q. R. fourth	36. R. takes P. (check)

* This would lose Black the game, as White could liberate his Rook by playing Kt. to Q. second, &c. Black, instead of taking as above, should first play the R. to K. R. sq., &c.—ED.

37. Kt. to Q. second	37. P. to K. B. fifth
38. R. to Q. R. third	38. R. to K. Kt. sixth
39. Kt. to Kt. third (check)	39. K. to Q. fourth
	and Black will win.

This last play is not exhaustive, but I believe Black's Pawns would win, let White play as he may.

D.

Beginning at White's 28th move.

28. Kt. to Q. second	28. K. R. to K. eight
29. Kt. to Q. Kt. third	29. Q. R. to K. B. eighth (ch.)
30. K. to Kt. third	

And Black has a good game, for he will advance the Pawns on the King's side, or bring the King up, while White can hardly move anything. For instance :—

P. to K. Kt. fourth

Black cannot move the Bishop, and challenge exchanges, for mate would follow in three moves. Nor can his Rook move to any purpose. Suppose

31. P. to K. R. third	31. P. to K. R. fourth*
32. K. to R. second	32. P. to R. fifth and mates
	next move.

If

31. Q. R. P. to R. fourth	31. P. to K. B. fourth
32. P. to Q. R. sixth	32. P. to K. R. fourth
33. P. to Q. R. fifth	33. P. to K. R. fifth (check)
	and mates next move.

There may be other moves for White slightly better, but I do not think White can save the game.

W. C. GREEN.

Cambridge, June 5, 1866.

* Suppose White now plays B. to Kt. second, would he not have the better game of the two?—ED.

MR. HEALEY'S PROBLEMS:

When we pointed out in our last number some errors which occur in this interesting work we did so mainly with a view to their correction in a future edition, and certainly not with any idea of detracting from the merits of the collection, the excellence of which we have always been prompt to acknowledge. Mr. Henry White, who takes a great interest in this branch of Chess, and more particularly in the volume of which we are speaking, had requested us to notice these occasional blemishes, some of which he had himself discovered. Mr. Healey has kindly supplied us with the alterations necessary to correct the faulty positions. Before giving them, however, we must express our regret at having inadvertently noticed two of the defective problems more than once. Mr. Healey's corrections are as follows:—

Problem 14 is erroneous simply through a misprint. A black pawn should be placed on Black's K. R. third square.

Problem 30. Place a black pawn on Black's Q. Kt. second square.

Problem 31. Place a black pawn on Black's K. R. third square.

Problem 85. Place a black pawn on Black's Q. R. fourth square.

Problem 87. Transfer White's King from Q. R. square to Q. R. second.

Problem 89. Place a black pawn at Black's K. B. third square.

Problem 90. Transfer White's Queen from Q. third to K. R. square.

Problem 139. Place a black pawn at Black's Q. B. third square.
Problem 151. Place a black pawn at Black's K. R. fifth square.
Problem 180. Place a black pawn at Black's K. B. second square.

Problem 185. Place a black bishop at Black's K. square.

According to the author, Problems 116, 126, 129, 149, and 181 are perfectly correct.

CORRESPONDENCE.

TO THE EDITOR OF THE "CHESS PLAYER'S MAGAZINE."

Sir,—In the May number of the "Chess Player's Magazine" occurs a game (No. 156) between Messrs. Sich and Lowenthal, the latter giving the odds of Pawn and two moves. Mr. Sich loses, but it appears to me he might have won. The position of the men after White's 22nd move is as follows:—

White.
K. at Kt. square
Q. at Q. B. fifth
Rs. at K. B. and K. B. third
B. at Q. third
Ps. at K. R. second, K. Kt. second, Q. B. second, Q. Kt. second, Q. R. second.

Black.
K. at K. Kt. square
Q. at K. Kt. second
Rs. at K. B. and Q. R. sqrs.
B. at Q. second
Kt. at K. square
Ps. at K. R. third, K. B. fifth, K. third, Q. B. second, Q. Kt. fourth, Q. R. second.

Black now moves—
23. Q. to Q. fourth.

22. Q. to K. Kt. fourth

If, instead of this move, White had played R. to K. Kt. third, how could Black save the game? He cannot exchange Queens. If Pawn take Rook, then White mates by taking K. R. with his Queen. Nothing remains, therefore, for Black but to submit to the loss of his Queen for the Rook. After this White must win easily. Will you kindly answer this in your next number?

EVA.

GAMES.

GAME 166.
GRAND CHALLENGE CUP TOURNEY.

The following game was played during the meeting of the Chess Association, at the St. James's Hall, by the Rev. G. MacDonnell against Mr. De Vere:—

(*French Opening.*)

White. (MR. MACDONNELL.)	Black. (MR. DE VERE.)
1. P. to K. fourth	1. P. to K. third
2. P. to Q. fourth	2. P. to Q. fourth
3. P. takes P.	3. P. takes P.
4. B. to Q. third	4. Kt. to Q. B. third
5. B. to K. third	5. B. to K. third
6. Kt. to K. B. third	6. Kt. to K. B. third
7. Kt. to Q. B. third	7. B. to Q. third
8. Castles	8. Castles
9. P. to K. R. third	9. Q. to Q. second
10. K. Kt. to Kt. fifth	10. Q. B. to B. fourth
11. B. takes B.	11. Q. takes B.
12. P. to K. Kt. fourth (*a*)	12. Q. to Q. second
13. P. to K. B. fourth	13. Q. R. to K. sq. (*b*)
14. Q. to Q. second	14. Kt. takes Kt. P. (*c*)
15. P. takes Kt.	15. Q. takes P. (check)
16. K. to B. second	16. R. takes B. (*d*)
17. Q. takes R.	17. B. takes P.
18. Q. to R. third (*e*)	18. Q. takes Kt.
19. Kt. to K. second	19. R. to K. sq.
20. P. to Q. B. third	20. B. to K. sixth (ch.)
21. K. to K. sq.	21. B. takes P. (*f*)
22. Q. R. to Q. sq.	22. B. to K. sixth (*g*)
23. R. to to K. B. fifth	23. Q. to K. Kt. third
24. Q. R. takes Q. P.	24. B. to Kt. third

25. Q. to K. B. third	25. Q. to K. Kt. eight (ch.)
26. Q. to B. sq.	26. Q. to K. sixth
27. K. to Q. sq.	27. Kt. to K. second (h)
28. Kt. to Q. fourth (i)	28. Kt. takes Q. R.
29. R. takes Kt.	29. Q. to K. fifth
30. R. to K. B. fifth	30. B. takes Kt.
13. P. takes B.	31. Q. to Kt. eighth (ch.)
32. K. to Q. second	32. Q. takes Q. (ch.)

And White resigns.

NOTES.

(a) A weak move, and fatal in its consequences, as will be presently seen.

(b) A precursor to a masterly combination; White will now be compelled to move the Q. to Q. second, for if B. plays to either B. or Q. second, a Pawn is obviously lost, and, if to Q. B. square, the development of the game is thereby retarded. The Queen could not have been played to either K. B. third or Q. third, for if the first be adopted Black wins the Kt. by P. to K. R. third, and if the latter, Kt. to Q. Kt. fifth, winning at least a Pawn.

(c) An ingenious sacrifice, which leads to a combination of remarkable interest.

(d) Black continues the attack with great spirit and energy.

(e) If Q. to B. third Black wins the Queen at least.

(f) All this is finely conceived. On examination the sacrifice will be found perfectly justifiable; for if White were to take the proffered Bishop the loss of a Rook, at least, would be inevitable—e. g.,

	22. P. takes B.
23. Kt. takes P.	23. R. to K. B. second (best)
24. Q. to K. Kt. eighth (check), winning Rook, and Knight or Queen.	

(g) Q. to K. second deserves consideration.

(h) Cleverly played.

(i) If 28. R. to K. fifth

	28. Kt. takes R.
29. R. takes Q.	29. Kt. takes Q. (check),

Regaining Queen, &c.

GAME 167.

The following interesting game was played during the meeting of the British Chess Association at the St. James's Hall. Messrs. Steinitz, Medley, and Hampton in consultation against Capt. H. A. Kennedy, the Rev. E. C. Ranken, and Mr. Lowenthal.

(*King's Gambit Declined.*)

White. (Messrs. STEINITZ, MEDLEY, and HAMPTON.)	Black. (Capt. KENNEDY, Messrs. RANKEN and LOWENTHAL.)
1. P. to K. fourth	1. P. to K. fourth
2. P. to K. B. fourth	2. K. B. to Q. B. fourth
3. K. Kt. to B. third	3. P. to Q. third
4. K. B. to Q. B. fourth	4. K. Kt. to K. B. third
5. P. to Q. third	5. Kt. to Q. B. third
6. P. to Q. B. third	6. B. to Q. Kt. third

7. Q. to K. second	7. B. to K. Kt. fifth
8. Kt. to R. third (a)	8. P. takes P.
9. B. takes P.	9. Kt. to K. R. fourth
10. B. to Q. second	10. Q. Kt. to K. fourth
11. Castles (Q. R.)	11. Q. to K. B. third
12. K. R. to B. square	12. B. takes Kt.
13. P. takes B.	13. Kt. to B. fifth (b)
14. B. takes Kt.	14. Q. takes B. (check)
15. K. to Kt. square	15. Castles (Q. R.)
16. B. to Kt. third	16. K. R. to K. square
17. P. to Q. fourth	17. Kt. to K. Kt. third
18. Q. to Kt. second	18. K. to Kt. square
19. Q. to K. Kt. third	19. K. R. to K. second.
20. Kt. to Q. B. second	20. P. to Q. B. third
21. Kt. to Q. Kt. fourth	21. B. to Q. B. second
22. Kt. to Q. third	22. Q. to K. R. third
23. Q. R. to K. square	23. Q. R. to K. square
24. B. to B. second	24. P. to K. B. third (c)
25. Q. R. to K. second	25. P. to Q. fourth
26. Q. to Kt. second (d)	26. Kt. to R. fifth
27. Q. to K. R. square	27. Q. to K. R. fourth
28. Kt. to B. square	28. Kt. to Kt. third
29. R. from K. 2nd to K. sq. (e)	29. Q. takes R. P.
30. Q. takes Q.	30. B. takes Q.
31. R. to K. R. square	31. B. to B. fifth
32. R. takes P.	32. B. to K. R. third
33. Kt. to K. second	33. Kt. to R. fifth
34. R. to K. B. square	34. Kt. to B. fourth
35. B. to Q. third	35. Kt. to Q. third
36. Kt. to Kt. third	36. P. takes P.
37. P. takes P.	37. Kt. takes P.
38. Kt. takes Kt.	38. R. takes Kt.
39. B. takes R.	39. R. takes B.
40. R. to K. R. second	40. K. to B. square (f)
41. K. to B. second	41. K. to Q. square
42. K. to Q. third	42. R. to K. square
43. R. to K. second	43. R. to B. square
44. K. to K. fourth	44. K. to K. second
45. K. to B. fifth (dis. check)	45. K. to B. second
46. R. to K. sixth	46. B. to Kt. fourth (g)
47. P. to Q. fifth (h)	47. P. takes P.
48. R. to Q. sixth	48. K. to K. second
49. R. takes P.	49. B. to R. third

50. P. to B. fourth	50. R. to Q. B.'s square
51. P. to B. fifth	51. P. to R. fourth
52. P. to Kt. third	52. R. to B. second
53. R. to R. eighth	53. B. to K. sixth
54. P. to B. sixth	54. R. takes P.
55. R. takes P.	55. K. to B. second
56. R. to Q. Kt. eighth	56. R. to B. second
57. R. to Kt. fifth	57. P. to Q. Kt. third
58. P. to R. fourth	58. R. to K. second
59. P. to Kt. fourth	59. P. to Kt. third (check)
60. K. to Kt. fifth	60. P. to B. fourth (check)
61. K. to B. third	61. R. to K. third (i)
62. P. to R. fifth	62. P. takes P.
63. R. takes P.	63. B. to Q. fifth (k)
64. P. to Kt. fifth	64. R. to K. sixth (check)
65. K. to Kt. second	65. P. to K. B. fifth
66. R. to R. sixth (l)	66. R. to Kt. sixth (check)
67. K. to R. second	67. K. to Kt. second.
68. P. to Kt. sixth	68. B. to Kt. eighth (check)
69. K. to R. square	69. P. to B. sixth
70. P. to Kt. seventh	70. B. to Q. fifth
71. R. to Kt. eighth (check)	71. K. to R. second
72. R. to R. eighth (check)	72. B. takes R.
73. P. Queens	73. R. to R. sixth (check)
74. Q. interposes	74. R. takes Q. (check)
75. K. takes R.	75. B. to K. fourth (check)
76. K. to R. third	76. P. to Kt. fourth
77. R. to R. third	77. P. to B. seventh
78. K. to Kt. second	

Drawn game.

NOTES.

(a) This appears to be a weak move; P. to K. B. third would have been much more preferable.

(b) Black has now a good game.

(c) In order to be enabled to advance the Queen's Pawn with safety.

(d) The best move.

(e) The White allies exercised sound judgment in sacrificing the Pawn, as by doing so they not only relieved themselves from their cramped position, but turned the tables rather in their favour.

(f) R. to K. square would have been the correct play here.

(g) The only move to prevent loss.

(h) Very well played.

(i) The effect of this move will become apparent as the game advances.

(k) The position here is very interesting and instructive, and is played on both sides with great care.

(l) Threatening mate in two moves.

(From the *Schachzeitung*).

(*Evans' Gambit.*)

GAME 168.

The two following games serve to illustrate what may, perhaps, prove to be the best defence in the Mortimer's form of the Evan's Gambit:—

White. (Mr. MORTIMER).	Black. (Mr. ROSENTHAL.)
1. P. to K. fourth	1. P. to K. fourth
2. K. Kt. to B. third	2. Q. Kt to B. third
3. K. B. to Q. B. fourth	3. K. B. to Q. B. fourth
4. P. to Q. Kt. fourth	4. B. takes Q. Kt. P.
5. P. to Q. B. third	5. B. to Q. B. fourth
6. Castles	6. P. to Q. third
7. P. to Q. fourth	7. P. takes P.
8. P. takes P.	8. B. to Q. Kt. third
9. Q. Kt. to B. third	9. Q. B. to K. Kt. fifth
10. Q. to Q. R. fourth	10. B. to Q. second
11. Q. to Q. Kt. third	11. Kt. to Q. R. fourth
12. K. B. takes P. (check)	12. K. to B. square
13. Q. to Q. B. second	13. K. takes B.
14. P. to K. fifth	14. P. to K. R. third
15. P. to Q. fifth	15. K. Kt. to B. third
16. P. to K. sixth (check)	16. K. to Kt. square (*a*)
17. P. takes B.	17. Q. takes P. (*b*)
18. P. to K. R. third	18. P. to K. Kt. fourth
19. K. R. to K. square	19. K. to Kt. second
20. R. to K. sixth	20. K. R. to K. B. square
21. Q. to K. B. fifth	21. Kt. to Q. B fifth
22. Kt. to K. fourth (*c*)	22. Kt. takes Kt. (*d*)
23. R. to K. Kt. sixth (ch.)	23. K. to R. second
24. Q. takes Q. (check)	24. K. takes R.
25. Q. to K. sixth (check)	25. Kt. to K. B. third
26. P. to K. R. fourth (*e*)	26. Q. R. to Q. square
27. P. to K. R. fifth (check)	27. K. takes P.
28. Q. to K. B. fifth	28. B. takes K. B. P. (ch.) (*f*)
29. K. to R. square	29. Kt. to K. Kt. fifth
30. Q. to Q. third	30. R. takes Kt.
31. P. takes R.	

And Black mates in four moves.

NOTES.

(*a*) This is unquestionably less dangerous than taking Pawn with Bishop and bringing the King out into the middle of the board.

(*b*) Mr. Mortimer's analysis breaks off here with the remark that White has unquestionably the better game, his position being more than an equivalent for the single Pawn. The result of this and the companion game, however, seems to render this somewhat doubtful.

Position after Black's 21st move.

BLACK.

WHITE.

(c) White does not take sufficient advantage of his position. Had he played Kt. takes Kt. P., he could hardly have failed to win the game, e.g.—

22. Kt. takes Kt. P.	22. P. takes Kt. (or A.)
23. Q. takes P. (check)	23. K. to R. square
24. R. takes Kt.	24. R. takes R. (best)
25. Q. takes R. (check)	25. K. to Kt. square (best)
26. B. to K. R. sixth, with a very superior game.	

A.

	22. Kt to K. fourth (or B.)
23. Q. Kt. to K. fourth	23. B. to Q. 5 (we see nothing better)
24. Kt. takes Kt.	24. B. takes R. (best)
	[If 24. P. takes Kt.
25. Kt. to R. fifth (check)	25. K. to R. square
26. R. to R. sixth (check)	26. K. to Kt. square
27. Q. takes P. (check)	27. K. to B. second
28. R. to B. sixth (check)	28. K. to K. square (best)
29. Kt. to K. Kt. seventh (check) wins.]	
25. Kt. to R. fifth (check)	25. K. to R. square
26. R. takes P. (check)	26. K. to Kt. square
27. Kt. to K. B. sixth (check)	27. R. takes Kt.
28. Q. takes R.	28. Q. to K. Kt. second (best)
29. Q. to K. sixth (check) wins.	

B.

	22. B. to Q. fifth
23. Kt. to K. second	23. B. takes R. (or C.)
24. Kt. to K. B. fourth	24. P. takes Kt. (best)
25. Q. takes P. (check)	25. K. to R. second (best)
26. Kt. to Kt. sixth, and play as Black may, White must win.	

C.

	23. P. takes Kt.
24. Q. takes P. (check)	24. K. to R. square.
25. Kt. takes B., and White must win.	

(d) The best move. Black now loses his Queen, but he obtains a fair equivalent, and the attack and position are henceforth in his favour.

(e) White, if we mistake not, ought at once to have withdrawn the Queen from her dangerous position, abandoning for a time the attempt to keep up an attack.

(f) The terminating moves are beautifully played by M. Rosenthal. From this point he has a won game.

Consultation game, played by telegraph between Dublin and London, Oct. 5, 1865. Dublin, Messrs. Mills, Rynd, and Thacker. London, Messrs. Baker, Howard, and Kebble.

GAME 169.
(Evan's Gambit.) :

[Moves 1 to 17 the same as in the last game.]

White. (DUBLIN).	Black. (LONDON.)
18. P. to K. R. third	18. Q. R. to K. square (a)
19. Kt. to K. R. fourth	19. P. to K. Kt. fourth
20. Kt. to K. Kt. sixth	20. R. to K. R. second
21. K. to R. square	21. Kt. to Q. B. fifth
22. P. to K. B. fourth	22. Kt. to K. sixth (b)
23. B. takes Kt.	23. R. takes B.
24. Q. R. to K. square	24. Q. to K. square
25. R. takes R.	25. Q. takes R.
26. K. to R. second	26. P. to K. R. fourth (c)
27. P. to K. Kt. third (d)	27. P. to K. R. fifth
28. Kt. P. takes P.	28. P. takes R. P.
29. Kt. to K. second (e)	29. Kt. to K. fifth
30. R. to K. Kt. square	30. K. to B. second
31. R. to K. Kt. second	31. K. to K. square
32. Q. to Q. R. fourth (check)	32. K. to Q. square
33. Kt. to K. B. eighth	33. Kt. to Q. seventh
34. Q. to Q. square	34. Kt. to K. B. sixth (check)
35. K. to R. square	35. Kt. to K. eighth (f)

And Black must win.

NOTES.

(a) This we believe to be a better move than P. to K. Kt. fourth, as played in the last game.

(b) The Black allies rightly seek exchange, foreseeing the weakness of White's Q. P. in the end game, and having an eye also to a more decisive blow by R. takes K. R. P. (check).

(c) Threatening Kt. to K. Kt. fifth (check) with fatal effect.

(d) The best move.

(e) Could White take this move better? It seems an error to admit Black's Kt. into their game.

(f) An excellent stroke of play, which must have proved decisive in a few more moves. At this point, owing to the lateness of the hour, the game was abandoned. But what can White do? They are threatened with mate in three moves; while if

36. Q. takes Kt.	36. Q. takes R. P. (check)
37. R. to R. second	37. Q. to K. B. sixth (check)
38. R. to Kt. second	38. P. to K. R. sixth, and wins.

The most feasible move apparently is—

36. Kt. to Kt. square	36. Kt. takes R.
37. Kt. takes R.	37. Kt. takes K. B. P.

and Black must win easily. They now threaten Q. to K. B. seventh.

GAME 170.

In the following game the Rev. W. Wayte gives the odds of the Pawn and move to Mr. Fenton, of the Bath Chess Club:—

White. (Mr. FENTON.)	Black. (Mr. WAYTE.)
1. P. to K. fourth	1. P. to Q. third
2. P. to Q. fourth	2. K. Kt. to B. third
3. Q. Kt. to B. third	3. P. to K. fourth
4. P. to Q. fifth (a)	4. B. to K. second
5. P. to K. R. third	5. Castles
6. K. Kt. to B. third	6. P. to Q. B. third
7. P. takes P.	7. P. takes P.
8. B. to Q. B. fourth (ch.)	8. K. to R. sq.
9. Castles	9. B. to Q. R. third
10. B. to Q. third	10. B. takes B.
11. P. takes B.	11. Q. Kt. to Q. second (b)
12. Kt. to K. Kt. fifth	12. Q. to Q. Kt. third (c)
13. Kt. to K. sixth	13. R. to K. B. second
14. B. to K. third	14. Q. to Q. Kt. second (d)
15. P. to K. B. fourth	15. P. to K. R. third
16. P. takes P.	16. Q. Kt. takes P.
17. Q. Kt. to K. second	17. Q. to Q. second
18. Q. to Q. Kt. third	18. P. to Q. fourth
19. P. takes P.	19. P. takes P.
20. K. Kt. to. K. B. fourth	20. B. to Q. sq. (e)
21. B. to Q. fourth	21. Kt. to Q. B. third
22. B. takes K. Kt.	22. B. takes B.
23. Kt. takes P.	23. B. takes Q. Kt. P.
24. Q. takes B.	24. R. takes R. (ch.)
25. R. takes R.	25. Q. takes Kt.
26. Q. to Q. Kt. seventh	26. R. to K. sq.
27. Kt. to K. B. fourth	27. Q. to Q. fifth (ch.)

28. K. to R. sq.	28. Kt. to K. fourth
29. Q. to Q. Kt. fifth (*f*)	29. R. to K. B. sq. (*g*)
30. R. to K. sq.	30. R. takes Kt.
31. Q. takes Kt. (*h*)	31. R. to K. B. eighth (ch.)
32. K. to R. second	32. Q. to K. Kt. eighth (ch.)
33. K. to Kt. third	33. R. takes R.

And White resigns.

NOTES.

(*a*) K. Kt. to B. third is a better move.

(*b*) Black would have saved himself some trouble by now moving P. to K. R. third.

(*c*) Compulsory. It was necessary to prevent the adverse Q. from going to Q. Kt. third.

(*d*) Taking the Q. Kt. P., either on this move or the next, would have been dangerous.

(*e*) The only move to avoid the loss of a Pawn. Black's position was a difficult one.

(*f*) Threatening, if Black played away the Rook, to take Kt. with Q. Black manages, however, "out of the nettle danger to pluck the flower safety."

(*g*) The winning move, play as White may.

(*h*) If R. takes Kt. mates follows in three moves.

GAME 171.
(*Bishop's Gambit*).

White. (MR. WAYTE.)	Black. (MR. THOROLD.)
1. P. to K. fourth	1. P. to K. fourth
2. P. to K. B. fourth	2. P. takes P.
3. K. B. to Q. B. fourth.	3. K. Kt. to B. third (*a*)
4. Q. Kt. to B. third	4. P. to Q. fourth (*b*)
5. Kt. takes P.	5. Kt. takes Kt.
6. B. takes Kt.	6. B. to Q. third
7. K. Kt. to B. third	7. Castles (*c*)
8. Castles	8. P. to Q. B. third
9. B. to Q. Kt. third	9. B. to K. third
10. P. to Q. fourth	10. B. takes B.
11. R. P. takes B.	11. Kt. to Q. second
12. P. to K. fifth	12. B. to Q. B. second
13. B. takes P.	13. B. to Q. Kt. third
14. P. to Q. Kt. fourth	14. Q. to K. second
15. P. to Q. B. third	15. P. to K. R. third
16. Q. to K. sq.	16. P. to Q. R. fourth
17. P. takes P.	17. R. takes P.
18. R. takes R.	18. B. takes R.
19. Q. to K. Kt. third (*d*)	19. Q. to K. third

20. B. to K. third	20. B. to Q. Kt. third
21. Kt. to K. R. fourth	21. P. to K. B. fourth
22. Kt. to K. Kt. sixth	22. R. to K. B. second (e)
23. Kt. to K. B. fourth	23. Q. to K. sq.
24. P. to K. sixth	24. R. to K. second
25. P. takes Kt.	25. Q. takes P.
26. Kt. to K. R. fifth	26. Q. to K. third
27. B. to Q. second	27. Q. to K. B. second
28. Q. to K. B. third	28. P. to K. Kt. third
29. Kt. to K. Kt. third	29. P. to Q. B. fourth
30. P. takes P.	30. B. takes P. (check)
31. K. to R. sq.	31. R. to Q. second
32. B. takes P.	32. Q. to Q. B. fifth
33. R. to Q. sq.	33. R. to K. second
34. Kt. takes P.	34. P. takes Kt. (f)

And White mates in six moves.

NOTES.

(a) Probably the best defence in the Bishop's Gambit.

(b) It is better, if Black intends to sacrifice the Q. P., to do so at the third move. Q. Kt. to B. third would now be stronger. See the Games of the Congress, p. 99.

(c) After this move the Gambit Pawn is indefensible, since P. to K. Kt. fourth would now be too hazardous.

(d) The attack is now rapidly becoming irresistible.

(e) This loses a piece, but R. to K. sq. would have been answered by B. takes K. R. P. with decisive effect.

(f) R. to K. B. second would have been unavailing; White would have replied with B. to K. Kt. fifth, prepared to check with Q. either at K. R. third or K. R. fifth, according to Black's play.

The following casual game was recently at the Divan in the Strand by Mr. Minchin against Herr Steinitz :—

GAME 172.

(*Evans's Gambit.*)

White. (Mr. MINCHIN.)	*Black.* (HERR STEINITZ.)
1. P. to K. fourth	1. P. to K. fourth
2. K. Kt. to B. third	2. Q. Kt. to B. third
3. K. B. to Q. B. fourth	3. K. B. to Q. B. fourth
4. P. to Q. Kt. fourth	4. B. takes P.
5. P. to Q. B. third	5. B. to Q. B. fourth
6. P. to Q. fourth	6. P. takes P.
7. P. takes P.	7. B. to Q. Kt. fifth (check) (a)
8. K. to B sq..	8. Q. to K. second (b)
9. P. to K. fifth	9. P. to K. B. third

10. P. takes P.	10. Kt. takes P.
11. Q. B. to K. Kt. fifth	11. P. to Q. Kt. third
12. P. to Q. R. third	12. B. to Q. third
13. R. to Q. R. second (c)	13. Q. to K. B. sq.
14. R. to K. second (check)	14. B. to K. second
15. Q. Kt. to B. third	15. Q. B. to Kt. second
16. K. Kt. to K. fifth	16. Castles (Q. R.) (d)
17. Kt. to K. B. seventh	17. P. to Q. fourth
18. Kt. takes Q. R.	18. Q. takes Kt.
19. Q. B. takes Kt.	19. B. takes B.
20. B. takes P.	20. B. takes P.
21. R. to Q. second (e)	21. B. takes Kt.
22. B. to K. sixth (check)	22. K. to Q. Kt. sq.
23. R. takes Q.	23. R. takes R.
24. Q. to Q. R. fourth (f)	24. R. to Q. fifth
25. Q. to Q. B. second	25. B. to Q. R. third (check)
26. K. to Kt. sq.	26. R. to Q. seventh
27. Q. to Q. B. sq.	27. Kt. to Q. fifth
28. B. to K. Kt. fourth	28. Kt. to K. seventh (check)
29. B. takes Kt.	29. B. takes B.
30. P. to K. R. fourth	30. R. to Q. eighth (check)
31. K. to R. second	31. R. takes Q.
32. R. takes R.	32. B. to K. B. third (g)

And Mr. Steinitz wins.

NOTES.

(a) B. to Kt. third is here generally preferred.
(b) Mr. Steinitz is of opinion that this is the best defence Black can adopt at this point, as it not only brings the Queen into play, but also provides for the safety of the King's Bishop.

Position after White's 21st move.

BLACK.

WHITE.

(c) In order to bring the Rook into immediate co-operation.
(d) Mr. Steinitz willingly gives up the exchange to free his game.
(e) If—

21. B. takes Kt.	21. B. takes B.
22. R. to Q. second	22. Q. to K. Kt. fourth
23. R. takes B.	23. Q. takes Kt. P. (check)
24. K. to K. second	24. R. to K. square (check)
25. K. to Q. second	25. Q. takes B. P. (check)

And White cannot save the game.

(f) Had White played the Queen to Kt. third Black would have replied with B. to R third (check), followed by R. to Q. seventh, &c. Q. to Q. Kt. square might have given Black some trouble, but he would win in any case.

(g) The termination is a good example of Herr Steinitz's play.

CHESS INTELLIGENCE.

SHEFFIELD ATHENÆUM CHESS CLUB.

A tournament has, during the past three months, been held in connection with this Club. The prize consisted of a handsome set of Chessmen, with board, which were presented to the Club by Dr. J. C. Hall. The tournament was conducted on the handicap principle, and on the plan of each competitor contesting one game, exclusive of draws, with every other combatant. The contest created much interest, and the plan upon which it was conducted gave general satisfaction. The following was the system of handicapping:—

1st Division gave Pawn and move to 2nd Division.
" " " Pawn and two moves to 3rd Division.
" " " Knight to 4th Division.
" " " Knight and Bishop to 5th Division.
2nd " " Pawn and move to 3rd Division.
" " " Pawn and two moves to 4th Division.
" " " Knight and move to 5th Division.
3rd " " Pawn and move to 4th Division.
" " " Knight to 5th Division.
4th " " Pawn and two moves to 5th Division.

The following shows the result:—

1ST DIVISION.

	Won.	Lost.
Mr. W. Cockayne	9	7
" Latham	19	4
" Mort	17	5

2ND DIVISION.

	Won.	Lost.
" Bennett	19	4
" Champion	12	9
" Cocking	17	5
" Greening	10	10
" Pearson	8	15

3RD DIVISION.

	Won.	Lost.
" Herbert	8	8
" Padley	5	9
" Shallcross	6	9
" Shaw	9	8
Mr. Taylor	4	5

4TH DIVISION.

	Won.	Lost.
" Algar	5	9
" Allott	6	17
" Anderson	10	10
" Brownell	6	10
" E. Cockayne	13	8
" B. Cockayne	5	8
" Edwards	7	10
" S. Smith	8	8
" Staniforth	9	10

5TH DIVISION.

	Won.	Lost.
" Mr. Berly	11	12
" Cubley	0	23

The deciding game between Messrs. Latham and Bennett was won by Mr. Latham, who thus became the winner of the prize.

WEST YORKSHIRE CHESS ASSOCIATION.

We subjoin the following from the *Huddersfield Examiner*, June 2, 1866:—

The eleventh annual meeting of this association was held at the Victoria Hotel, Leeds, on May 26. The room was open for chess-play at twelve o'clock, but it was after four in the afternoon before play in the tournaments commenced, and, as our readers will see, this did not leave time for the various matches being brought to a satisfactory termination. There were about fifty players present from different parts of the Riding, the principal of which were Messrs. Cadman, Myers, Luccock, Winterbottom, Pullan, &c., from Leeds; Messrs. Watkinson, Marsden, and Finlinson, from Huddersfield; Messrs. Hunter, Tomlinson, Young, and Robinson, from Wakefield; and Messrs. Broughton, Fieldsend, Milligan, Ferrand, and Heselton, from Bradford. Amongst the visitors who honoured the gathering with their presence were the Rev. A. B. Skipworth, B.A., of Bilsdale, Dr. Wilson, of Claycross, and G. H. Taylor, Esq., of Houghton-le-Spring.

Mr. Rhodes, the esteemed president of the association for the year, was prevented from being present by domestic affliction.

Several tournaments were formed in the course of the afternoon.

The first class tournament was entered by the following gentlemen, who, in the first round were paired by lot as follows:—Mr. Watkinson against Mr. Marsden, both of Huddersfield; Mr. Skipworth, of Bilsdale, against Mr. Young, of Wakefield; Mr. Taylor, of Houghton-le-Spring, against Mr. Mort, of Sheffield; Mr. W. Fieldsend, of Bradford, against Mr. Pope, of Leeds.

Mr. Marsden declined entering the lists against Mr. Watkinson, and so the latter gentleman walked over the course. Mr. Skipworth, after a sharp skirmish, defeated Mr. Young. Mr. Fieldsend won off Mr. Pope. The first game between Mr. Taylor and Mr. Mort was a very fine one, and, after some very critical and interesting play, ended in a draw. The second game was scored by Mr. Taylor, as his opponent had to leave by train, and according to the decision of the committee this was deemed equivalent to losing the game. In the second round, Mr. Watkinson was paired against Mr. Skipworth, and Mr. Taylor against Mr. Fieldsend. To take the latter couple first, Mr. Taylor conquered Mr. Fieldsend after a stiff contest. After a long encounter between Mr. Watkinson and Mr. Skipworth, the game appearing pretty equal, Mr. Watkinson was obliged to leave the game unfinished, in order to leave by the last train, and so Mr. Skipworth was adjudged to be the winner. This left Mr. Skipworth and Mr. Taylor to contend for the first prize, and Mr. Skipworth making a mis-calculation, it was ot once taken advantage of by his opponent, and thus Mr. Taylor came off the final winner.

To show the very unsatisfactory nature of our game tournaments, especially when commenced at such a late hour, it may be stated that Mr. Taylor is in the habit of receiving the large odds of the Knight from Mr. Watkinson.

In the second tournament, Mr. Winterbottom, of Leeds, won the first prize, and Mr. Ball, of York, the second. In the third tournament Messrs. Robinson, of Wakefield, and Finlinson, of Huddersfield, were the winners in the second round, and time not allowing the game to be played out, they agreed to divide the prize.

There was a very pleasant interruption of the chess-play at six o'clock in the shape of a substantial tea, which was done ample justice to by the assemblage, after which the routine business of the association was transacted, Wakefield being unanimously chosen as the next place of meeting.

The Rev. A. B. Skipworth has spent a day or two in Huddersfield during his visit to this part of the country, and a match to consist of the first winner of seven games has been commenced between Mr. Watkinson and himself. Only one game has been contested which terminated in favour of the Huddersfield player. The match will not, however, be continued for some months.

CROYDON WORKMEN'S CLUB.—On Friday, June 15, an interesting meeting was held at the above workmen's club. In connection with this institution a Chess club has been for some time in operation. The late president of the club having retired in consequence of his departure from that town, Mr. W. G. Medley has been unanimously elected president of the club. On the above-mentioned day the newly chosen president made his first visit to the club, and was installed in his office. The hon. secretary, Mr. Lawnes, introduced Mr. Medley to the members of the institution, who had mustered in large numbers on the occasion. In his introductory remarks Mr. Lawnes congratulated the society upon having the good fortune to secure so distinguished an amateur for their chief, whose influence and position in the Chess world could not otherwise than prove beneficial to the interests of the club. Mr. Medley, in thanking the members for the kind reception they had given him, observed that, when offered the presidentship, he had scruples about accepting that honour, considering his many other duties and occupations. The consideration, however, of being able to contribute to the cause of Chess determined him to accept the post, and he assured the members that he would exert his best endeavours to promote the interests of Chess not only in the club, but also in the whole district. Mr. Lowenthal was also present on the occasion, and played some games with the strongest members. A vote of thanks to Mr. Medley and Mr. Lowenthal terminated the proceedings.

A friendly match at Chess took place at Ipswich on Friday evening last, between the Ipswich and Colchester Clubs. Fortune, on this occasion, as usual (according to the Napoleonic dictum), declared herself in favour of the side possessing the largest battalions. Several games, however, were stubbornly contested, and excited much interest. One played by the Rev. C. S. Lock, president of the Colchester Club, and Mr. J. Gocher, the Ipswich champion ; and two other games between the same comba'ants, one of which was scored by the Essex, the other by the Suffolk player. Dr. Bree (C.) won two games and lost one, against Mr. Vulliamy (I.); Dr. Wallace (C.) and Dr. Chevallier (I.) each scored a game; Mr. A. M. White (C.) lost two games to Mr. T. Gocher (I.), drawing the third ; Dr. Williams (C.) lost three games to Mr. Cooke (I.); Mr. Pennyfeather (C.) had to yield two games to Mr. Staddon (I.); and Mr. Brightwell (C.) having lost one to his antagonist, Mr. Slater (I.), was compelled to leave the second unfinished, though it is right to say that it was very much in Mr. Brightwell's favour when it had to be abandoned. We hope shortly to hear that a return match has been arranged, when the Colchester club will have an opportunity of reciprocating the courteous hospitality of their *friendly foes* at Ipswich.—*From a Special Correspondent.*

THE RETURN MATCH BETWEEN THE WORCESTER AND BIRMINGHAM CHESS CLUBS.—On Whit Monday nine members of the Worcester club visited Birmingham, and contested a series of games against the same number of Birmingham players. The combatants were matched against each other according to strength; and it was arranged that three games should be contested at each board. The subjoined score, however, will show that time did not in all cases allow this plan to be carried out:—

Won by Birmingham.		Won by Worcester.		Drawn or Unfinished.
3	Mr. T. Avery	0	Lord Lyttelton	...
1	Rev. S. W. Earnshaw	1	Mr. Parrott	...
1	Mr. H. A Fry	2	Rev. J. F. Eld	...
0	Dr. Freeman	1	Mr. Harrison	1
1	Rev. T. Yarranton	2	Mr. Zacchary	...
2	Mr. H. S. Hill	1	Mr. Wood	...
1	Mr. J. Halford	1	Mr. Gillain	1
1	Mr. E. Warren	0	Mr. Woodward	1
2	Mr. S. Kempson	1	Mr. Sylvester	...
12		9		3

Majority for Birmingham—three games.

PLAYING FOR A MAN'S HEAD.—During the "Terror" few came to play at the Café de la Régence. People had not the heart, and it was not pleasant to see through the panes the cars bearing the condemned through the Rue St. Honoré to execution. Robespierre often took a seat, but few had any wish to play with him, such terror did the insignificant looking little man strike into every one's heart. One day a very handsome young man sat opposite him, and made a move as a signal for a game; Robespierre responded, and the stranger won. A second game was played and won, and then Robespierre asked what was the stake. "The head of a young man," was the answer, "who would be executed to-morrow. Here is the order for his release, wanting only your signature; and be quick—the executioner will give no delay." It was young Count B. that was thus saved. The paper was signed, and the great man asked, "But who are you citizen?" "Say citizeness, monsieur; I am the count's betrothed. Thanks and adieu."—*Dublin University Magazine.*

DISTINGUISHED VISITORS. In the course of last month we had the pleasure of receiving in London some distinguished visitors— M. Arnaud de Riviere, the French champion, Herr Hirschfeldt, and Herr Meyer, the famous problem composer. These gentlemen visited the different Chess Clubs, and engaged in several interesting games.

Problem No. 86. By C. R. Alexander, Esq.

BLACK.

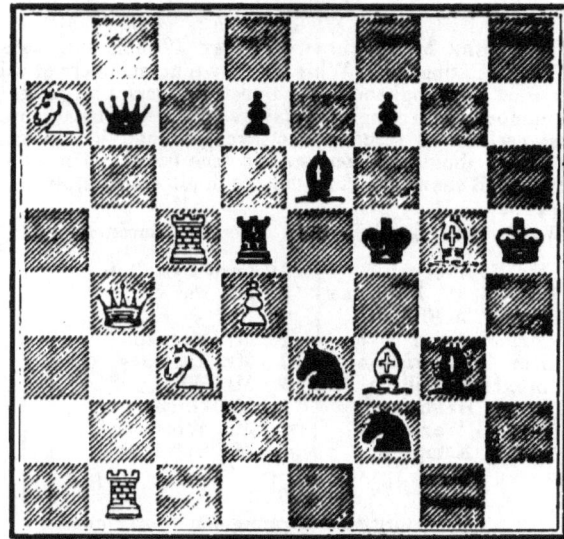

WHITE.

White to play, and mate in four moves.

Problem No. 87. By T. Smith, Esq.

BLACK.

WHITE.

White to play, and mate in four moves.

Problem No. 88. By Herr KLETT.

White to play, and mate in four moves.

Problem No. 89. By Herr H. MEYER, of Hanover.

White to play, and mate in three moves.

Chess Study No. 22 By W. T. Pierce, Esq.

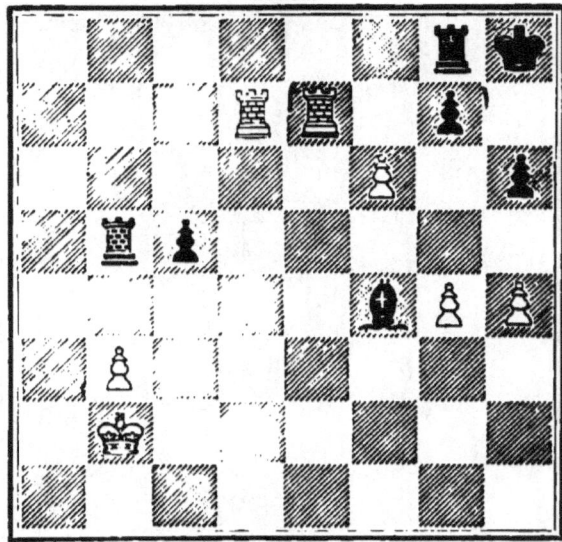

White to move, and draw.

Chess Study No. 23. By Herr Kling.

White to move, and win.

The Chess Player's Magazine.

THE ENGLISH CHALLENGE CUP.

WHATEVER other results may spring from the meeting of the British Chess Association in 1866, it will ever be memorable for the establishment of the Challenge Cup, open to all English players. There have been ere now, we believe, cups competed for at the London Chess Club, the famous Cochrane having successfully fleshed his maiden sword on one or more of these occasions. These contests, however, unless we are mistaken, were strictly private, and emanated from the liberality of a single person; they were not of an open character, nor did they at any time receive the ratification of a public body. But now the Association steps forward and institutes what ought to be to British Chess that which the classic games were to the athletes of ancient Greece. There are few Chess-players perhaps who will be inclined to deny that the Association ought to do something for English Chess, apart from general encouragement of the game, if it can do so advantageously; the difficulty is to decide on the best course. We do not think that a central body could do better than it has done by the institution of this Cup. For, as the Queen's Prize at Wimbledon for Volunteers leads to a great number of local contests in order to determine who are the best shots in the respective corps, that they may take part in the grand meeting at head-quarters, so this Chess Cup, when it comes to be more bruited about, is likely to lead to similar enterprise in the provincial clubs. All cannot contend, that is clear; we hope, therefore, to see the day when every good club will be represented by at least one champion. It would be absurd to run away with the notion, that because there were but few entries upon this the first occasion, therefore little interest is, or will be, taken in the matter. The Grand Challenge Cup at Henley Regatta sprang out of even smaller beginnings. Upon the whole, it is better that the contest should have been of a somewhat narrow character this time, as it enabled the committee to experimentalise on mere details without endangering the permanent success of the institution. It would have been a somewhat perilous honour for the winner to style himself the champion of English Chess,

> "Assume the god,
> Affect to nod,
> And seem to shake the spheres,"

before all opposition to the undertaking was disarmed by showing its perfectly fair and impartial nature. The winner, whoever he may turn out to be, has, however, a right to demand that his success be not grudged or carped at by those who were absent. There are, of course, reasons in abundance—such as want of leisure, ill-health, and other casualties—why particular amateurs cannot play at a given time; this, therefore, is an excellent excuse for their non-appearance, but would be none at all for envying another's laurels. We must take the winner as the best in the field; true, a champion "rose would smell as sweet by any other name," but then many a flower of this description is what Horace would call "*sera rosa*," or a late rose.* All honour, at the same time, to those flowers, if they really are roses, which either have too tardily come into bloom, or have suffered decay. None of us can expect to be always in full-blown perfection; let us then agree to clear ourselves off, and make room for the younger and more vigorous.

We will take it for granted that every generous spirit is prepared to do justice to the several winners of such cups; it is essential, therefore, to insure, as far as is possible, the best quality coming into competition. Matters of detail may, as a rule, be safely left in the hands of the managing committee which inaugurates and subsequently carries out such contests. The journalist has, how-

---

* Moore, as some of our readers will remember, thus translates the passage from Horace—

> "Rosa quo locorum,
> Sera moretur."
> "At which of his places old Rose is delaying."

ever, his duty to perform in subjects of public interest. We will, consequently, mention one or two conditions which appear to be indispensable to give permanence to the praiseworthy scheme of the Association. It is, above all things, necessary that, whenever a contest for a cup take place, the series of matches be played off at once consecutively. The reason is obvious. Many an amateur would gladly give a certain definite time, say July or August, though the hottest months are scarcely the best that can be chosen for Chess—but this is comparatively immaterial—to such an engagement; but if, instead of being continuous, it is broken off by intervals, circumstances would place this completely out of his power. This would be especially the case with good country players. We may again borrow an illustration from the Queen's Prize for the rifle corps at Wimbledon. This has been gained by Volunteers from Shropshire and Scotland, the openness of the prize being its most prominent feature. It is clear that unless the shooting were to be continued from day to day, these valuable supporters of the meeting could never stop at head-quarters until the matches were finished. *Mutatis mutandis*, it would be so with the Chess Cup. Under a railway system, country play is far too important an element in English Chess to be neglected. In other words, we want to see in the field the best play that can possibly be found in the British dominions, whether it be in the metropolis, in the provinces, or even in the colonies. The Challenge Cup cannot be put upon too broad a basis if it is to be a permanent institution, and if the country at large is to take an interest in the matter.

According to the present arrangements, the Cup is to be competed for biennially, and not to become the property of the winner unless gained twice consecutively. We cannot think this an improvement on the model of the Grand Challenge Cup at Henley Regatta. There the contest is annual, and the winner must gain the Cup three times in succession before he can call it absolutely his own. The experience of these practical Henley men is worth the consideration of the managing committee of the Association. We are aware of the difficulty which will be started. It is thought that the Association itself cannot meet to effect any good more frequently than once in two years, and that the Cup must therefore apse with the interregnum. This does not, however, seem to be a forced conclusion, as a meeting might take place for the purpose of having the Cup played for, and not for any other object. Besides, is it wise to decide that the meetings of the Association shall be biennial, and not annual? We apprehend that a mistaken idea has taken hold of some of the most zealous and loyal promoters of such assemblages. They always keep in eye a great field-day, whereas there may be in addition meetings of minor importance, yet not devoid of considerable utility. And there is this danger—if the Association become biennial, its supporters may become biennial also. Now what is needed by a British Chess Association is a list of permanent annual subscribers, so that it may calculate to a nicety the strength on which it can rely in the hour of action. We will connect what we have just said with our more immediate subject. The Challenge Cup is a new feature in the proceedings of the Association, and will of itself, we venture to prophesy, if properly managed, make a meeting. It is not the particular regatta or meeting which causes the success of the cups, but the cups which cause the success of the regatta.

We would leave the question as we have placed it. After all, matters of detail are best tested, and can only be ascertained with safety, by actual experience. The committee which has so ably planned will no doubt carry out in a satisfactory manner the necessary arrangements, preserving the original design where it is apparently faultless, and improving where improvement seems to be necessary. One thing is certain. The highest praise ought to be bestowed upon the public-spirited body which has asserted a principle destined, unless our hopes deceive us, to exercise the most important influence on the future condition of English Chess.

WHY NOT?

Is it not quite time for some Chess D'Israeli to give us a hot-pressed volume on the "Quarrels of Chess-players?" It has been the fashion for ever so long to speak of our fraternity as an *irritabile genus*, and under this decent Latin characterisation to convey the impression that not pure intellect alone is the god of the Chessboard, but that the cultivation of the pensive game hath its mingling of asperities and clashings with the better things that belong to it in as good a proportion as will be found in the more turbulent pursuits of the active world around. In truth, it is clear enough to any one conversant with the subject that passion and feeling, which contribute so largely to make up the springs of human action in other things, find scope and play in the circumstances of a Chess party as readily as under the conditions of any situation besides that can be named. It can hardly be doubted that it is a necessary law of human nature that every player is in some degree elated by victory, and that defeat is in no single case without its pang. That the feeling is keener with some than with others, and that while some exhibit it most discreditably, others are able to hide it completely under an outward composure, is perfectly true; but the necessary existence of the trait, as here intimated, is as clearly ascertained as anything of the kind can be. Failure is depletion. Success is the wine of life. Triumph is glorious champagne, with power to make a man's eye sparkle, and, taken in a certain measure, to intoxicate the strongest. There are some happy constitutions that can take heart of grace after a fall, and rise with fresh determination: these, in Chess and in life, generally win at last. But most of us are disheartened and weakened by failure, and its sure result in any case is pain. Success, on the other hand, invigorates, prompts to higher efforts, leads on to grander achievements, and is ever sweet to the taste of him it inspires. So at Chess every one is immediately affected, pleasantly or unpleasantly, by the issue of his play. The Prussian who felt Mr. Morphy's pulse at the conclusion of a lost game in an important match, and expressed his surprise at its calmness, by no means threw away his admiration; for self-possession in a trying situation, being the peculiar attribute of good-breeding, is of far higher account than any degree of skill in manœuvring the Chess forces; but the hero who at the time referred to stirred the sympathies of the French capital does not wear his heart upon his sleeve, and what motions were swelling too far below the surface for the public probe of eye or finger to reach, none may declare. That he felt the passing disaster less than other men would, from the consciousness of power and assurance of victory within him, may easily be believed; yet, doubtless, he endured some pain; and if he had been made of more penetrable stuff, friends and foes alike must have witnessed it.

It is one of the most noble triumphs of principle and will over the inferior part of human nature, so rampant in its perversions, when one has arrived at the ability to play Chess under any and all circumstances without ever forgetting to be a gentleman. As *he that ruleth his own temper is better than he that taketh a strong city*, so the ever-courteous and self-contained Chess-player hath a higher and rarer excellence than he that is a master in strategy and winner of games. This excellence is indeed difficult of attainment to a man of an irritable temperament; but not even to him is it impossible. If it were impossible, he ought to stop playing Chess, for then the game would be productive of more evil than good in his case. It is a serious mistake to suppose that study and the finest practice are incompatible with moral scrupulosity in this matter. Complete absorption in Chess studies is certainly unlawful; but not only would conscience and good manners suffer from this cause, but all the interests of life would be sacrificed with them. A due interest and diligence in the culture of the game will not only be found consistent with politeness and moral worth, but will even prove a special means for developing and strengthening both these important qualities. *Our* " divine philosophy . . . . is not harsh and crabbed," to continue the quotation no further, but hath its chords and sympathies, and its healthful points of contact with our fellow-creatures' world, as to be a good and true philosophy it must. If our players—and especially our strong players—will bear this in mind, and make their moral as well as their intellectual preparation for every Chess match they engage in, the " Quarrels of Chess-players" will be happily but a record of the past, and our D'Israeli will find the " Amenities" and " Curiosities" of the game and its history so large and growing a pile of materials, that after the issue of more than one bulky volume he will needs revive the " Chess-player's Annual," that all the good things may be saved and enjoyed.

N. R. W.

CHESS LITERATURE.

PONZIANI.—*Il Giuoco incomparabile degli Scacchi; per cura di M. Castelli.* Very large 8vo. Venezia, 1861.

The stream-tide of the "Incomparable Game of Chess" has been steadily flowing for many centuries from the east and south towards the west and north. Its circuitous route resembles that of the Gulf Stream from Mexico, only it begins in a contrary direction. From India, where the game had its undoubted origin, it flowed westwards through Persia, Arabia, and the north of Africa, whence it passed over into Spain more than a thousand years ago. About the end of our fifteenth and during the sixteenth centuries a few Peninsular authors favoured us with certain meagre treatises on the game, such as those of Lucena, Damiano, and Ruy Lopez. Before the time of these writers there existed not in Europe any work on the subject worth a moment's consideration on the part of the Chess student, with the exception of a few manuscript treatises in the languages of Persia and Arabia, which were to European readers at that early period so many sealed books.

In the seventeenth and eighteenth centuries Italy took the lead in the practice, theory, and literature of the noble game. Those were the days when there were Chess giants in that fair and sunny land! The 17th century produced Gianutio, Salvio, Carrera, and Greco; and in the latter half of the 18th, appeared Ercole dal Rio, Lolli, Cozio, and Ponziani. During this long period of three centuries, we *Tramontanes* contributed little or nothing towards the promotion or illustration of the *Giuoco incomparabile*. To be sure, Germany could boast of the ponderous work of Gustavus Silenus, and France that of Philidor—excellent works in their way, but by no means to be compared to those of the Italian masters.

The edition of Ponziani's valuable work now before us is the seventh. The first was printed at Modena in 1769, which was followed by a second and greatly improved one, at the same place, in 1782. Three very inferior editions were published at Venice between 1769 and 1812, being merely repetitions of the author's first. A sixth edition appeared at Rome in 1829, being a reprint of that of Modena, 1782; and lastly the work now before us, which far excels all its predecessors in every respect, being a careful reprint of the best Modenese edition—that of 1782. Ponziani's own games are given on a series of folding plates or tables, twenty-six in number. The notation adopted is that employed by Alexandre in his "Encyclopædia," Allgaier, Jaenisch, and other continental writers—a notation at once perspicuous and economical. The notes and observations occupy forty-four pages by themselves, enriched by numerous additional ones by the present editor. The third section of this work, from p. 107 to p. 152, is devoted to end-games, concluding with fifty select problems or positions, most if not all of which have been appropriated by more recent writers, either in our own country or on the continent.

In addition to the whole text of Ponziani's best edition, the Venetian editor has given us an appendix, in eight folding tables, with notes corresponding, on the same plan as that described above. This additional portion is devoted to the following Gambits—viz., the Evans, the Bishop's Gambit, the Cochrane, Muzio, and Allgaier Gambits, and, lastly, what the compiler calls "Il Gambitto Grande." All these are selected from the best authorities, both English and continental, and form a valuable supplement to the work of the junior Modenese, to whom most of them were unknown.

The mere English reader may form some faint idea of the great merits of Ponziani's work by a perusal of a very meagre translation of it, published in 8vo, London, 1820, by some sapient wight who calls himself J. S. Bingham, Esq. This nomenclature is supposed to be fictitious. The translator seems to have taken for his text the very worst edition he could have selected—viz., that of Venice, 1812. He further labours under the hallucination that he is translating the work of Ercole dal Rio—not that of Ponziani. From the circumstance that both Dal Rio and Ponziani were citizens of the ancient town of Modena, and published each his work anonymously, the former is not unfrequently confounded with the latter, and *vice versâ*.

In conclusion, we may mention one slight drawback, which applies not only to the work of Ponziani, but to those of the Italian masters in general, with the sole exception of Greco's Treatise. This drawback, however, affects merely the *openings*, which are somewhat modified by the pre-supposition that either party *may* Castle according to the mode adopted in Italy. The Castling, however, being once effected, we may safely apply to the work of Ponziani what Mr. Cochrane says with regard to that of Dal Rio—viz., "For my own part, I have little hesitation in saying that the brilliancy of play and accuracy in calculation which are apparent in the games of the [senior] Modenese have certainly never been excelled—perhaps never equalled."

D. F.

BRITISH CHESS ASSOCIATION. CONGRESS 1866.

In continuation of our report last month of this important meeting we now describe the later part of the proceedings—namely, from Monday, the last day of the meeting at St. James's Hall. The matches and the tournaments were continued at the London and St. George's Chess Clubs, attracting a large number of members and visitors, and the first round in the Handicap Tournament was concluded in favour of Herr Steinitz, Mr. V. Green,* Mr. Chinnery, Mr. Minchin, Mr. Mocatta, Mr. Mongredien, jun., Mr. S. Green, and Mr. MacDonnell. The winners were then paired off as follows:—

   Herr Steinitz .... v. Mr. MacDonnell.
   Mr. Chinnery .... v. ,, Mocatta.
   ,, Minchin .... v. ,, S. J. Green.
   ,, Mongredien, jun., v. ,, V. Green.

In this round Herr Steinitz has won one game of his opponent, whilst the other matches terminated in favour of Messrs. Mocatta, S. J. Green, and Mongredien. The winners have thus been paired: Mr. S. J. Green against Mr. Mongredien, jun., and Mr. Mocatta against the remaining candidate.

GRAND CHALLENGE CUP.—There were several highly-interesting contests in this tourney, the combatants being naturally stimulated to exertion by the handsome and valuable trophy for which they contended; in one or two instances, however, the players failed to exhibit powers of which they have repeatedly given evidence. The prize was eventually won by Mr. De Vere, who played his various games in a manner which entitles him to our praise for his originality and power of combination, and which fully merited the reward. If Mr. De Vere would set himself to the task of acquiring a perfect knowledge of the "openings," we would predict for him a brilliant career.

THE FIRST ANNUAL DINNER after the re-organisation of the British Chess Association took place at Willis's Rooms, King-street, St. James's, on Thursday, the 12th of July, under the presidency of Lord Lyttelton, Earl Dartrey being in the vice-chair. There was a good attendance of members, amongs whom were Sir T. Metcalfe, M. Wyvill, Esq., M.P., Colonel Ross, the Revs. MacDonnell and Salter, Herr Steinitz, and Messrs. Mongredien, De Vere, Strode, Medley, Hampton, Hewitt, Barber, and Lowenthal, &c. &c. After the usual introductory toasts, the noble president proposed "Success to the British Chess Association," and specially congratulated the members upon the satisfactory results of their first Congress after the re-organisation of their Society. The meeting, considered as the beginning of such efforts, had exceeded most of their expectations. His lordship then showed the great advantages accruing from such meetings to the Game of Chess, and hoped that the Managing Committee would never lose sight of the main object in view—namely, the diffusion of the game. As far

* Scoring his games against Mr. Gover, who was obliged by other engagements to retire from the contest.

as his lordship himself was concerned he might be permitted to say that he was anxious to see a knowledge of the game spread as widely as possible, and to that end the establishment of the British Chess Association upon a permanent basis, which had just now been accomplished, was a most important step. Anything he (Lord Lyttelton) could do to assist the Committee of this Association he would willingly perform. Various other toasts were subsequently proposed and responded to by Earl Dartrey, Sir T. Metcalfe, Mr. Wyvill, Mr. Mongredien, Mr. MacDonnell, Mr. Medley, Herr Steinitz, Mr. Lowenthal, &c., &c.

CHESS INTELLIGENCE.

MATCH BETWEEN ANDERSSEN AND STEINITZ.

This contest, which has been long looked forward to with interest by all Chess-players, commenced immediately after the arrival in London of the distinguished Professor Herr Anderssen about the third week in July. It will, perhaps, be remembered that we stated the match was for £100 a side; we may now add that the stakes are provided by Mr. Forster on the part of Herr Steinitz, and by some of the leading members of the Westminster Chess Club on the part of Herr Anderssen. The conditions are that the winner of the first eight games shall be declared the victor; that the games be played at the London, St. George's, and Westminster Chess Clubs alternately; and that these three Clubs give £20 to the loser. Up to the time of going to press seven games had been played, and the score stood as follows:—

    Herr Anderssen.............................. 3
    Herr Steinitz................................. 4

We reserve our criticism of the play until the match shall have been concluded.

WESTMINSTER CHESS CLUB.—A club under this title has just been formed at the Gordon Hotel, Covent Garden, by some of the leading Chess amateurs who used to meet at Simpson's Divan in the Strand, which has recently been converted into a dining-hall. A strong committee has been formed, consisting, as we understand, of Messrs. Staunton, MacDonnell, Cunningham, Hewitt, Barnes, Bird, Walsh, and several others, and Messrs. Boden, Duffy, and Burden have been appointed secretaries. We are glad to be able to report that the club has already a large number of members, and there can be little doubt that with so many eminent Chess-players and influential amateurs it must soon take rank among the most important of the metropolitan Chess institutions.

NOTICES TO CORRESPONDENTS.

DR. B., COLCHESTER.—We are grateful to you for calling our attention to an error in our last Number, which we hereby rectify by stating that in the match between the Ipswich and Colchester Clubs Mr. Locke won two games of Mr. Gocher. We shall examine into Dr. B.'s other statement.

GAMES.

MATCH BETWEEN ANDERSSEN AND STEINITZ.

GAME 173.

First Game. (*Evans's Gambit.*)

White. (MR. ANDERSSEN.)	Black. (MR. STEINITZ.)
1. P. to K. fourth	1. P. to K. fourth
2. Kt. to K. B. third	2. Kt. to Q. B. third
3. B. to B. fourth	3. B. to B. fourth
4. P. to Q. Kt. fourth	4. B. takes P.
5. P. to Q. B. third	5. B. to B. fourth
6. P. to Q. fourth	6. P. takes P.
7. Castles	7. P. to Q. third
8. P. takes P.	8. B. to Kt. third
9. P. to Q. fifth	9. Kt. to R. fourth
10. B. to Kt. second	10. K. Kt. to K. second (*a*)
11. B. to Q. third	11. Castles
12. Q. Kt. to B. third	12. P. to Q. B. third (*b*)
13. Q. Kt. to K. second	13. P. to K. B. fourth
14. Q. R. to B. square	14. K. B. P. takes P.
15. K. B. takes P.	15. Q. B. to B. fourth
16. B. takes B.	16. R. takes B.
17. P. takes P.	17. P. takes P. (*c*)
18. Q. Kt. to Q. fourth	18. R. to B. third
19. Kt. takes P.	19. K. Kt. takes Kt.
20. B. takes R.	20. Q. takes B.
21. R. takes Kt.	21. Kt. takes R.
22. Q. to Q. fifth (check)	22. Q. to B. second
23. Q. takes Kt.	23. R. to Q. square
24. P. to Q. R. fourth	24. P. to Q. fourth
25. R. to Q. square	25. P. to Q. fifth
26. R. to Q. third	26. Q. to B. fourth (*d*)

27. Q. to B. fourth (check)	27. K. to R. square
28. P. to K. R. third	28. R. to Q. B. square
29. Q. to Q. Kt. third	29. P. to K. R. third
30. P. to K. Kt. fourth	30. Q. to K. B. third
31. Q. to Q. fifth	31. R. to B. sixth
32. Kt. to K. fifth	32. R. to B. fourth (e)
33. Q. to R. eighth (check)	33. K. to R. second
34. Q. to K. fourth (check)	34. K. to Kt. square
35. Kt. to Kt. sixth	35. R. to B. sixth
36. Q. to K. eighth (check), and wins.	

NOTES.

(a) This counter-stroke, as was demonstrated by Mr. Paulsen, is the best resource in the second player's power.

(b) An invention of Mr. Steinitz, but "P. to Q. B. fourth" as adopted by Mr. Paulsen in positions of an analogous character, from the little examination we have been able to give, appears to be stronger.

(c) Apparently this confers on Black the advantage of two passed Pawns, but had he made the capture with the Q. Kt., he would have brought a valuable officer into immediate co-operation with the rest of his forces. In reality, a Pawn is lost without any compensation by the mode of play adopted.

Position after Black's 20th move.

BLACK.

WHITE.

(d) "Q. to Q. R. seventh" would equally menace the hostile Rook, and have also the advantage of preserving the diagonal to Black's own King, confining the White Queen, and placing the Q. R. P. in ultimate danger.

(e) Had he simply exchanged Rooks, he would have sustained no disadvantage. The move made is fatal on account of the Queen's check.

GAME 174.

Second Game. *(King's Knight's Gambit.)*

White. (MR. STEINITZ.)	Black. (MR. ANDERSSEN.)
1. P. to K. fourth	1. P. to K. fourth
2. P. to K. B. fourth	2. P. takes P.
3. K. Kt. to B. third	3. P. to K. Kt. fourth
4. B. to B. fourth	4. P. to Kt. fifth
5. Kt. to K. fifth	5. Q. to R. fifth (check)
6. K. to B. square	6. K. Kt. to R. third
7. P. to Q. fourth	7. P. to Q. third
8. Kt. to Q. third	8. P. to B. sixth
9. P. to Kt. third	9. Q. to R. sixth (check) (a)
10. K. to K. square	10. Q. to R. fourth (b)
11. Kt. to Q. B. third (c)	11. P. to Q. B. third
12. B. to Q. second	12. Q. to Kt. third
13. Kt. to B. fourth	13. Q. to B. third
14. B. to K. third	14. Kt. to Q. second
15. K. to B. second	15. K. Kt. to Kt. square
16. P. to K. fifth	16. Q. to K. second (d)
17. P. to K. sixth	17. P. takes P.
18. Kt. takes P.	18. Q. Kt. to K. B. third
19. B. to B. fourth	19. B. takes Kt.
20. B. takes B.	20. K. to Q. square
21. R. to K. square	21. Q. to Kt. second
22. P. to Q. fifth	22. P. to Q. B. fourth
23. Kt. to Q. Kt. fifth	23. Q. Kt. to K. square
24. Q. to Q. second	24. K. Kt. to B. third
25. Q. to R. fifth (check)	25. P. to Kt. third
26. Q. to R. fourth	26. Q. to Q. Kt. second
27. B. to K. Kt. fifth	27. B. to K. second
28. B. to B. seventh	28. Q. to Q. second
29. K. B. takes Q. Kt.	29. R. takes B.
30. R. to K. sixth	30. P. to Q. R. third
31. Q. R. to K. square	31. Q. takes Kt.
32. Q. takes Q.	32. P. takes Q.
33. B. takes Kt.	33. R. to R. second
34. R. takes P. (check)	34. R. to Q. second
35. K. R. to K. sixth	35. B. takes B.
36. R. takes R. (check)	36. K. to B. second
37. K. R. to K. sixth	37. B. takes P.

38. R. to K. seventh	38. B. to Q. fifth (check)
39. K. to B. square	39. R. takes R.
40. R. takes R. (check)	40. K to Q. third
41. R. takes R. P.	41. K. takes P.
42. R. to R. fourth	42. K. to Q. B. fifth
43. R. takes P.	43. K. to B. sixth
44. P. to R. fourth	44. K. takes P.
45. P. to R. fifth	45. B. to K. sixth
46. R. to B. fourth	46. P. to B. fifth
47. P. to R. sixth	47. B. takes R.
48. P. takes B.	48. P. to B. sixth
49. P. to R. seventh	49. K. to Kt. eighth
50. P. to R. eighth (Queens)	50. P. to B. seventh
51. Q. to R. seventh	51. K. to Kt. seventh
52. Q. to Kt. seventh (check)	52. K. takes P.
53. Q. to B. sixth, and wins (e)	

NOTES.

(a) It is scarcely conceivable that in a match of such importance so experienced a master should have made so obvious a slip—a result in this case clearly owing to carelessness. The blunder is the more unfortunate as it loses the game against a good player.

(b) There is no better resource to save the Queen. If she stops where she is, she is gained by "Kt. to K. B. fourth," and if she advance to K. Kt. seventh, by "Kt. to K. B. second," followed by "B. to K. B. square."

(c) "K. Kt. to K. B. fourth" is more immediately attacking.

(d) If he had captured the Pawn, the following variation might have occurred :—

	16. P. takes P.
17. P. takes P.	17. Kt. takes P. (we see no better move)
18. B. to Q. fourth	

Winning without difficulty.

(e) Mr. Steinitz took full advantage of his opponent's unhappy mistake, and played the whole of the game with great skill and energy.

GAME 175.

Third Game. (*Evans's Gambit.*)

White. (Mr. Anderssen.)	Black. (Mr. Steinitz.)
1. P. to K. fourth	1. P. to K. fourth
2. Kt. to K. B. third	2. Q. Kt. to B. third
3. B. to B. fourth	3. B. to B. fourth
4. P. to Q. Kt. fourth	4. B. takes P.

5. P. to Q. B. third	5. B. to B. fourth
6. P. to Q. fourth	6. P. takes P.
7. Castles	7. P. to Q. sixth (*a*)
8. Q. takes P. (*b*)	8. P. to Q. third
9. Q. B. to Kt. fifth	9. K. Kt. to K. second
10. Q. Kt. to Q. second	10. P. to K. R. third
11. Q. B. to R. fourth	11. Castles
12. Q. Kt. to Kt. third	12. B. to Kt. third
13. P. to K. R. third	13. B. to K. third
14. Q. R. to Q. square	14. Q. to Q. second
15. B. to Q. fifth	15. Kt. to Kt. third
16. B. to Kt. third	16. Q. R. to K. square
17. P. to Q. B. fourth	17. B. takes B.
18. K. P. takes B.	18. Q. Kt. to K. fourth
19. Kt. takes Kt.	19. Kt. takes Kt.
20. Q. to Q. B. third (*c*)	20. Kt. to Kt. third
21. P. to B. fifth	21. P. takes P.
22. Kt. takes P.	22. Q. to K. B. fourth
23. Kt. takes P.	23. R. to K. seventh
24. P. to Q. sixth	24. P. takes P.
25. Kt. takes P.	25. Q. to K. third
26. P. to Q. R. fourth	26. B. to Q. square
27. Q. to B. fifth (*d*)	27. P. to K. B. fourth (*e*)
28. Q. takes R. P. (*f*)	28. P. to B. fifth
29. B. to R. second	29. Kt. to R. fifth
30. Q. to Kt. seventh	30. Q. to Kt. third
31. R. to Q. fourth (*g*)	31. B. to Kt. third
32. Q. R. to Q. square	32. B. to K. third
33. P. to Q. R. fifth	33. B. to B. fourth
34. P. to Q. R. sixth	34. R. to K. second (*h*)
35. Q. to Q. fifth (check)	35. K. to R. square
36. P. to R. seventh (*i*)	36. B. takes P.
37. K. R. to K. square	37. R. takes R. (check)
38. R. takes R.	38. K. to R. second
39. Q. to K. fourth	39. R. to B. third
40. Kt. to Kt. fifth	40. R. to K. third
41. Q. takes Q. (check)	41. R. takes Q.
42. Kt. takes B.	42. R. takes P. (check)
43. K. to R. square	43. R. takes B. (check)
44. K. takes R.	44. Kt. to B. sixth (check)
45. K. to Kt. second	45. Kt. takes R. (check)
46. K. to B. square	46. Kt. to K. sixth

47. Kt. to B. sixth	47. K. to Kt. third
48. K. to K. second	48. Kt. to B. fourth
49. K. to B. third	49. Kt. to K. third
50. Kt. to K. fifth (check)	50. K. to B. fourth
51. Kt. to Q. third (*k*)	51. P. to Kt. third
52. Kt. to K square	52. Kt. to Q. fifth (check)
53. K. to Kt. second	53. K. to K. fifth
54. K. to B. square	54. P. to B. sixth
55. K. to Kt. square	55. P. to Kt. fourth
56. K. to R. second	56. P. to R. fourth
57. K. to Kt. third	57. Kt. to B. fourth (check)
58. K. to R. second	58. P. to Kt. fifth
59. P. takes P.	59. P. takes P.
60. K. to Kt. square.	60. K. to Q. fifth
61. Kt. to B. second (check)	61. K. to Q. sixth
62. Kt. to R. third (*l*)	62. P. to Kt. sixth
63. Kt. to Kt. fifth	63. P. to Kt. seventh

And wins.

NOTES.

(*a*) This defence is decidedly inferior to that springing from "P. to Q. third."

(*b*) Not nearly so strong as "Q. to Q. Kt. third." Curiously enough, so far as our memory serves us, Mr. Anderssen himself published in the *Berliner Schachzeitung* of 1851 an elaborate analysis demonstrating the inferiority of the move in the text.

(*c*) Threatening to win a piece by the advance of the Q. B. Pawn.

Position after White's 39th move.

(d) In manœuvring to gain the Pawn on his extreme left, White loses valuable time and position. It must be admitted, however, that just at this point the game assumes an extremely critical form.

(e) The best and promptest way of meeting his opponent's false attack.

(f) It is evident that he could not have taken the K. B. Pawn with his Knight, on account of the simple reply, "B. to Q. Kt. third."

(g) "Q. to Q. fifth (check)" would have given White some resource. The move made only increases his difficulties.

(h) A much safer mode of prosecuting the attack than the capture of the Knight would be.

(i) To save the Knight. Had he played that piece to Q. Kt. seventh, Black might have replied with R. to Q. second, and the White Queen could not have been removed to any square on which she would have been safe herself, and the threatened mate also averted. The finest part of this game is Black's continually skilful attack on the Knight, coupled with his forbearance from taking it inopportunely.

(k) It was afterwards suggested that Mr. Anderssen would have had a better chance of drawing the game if he had now moved his Knight to Q. B. fourth.

(l) This, of course, loses the game: Kt. to Kt. fourth (check) would have given him a chance to draw.

GAME 176.
Fourth Game.

White. (Mr. Steinitz.)	Black. (Mr. Anderssen.)
1. P. to K. fourth	1. P. to K. fourth
2. P. to. K. B. fourth	2. P. takes P.
3. K. Kt. to B. third	3. P. to K. Kt. fourth
4. B. to B. fourth	4. P. to Kt. fifth
5. Kt. to K. fifth	5. Q. to R. fifth (check)
6. K. to B. square	6. K. Kt. to R. third
7. P. to Q. fourth	7. P. to Q. third
8. Kt. to Q. third	8. P. to B. sixth
9. P. to Kt. third	9. Q. to K. second
10. Kt. to B. second (a)	10. B. to K. third
11. Q. Kt. to R. third	11. B. takes B.
12. Kt. takes B.	12. Q. to K. third
13. P. to Q. fifth	13. Q. to Kt. third
14. P. to K. R. third	14. Q. Kt. to Q. second
15. B. takes Kt.	15. B. takes B.
16. P. takes P.	16. P. to Q. Kt. fourth
17. Q. Kt. to R. third	17. Kt. to K. fourth
18. Kt. takes P.	18. Q. R. to Kt. square
19. Kt. to Q. fourth	19. B. to K. sixth (b)
20. Kt. takes P.	20. Q. to K. R. third
21. K. to Kt. second	21. B. takes Kt. (c)

22. Kt. takes Kt.	22. B. takes P. (d)
23. Kt. to Q. third	23. B. to R. fifth
24. Q. to K. second	24. Q. to K. second
25. Q. R. to K. B. square	25. B. to Kt. fourth
26. Q. R. to B. fifth	26. P. to K. B. third
27. K. R. to K. B. square	27. Castles (e)
28. P. to Q. Kt. third	28. Q. R. to K. square
29. K. R. to K. square	29. K. to R. square
30. Kt. to B. second	30. B. to R. fifth
31. R. to R. fifth	31. B. takes Kt.
32. Q. takes B.	32. K. R. to Kt. square
33. Q. to B. fifth	33. K. R. to Kt. second
34. Q. R. to R. sixth	34. Q. R. to K. Kt. square (f)
35. K. R. to K. R. square	35. K. R. takes P. (check)
36. K. to B. third	36. K. R. to Kt. sixth (check)
37. K. to K. second	37. K. R. to Kt. second
38. R. takes K. B. P.	38. K. R. to Kt. seventh (check)
39. K. to Q. third	39. Q. R. to Kt. sixth (ch.) (g)
40. K. to B. fourth	40. R. to K. sixth (h)
41. R. to B. eighth (check)	41. R. to Kt. square
42. R. takes R. (check)	42. K. takes R.
43. R. to Kt. square (check), and wins.	

NOTES.

(a) This is a novelty which certainly deserves analysis, as it not only defends White's own centre Pawn, but threatens, moreover, to break up the hostile Pawns by P. to K. R. third. The move usually recommended at this point is 'K. to K. B. second."

(b) Good play, we believe, if correctly followed.

(c) Here Mr. Anderssen, we suspect, should have taken the other Knight, compelling the exchange of all the pieces except the Rooks. He could then have captured the Q. Kt. Pawn with his Rook, and his game would have been at least as good as that of his opponent.

(d) "Q. takes Kt." appears to be stronger.

(e) However hazardous this may seem, the menaced advance of the centre Pawn perhaps rendered it imperative.

(f) Although after this move White's K. Kt. Pawn can scarcely be maintained, unless he submit to a somewhat servile defence, it would, unless we are mistaken, have been sounder play to have defended his own K. B. Pawn by "R. to K. B. square."

(g) Mr. Anderssen subsequently admitted that this was a mistake, and thought that he would have obtained the advantage by first moving his Pawn to Q. R. fourth. We doubt his gaining any such result by the mode of play suggested, as White might simply have rejoined with P. to Q. B. third, as observed by Mr. Steinitz himself. It is likely that Mr. Anderssen based his suggestion on the idea that White would answer the sally of the Q. R. Pawn with "R. to K. B. seventh," in which case he would inevitably have been mated, for

39. If R. to K. B. seventh
40. K. to B. fourth
41. K. to Kt. fifth

38. P. to Q. R. fourth
39. Then Q. R. to Kt. sixth (check)
40. K. R. takes P. (check)
41. Q. to K. square (check)

And mate follows directly.

(*h*) Black's attack is now over, and it is of no consequence whether he advance or withdraw the Rook.

GAME 177.

Fifth Game. (*Evans's Gambit.*)

White. (Mr. Anderssen.)	Black. (Mr. Steinitz.)
1. P. to K. fourth	1. P. to K. fourth
2. K. Kt. to B. third	2. Q. Kt. to B. third
3. B. to B. fourth	3. B. to B. fourth
4. P. to Q. Kt. fourth	4. B. takes P.
5. P. to Q. B. third	5. B. to B. fourth
6. P. to Q. fourth	6. P. takes P.
7. Castles	7. P. to Q. third
8. P. takes P.	8. B. to Kt. third
9. P. to Q. fifth	9. Kt. to R. fourth
10. B. to Kt. second	10. K. Kt. to K. second
11. B. to Q. third	11. Castles
12. Kt. to Q. B. third	12. P. to Q. B. third
13. Q. to Q. second	13. P. to K. B. fourth
14. Q. R. to K. square	14. B. P. takes K. P.
15. Kt. takes P.	15. Kt. takes P.
16. Q. Kt. to Kt. fifth (*a*)	16. P. to K. R. third
17. Kt. to K. sixth	17. B. takes Kt.
18. R. takes B.	18. Q. to Q. second (*b*)
19. R. to K. Kt. sixth	19. Kt. to K. B. fifth (*c*)
20. R. takes Kt. P. (check)	20. Q. takes R.
21. B. takes Q.	21. K. takes B.
22. Kt. to R. fourth (*d*)	22. Kt. takes B.
23. Q. takes Kt.	23. R. to B. third
24. Kt. to B. fifth (check)	24. K. to B. square
25. Q. to K. R. third (*e*)	25. Q. R. to K. square
26. Q. to Kt. fourth	26. Q. R. to K. third
27. Q. to Kt. seventh (check)	27. K. to K. square
28. P. to K. Kt. fourth	28. P. to Q. fourth
29. K. to Kt. second	29. Kt. to B. fifth
30. Q. takes Q. Kt. P.	30. R. to K. seventh

31. Q. to K. Kt. seventh (*f*)	31. K. R. to K. third
32. P. to K. R. fourth	32. P. to Q. fifth
33. Q. to Kt. eighth (check)	33. K. to Q. second
34. Q. to B. seventh (check)	34. K. to B. square
35. Kt. to Kt. seventh	35. Kt. to Q. sixth (check) (*g*)
36. K. to Kt. square (*h*)	36. R. to K. fifth
37. P. to K. B. third (*i*)	37. P. to Q. sixth
38. P. takes R.	38. Kt. takes P. (dis. check)
39. R. to B. second	39. B. takes R. (check)
40. K. to R. square (*k*)	40. B. to K. eighth (check)
41. K. to Kt. second	41. R. to Kt. eighth (check)
42. K. to B. third	42. Kt. to K. fourth (check)
43. K. takes B.	43. Kt. takes Q.
44. K. takes R.	44. P. to Q. seventh, and wins

NOTES.

(*a*) White has now a very attacking position.

(*b*) Had he played the Knight at once to K. B. fifth, White could have rejoined with "R. takes Q. P." It must be confessed that at this point Black has so critical a game that it is difficult to suggest a good resource.

(*c*) Observing the hopelessness of his situation, Mr. Steinitz sacrifices his Queen to avoid the more immediate pressure.

(*d*) Having so great an advantage, Mr. Anderssen now plays very carelessly. He should never have allowed his attacking Bishop to be exchanged for the hostile Rook, but should have withdrawn him to Q. Kt. square.

(*e*) White loses time with his Queen. He should have brought his Rook into co-operation at K. square.

(*f*) "K to K. B. third" appears to be much stronger.

(*g*) Though something highly ingenious comes out of this—shall we say desperate?—resource, it ought not to have availed him.

(*h*) Again "K to K. B. third" is decisive.

(*i*) If he had taken the Kt., Mr. Steinitz, whose conception in the strait in which he was in deserves great commendation, would obviously have drawn the game by "R. takes P.," and on the King moving, "R. takes R. P. (check)." The move in the text which is played to win the game effectually loses it.

(*k*) Had he brought his King to Kt. second, Black's best mode of prosecuting the attack is "B. to K. eighth (dis. check)."

GAME 178.

Handicap Tournament. First round between Mr. De Vere and Herr Steinitz. First Game.

(*Ruy Lopez Knight's Game.*)

White. (Mr. De Vere.)	*Black.* (Mr. Steinitz.)
1. P. to K. fourth	1. P. to K. fourth
2. Kt. to K. B. third	2. Kt. to Q. B. third
3. B. to Q. Kt. fifth	3. Kt. to K. B. third

4. Castles	4. Kt. takes P.
5. R. to K. square	5. Kt. to Q. third
6. B. takes Kt.	6. Q. P. takes B.
7. Kt. takes P.	7. B. to K. second
8. P. to Q. third	8. Castles
9. Q. Kt. to B. third	9. Kt. to K. B. fourth
10. Kt. to K. B. third (a)	10. B. to K. third
11. B. to B. fourth	11. B. to Q. third
12. Q. to Q. second	12. Q. to B. third (b)
13. B. takes B. (c)	13. P. takes B.
14. Q. to B. fourth	14. P. to Q. fourth
15. P. to K. Kt. fourth	15. Kt. to R. third (d)
16. Q. takes Q.	16. P. takes Q.
17. P. to K. R. third	17. K. R. to K. square
18. Kt. to K. second (e)	18. B. to Q. second
19. Kt. to B. fourth	19. K. to B. square
20. K. to B. square	20. Kt. to Kt. square
21. Kt. to R. fifth	21. R. to K. third
22. Kt. to Q. fourth	22. R. to Q. third
23. P. to K. B. fourth	23. P. to Q. B. fourth
24. Kt. to B. third (f)	24. P. to Q. R. fourth
25. Q. R. to Q. square	25. P. to Q. R. fifth
26. P. to K. B. fifth	26. P. to Q. R. sixth
27. P. to Q. Kt. third	27. Kt. to K. second
28. P. to Q. B. fourth	28. Kt. to Q. B. third (g)
29. Kt. to K. B. fourth	29. Kt. to Q. Kt. fifth
30. R. to Q. second	30. P. takes P.
31. Kt. P. takes P.	31. B. to Q. B. third
32. K. to B. second	32. Q. R. to Q. square
33. K. R. to Q. square	33. B. to Q. R. fifth
34. R. to Q. B. square	34. Kt. takes Q. P. (check)
35. Kt. takes Kt.	35. R. takes Kt.
36. R. takes R.	36. R. takes R.
37. K. to K. second	37. R. to Q. third
38. R. to Q. B. third	38. B. to Q. eighth (check) (h)
39. K. to K. B. second	39. B. takes Kt.
40. K. takes B.	40. R. to Q. fifth
41. R. takes P.	41. R. takes B. P.
42. R. to Kt. third	42. R. to R. fifth
43. R. takes P.	43. R. takes P.
44. R. to Q. B. seventh	44. R. to Q. B. seventh
45. K. to K. fourth	45. K. to Kt. second

46. K. to Q. fifth	46. R. to Q. B. sixth
47. R. takes P.	47. R. takes P.
48. K. to K. fourth	48. P. to R. fourth
49. P. takes P.	49. R. takes P.
50. R. to Q. B. sixth	

Drawn game.

NOTES.

(*a*) Black's last and White's present move were made, the one to retard, the other to facilitate, the advance of the first player's centre Pawn.

(*b*) This move effectually prevents the immediate advance of White's Q. Pawn, but it is nevertheless open to objection, as will be seen presently.

(*c*) "Kt. to K. fourth" would not be nearly as effective in performance as it appears to be in promise. Black could, in answer, safely take the Q. Kt. P., for, suppose

13. Kt. to K. fourth	13. Q. takes Q. Kt. P.
14. Kt. takes B.	14. Kt. takes Kt.
15. B. takes Kt.	15. P. takes B.
16. K. R. to Q. Kt. square	16. Q. to K. B. third,

and will remain with a Pawn ahead. A transposition of these latter moves would not affect the position. We may also remark that the first player cannot advance his centre Pawn at this juncture without surrendering it to his antagonist, *e.g.*—

13. P. to Q. fourth	13. Kt. takes P.
14. B. to K. Kt. fifth.	

It is needless to trace the result of Kt. takes Kt.

	14. Kt. takes Kt. (check)
15. P. takes Kt.	15. Q. to K. Kt. third

With a winning advantage.

(*d*) We believe that "Q. to K. Kt. third" would not have compromised Black's game to the same extent.

Position after White's 38th move.

BLACK.

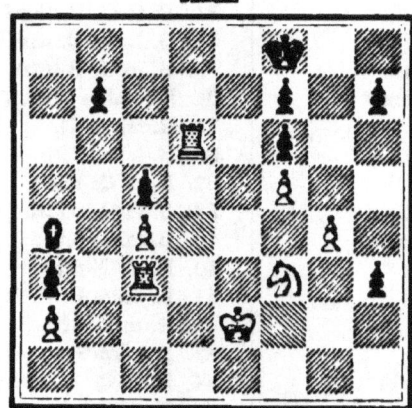

WHITE.

(e) "K. Kt. to K. R. fourth" appears to be stronger, as it not only holds back the hostile Bishop's Pawn, but also threatens to advance White's own Pawns on the right wing.

(f) At this point the first player has an excellent game. By losing time, however, with his Queen's Rook at his next move, he throws away most of his advantage.

(g) By the series of moves, of which this is the most important, Black much improves his position.

(h) "R. to Q. R. third" would have enabled Black to maintain, at any rate temporarily, the numerical superiority which he had obtained.

GAME 179.

HANDICAP. Second Game.

(*French Opening.*)

White. (MR. STEINITZ.)	Black. (MR. DE VERE.)
1. P. to K. fourth	1. P. to K. third
2. P. to Q. fourth	2. P. to Q. fourth
3. Q. Kt. to B. third	3. K. B. to Kt. fifth
4. P. takes P.	4. P. takes P.
5. K. Kt. to B. third	5. K. Kt. to B. third
6. K. B. to Q. third	6. Q. Kt. to B. third
7. Castles	7. Castles
8. Q. Kt. to K. second	8. Q. Kt. to K. second
9. K. Kt. to K. fifth	9. Q. Kt. to K. Kt. third (*a*)
10. P. to K. B. fourth	10. K. Kt. to K. fifth
11. P. to Q. B. third	11. K. B. to Q. R. fourth
12. B. takes Kt.	12. P. takes B.
13. Q. Kt. to Kt. third (*b*)	13. Kt. takes Kt.
14. B. P. takes Kt.	14. K. B. to Kt. third
15. B. to K. third (*c*)	15. P. to K. B. fourth
16. P. takes P. (*en pas.*)	16. R. takes P.
17. Q. to K. R. fifth (*d*)	17. P. to K. Kt. third
18. Q. to K. R. sixth	18. B. to K. B. fourth
19. B. to K. Kt. fifth	19. Q. to K. B. square
20. Q. to K. R. fourth	20. R. to K. third
21. R. takes B. (*e*)	21. P. takes R.
22. R. to B. square	22. P. to K. sixth
23. R. takes P.	23. Q. to Q. third
24. B. to K. B. sixth	

And Black resigns.

NOTES.

(*a*) At this point, in all openings of this description, it is much better to post the Q. B. at K. B. fourth square, as the first player's attack is thereby paralysed, and Black's game also properly developed.

(b) "Q. to Q. B. second" seems to be simpler and more immediately effective.

(c) "Kt. takes P." would have gained nothing, as Black could have rejoined with "Q. to Q. fourth," winning the K. P. directly.

(d) There is no means of saving the isolated Pawn.

(e) The opening player has now a won game, and finishes the *partie* with great skill and ability.

GAME 180.

Third Game. (*Ruy Lopez Knight's Game*.)

White. (Mr. De Vere.)	Black. (Mr. Steinitz.)
1. P. to K. fourth	1. P. to K. fourth
2. K. Kt. to B. third	2. Q. Kt. to B. third
3. K. B. to Q. Kt. fifth	3. K. Kt. to B. third
4. Castles	4. K. B. to K. second
5. Q. Kt. to B. third	5. P. to Q. third
6. P. to Q. fourth	6. P. takes P.
7. K. Kt. takes P.	7. Q. B. to Q. second
8. Kt. takes Kt.	8. P. takes Kt.
9. B. to Q. R. fourth (a)	9. Castles
10. P. to K. B. fourth	10. P. to Q. fourth
11. P. to K. fifth	11. B. to Q. B. fourth (check)
12. K. to R. square	12. Kt. to K. Kt. fifth
13. Q. to K. square	13. Kt. to K. R. third
14. Q. B. to K. third	14. B. to Q. Kt. third
15. Q. R. to Q. square (b)	15. Q. to K. second
16. B. takes B.	16. R. P. takes B.
17. B. to Q. Kt. third	17. Q. R. to K. square
18. Q. to Q second	18. P. to K. B. third
19. P. takes P.	19. Q. takes P.
20. P. to K. Kt. third	20. B. to R. sixth
21. K. R. to K. square	21. Q. to Kt. third
22. R. takes R.	22. R. takes R.
23. R. to K. square	23. Kt. to K. Kt. fifth
24. R. takes R. (check)	24. Q. takes R.
25. Q. to K. second	25. Q. to K. Kt. third
26. K. to K. Kt. square (c)	26. K. to B. square
27. Kt. to Q. square	27. Q. to Q. third (d)
28. Kt. to B. second	28. Kt. takes Kt.

29. K. takes Kt.	29. Q. to B. fourth (check)
30. Q. to K. third	30. P. to Q. fifth
31. Q. to K. fifth	31. Q. takes Q.
32. P. takes Q.	32. K. to K. second
33. K. to B. third	33. P. to Q. B. fourth
34. P. to Q. R. fourth	34. B. to B. fourth
35. P. to Kt. fourth	35. B. to Kt. third
36. P. to K. R. fourth	36. P. to Q. B. fifth
37. B. takes P.	37. B. takes P.
38. P. to Q. Kt. third	38. P. to Q. B. fourth
39. B. to Q. fifth	39. B. to Q. eighth (check)
40. K. to K. B. fourth	40. B. to B. seventh
41. P. to K. Kt. fifth	41. B. to K. Kt. third
42. B. to K. fourth	42. B. takes B.
43. K. takes B.	43. K. to Q. second
44. P. to Q. Kt. fourth (*e*)	44. P. takes P.
45. K. takes P.	45. K. to K. third
46. K. to B. fourth	46. K. takes P.
47. K. takes P.	47. K. to Q. third
48. K. to Q. Kt. fifth	48. K. to Q. B. second
49. K. to Q. R. sixth	49. K. to Q. B. third
50. K. to Q. R. seventh (*f*)	50. P. to Q. Kt. fourth

And the game was drawn.

NOTES.

(*a*) As will be seen presently, it would have been far better to have kept command of the centre by " B. to Q. B. fourth."

(*b*) Evidently threatening to take the Q. Pawn with his Knight.

(*c*) This is good play, as White now menaces to play "Kt. to K. fourth," a move which he could not have made previously with any advantage, on account of Black's having the resource of Kt. to K. B. seventh at the right moment.

(*d*) The second player posted his Queen on this square in all probability with the double motive of either checking with her at Q. B. fourth or of advancing his Q. B. Pawn, if the opportunity was offered him.

(*e*) The end-game now becomes singularly instructive, White's conception being throughout very ingenious.

(*f*) It was suggested that Mr. De Vere might here have won by advancing his Pawn to K. R. fifth. That resource, however, with the best play would only have led to a drawn game. Suppose—

50. P. to K. R. fifth	50. P. to K. Kt. third

The only move to draw, for if—50. K. to Q. B. second.

51. K. to Q. R. seventh	51. K. to B. third (best)
52. K. to Kt. eighth	52. K. to B. fourth (best)
53. K. to B. seventh, and wins	

51. P. to R. sixth	51. P. to Q. Kt. fourth
52. P. takes P. (check)	52. K. takes P.

53. K. to Kt. seventh	53. K. to B. fourth
54. K. to B. seventh	54. K. to Q. fourth
55. K. to Q. seventh	55. K. to K. fourth
56. K. to K. seventh	56. K. to Q. fourth
57. K. to B. seventh	57. K. to Q. third
58. K. to Kt. seventh	58. K. to K. second
59. K. takes P.	59. K. to B. second

And the game is drawn.

Position after White's 44th move.

BLACK.

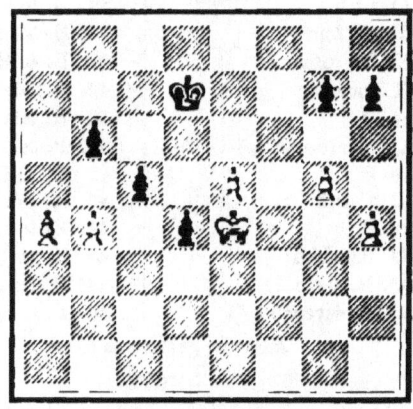

WHITE.

GAME 181.

Fourth Game. (*Fianchetto di Rè.*)

White. MR. STEINITZ.	*Black.* MR. DE VERE.
1. P. to K. fourth	1. P. to K. Kt. third
2. P. to Q. fourth	2. B. to Kt. second
3. Kt. to K. B. third	3. P. to Q. Kt. third
4. B. to Q. third	4. P. to K. third
5. Kt. to Q. B. third	5. B. to Q. Kt. second
6. B. to K. third	6. P. to Q. third
7. Q. to Q. second	7. Kt. to Q. second
8. Castles (Q. R.)	8. Kt. to K second
9. P. to K. R. fourth	9. P. to K. R. fourth (*a*)
10. K. Kt. to Kt. fifth	10. P. to K. fourth
11. K. B. to Q. B. fourth	11. Castles
12. P. to K. Kt. fourth	12. K. P. takes P.

13. Q. B. takes P.	13. B. takes B.
14. Q. takes B.	14. Q. Kt. to K. fourth (*b*)
15. B. to K. second	15. P. takes P.
16. P. to R. fifth	16. Kt. to Q. fourth
17. P. takes Kt. (*c*)	17. Q. takes Kt. (check)
18. K. to Kt. square	18. Q. R. to K. square (*d*)
19. Q. R. to K. Kt. square	19. P. to Q. B. fourth
20. Q. to Q. R. fourth	20. Q. to K. B. fourth
21. Q. takes R. P.	21. B. takes P.
22. Kt. takes B.	22. Kt. to Q. B. third
23. Q. to Q. R. fourth	23. Q. takes Kt.
24. P. takes P.	24. R. to K. fifth (*e*)
25. P. takes P. (check)	25. K. takes P.
26. Q. to R. sixth	26. Kt. to Kt. fifth
27. Q. to R. seventh (check)	27. K. to K. third
28. B. to Q. Kt. fifth (*f*)	28. R. to K. B. second
29. R. to R. sixth (check)	29. K. to K. fourth
30. R. to R. fifth (check)	30. K. to K. third
31. R. takes Q.	31. R. takes Q.
32. R. to Q. second	32. P. to Q. B. fifth
33. Q. R. to Q. square	33. P. to Q. fourth
34. P. to R. third	34. R. to R. fourth (*g*)
35. P. takes Kt.	35. R. takes B.
36. P. to Q. B. third	36. K. to K. fourth
37. K. to R. second	37. K. to B. fifth
38. R. to Q. fourth	38. K. to B. sixth
39. K. to R. third, and wins	

NOTES.

(*a*) This throws away an opportunity. By the nature of the opening Black has for a time a constrained game, but he might here have relieved himself by playing P. to Q. B. fourth, however hazardous that move may appear at a superficial glance.

(*b*) A good move, as it not only attacks the Knight's Pawn, which we believe to have been advanced prematurely, but also threatens to win the hostile Bishop unless due care is taken.

(*c*) He would have gained nothing by "Kt. takes K. B. P."

(*d*) This appears to be good on principle, as it brings the Rook into co-operation in the centre, but it is notwithstanding of doubtful expediency. Black's left wing is already weak, and he now materially enfeebles the extreme right of his position.

(*e*) Had he taken the offered Bishop, White would have won the game off-hand by "P. takes P. (check)."

(*f*) "R. to K. R. seventh" seems to be much more effective.

(*g*) Black has escaped the disasters with which he was menaced. By his manœuvres from this point, however, he imprisons his Rook unnecessarily.

GAME 182.

Challenge Cup. Between Mr. Bird and Mr. De Vere. First Game.

(*Ruy Lopez Knight's Game.*)

White. (Mr. De Vere.)	Black. (Mr Bird.)
1. P. to K. fourth	1. P. to K. fourth
2. K. Kt. to B. third	2. Q. Kt. to B. third
3. K. B. to Q. Kt. fifth	3. Q. Kt. to Q. fifth
4. Kt. takes Kt.	4. P. takes Kt.
5. Castles	5. K. B. to Q. B. fourth
6. P. to Q. third	6. Kt. to K. second
7. Q. to K. R. fifth	7. K. B. to Q. Kt. third
8. Q. B. to K. Kt. fifth	8. Castles
9. K. B. to Q. B. fourth	9. Q. to K. square
10. P. to K. B. fourth	10. K. to R. square
11. P. to K. fifth	11. P. to Q. third
12. B. takes Kt. (*a*)	12. Q. takes B.
13. Kt. to Q. second	13. B. to K. third
14. P. takes P.	14. P. takes P.
15. Q. R. to K. square	15. P. to Q. fourth (*b*)
16. B. takes P.	16. Q. to Q. B. fourth
17. R. to K. fifth	17. B takes B. (*c*)
18. R. takes B.	18. Q. takes Q. B. P.
19. Kt. to K. B. third	19. Q. takes Q. P.
20. P. to K. B. fifth	20. Q. to K. seventh.
21. R. to K. square	21. P. to Q. sixth (dis. check)
22. K. to R. square	22. Q. to K. B. seventh (*d*)
23. P. to K. B. sixth	23. P. takes P.
24. Q. to K. R. sixth	24. K. R. to Kt. square
25. Q. takes B. P. (check)	25. R. to Kt. second
26. P. to K. Kt. third (*e*)	26. Q. R. to K. Kt. square
27. R. takes Q. P.	27. B. to Q. R. fourth
28. K. R. to Q. square	28. Q. R. to K. square
29. P. to Q. Kt. fourth	29. Q. to Q. Kt. third
30. Q. takes Q.	30. B. takes Q.
31. Q. R. to Q. seventh	31. P. to B. third
32. P. to Q. R. fourth	32. Q. R. to K. second
33. Q. R. to Q. sixth	33. K. R. to B. second
34. Kt. to K. R. fourth	34. P. to K. B. fourth
35. Q. R. to Q. fifth	35. K. R. to B. square
36. Kt. takes P.	36. Q. R. to K. fifth

37. P. to R. fifth	37. B. to Q. B. second
38. Q. R. to Q. seventh	38. Q. R. to Q. B. fifth
39. Kt. to K. third	39. Q. R. to Q. B. third
40. Kt. to Q. fifth	40. B. to Q. third
41. P. to Q. Kt. fifth	41. R. to Q. B. seventh
42. R. takes B.	42. K. R. to K. B. seventh
43. Kt. to K. B. fourth	43. And Black resigns

NOTES.

(a) "Kt. to Q. second" seems stronger, as White's game would have been thereby developed most rapidly, and his Bishop have remained in his powerful position. As a rule, the player who has this kind of attack only relieves his opponent by the exchange of pieces.

(b) Black evidently sacrifices his Pawn with the view of playing his Queen to her B. fourth, thinking that by pinning the hostile Bishop for a time he must obtain an equivalent for his lost Pawn; but he appears to have forgotten the consequences flowing from White's reply of "R. to K. fifth."

(c) If "P. to K. Kt. third," the rejoinder should be "Q. to K. B. third."

(d) Black appears to have no better move. Had he played "Q. to Q. B. seventh," the following would have been a probable continuation:—

	22. Q. to Q. B. seventh.
23. P. to K. B. sixth.	23. P. takes P.
There seems to be no other resource.	
24. Q. to K. R. sixth	24. R. to K. Kt. square
25. Q. takes P. at K. B. sixth (check)	25. R. to Kt. second
26. R. to K. Kt. fifth	26. Q. R. to K. Kt. square

White mates in three moves.

(e) This quiet-looking mode of play was essential, and is also, if rightly looked at, eminently attacking. If he had made the plausible move of "R. to K. Kt. fifth," Black would have at once gained the day by "B. to Q fifth." Hence we see the importance of Black's twenty-second move, "Q. to K. B. seventh," bringing his own Queen into co-operation with his Bishop, and hampering every one of the hostile pieces.

CORRESPONDENCE.

TO THE EDITOR OF "THE CHESS PLAYER'S MAGAZINE."

Bilsdale Rectory, July 23rd, 1866.

DEAR SIR,—As my visit to Huddersfield has merited notice in your columns, perhaps you will allow me to say with reference to the paragraph which appeared in your last Magazine, that *four* games were played at Huddersfield between Mr. Watkinson and myself. I won the two first, Mr. Watkinson the two last. The last game, which happened to be the first of a little match which we have arranged to play, was the only game alluded to in the paragraph under notice. In justice to myself I make public this remaining part, of which your correspondent failed to speak.

I am, dear Sir, faithfully yours,

A. B. SKIPWORTH.

Problem No. 90. By Lieutenant Ph. Klett, in Stuttgart.

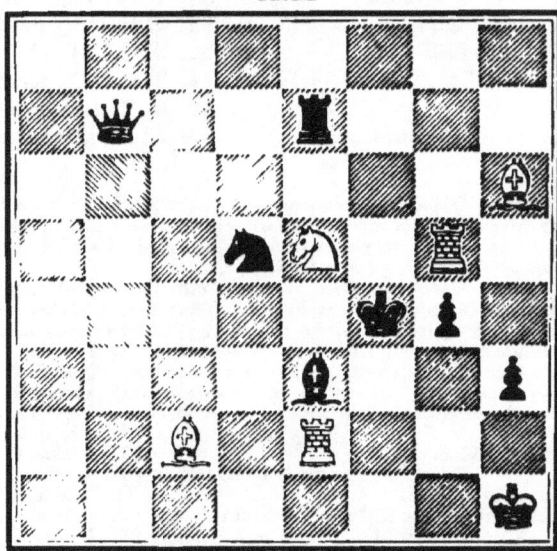

White to move, and mate in five moves.

Problem No. 91. By Herr Kockelkorn.

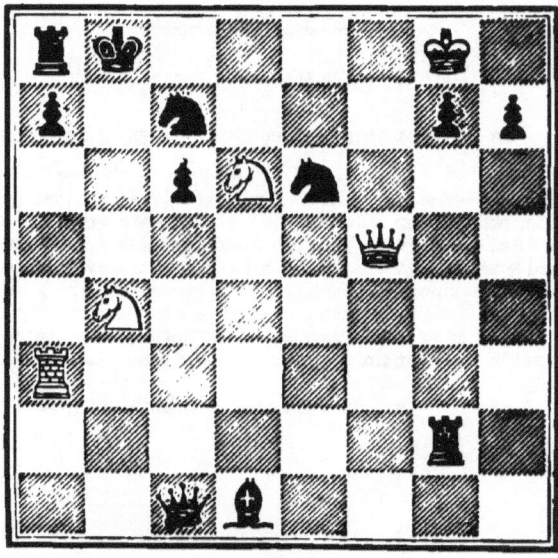

Problem No. 92. By Herr GEORG MEHRTENS, of Hanover.

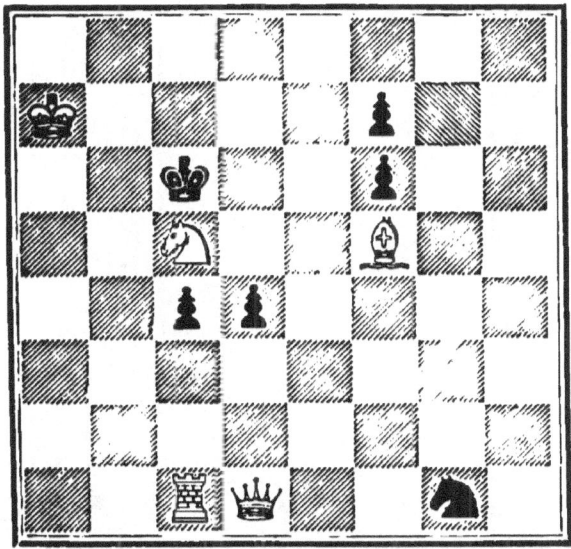

White to play, and mate in three moves.

Problem No. 93. By C. R. ALEXANDER.

White to play, and mate in four moves.

Problem No. 94. By Herr A. KELLES, of Elberfeld.

BLACK.

WHITE.

White to play, and mate in four moves.

Problem No. 95. By Herr BROUNE, of Graz.

BLACK.

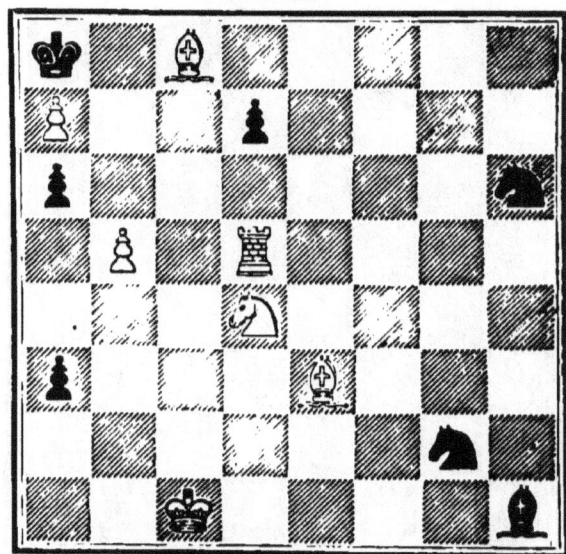

WHITE.

White to play, and mate in five moves.

THE Chess Player's Magazine.

CHESS AND GYMNASTICS.

"Is Chess indeed too serious an occupation for a game, and too much of a game to be a serious occupation?"

SINCE some celebrated person, whose name we do not remember, pronounced this *ipse dixit*, every one to whom this noble game seems too profitless a pursuit, or whose mental powers are below the necessary standard to follow it up, appeals to the above saying as an authority to condemn Chess. If this produced no worse results than to keep these persons from playing at Chess, the evil would not be very great; for he whose intellect is too clouded to allow of profound thinking, or they who believe that only such pursuits are worth cultivating which bring in an immediate cash return, may, without detriment, keep aloof from the chequered field.

Like all similar play upon words, however witty, the present one carries the same great germ of mischief within it, as it tends to mislead the general opinion prevalent on the subject. This somewhat accounts for the fact that this wonderful game, great as has been its development of late years, has still not received that acknowledgment of its intrinsic value to which it is justly entitled. Nor will it do so until the following axiom, in the truth of which all masters of Chess are convinced, receives general acceptation, and that axiom is, *that Chess is for the mind what gymnastics are for the body.*

To prove our statement, we shall endeavour, in a few light sketches, to show the evident analogy which exists between Chess and gymnastics. The purpose of the latter is not limited to hardening and training the body for some special service, but rather to generally strengthen and develop the human frame, and give it agility, power, and suppleness. As gymnastics bring all the powers of the body into play and invigorate it, in like manner does Chess exercise the powers of the mind—memory and imagination, and, above all, the talent of combination, becomes improved. We place great emphasis on this latter effect produced by Chess, because combination, although of the greatest importance in the improvement of acquired knowledge, is scarcely ever called into action in the process of learning the science. There are many remarkable instances of individuals stored with all the wisdom of the ages, who, from their utter incapacity to make combinations in a proper manner, were unable to advance scientific interests in general by a single iota; and their failure may be attributable in great measure to the fact that they had not devoted themselves to the cultivation of Chess in their youthful days. A good Chess-player only can know how much depends upon combination, how useless theory is to him who cannot quickly and rightly combine, and the large extent to which the power of combination receives development and improvement by exercise.

Many who are incapable of emulating the celebrities of the Chess world generally console themselves with attributing an "ability" for games (*la bosse du jeu*) to a superior player. But this so-called ability is really nothing else but a general aptitude for anything, and, although discernible under all circumstances, it is nowhere so patent and so readily perceptible as in Chess.

It scarcely needs proof that all great Chess-players, not devoting themselves exclusively to the game, have been and are invariably eminent in their various callings and professions. Conspicuous among these were Charles XII., Gustavus Adolphus of Sweden, Deschappelles, Petrow the privy councillor, Anderssen, Janisch, Max Lange, Suhle, and last, but not least, the late lamented Henry Thomas Buckle.

To such as argue that superior intelligence is the cause rather than the effect, and that these great masters were such strong players because Nature had endowed them with superior powers, we simply reply that, in such instances, cause and effect are dependent upon each other. Nobody can become an athlete unless Nature has gifted him with muscular power, but without due exercise, muscular power by itself would not make an athlete.

If we trace the analogy which exists between gymnastics and

Chess still further, we find that the great advantage that gymnastics possess for the body is enabling it to perform great feats, and the trained gymnast to do with the greatest ease that which the neophyte can only perform, nay, attempt, with the utmost difficulty. It is the same with Chess. Precisely as the gymnast considers it ridiculous that a person shall return home fatigued from a short excursion, so the mind of a regular Chess-player does not easily tire, as can be demonstrated by the fact that most celebrated amateurs, after a day of heavy head-work, sit down in the evening to enjoy, as a recreation, a game of Chess, and by the depth of their combinations and the brilliancy of their conceptions, astonish the lookers-on.

The analogy remains unaltered as respects the charm or the pleasure of the game. Gymnastics would never have become popular unless it afforded considerable amusement to young men; nor would Chess have been widely diffused were it not for the intense interest which it excites, an interest which receives violent stimulus with increasing knowledge of the game.

We recommend to the serious consideration of all teachers of the young the necessity of their obtaining a keener perception of the favourable influence which the study of Chess must have upon the youthful mind in developing the mental powers. In most sciences, the gift of memory alone suffices to pass successfully, but in Chess, memory by itself will not much help the learner; but, even with regard to memory, Chess has a considerable advantage over other studies. There are, according to our idea, three distinct kinds of memory—that of the ear, of the eye, and, lastly, that which may be purely called logical. The first-named, because less durable, is least valuable, and is chiefly exercised by children, who cannot learn a task without repeating it aloud. The second, somewha more preferable, is not either safe or sure. That memory only really to be relied upon, because indestructible, is the logical one by which we retain an idea or a fact, inasmuch as it enables us to remember the connection which it has with other facts and ideas. In Chess, the first kind of memory is thoroughly useless and inapplicable, the second only of limited use, while the third is in much requisition, and is widely and wonderfully improved by the cultivation of Chess. In conclusion, we will only make this remark, that it is fortunate that, in the education of the young, Chess and gymnastics may be employed as reciprocal antidotes to the evil results consequent upon over-indulgence in either. Too much devotion to Chess may have a deleterious effect on the body, and gymnastics can remedy it; while Chess will do a similar service, if needed.—From the *Berliner Schachzeitung*.

CORRESPONDENCE.

TO THE EDITOR OF "THE CHESS PLAYER'S MAGAZINE."

MY DEAR SIR,—I feel as if I should rest better in "the cradle of the rocky deep," to which I am about committing myself, if I seize this present spare moment, on the eve of my departure from England, to relieve my "stuffed bosom" of some of the Chess thoughts that have sprung up upon looking over the last two numbers of your Magazine. Perhaps the first of these lucubrations to be recorded is not, to speak precisely, a Chess thought, though excited by the perusal of a Chess paper. It relates to "Shakspeare's Silence about Chess," the theme on which the veteran player and ever-pleasant writer, Captain Kennedy, discourses to your readers in the July number. I bethink me how wonderful is this Shakspeare, who not only moves the world with his utterances, but whose very silence furnishes matter for disquisition among the curious and learned, sets antiquaries together by the ears, and makes thoughtful men seriously inquire if what he has not touched on could possibly have had existence in his day, or even if what he did not foresee can really be of any value. And then I find myself asking, is it indeed true that Shakspeare has nowhere noticed Chess? Are there not more passages than one in his writings in which terms and illustrations would seem to have been borrowed from the game? Does not *Taming of the Shrew*, in particular, contain a sharp and clear allusion to it? Not being able to speak by the book at the moment, however, I turn over all such questions to *Notes and Queries*, and Captain Kennedy, and Mr. Staunton in his next edition of the bard. Far be it from me, anyhow, to play the "venturous part" of one who would "tamper with such dangerous art" as that of the Shakspearean critics. I will only observe here, as something suggestive, that Shakspeare makes Hamlet admonish Horatio that there are more things, not only "in heaven," but on earth, than are dreamt of in our philosophy; acknowledging, at the same time, that I have not the slightest conception as to whether by "our philosophy" is to be understood Shakspeare's philosophy, or Hamlet's and Horatio's, or human philosophy in general—another knotty question which I hand over in like manner to the critics. Look to it, gentlemen.

"Non nostrum inter vos tantas componere lites."

I have no more to say on the subject, except to make the suggestion, if you will allow me, that Chess may be one of those things about which Shakspeare would have said more if he had known more. Chess was not as generally known and practised in the days of Elizabeth and James as it has since grown to be. Shakspeare probably knew something of it, but not much, along with the "little Latin and less Greek" which Ben Jonson gives him credit for. Why, with his many-sided mind, his deep insight, and royal imagination, he has not left a clearer recognition of it upon record, may well excite surprise and be a point for discussion.

My next reflection is a regular Chess thought, for it is directly upon the striking variation of Mr. Mortimer in the Frazer Attack of the Evans's Gambit. The conception of the brilliant Dundee player is certainly handsome and attractive; but, as it seemed to me long ago, it is demonstrably unsound as he follows it up, the sacrifice of the Bishop being succeeded by such moves with the Queen as to throw the first player himself upon the defensive, and enable his adversary, by the rapid development of the latter's game, to obtain a secure position, and one from which, considering the advantage of the piece, it may be reasonably said he ought to win. Seeing this, as I have intimated, and lacking, it would seem, the right kind of Chess brains for an inventor, I was minded to give up the Frazer Attack altogether; and, indeed, did abandon it in actual play with strong opponents, when, most unexpectedly, a countryman of mine came to the rescue, wiped off the reproach from this beautiful variation, and struck the right nail on the head so stoutly that the Chess welkin is yet ringing with the sound. The more one looks at Mr. Mortimer's move of 13. Q. to B. second, the more strongly, it seems to me, he will be impressed with its correctness, and, consequently, of the soundness of Mr. Frazer's Attack by 9. Q. Kt. to B. third. It is true that you, Mr. Editor, to whose judgment I am accustomed to bow in all such matters, speak somewhat doubtfully of it in your second note to Game 168, but you only mention the result of the two games given as making an unfavourable show for the Attack, which, under the circumstances, can hardly be considered as more than a negative argument against it at best; while your subsequent analysis of the first game shows by several trains of play that White ought to have won; and the loss of the second may be attributed to the error which you point out in your fifth note. I am pleased to understand from Mr. Steinitz that he holds the view I have expressed concerning this form of the Attack.

There is another opening upon which, in the third place, I had designed to offer you a few remarks in this communication, but considerations of time and space oblige me to a postponement. I cannot conclude, however, without expressing the lively satisfaction with which I have witnessed the play of Messrs. Steinitz and Anderssen in the match now going on at the London and Westminster Clubs. It is not alone the skill they display—that is a matter of course with such champions—but the gallantry with which both choose those bold open games which are such true Chess, and which, unfortunately, are such a rare treat in great matches; this it is that will mark the Steinitz-Anderssen match as one deserving to be held in the highest honour among the recorded contests of the masters. Professor Anderssen has indeed long been distinguished for the knightly character of his play, and the accomplished adversary with whom he now joins issue seems resolved to couch as brave a lance as he. Neither can be dishonoured by losing a match in which each has set such a noble example before the Chess public in extending the science and upholding the loftier MORALS of the game.

With much respect and regard, dear Sir, yours,

NATHANIEL RAMSAY WATERS.

London, Aug. 10th, 1866.

GAMES.

GAME 183.

CHALLENGE CUP.—First Game.

(*King's Gambit Declined.*)

White. (MR. MINCHIN.)	Black. (MR. MACDONNELL.)
1. P. to K. fourth	1. P. to K. fourth
2. P. to K. B. fourth	2. B. to Q. B. fourth
3. Kt. to K. B. third	3. P. to Q. third
4. P. to Q. B. third	4. B. to K. Kt. fifth
5. B. to K. second	5. B. takes Kt.
6. B. takes B.	6. Kt. to K. B. third
7. P. to Q. fourth	7. P. takes P.
8. P. takes P.	8. B. to Q. Kt. fifth (check) (*a*)
9. Kt. to Q. B. third (*b*)	9. Castles
10. Castles (*c*)	10. Kt. to Q. B. third
11. B. to K. third	11. B. takes Kt.
12. P. takes B.	12. Q. to K. second
13. P. to K. fifth	13. P. takes P.
14. K. B. P. takes P.	14. K. Kt. to Q. second
15. B. takes Kt. (*d*)	15. P. takes B.
16. Q. to K. B. third	16. P. to Q. B. fourth
17. Q. to K. Kt. third	17. P. takes Q. P.
18. Q. B. P. takes P.	18. P. to K. B. third
19. P. takes P.	19. Kt. takes P.
20. B. to K. Kt. fifth	20. Q. to Q. second
21. Q. to K. R. fourth	21. Kt. to K. Kt. fifth
22. R. takes R. (check)	22. R. takes R.
23. R. to Q. square	23. P. to K. R. third
24. B. to Q. B. square	24. Q. to K. B. fourth
25. Q. to K. square	25. Kt. to K. B. seventh
26. B. to Q. R. third	26. R. to K. B. third
27. R. to Q. second	27. Kt. to K. R. sixth (check) (*e*)
28. P. takes Kt.	28. Q. to K. B. sixth
29. R. to K. Kt. second	29. Q takes B.
30. Q. to K. eighth (check)	30. R. to K. B. square
31. Q. to K. sixth (check)	31. K. to R. square

32. R. to K. B. second	32. Q. to Q. B. eighth (check)
33. K. to Kt. second	33. R. takes R. (check)
34. K. takes R.	34. Q. to K. B. fifth (check)
35. K. to Kt. second	35. Q. takes Q. P.
36. Q. to Q. B. eighth (check)	36. K. to R. second
37. Q. to K. B. fifth (check) (*f*)	37. P. to K. Kt. third
38. Q. to K. sixth	38. P. to K. R. fourth
39. P. to K. R. fourth	39. Q. to K. Kt. fifth (check)
40. Q. takes Q.	40. P. takes Q.
41. K. to Kt. third	41. K. to R. third
42. K. takes P.	42. P. to Q. B. fourth
43. K. to K. B. fourth	43. K. to R. fourth, and wins.

NOTES.

(*a*) The correct play is to bring the Bishop back to Kt. third.

(*b*) "K. to B. square" would gain an immediate advantage.

(*c*) "P. to K. fifth" would have been an excellent mode of continuing the attack.

(*d*) White has two Bishops, and both well posted, against two Knights which are comparatively out of play. Consequently he errs in exchanging one of these formidable pieces for the hostile Knight, although he doubles the Pawns thereby. "B. to K. fourth" would have been much more to the purpose.

(*e*) As the second player is sure to win the enemy's Bishop in return, he may safely sacrifice the Knight, cutting up White's Pawns.

Position after White's 28th move.

BLACK.

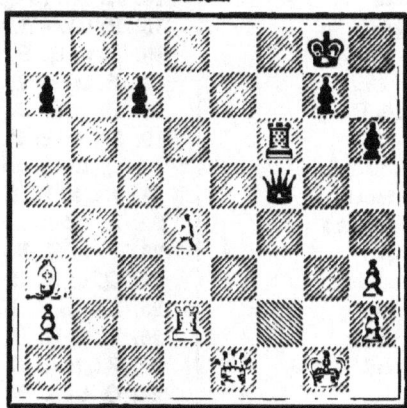

WHITE.

(*f*) Taking the Q. B. P. would have been stronger. White should not have permitted the subsequent exchange of Queens.

GAME 184.
Second Game.
(Ruy Lopez Knight's Game.)

White. (Mr. MacDonnell.)	Black. (Mr. Minchin.)
1. P. to K. fourth	1. P. to K. fourth
2. K. Kt. to B. third	2. Q. Kt. to B. third
3. K. B. to Q. Kt. fifth	3. P. to Q. R. third
4. K. B. to Q. R. fourth	4. K. Kt. to B. third
5. Castles	5. K. B. to K. second
6. P. to Q. fourth	6. Castles (a)
7. P. to Q. fifth	7. Q. Kt. to Kt. square
8. K. R. to K. square	8. P. to Q. third
9. P. to K. R. third	9. P. to K. R. third
10. P. to Q. B. fourth	10. Kt. to K. R. second
11. K. B. to Q. B. second	11. P. to K. B. fourth
12. P. takes P.	12. B. takes P.
13. Q. Kt. to B. third	13. Q. Kt. to Q. second
14. Q. B. to K. third	14. K. Kt. to Kt. fourth
15. Q. B. takes Kt.	15. K. B. takes B.
16. K. B. takes B.	16. R. takes B.
17. Q. Kt. to K. fourth	17. B. to K. R. fifth (b)
18. P. to Q. Kt. fourth	18. Q. to K. second
19. P. to Q. R. fourth	19. Q. R. to K. B. square
20. P. to Q. R. fifth	20. K. R. to K. B. fifth
21. Q. R. to R. third	21. Kt. to K. B. third
22. Q. Kt. to Q. second	22. Q. to K. B. second (c)
23. P. to K. Kt. third	23. Q. to K. Kt. third
24. K. to K. R. second	24. Kt. to K. R. fourth
25. K. R. to K. Kt. square	25. Q. to K. B. fourth
26. Kt. takes B.	26. R. takes P. (check)
27. R. to Kt. second	27. R. takes R. (check)
28. Kt. takes R.	28. Q. to K. B. seventh
29. Q. Kt. to K. fourth, and wins	

NOTES.

(a) An exceptionable move, leading to a position which increases the difficulties of the defence.

(b) The retreat of the Bishop to K. second was probably better than his advance.

(c) This must lose a piece eventually.

GAME 185.

The two following slight skirmishes are offered in support of the thesis that there arises a perfectly satisfactory defence to the Ruy Lopez Knight's Game.

First Game. (*Ruy Lopez Knight's Game.*)

White. (Mr. Skipworth.)	Black. (Mr. Wayte.)
1. P. to K. fourth	1. P. to K. fourth
2. K. Kt to B. third	2. Q. Kt. to B. third
3. K. B. to Q. Kt. fifth	3. P. to Q. R. third
4. B. to Q. R. fourth	4. K. Kt. to B. third
5. Castles	5. B. to K. second
6. P. to Q. third (*a*)	6. P. to Q. Kt. fourth
7. B. to Q. Kt. third	7. P. to Q. third
8. B. to K. Kt. fifth (*b*)	8. Kt. to Q. R. fourth (*c*)
9. B. takes Kt.	9. B. takes B.
10. P. to Q. B. third	10. Kt. takes B.
11. P. takes Kt.	11. Castles
12. Q. Kt. to Q. second	12. B. to K. second (*d*)
13. K. Kt to K. square	13. P. to K. B. fourth
14. P. to K. B. third (*e*)	14. P. to K. B. fifth
15. Q. to K. second	15. R. to K. B. third
16. K. to R. square (*f*)	16. R. to K. R. third
17. K. Kt. to Q. B. second	17. B. to K. R. fifth
18. K. to Kt. square	18. B. to K. Kt. sixth (*g*)
19. P. to K. R. third	19. Q. B. takes K. R. P.
20. P. takes B.	20. R. takes P.
21. Q. to K. Kt. second	21. Q. to K. R. fifth

And White resigns.

NOTES.

(*a*) P. to Q. fourth, or Q. Kt. to B. third, is usually recommended; but the move in the text (a favourite one of Mr. Paulsen's in this opening) is perhaps equally good.

(*b*) We doubt the policy of this move, and of the subsequent capture of the K. Kt.

(*c*) In this opening Black should always endeavour to get rid of the adverse K. B. If this move were not made now, the Bishop would be played to Q. fifth, and Black would be compelled to lose time.

(*d*) At this point we already prefer Black's game. He has two Bishops against two Knights, and his K. B. P. will get first into the field.

(*e*) This Pawn should have been advanced two steps. White's game now becomes completely locked, and his opponent has ample time to mature his attack.

(*f*) White appears to have anticipated 16 P. to Q. fourth. This loss of time, however, mattered little, as White has no good move on the board.

(*g*) If this Bishop be taken, Black simply retakes with Pawn, and mate is inevitable.

Position after Black's 18th move.

BLACK.

WHITE.

GAME 186.

Second Game.

(*Ruy Lopez Knight's Game.*)

White. (Mr. Skipworth.)	Black. (Mr. Waytr.)
1. P. to K. fourth	1. P. to K. fourth
2. K. Kt. to B. third	2. Q. Kt. to B. third
3. K. B. to Q. Kt. fifth	3. P. to Q. R. third
4. B. to Q. R. fourth	4. K. Kt. to B. third
5. Castles	5. B. to K. second.
6. P. to Q. fourth	6. P. takes P.
7. P. to K. fifth	7. Kt. to K. fifth
8. R. to K. square	8. Kt. to Q. B. fourth
9. B. to Q. Kt. third (*a*)	9. Kt. takes B. (*b*)
10. R. P. takes Kt.	10. Castles
11. Kt. takes P.	11. Kt. takes Kt.
12. Q. takes Kt.	12. P. to Q. fourth
13. Kt. to Q. B. third	13. B. to K. third
14. P. to Q. Kt. fourth	14. Q. to Q. second
15. Kt. to K. second	15. P. to Q. B. third
16. P. to Q. B. third	16. P. to K. B. third (*c*)

17. Kt. to K. B. fourth	17. Q. R. to K. square
18. Kt. takes B. (d)	18. Q. takes Kt.
19. B. to K. B. fourth	19. B. to Q. third
20. R. to K. third (e)	20. P. takes P.

Winning a piece and the game.

NOTES.

(a) The "Handbuch" gives—9. B. takes Kt. 9. Q P. takes B. 10. Kt. takes P. 10. Castles, with an even game. The move in the text is also noticed, but is inferior.

(b) By 9 Kt. to K. third, followed by B. to Q. B. fourth, Black might have retained the Pawn. By giving it up, however, he obtains a free, well-opened game, every way equal to his opponent's.

(c) Insuring a fine opening for his Rooks.

(d) This loses a Pawn.

(e) This was of course an error, but the game was already much in Black's favour.

GAME 187.

The following is one of the Match Games played lately at the Bristol Chess Club between Mr. E. Thorold and Mr. Fedden:—

(Allgaier Gambit.)

White. (Mr. Fedden.)	*Black.* (Mr. Thorold.)
1. P. to K. fourth	1. P. to K. fourth
2. P. to K. B. fourth	2. P. takes P.
3. K. Kt. to B. third	3. P. to K. Kt. fourth
4. P. to K. R. fourth	4. P. to K. Kt. fifth
5. Kt. to K. fifth	5. K. B. to Kt. second
6. Kt. takes Kt. P.	6. P. to K. R. fourth
7. Kt. to K. B. second	7. K. Kt. to K. second
8. P. to Q. fourth	8. Kt. to K. Kt. third
9. Q. Kt. to B. third	9. P. to Q. third
10. Kt. to Q. fifth	10. Q. Kt. to B. third
11. P. to Q. B. third	11. Kt. takes K. R. P.
12. Q. B. takes P.	12. Q. B. to K. third
13. Q. Kt. to K. third (a)	13. Kt. to K. Kt. third
14. P. to K. Kt. third	14. P. to Q. fourth
15. P. takes P.	15. Q. B. takes P.
16. R. takes P.	16. Kt. takes B.
17. P. takes Kt.	17. Q. to K. second
18. K. to Q. second	18. B. to K. fifth

19. B. to K. R. third	19. Q. R. to Q. square
20. R. takes R. (check)	20. B. takes R.
21. Q. to Q. R. fourth (*b*)	21. B. takes P.
22. Kt. takes B.	22. Q. takes Kt.

And wins.

NOTES.

(*a*) At the conclusion of the game, a looker-on suggested that White might at this point have played—13. Kt. takes Q. B. P. (check), and this opinion appears to be well grounded.

(*b*) 21. Q. to K. Kt. fourth would appear to be a better move. Indeed the one in the text leads at once to fatal consequences.

MATCH BETWEEN ANDERSSEN AND STEINITZ.

This match has terminated in favour of Mr. Steinitz. Final score:—Mr. Anderssen, 6; Mr. Steinitz, 8; drawn, 0. In our next number we shall give an elaborate critique of the play exhibited on the occasion.

GAME 188.

Sixth Game. (*Sicilian Opening.*)

White. (Mr. STEINITZ.)	Black. (Mr. ANDERSSEN.)
1. P. to K. fourth	1. P. to Q. B. fourth
2. P. to K. Kt. third	2. Q. Kt. to B. third
3. B. to K. Kt. second	3. P. to K. fourth
4. K. Kt. to K. second	4. Kt. to K. B. third
5. Q. Kt. to B. third	5. P. to Q. third
6. Castles	6. B. to K. second
7. P. to K. B. fourth	7. P. to K. R. fourth
8. P. to K. R. third	8. B. to Q. second
9. Kt. to Q. fifth	9. Q. to Q. B. square
10. Kt. takes Kt. (check)	10. B. takes Kt.
11. P. to B. fifth	11. Kt. to K. second
12. P. to Q. B. fourth	12. Q. to Q. square
13. Kt. to Q. B. third	13. Q. B. to B. third
14. P. to Q. third	14. Q. to Q. second
15. P. to Q. R. third	15. P. to Q. R. fourth
16. P. to Q. Kt. third	16. P. to Q. Kt. fourth
17. B. to K. third	17. P. to Q. Kt. fifth
18. P. takes P.	18. B. P. takes P.
19. Kt. to Q. R. fourth	19. B. takes Kt.
20. R. takes B.	20. Kt. to Q. B. third
21. Q. to Q. second	21. B. to Q. square

22. P. to Q. fourth	22. B. to Q. Kt. third
23. P. to Q. fifth	23. Q. to Q. R. second
24. B. takes B.	24. Q. takes B. (check)
25. K. to R. square	25. Kt. to Q. square (a)
26. Q. to K. Kt. fifth	26. K. to B. square
27. P. to K. B. sixth	27. P. to K. Kt. third
28. P. to K. R. fourth	28. Kt. to Q. Kt. second
29. B. to K. R. third	29. Q. R. to Q. square (b)
30. Q. R. to Q. R. second	30. K. to K. square
31. R. to Q. square	31. R. to Q. R. square
32. Q. to Q. second	32. Kt. to Q. B. fourth
33. Q. to K. third	33. K. to Q. square
34. B. to K. sixth (c)	34. Q. to Q. Kt. second (d)
35. K. to Kt. square	35. P. to Q. R. fifth (e)
36. P. takes P.	36. P. to Kt. sixth
37. Q. R. to Q. R. square	37. P. to Kt. seventh
38. Q. R. to Q. Kt. square	38. R. takes Q. R. P.
39. B. to K. R. third (f)	39. K. to Q. B. second (g)
40. B. to K. B. square	40. K. R. to Q. R. square
41. R. to Q. second	41. Q. R. to Q. Kt. fifth
42. K. to R. second	42. K. R. to Q. R. eighth
43. K. R. to Q. square	43. R. to Q. Kt. sixth
44. Q. to K. R. sixth	44. R. takes R.
45. R. takes R.	45. Q. to Q. Kt. fifth
46. Q. to K. B. eighth (h)	46. Q. to Q. seventh (check)
47. B. to Kt. second	47. Q. to Q. sixth
48. Q. takes K. B. P. (check)	48. Kt. to Q. second
49. P. to Q. B. fifth	49. Q. takes K. Kt. P. (check)
50. K. to Kt. square	50. R. to Q. B. sixth
51. P. takes P. (check)	51. K. to Kt. third
52. R. takes P. (check)	52. K. to B. fourth
53. R. to Q. Kt. square	53. R. to Q. B. seventh
54. R. to Q. Kt. fifth (check)	54. K. to Q. B. fifth, and wins (i)

NOTES.

(a) The plausible move of "Kt. to Q. fifth" would not be so effective. Black now threatens to occupy Q. B. fourth square at the right moment, attacking both the left wing and the centre of the enemy's position.

(b) We do not see valid objections against "Kt. to Q. B. fourth," as the replies of "R. to K. B. fifth" and "B. to K. sixth" do not appear to gain White any advantage.

(c) Ingeniously conceived, but not critically sound; for though the Bishop cannot be taken at once without danger to the second player, that piece will subsequently be in jeopardy, and also be unable to aid in the defence of his own King's beleaguered quarters until it is too late.

Position after White's 34th move.
BLACK.

WHITE.

(*d*) Not only relieving his Queen, but threatening also to capture the hostile Bishop and then the King's Pawn with the Knight, having every way the best game.

(*e*) A careful examination will show that "P. takes B.," followed by "Q. or Kt. takes K. P.," would have been very dangerous, especially when it is remembered that Mr. Anderssen was several games behind his opponent at this important crisis in the match.

(*f*) The Bishop must retreat now to avoid a worse fate.

(*g*) Better, we believe, than the simple capture of the Q. B. Pawn. After this move Black is in no peril of losing his passed Pawn, and all his pieces are brought into co-operation at the point of attack.

(*h*) Under the circumstances Mr. Steinitz plays quite properly in persevering

Position after Black's 50th move.
BLACK.

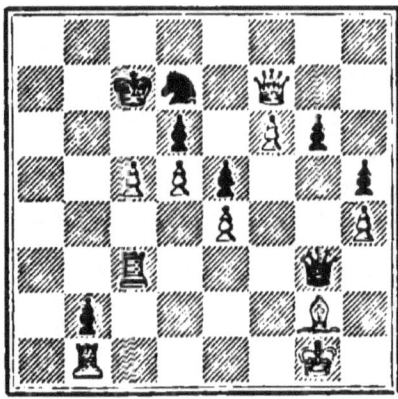

WHITE.

in his counter-attack, as he has thereby a chance of saving or even winning the game, unless his opponent is watchful. He could not attempt to defend himself, none of his pieces being able to quit their present positions for that purpose without immediate loss, whilst Black on his side threatens to occupy Q. B. sixth with his Knight.

(*i*) Mr. Anderssen conducts the whole of this game in his best style.

GAME 189.

Seventh Game. (*Evans's Gambit.*)

White. (Mr. Anderssen.)	Black. (Mr. Steinitz.)
1. P. to K. fourth	1. P. to K. fourth
2. Kt. to K. B. third	2. Kt. to Q. B. third
3. B. to B. fourth	3. B. to B. fourth
4. P. to Q. Kt. fourth	4. B. takes P.
5. P. to Q. B. third	5. B. to B. fourth
6. Castles	6. P. to Q. third
7. P. to Q. fourth	7. P. takes P.
8. P. takes P.	8. B. to Kt. third
9. P. to Q. fifth	9. Kt. to R. fourth
10. B. to Kt. second	10. K. Kt. to K. second
11. B. to Q. third	11. Kt. to Kt. third
12. Q. Kt. to B. third	12. Castles
13. Q. to Q. second	13. B. to Q. second
14. Kt. to K. second	14. P. to Q. B. fourth
15. Kt. to Kt. third	15. B. to B. second (*a*)
16. B. takes Kt. P.	16. P. to B. third (*b*)
17. B. takes R.	17. Q. takes B.
18. Kt. takes B. fifth	18. P. to Q. Kt. fourth
19. Q. R. to Q. B. square	19. Kt. to Kt. second
20. K. to R. square	20. P. to Q. R. fourth
21. P. to K. Kt. fourth	21. R. to K. square
22. P. to Kt. fifth	22. P. to B. fifth
23. P. takes P.	23. Q. takes P.
24. Kt. to Kt. fifth	24. Kt. to K. fourth
25. B. to Kt. square	25. Kt. to Q. B. fourth
26. R. to K. Kt. square	26. K. to R. square.
27. Q. to Q. B. third	27. B. takes Kt.
28. P. takes B.	28. P. to Kt. fifth
29. Q. to K. Kt. third	29. B. to Q. square
30. Kt. takes R. P.	30. Q. to B. second (*c*)
31. P. to B. sixth	31. Q. takes Q. P. (check)

32. R. to Kt. second	32. R. to Kt. square
33. Kt to Kt. fifth	33. B. takes P.
34. Kt. to B. seventh (check)	

And Black surrenders.

NOTES.

(*a*) Hastily played. "P. to K. B. third" would have rendered his game perfectly safe, whilst the move in the text subjects him to immediate disadvantage.

(*b*) If he had taken the Bishop he must have lost his Queen in order to avert the menaced mate.

Position after Black's 30th move.
BLACK.

WHITE.

(*c*) The capture of the Knight would have been directly fatal. Suppose

	30. K. takes Kt.
31. Q. to K. R. third (check)	31. Q. to K. R. third
32. P. to K. B. sixth (dis. ch.)	32. One of the Knights to Q. sixth

White mates in two moves.

GAME 190.

Eighth Game. (*King's Knight's Gambit.*)

White. (Mr. Steinitz.)	*Black.* (Mr. Anderssen.)
1. P. to K. fourth	1. P. to K. fourth
2. P. to K. B. fourth	2. P. takes P.
3. K. Kt. to K. B. third	3. P. to K. Kt. fourth
4. B. to Q. B. fourth	4. P. to K. Kt. fifth
5. Kt. to K. fifth	5. Q. to R. fifth (check)

6. K. to B. square	6. K. Kt. to R. third
7. P. to Q. fourth	7. P. to Q. third
8. K. Kt. to Q. third	8. P. to B. sixth
9. P. to K. Kt. third	9. Q. to K. second
10. Q. Kt. to B. third (a)	10. B. to K. third
11. P. to Q. fifth	11. Q. B. to B. square
12. P. to K. fifth (b)	12. P. takes P.
13. Kt. takes P.	13. Q. takes Kt.
14. Q. B. to K. B. fourth	14. Q. to K. Kt second (c)
15. Kt. to Q. Kt. fifth	15. B. to Q. third (d)
16. Q. to K. square (check)	16. K. to Q. square
17. B. takes B.	17. P. takes B.
18. Q. to Q. Kt. fourth	18. Kt. to K. B. fourth
19. B. to Q. third	19. Kt. to Q. R. third
20. Q. to Q. R. third	20. Kt. to Q. B. fourth
21. B. takes Kt.	21. Q. to K. R. third (e)
22. B. to Q. third	22. R. to K. square
23. P. to K. R. fourth	23. Q. to Q. seventh
24. R. to K. Kt. square	24. R. to K. seventh, and wins.

NOTES.

(a) "K. to B. second," as we observed in our last number, is the usual move. Mr. Steinitz's new mode of play, "Kt. to K. B. second," has certainly some advantages, as it threatens to break up Black's Pawns, besides protecting White's own centre. Whether the move in the text is equal to either we are not yet prepared to assert confidently.

(b) Although this move was hazardous in a match, as the result seems to demonstrate, it is clear that Mr. Steinitz did not make it without some deliberation. The sacrifice of the Knight which follows, is, of course, an essential portion of the first player's plan.

(c) "Q. to K. R. fourth" appears equally sound, and menaces also a dangerous attack on the enemy's quarters.

(d) A careful examination will show that Mr. Anderssen offered the exchange in all probability for two reasons. Firstly had he adopted the defensive move of Kt. to Q. R. third, Mr. Steinitz would have obtained an attack of more or less intensity. Secondly, if White had now taken the Bishop, and then proceeded to capture the Rook, Black, by the simple rejoinder of "Q. takes Q. Kt. P.," would have acquired a powerfully assailing position. It appears, indeed, that there are several answers which can be made to such a capture of the Knight's Pawn, but, after much consideration, we have found none of them satisfactory. In our previous note we suggested that Q. to K. R. fourth would have been good play for White at his 14th move; and so it would have been, but the reader will do justice to the genius of the master who preferred the more profound line of action hinted at in our present remarks.

(e) Black will not waste time by making useless captures when he sees his way to immediate victory.

Position after Black's 21st move.

WHITE.

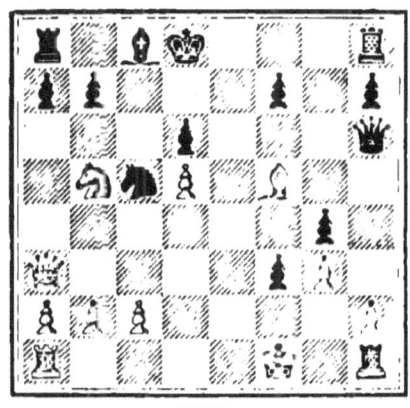

BLACK.

GAME 191.

Ninth Game. (*Evans's Gambit.*)

White. (MR. ANDERSSEN.)	Black. (MR. STEINITZ.)
1. P. to K. fourth	1. P. to K. fourth
2. K. Kt. to B. third	2. Q. Kt. to B. third
3. B. to B. fourth	3. B. to B. fourth
4. P. to Q. Kt. fourth	4. B. takes Kt. P.
5. P. to Q. B. third	5. B. to B. fourth
6. Castles	6. P. to Q. third
7. P. to Q. fourth	7. P. takes P.
8. P. takes P.	8. B. to Kt. third
9. P. to Q. fifth	9. Q. Kt. to R. fourth
10. B. to Q. third	10. K. Kt. to K. second
11. B. to Kt. second	11. Castles.
12. Q. Kt. to B. third	12. Kt. to Kt. third
13. Q. Kt. to K. second	13. P. to Q. B. fourth
14. Q. to Q. second	14. B. to Q. B. second
15. Q. R. to Q. B. square	15. Q. R. to Q. Kt. square
16. Kt. to K. Kt. third	16. P. to K. B. third (*a*)
17. Q. Kt. to K. B. fifth	17. P. to Q. Kt. fourth
18. K. to R. square	18. P. to Q. Kt. fifth
19. K. R. to K. Kt. square	19. B. takes Kt. (*b*)

30. R. takes B.	30. Kt. takes R.
31. B. takes R.	31. K. to B. second
32. B. to K. fifth	32. Q. to R. fourth
33. Q. to K. B. fourth (check)	33. K. to Kt. square (*e*)
34. R. to K. R. square	34. Kt. to Kt. fifth (check)
35. K. to Kt. square	(*f*)

And, after a few more moves, White won the game.

NOTES.

(*a*) "P. to K. R. third" would perhaps have saved the Pawn which Black sacrifices, though White would have gained in that case an attacking position.

(*b*) If he had captured the Pawn with his Bishop the first player might have taken his Knight, and, on his own Knight falling, have checked with the Queen at Q. Kt. fourth.

Position after Black's 23rd move.

BLACK.

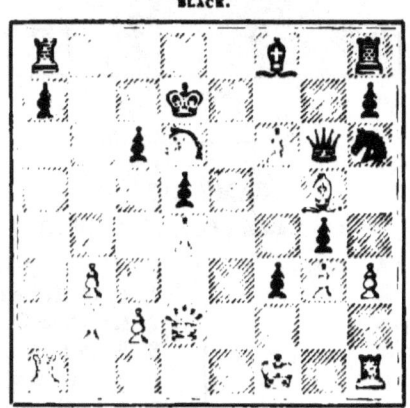

WHITE.

(*c*) It is evident that he could not have taken the Rook at this point without loss.

(*d*) This move is exceedingly disastrous.

(*e*) Had he played "K. to K. second," White could have rejoined with "R. to K. R. square," as in the actual game.

(*f*) "Q. takes R." would involve mate in five moves.

(*g*) No real resource springs from "P. to K. B. seventh (check)," followed by "P. to K. B. eight," becoming a Q. (check).

GAME 193.

Eleventh Game. (*Evans's Gambit.*)

White. (MR. ANDERSSEN.)	*Black.* (MR. STEINITZ.)
1. P. to K. fourth	1. P. to K. fourth
2. K. Kt. to B. third	2. Q. Kt. to B. third
3. B. to Q. B. fourth	3. B. to Q. B. fourth

4. P. to Q. Kt. fourth	4. B. takes P.
5. P. to Q. B. third	5. B. to B. fourth
6. Castles	6. P. to Q. third
7. P. to Q. fourth	7. P. takes P.
8. P. takes P.	8. B. to Kt. third
9. P. to Q. fifth	9. Kt. to Q. R. fourth
10. Q. B. to Kt. second	10. K. Kt. to K. second
11. K. B. to Q. third	11. Castles
12. Q. Kt. to Q. B. third	12. P. to Q. B. third
13. Q. to Q second	13. P. takes P.
14. Q. Kt. takes P.	14. Kt. to K. Kt. third
15. Kt. takes B.	15. Q. takes Kt.
16. Q. R. to Kt. square	16. Q. to Q. square
17. Kt. to Q. fourth (a)	17. K. Kt. to K. fourth
18. Q. B. to R. square	18. Kt. takes B.
19. Q. takes K. Kt.	19. Q. Kt. to Q. B. third
20. Kt. to Q. Kt. fifth (b)	20. Q. to K second
21. Kt. takes P.	21. R. to Q. square
22. Q. to K. Kt. third	22. P. to K. B. third
23. Q. R. to Q. square (c)	23. B. to K. third
24. K. R. to K. square	24. B. takes P.
25. Kt. to K. B. fifth	25. Q. to B. square
26. Kt. to Q. sixth (d)	26. R. to Q. second
27. R. to Q. second	27. Q. R. to Q. square
28. K. R. to Q. square	28. B. to K. third
29. P. to K. R. fourth (e)	29. P. to Q. R. fourth
30. B. to Q. B. third	30. P. to Q. R. fifth
31. R. to Q. third	31. P. to Q. R. sixth
32. P. to K. R. fifth	32. P. to K. R. third
33. Q. R. to Q. second	33. P. to Q. R. seventh
34. B. to Q. Kt. second	34. Kt. to K. fourth
35. B. to Q. R. third (f)	35. R. takes Kt.
36. B. takes R.	36. R. takes B.
37. R. takes R.	37. Q. takes R.
38. R. to Q. B. square	38. Q. to Q. fifth
39. Q. to Q. R. third	39. Kt. to K. Kt. fifth
40. R. to K. B. square	40. Kt. takes P.
41. K. to R. second	41. Kt. to K. Kt. fifth (check)
42. K. to R. square	42. Q. to K. fourth
43. P. to Kt. third	43. Q. takes R. P. (ch.) and wins.

NOTES.

(a) "B. to Q. B. third" might perhaps have led to a more enduring attack.

(b) "Kt. takes Kt.," followed by "Q. to Q. B. third," seems to be stronger.

(c) It would have been better to have captured the Bishop with the Knight than to have thus withdrawn the Rook from a good square.

(d) Although there are some objections to be urged against "R. to Q. sixth," it would, we believe, have been preferable to the move in the text.

(e) If this was done for the purpose of breaking up the hostile Pawns on the King's side, evidently it can have no effect, as when the Pawn reaches the fifth square Black will obviate all difficulty by "P. to K. R. third." "R. to Q. third," to tempt the enemy's Kt. on to Q. Kt. fifth, with the view of subsequently advancing the K. Pawn, might have given White more resource, but in any case, we imagine, the passed Pawns would have insured Black the victory.

(f) This is worthless, but "Q. to Q. R. third" would also have been unavailing.

THE NORTH OF ENGLAND CHESS MEETING.

The Chess Meeting held last week at Redcar has been a great success. Though we much regret the absence of several patrons of the Association, owing to a busy and attractive week in York, occasioned by the visit of the Prince and Princess of Wales, yet we rejoice in an assemblage of Chess talent. Among the company present we noticed: Lord Benholme, Rev. Canon and Mrs. Dixon, Mr. and Mrs. Staunton (London), Mr. and Mrs. Browne (Bournemouth), Rev. W. Beckett (Heighington), Rev. J. F. Newton, Rev. W. Wayte (Eton), Mr. Morley (Birkby Rectory), Rev. G. B. Morley, Fellow of St. Catherine's College, Cambridge, Rev. Chas. and Mrs. Bailey, Mr. and Mrs. Thorold (Bath), Miss Thorold (Sheffield), Rev. F. R. Drew (Malvern), Mr. and Miss Oxley (Redcar), Rev. Jno. and Mrs. Owen (Hootan, Chester), Dr. Wilson (Claycross), Rev. John and Mrs. Seaton, Mr. Fieldsend (Bradford), Mr. S. Tomkins (London), Rev. W. Milburne, Rev. D. Salter, Rev. B. N. R. and Mrs. Batty, Mr. Wisker (Hull), Dr. and Mrs. Bennett (Redcar), Rev. A. B. and Mrs. Skipworth (Bilsdale), Mr. G. F. Bodington, Mr. Hamel (Nottingham), Mr. De Vere (London), Mr. Rhodes, Mr. Cadman and Mr. Myers (Leeds), Mr. Grimshaw (Whitby), Mr. Kidson (Liverpool), Mr. Watson (Saltburn), Mr. Coates (Redcar), Mr. Semple (Stockton), Mr. Park (Hartlepool), and Mr. and Mrs. T. H. Cook. There were many other ladies and gentlemen whose names we were unable to ascertain. The continental war delayed Herr Anderssen's visit to England, in consequence of which his match with Herr Steinitz commenced at so late a period that it was not concluded at the time of the Redcar meeting. Neither, therefore, could be present. In the several classes the combatants played a single game with each other, and the prizes were awarded according to the gross score. In Class I. eight gentlemen competed —Messrs. De Vere, Thorold, Wayte, Wisker, Wilson, Skipworth,

Salter, and Owen. The prize was carried off by Mr. De Vere, who only lost one game, and that to Mr. Thorold. Messrs. Owen, Wisker, and Thorold were equal for the second place, each having lost two games. There were twelve competitors in Class II.—Lord Benholme, Messrs. Morley, Hamel, Kidson, Fieldsend, Bennett, Beckett, Grimshaw, Park, Drew, Semple, and Bodington. The prize was won by Mr. Drew, who did not lose a single game. Next in order of merit stood Messrs. Hamel and Kidson, each of whom won eight games; then Lord Benholme and Mr. Semple, winners of seven games. The Rev. G. B. Morley won in Class III., and Miss Thorold won in the Ladies' Class. Mr. Skipworth and Dr. Bennett were compelled in the early part of the week to resign all further competition, on account of their frequent interruptions in the discharge of the somewhat arduous duties which devolved upon them as the chief promoters and managers of this meeting. The prize for problems was awarded by Messrs. Staunton, Wayte, and De Vere (the committee chosen to make the award) to Mr. Grimshaw, of Whitby. In the absence of Herr Steinitz, the Rev. W. Wayte kindly undertook the blindfold play, conducting five games simultaneously against Mrs. Seaton, Messrs. Semple, Fieldsend, Morley, and Beckett. At the close of a five hours' sitting Mr. Wayte had won three of the games, and the remaining two, with Mr. Morley and Mr. Semple, were given up as drawn. About thirty ladies and gentlemen made the excursion to Saltburne, and luncheon was served at the Zetland Hotel. The Rev. Canon Dixon, in the absence of Lord Zetland, the president, presided, supported on his right by Lord Benholme. Mr. Skipworth occupied the vice-chair. After the usual loyal toasts, " The Army and Navy," "The Archbishop and Clergy," Lord Benholme proposed " Success to the North Yorkshire and Durham Chess Association," whose inaugural meeting was being held at Redcar. Mr. Skipworth, in returning thanks, stated the circumstances which led to the formation of the Association, and spoke briefly on the advantages of Chess, especially on its introduction into the homes of the working people, where it must tend to bring into active exercise their thinking powers, and so help to prepare their minds for useful and solemn teaching. The last but by no means the least interesting feature of this successful meeting was a Consultation Game—Mr. Staunton and the Rev. D. Salter against the Revs. J. Owen and A. B. Skipworth. After playing more than six hours the game was given up as drawn. Mr. Staunton during the week played several games, giving the odds of a rook, and won in every instance.

It is proposed to hold the next meeting of the Association in York, in August, 1867; and it was resolved to invite the Earl of Zetland to be again the President, and the Lady De L'Isle and Dudley to be again the Lady Patroness.

Problem No. 96. — By Herr E. Vorwerk, of Druse.

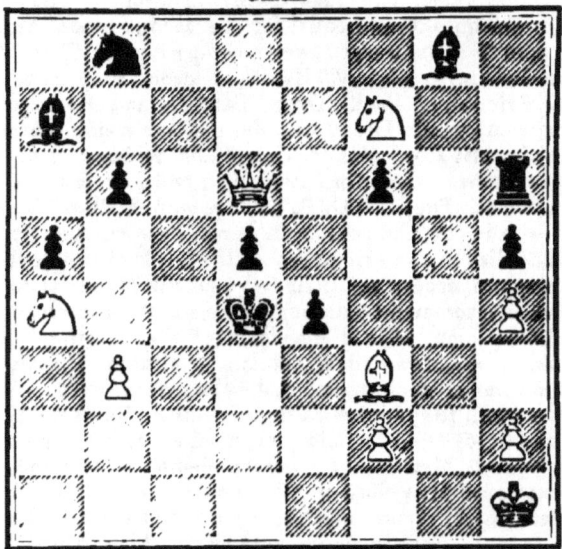

White to move, and mate in three moves.

Problem No. 97. By J. J. Watts, Esq.

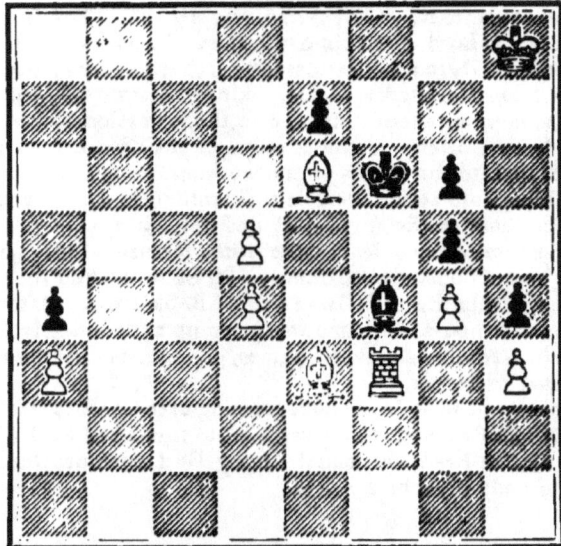

White to play, and mate in five moves.

If Black Pawn stood on Q. R. fourth, instead as in the above on Q. R. fifth, the mate can be effected in four moves.

Problem No. 98. By E. Heath, Esq.
BLACK.

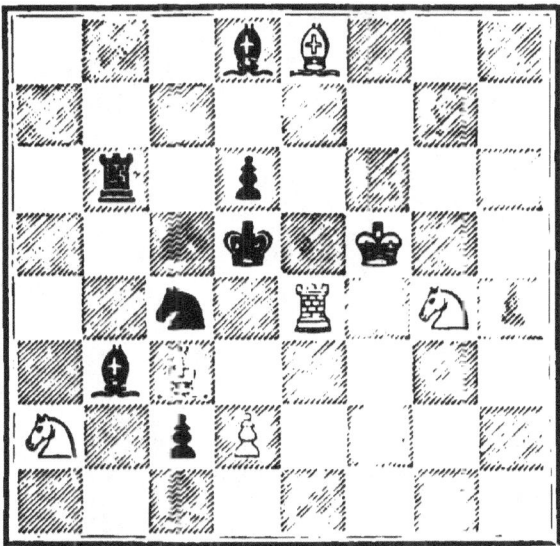

WHITE.
White to play, and mate in three moves.

Problem No. 99. By T. Smith, Esq.
BLACK.

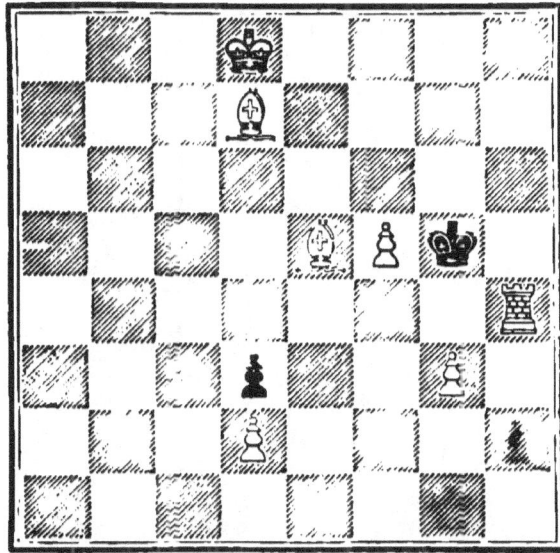

WHITE.
White to play, and mate in three moves.

Problem No. 100. By Herr Meyer, late of Hanover.

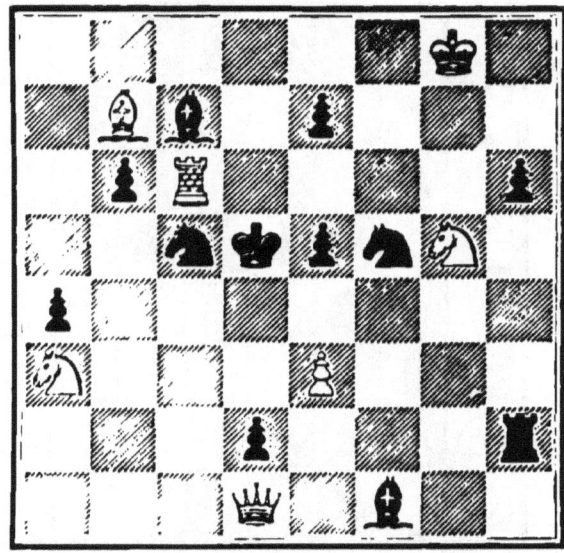

WHITE.

White to play, and mate in three moves.

Chess Study, No. 24. By Herr Horwitz.

WHITE.

Black to move and win.

SOLUTIONS TO PROBLEMS.

No. 78.—By Dr. Conrad Bayer.

White.
1. P. to B. third (check)
2. R. to R. fifth (check)
3. B. to K. third
4. R. to Q. B. fifth (mate)

Black.
1. K. to Q. fourth (A)
2. K. to B. fifth (best)
3. any move

(A)

2. R. to R. fifth (check)
3. P. takes Kt (Queens) (check)
4. Q. to B. seventh (mate)

1. K. to B. fourth
2. K. to Kt. third
3. K. to Kt. second

No. 79.—By T. Smith, Esq.

White.
1. Kt. to Q. sixth
2. K. to B. fifth
3. Kt. takes Kt.
4. K. to Kt. seventh (check)
5. R. mates.

Black.
1. B. to R. seventh (check)
2. Kt. takes Kt. (check) (A)
3. Kt. to K. fifth (check)
4. Kt. takes B.

(A)

3. B. takes Kt. (check)
4. R. to K. eighth (check)
5. R. mates.

2. R. takes Kt.
3. Kt. takes B.
4. Kt. takes R.

No. 80.—By T. Smith, Esq.

White.
1. K. Kt. takes P.
2. K. Kt. to Q. sixth
3. Kt. or R. mates.

Black.
1. P. takes B. (A)
2. any move

(A)

2. R. to Q. third (check)
3. Kt. mates.

1. Kt. takes Kt. P.
2. Kt. takes Kt.

No. 81.—By J. J. Watts, Esq.

White.
1. Q. to Q. sixth (check)
2. Kt. to Q. eighth (check)
3. Kt. mates.

Black.
1. Q. takes Q. or (A)
2. K. moves.

(A)

2. Kt. to K. fifth (check)
3. Q. takes Q. (mate)

1. K. takes Kt.
2. K. moves

No. 82.—By T. Smith, Esq.

1. Q. to Q. Kt. fourth
2. R. to K. seventh
3. Kt. to B. seventh (check)
4. Q. mates.

1. B. takes R. (best)
2. B. takes R. (A)
3. K. moves.

(A)

3. Q. takes P. (check)
4. Kt. to Kt. fifth (mate)

2. P. to B. fourth
3. K. to K. fifth

No. 83.—By S. Loyd, Esq.

White.
1. Kt. to Q. second
2. K. to Kt. fourth
3. Kt. to B. fourth
4. Kt. takes Q.
5. P. to R. fourth (mate)

Black.
1. Q. to Q. R. eighth (check) (A)
2. Q. takes P. (check) (a)
3. Q. takes Kt. P. (check)
4. any move

3. Kt. to Kt. third
4. K. takes Q.
5. P. to R. fourth (mate)

(a) 2. Q. to Kt. seventh (check)
3. Q. takes Kt. (check)
4. any move

(A)

2. K. to Kt. fourth
3. K. takes R.
4. Kt. takes Q.
5. P. to R. fourth (mate)

1. R. takes R. (check) (B)
2. R. to Kt. fourth (check)
3. Q. to Q. Kt. eighth (check)
4. any move

(B)

2. K. to Kt. fourth
3. R. takes B.
4. Kt. takes Q.
5. Mates.

1. B. takes P. (check)
2. B. to R. fourth (check)
3. Q. to Q. Kt. eighth (check)
4. any move

No. 84.—By E. B. O., of Hoboken.

White.
1. Kt. to K. sixth
2. Kt. takes R. or P. (check)
3. R. mates.

Black.
1. R. or P. takes R.
2. any move

2. Kt. to K. B. seventh
3. R. mates.

1. K. moves
2. any move

2. P. to K. fourth (check)
3. R. to Q. B. sixth (mate)

1. P. takes Kt.
2. K. moves

2. Kt. to B. fourth (check)
3. Kt. to B. seventh (mate)

1. P. to Kt. third
2. K moves

No. 85.—By Herr Landesman.

White.
1. P. to Q. B. sixth
2. K. to K. Kt. fourth
3. Kt. to K. B. fourth (mate)

Black.
1. Q. takes Q. or (A)
2. R. takes K. B. P. (check)

(A)

1. Q takes Q. B. P. or (B)
2. Kt. to Q. B. fifth (check)   2. Q. takes Kt.
3. Q. to Q. B. eighth (mate)
    If 2. K. to K. B. fourth, 3. Q. takes B. (mate).

(B)

1. Q. takes K. Kt. P. (check)
2. K. takes Q.   2. any move
3. Mate.

CHESS STUDIES.

No. 17.—By Mr. WATKINSON.

White.   *Black.*

1. R. to Kt. sixth (check)   1. K to R. sixth (best)
2. R. to K. Kt. square   2. P. takes R. (check)
3. K. takes Q.   3. R. to Kt. sixth
4. K. to B. square   4. R. to K. sixth
5. P. to Q. sixth   5. R. to K. third
6. P. to Q. seventh, and must win with a Q. against R.

No. 18.—By Herr KLING.

White.   *Black.*

1. P. to B. seventh   1. R to K. B. fourth or (A)
2. P. to R. fourth (check)   2. K. to Kt. fifth (best)
3. P. to R. fifth, and wins.

(A)

1. R. to Q. B. second
2. K. to Kt. second   2. K. to B. fourth or (B)
3. P. to R. fourth   3. K. to B. third (best)
4. K. to Kt. fourth, and wins.

(B)

2. K. to B. third
3. K. to Kt. fourth   3. P. moves
4. P. to R. third, and wins.

No. 19.—By W. T. PIERCE, Esq.

White.   *Black.*

1. B. to Q. B. third   1. R. to Q. B. seventh (a)
2. K. to Q. third   2. R. takes P.
3. B. to Q. fourth   3. R. to B. sixth (check)
4. R. to R. fourth, and wins.
(a) If 1. R. takes P., White wins by playing 2. B. to Q. fourth, and if R. to Kt. third, then K. to Q. fourth, and wins also.

No. 20.—By W. T. PIERCE, Esq.

White.   *Black.*

1. K. to B. second   1. K. to Kt. fifth (best)
2. K. takes B.   2. K. takes B.
3. B. to Kt. third (the only move to draw)
The game is evidently drawn, as White will now give up his B. for Q. B. P.,

and play his K. into the corner square, and Black cannot queen his P. as his B. does not govern the queening square.

SUICIDAL PROBLEM.

No. 9.—By the Rev. W. WATTS.

White.	*Black.*
1. Kt. to Q. second	1. K. to Q. eighth
2. Kt. to Q. Kt. third	2. K. to K. eighth
3. R. to Q. second	3. K. to K. B. eighth
4. Kt. to Q. fourth	4. K. to K. eighth
5. Kt. to K. B. third (check)	5. K. to B. eighth
6. R. to K. Kt. second	6. P. takes R. (mate)

NOTICES TO CORRESPONDENTS.

ERRATUM.—In our last number, in game No. 180, pages 249 and 250, there occurs an error in the last variation. It should run thus:—

51. P. to R. sixth	51. K. to Q. B. fourth
52. K. to Q. Kt. seventh	52. P. to Kt. fourth
53. P. takes P.	53. K. takes P.
54. K. to B. seventh	54. K. to B. fourth
55. K. to Q. seventh	55. K. to Q. fourth
56. K. to K. seventh	56. K. to K. fourth
57. K. to B. seventh	57. K. to Q. third

And the rest as in the text.

The principle upon which the game should be drawn is obvious, so the mistake—though we regret it—is of less consequence.

T. L. (Dublin).—We have received your kind communication, and regret that we cannot give it in full. The defence to the Evans's Gambit of B. to Q. third is condemned by the best authorities, yet it must be admitted that it may be played, at least, for change of openings. It was adopted, as you are of course aware, by MacDonnell against so great a master as De La Bourdonnais, and by Kieseritzki against Anderssen. These examples are sufficient for your judgment.

C. R.—We have received your communication, and have conveyed the substance of your letter to the proper quarters.

N. F. (Cardiff.)—With regard to Black's 36th move, in Game 147, your remarks are perfectly correct. It seems to have escaped our notice that had Black played R. takes Kt. he had a winning game.

W. W., Eton; A Cambridge Player; Hon. Secretary Sheffield Chess Club; Herrn Meyer, Hirschfeld, L. Paulsen; J. W., Huddersfield; Dr. Bree, Colchester; T. L., Lytham; A. B. S., Bilsdale; E. T., Bath; N.R.W., are thanked for their several kind contributions.

BERLINER SCHACHZEITUNG.—Wir sind Ihnen sehr verbunden für die gütige Aufnahme unserer Ankündigung des Adress-Buches und des Problem-Turniers, Bitten aber Sie darauf aufmerksam zu machen das unser Blatt nicht mehr Ch. Pl. Chron. sondern Ch. Pl. Magazine heisst.

LE SPHINX.—Merci pour l'insertion de nos annonces.

The Chess Player's Magazine.

THE MATCH BETWEEN ANDERSSEN AND STEINITZ.

THE match between Herren Anderssen and Steinitz is, if we are not mistaken, the first set encounter of any duration which has ever taken place between masters representing the rival schools of Austria and Prussia. Just at the time at which the young levies of Prussia were proving their superiority over the old experienced armies of the Austrian Empire, a quiet, unassuming Austrian player was avenging, in his own way, the defeat of Sadowa, and gaining victory over Professor Anderssen, the famous Prussian champion, a veteran of a hundred successful battles in the mimic war of Chess. Germany was divided against herself in both instances; there the contest was physical, and the laurels of the conqueror not unstained with blood; here it was mental, and the crown could be worn without causing misery, whilst a great neutral but friendly country looked on as arbiter of the lists, and afforded the fairest field for action, for there was no fear lest she should turn either the defeat of the one or the aggrandisement of the other to her own peculiar advantage. There were strange vicissitudes in the match. The first blow was struck by Anderssen, who was afterwards overpowered in four successive encounters; then regaining something of his pristine strength the Prussian scored, in his turn, the next four games, but falling away by degrees, in the later stages of the match, he finally succumbed to the prowess and good fortune of his youthful opponent. Our duty as journalists requires us to say a word or two respecting the issue and also the character of the play exhibited, at the hazard of performing a somewhat ungrateful and invidious task. At the commencement Anderssen was doubtless held in the highest esteem by most competent judges, yet those who affected to look upon the match when first made as a hoax, and those who asserted that Steinitz could not win a single game of such an adversary, never for one moment represented genuine public opinion. By a succession of victories, hardly tarnished by one defeat, when he was rendering odds to a skilful amateur who has since proved himself to be one of the best English players, Steinitz had gradually attained a distinguished place amongst the votaries of Chess. If it was doubted whether, under such circumstances, he could be put upon a par with Anderssen, it was because some of the previous victories of the latter were of the most brilliant character. It is impossible to exaggerate the services which the Breslau master has rendered to the cause of Chess. If he had been only a problematist and an analyst his fame would have been at the highest, but add to these considerable qualifications—the result of much study guided by seldom-erring instinct, an intuitive ingenuity—his practical skill, and who can fail to recognise that rare personage even amongst Chess masters—the *born* player? His spirit of chivalry has always been equal to his genius and ability. Ever ready to play, whether in his own country, or coming to gain and risk laurels in London, or courting defeat in Paris, he has, by example more than precept, laid down the golden rule that the true Chess-player is he who plays, not he who talks about the game. If we except consultation matches (in which, if our memory serves us right, he has also distinguished himself) his most remarkable performances during his career have been the triple victory in the tournaments of 1851 and 1862, and in the London Cup, the match with Harrwitz and that with Kolisch. Of these two last named, the first was one of the earliest and the last one of the latest of Anderssen's matches of which we have public record. When Anderssen played with Harrwitz the latter had returned for a while to Germany, fresh from the best English practice, and brimful of ingenuity. Consequently Harrwitz, at the commencement of the match, gained an advantage, but the earnest Anderssen, through the great qualities which he always possesses, though they are not invariably at his command, soon brought himself up to the level of his opponent, and in this unsatisfactory manner the match terminated, as it was never finished. It was at this period that Anderssen showed also his capacity for blindfold play, as he won a game from Harrwitz in the finest manner, both playing without sight of the board. With the Kolisch match we were less satisfied, for although Anderssen just obtained the victory, we have ever thought the play exhibited far below the standard of both masters. We have forborne to mention Anderssen's match with Paulsen, since that, as the match with Harrwitz, was abandoned when both players stood upon an equality. The circumstances connected with the tournaments of 1851 and 1862, and his match with Morphy, we may presume to be known to the majority of our readers; we have not space to recapitulate them; sufficient be it to say that Anderssen's play upon most occasions was of the highest order. We believe that his skill really reached its zenith about 1851. It was on account, then, of these great exploits of Anderssen, and for no other reasons, that the friends of Steinitz had misgivings when their young champion entered the lists against the Prussian veteran. But they were soon agreeably disappointed when they perceived that, whatever might be the capacity of Anderssen, Steinitz possessed moral qualities which rendered him at least a match for his powerful antagonist. A critic must now ask, in no captious spirit, has Anderssen's skill suffered material deterioration, or is Steinitz superior to any foreign player whom we have lately seen in the field? We believe that the truth, as is frequently the case, lies between these extreme opinions. Steinitz is much better than he was originally thought, and Anderssen is not now in his best form. We have said that the latter's play was at its zenith in 1851. We mean by this that his genius being always the same, he had just at that date been in constant good practice, and was in the highest condition so far as health was concerned. Before he entered the lists for the tournament of 1851 he had been properly trained in a series of encounters with such players as Szèn and Falkbeer, the former, it is true, a little *passée*, but the latter in full intellectual vigour, and perhaps better than we ever saw him in this country.

It was not necessary for Anderssen to be in quite the same condition to carry off the first prize in 1862 Then he had only to contend in one game against every individual player—a task, as experience will prove, by no means so wearying as a long set match with one opponent. There was not, however, any considerable fault to be found with his condition at that period. We cannot say the same of him upon the present occasion. It may be thought that we lay too much stress upon the possession of good condition as a necessary qualification for match-playing at Chess, but we really believe it to be more than half the battle. What said the great Athenian orator when asked the chief and also the second qualification for any one to shine in the art which he himself carried to perfection? "Delivery," was his answer, in both cases, "not genius or ability, but delivery." So in Chess, talent of the highest order, combined with the most complete knowledge, will not insure success unless a player is in good health, and also practice enough to bring such qualities out on the day of action. We have further to add that we have noticed in Anderssen, as in other superior minds, a tendency to periodical break-downs. However excellent his play, he cannot command it at the moment that he wishes half as much as the world has generally been disposed to believe. This failing—after all a natural defect on the side of genius, let any one call to mind Cochrane, Kieseritzki, and Horwitz —by no means detracts from his general capacity. We think Anderssen just the man, immediately after a defeat, to enter upon another match and vanquish even a stronger player than the one by whom he himself has been defeated. Steinitz's victory is not at all disparaged by the remarks which we have made respecting his opponent. A player can but win when he has the opportunity, and Steinitz did not win his games clumsily, but finely. It may be reserved for the Austrian to occupy even a higher position in Chess than that which his late distinguished antagonist has filled; he has youth in his favour, and up to this time has been constantly improving. We trust that he, in common with every other good player, may continue to improve.

It is the less necessary to speak critically of the games, as our published notes, we hope, have been sufficiently suggestive to lead a well-informed reader to form his own opinion upon them. Always wishing to assist any one who may be inexperienced, we should be loath to deprive him of availing himself in some degree of his own originality and sagacity. An impartial judge will readily pitch upon the games in which Anderssen outplays Steinitz and those in which he is outplayed, and will separate these again from those— we regret that there are such—in which he breaks down. Once or twice, but not more frequently, a little over-refinement will be detected in the play of Steinitz, but this is more than counterbalanced by his general steadiness and by his promptness in seizing the right moment for action. Certainly the match cannot be accused of dulness, as the majority of the games were Evans's and and Salvio's gambits, Anderssen having the attack in the first and the defence in the second of these brilliant openings. Wherever any striking novelty occurred, we believe that we called attention to it in our notes. We may, perhaps, be permitted to make one remark respecting those notes. If any deficiency be detected in them it arose from the necessity of the case, as we were anxious to lay before our readers the games as soon as they were played, and were therefore, on some occasions, obliged to eschew more elaborate and exhaustive analysis. We trust, however, that no serious error will be found in them, and that with all their shortcomings they may serve in some measure to illustrate one of the most interesting matches that has been contested within the last few years.

WAR CHESS.—We have received from the publisher, Mr. C. B. Richardson, 540, Broadway, New York, a new and interesting game, invented by Col. Charles Richardson, called "War Chess; or, the Game of Battle." The game, which is a very ingenious one, is played by two persons, with figures representing soldiers (cavalry, artillery, and infantry), forming two antagonistic armies, operating on a board, which represents a comparatively level country traversed by a river, passable at three points only—viz., a bridge and two fords. On one side of the river there is a figure representing a city, which is to be defended, and if captured, the player on that side loses the game. On the other side is a figure representing a waggon—"the supply train" of that army, which must be carefully guarded, as its loss is the defeat of the player of the side to which it belongs. A book of explanations accompanies each copy of the game, giving its composition, rules for playing, suggestions to players, remarks illustrating the power of the figures as compared with that of the troops represented; plates illustrating certain moves, &c., and indeed explicitly showing how the game is to be played. The game is beautifully gotten up, the pieces being of silvered and bronzed metal, and the board covered with handsomely embossed morocco. We have spent some time in studying out the peculiarities of the game, and can see that it will afford much amusement and give scope for considerable skill and strategy. It does not, of course, propose to supersede or rival Chess itself, but it is quite an addition to the catalogue of intellectual games, and we hope its capacities will be tested by our young players, whose ingenuity is always sharpened by every new exercise afforded to it. —*Evening Bulletin.*

GAMES.

Match between Anderssen and Steinitz.

GAME 194.

Twelfth Game. (*Sicilian Opening.*)

White. (Mr. Steinitz.)	Black. (Mr. Anderssen.)
1. P. to K. fourth	1. P. to Q. B. fourth
2. P. to K. Kt. third	2. Q. Kt. to B. third
3. K. B. to Kt. second	3. P. to K. fourth
4. K. Kt. to K. second	4. P. to Q. third
5. Castles	5. K. Kt. to B. third
6. P. to Q. B. third	6. Q. to Q. B. second
7. P. to Q. fourth	7. Q. B. to Q. second
8. Q. Kt. to R. third	8. P. to Q. R. third
9. Q. Kt. to Q. B. second	9. Q. to Q. B. square
10. Q. Kt. to K. third	10. K. B. to K. second
11. Q. Kt. to Q. fifth	11. K. B. to Q. square
12. Q. P. takes Q. B. P.	12. P. takes P.
13. B. to K. Kt. fifth	13. Kt. takes Kt.
14. B. takes B.	14. Kt. takes Q. B. P. (*a*)
15. Kt. takes Kt.	15. Q. takes B.
16. Q. to Q. sixth	16. Q. to K. second
17. Q. to Q. B. seventh	17. Castles
18. Kt. to Q. fifth	18. Q. to Q. square
19. Q. takes Q. Kt. P.	19. Q. R. to Q. Kt. square
20. Q. takes Q. R. P.	20. Q. R. takes Q. Kt. P.
21. Q. to Q. B. fourth	21. Q. to Q. R. fourth
22. K. R. to Q. B. square	22. K. R. to Q. R. square (*b*)
23. Q. takes Q. B. P.	23. Q. takes Q.
24. R. takes Q.	24. Kt. to Q. fifth
25. K. R. to Q. B. seventh	25. B. to K. third
26. P. to Q. R. fourth	26. P. to K. R. third
27. P. to K. R. third	27. Q. R. to R. fourth
28. Q. R. to R. third	28. K. to R. square
29. Q. R. to R. square	29. K. to R. second
30. Q. R. to R. third	30. P. to K. R. fourth
31. Q. R. to R. square	31. K. to R. third
32. Kt. to Q. B. third (*c*)	32. Q. R. to Q. B. seventh
33. Q. R. to K. square.	33. K. R. takes Q. R. P.
34. Kt. takes R.	34. R. takes R.

35. Kt. to Q. Kt. sixth	35. R. to Q. B. seventh
36. Kt. to Q. fifth	36. R. to Q. seventh
37. Kt. to K. third	37. P. to K. Kt. third
38. R. to Q. R. square	38. B. to Q. R. seventh
39. B. to K. B. square	39. P. to K. B. third
40. Kt. to Q. B. fourth	40. B. takes Kt.
41. B. takes B.	41. P. to K. R. fifth (*d*)
42. P. to Kt. fourth	42. Kt. to B. sixth (check)
43. K. to Kt. second	43. Kt. to Kt. fourth
44. B. to Q. fifth	44. R. to Q. sixth
45. R. to R. sixth (*e*)	45. Kt. takes R. P.
46. R. takes B. P.	46. K. to Kt. fourth
47. R. to Q. sixth	47. Kt. to B. fifth (check)
48. K. to R. second	48. R. to Q. seventh
49. K. to Kt. square	49. P. to R. sixth
50. R. to R. sixth	50. K. to R. fifth
51. B. to B. fourth	51. R. to Q. fifth
52. B. to Kt. fifth	52. K. takes Kt. P.
53. R. to R. third	53. K. to R. fifth
54. R. to R. eighth	54. P. to Kt. fourth
55. R. to K. eighth	55. R. to Q. eight (check)
56. K. to R. second	56. R. to Q. seventh
57. K. to Kt. square	57. P. to R. seventh (check)
58. K. takes P.	58. R. takes P. (check)
59. K. to R. square	59. P. to Kt. fifth
60. R. takes P.	60. P. to Kt. sixth
61. R. to K. eight	61. R. to R. seventh (check)

And White resigns.

NOTES.

(*a*) We suspect that some of Black's moves with his Queen at an earlier period lost a little time. At this point "Kt. to K. sixth" would perhaps have been a better resource, for although by the move in the text the second player wins a Pawn for the moment, he is placed immediately in difficulties.

(*b*) "Kt. to Q. fifth" looks promising, but careful examination will show that he is wanted to guard his own K. second.

(*c*) This appears to be the primary cause of the loss of White's passed Pawn; it is difficult, however, to suggest a really good move for him at this juncture.

(*d*) An excellent mode of putting White directly on the defensive.

(*e*) "R. to K. R. square" does not appear to be stronger.

GAME 195.

Thirteenth Game. (*Ruy Lopez Knight's Game.*)

White. (Mr. Anderssen.)	Black. (Mr. Steinitz.)
1. P. to K. fourth	1. P. to K. fourth
2. K. Kt. to B. third	2. Q. Kt. to B. third
3. K. B. to Q. Kt. fifth	3. K. Kt. to B. third
4. P. to Q. third	4. P. to Q. third
5. B. takes Kt. (check)	5. P. takes B.
6. P. to K. R. third	6. P. to K. Kt. third
7. Q. Kt. to B. third	7. K. B. to Kt. second
8. Castles	8. Castles
9. B. to K. Kt. fifth	9. P. to K. R. third
10. B. to K. third	10. P. to Q. B. fourth
11. Q. R. to Q. Kt. square	11. Kt. to K. square
12. P. to Q. Kt. fourth (*a*)	12. P. takes P.
13. Q. R. takes P.	13. P. to Q. B. fourth
14. Q. R. to Q. R. fourth	14. Q. B. to Q. second
15. R. to R. third (*b*)	15. P. to K. B. fourth
16. Q. to Q. Kt. square	16. K. to R. square
17. Q. to Q. Kt. seventh	17. P. to Q. R. fourth
18. K. R. to Q. Kt. square	18. P. to Q. R. fifth
19. Q. to Q. fifth	19. Q. to Q. B. square
20. K. R. to Q. Kt. sixth	20. Q. R. to R. second
21. K. to R. second	21. P. to K. B. fifth
22. B. to Q. second	22. P. to Kt. fourth
23. Q. to B. fourth	23. Q. to Q. square
24. K. R. to Kt. square	24. Kt. to B. third
25. K. to Kt. square	25. Kt. to R. second
26. K. to B. square	26. P. to R. fourth
27. Kt. to K. Kt. square (*c*)	27. P. to Kt. fifth
28. P. takes P.	28. P. takes P.
29. P. to K. B. third	29. Q. to K. R. fifth
30. Kt. to. Q. square	30. Kt. to Kt. fourth
31. B. to K. square	31. Q. to K. R. seventh
32. P. to Q. fourth	32. Kt. P. takes K. B. P.
33. Kt. P. takes P.	33. Kt. to K. R. sixth
34. B. to B. second	34. Kt. takes Kt.
35. Q. P. takes B. P.	35. Q. to R. sixth (check)
36. K. to K. square	36. Kt. takes P. (check)
37. R. takes Kt.	37. Q. takes R.
38. Kt. to Q. B. third	38. P. takes P.
39. B. takes P.	39. Q. R. to Q. B. second

40. Kt. to Q. fifth	40. R. takes B.
41. Q. takes R.	41. Q. takes P. (check)
42. K. to K. B. second	42. R. to Q. B. square
43. Kt. to B. seventh	43. Q. to K. sixth (check)

And White resigns.

NOTES.

(*a*) Had this move been played for the purpose of obtaining possession of an open file with his Rook, its principle would have been justifiable; but as Mr. Anderssen afterwards removes that piece to another file, it is certainly valueless.

(*b*) By this unaccountable loss of time, White enables his opponent to obtain an irresistible attack on the King's side. This unfortunate Rook, moreover, can never come to the assistance of his besieged sovereign.

(*c*) In the latter stages of this game, several moves may be suggested by way of improvement for White, but it would be worthless to dwell upon them in detail, so hopelessly is Mr. Anderssen lost through the imprisonment of his pieces on the left wing.

GAME 196.

Fourteenth and last Game in the Match. (*King's Gambit Declined.*)

White. MR. STEINITZ.	*Black.* (MR. ANDERSSEN.)
1. P. to K. fourth	1. P. to K. fourth
2. P. to K. B. fourth	2. B. to Q. B. fourth
3. Kt. to K. B. third	3. P. to Q. third
4. B. to Q. B. fourth	4. K. Kt. to B. third
5. P. to Q. third	5. Castles
6. Q. to K. second	6. B. to K. Kt. fifth
7. P. takes P.	7. P. takes P.
8. B. to K. third	8. Q. Kt. to Q. second
9. Q. Kt. to Q. second	9. P. to Q. B. third
10. B. to Q. Kt. third	10. P. to Q. Kt. fourth
11. Castles K. R.	11. Q. to Q. Kt. third
12. B. takes B.	12. Kt. takes B. (*a*)
13. K. to R. square	13. Q. R. to K. square
14. Q. to K. B. second	14. P. to Q. R. fourth
15. P. to Q. R. fourth	15. P. to K. R. third
16. Kt. to K. R. fourth	16. P. takes P.
17. B. takes P.	17. B. to K. third
18. P. to Q. Kt. third	18. Kt. to K. Kt. 5th (*b*)
19. Q. to K. Kt. square	19. Q. to Q. Kt. fifth
20. K. Kt. to K. B. third	20. B. to Q. second
21. Kt. to Q. B. fourth	21. Kt. takes B.
22. R. takes Kt.	22. Q. to Q. B. sixth

23. P. to K. R. third	23. Kt. to K. B. third
24. R. to Q. B. square	24. Kt. to K. R. fourth
25. Q. to K. square (c)	25. Q. takes Q. (check)
26. R. takes Q.	26. P. to K. B. third
27. R. takes P.	27. R. to K. third
28. P. to Q. fourth	28. R. to Q. Kt. square
29. P. takes P.	29. B. to K. square
30. Kt. to Q. fourth	30. R. to K. second
31. R. to Q. B. fifth	31. R. to Q. B. second
32. Kt. to Q. sixth	32. P. takes P.
33. Kt. takes B.	33. R. takes Kt.
34. R. takes P.	34. R. from K. sq. to Q. B. sq.
35. R. takes R.	35. R. takes R.
36. Kt. to K. B. third	36. R. takes P.
37. Kt. takes P.	37. R. to Q. B. sixth
38. P. to Q. Kt. fourth	38. R. to Q. Kt. sixth
39. Kt. to Q. B. sixth	39. Kt. to K. B. fifth
40. P. to K. fifth	40. Kt. to Q. sixth
41. R. to Q. R. square	41. Kt. takes Kt. P.
42. R. to R. eighth (check)	42. K. to R. second
43. R. to Q. Kt. eighth	43. Kt. takes Kt. (d)
44. R. takes R.	44. Kt. takes P.
45. R. to Q. Kt. sixth	45. Kt. to K. Kt. third
46. K. to R. second	46. Kt. to K. fourth
47. K. to Kt. third	47. Kt. to Q. second
48. R. to Q. sixth	48. Kt. to K. B. third
49. K. to K. B. fourth	49. Kt. to Kt. square
50. P. to Kt. fourth	50. Kt to K. second
51. P. to R. fourth	51. Kt. to Kt. third (check)
52. K. to Kt. third	52. Kt. to K. second
53. R. to K. sixth	53. Kt. to Kt. third (e)
54. P. to R. fifth	54. Kt. to R. square
55. R. to K. seventh	55. K. to Kt. square
56. K. to B. fourth	56. Kt. to B. second
57. K. to B. fifth	57. K. to B. square
58. R. to R. seventh	58. K. to Kt. square
59. R. to B. seventh	59. Kt. to Kt. fourth
60. K. to Kt. sixth	60. Kt. to K. third
61. R. to B. eighth (check)	61. Kt. to B. square (check)
62. K. to B. fifth	62. K. to B. second
63. R. to R. eighth	63. K. to Kt. square
64. K. to K. fifth	64. K. to B. second

65. R. to R. seventh (check)	65. K. to Kt. square
66. K. to Q. sixth	66. Kt. to R. second
67. K. to K. sixth	67. Kt to B. third
68. K. to B. fifth	68. K. to R. second
69. R. to K. seventh	69. Kt. to Q. fourth
70. R. to K. sixth	70. Kt. to B. second
71. R. to K. fifth	71. Kt. to R. third
72. K. to K. sixth	72. Kt. to Kt. fifth
73. K. to B. seventh	73. Kt. to Q. sixth
74. R. to K. eighth	74. Kt. to K. B. fifth
75. K. to B. eighth	75. Kt. to Q. fourth
76. R. to K. fifth	76. Kt. to K. B. fifth
77. K. to B. seventh	77. Kt. to R. sixth
78. R. to K. third	78. Kt. to Kt. fourth (check) (*f*)
79. K. to B. eighth	79. K. to R. square
80. R. to K. seventh	80. Kt. to R. second (check)
81. K. to B. seventh	81. Kt. to B. third
82. K. to Kt. sixth	82. Kt. to Kt. square
83. R. takes P.	83. Kt. to B. third
84. R. to Q. R. seventh	84. Kt. to Kt. square
85. R. to R. seventh (mate)	

NOTES.

(*a*) It would have been better, we think, to take with the Queen.

Position after Black's 28th move.
BLACK.

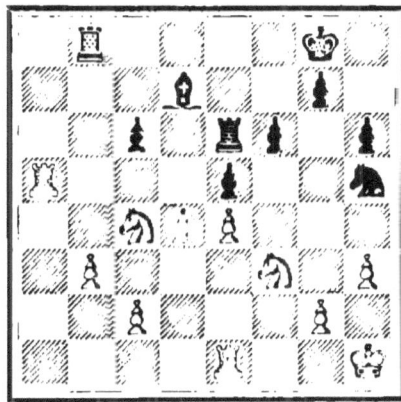

WHITE.

(*b*) Black doubtless plays this to drive the Queen for a moment to K. Kt. square, and thus gain an attack on the hostile Knight, but, as he will eventually have to provide for the defence of his weak Pawns on the Queen's side, his manœuvre is perfectly unavailing. We may observe that the whole of the play from the thirteenth move had a tendency to weaken his right wing.

(c) White could have taken the Q. R. P. at once with perfect safety.

(d) Considering the hopeless character of the game, Mr. Anderssen judiciously sacrificed the exchange, with the view of getting rid of White's most immediately threatening Pawns.

(e) The Knight should have simply returned to K. Kt. square, always remaining near his own King.

(f) A distinguished player present suggested "Kt. to K. B. fifth" at this point. It is certainly a much better resource.

Position after White's 78th move.

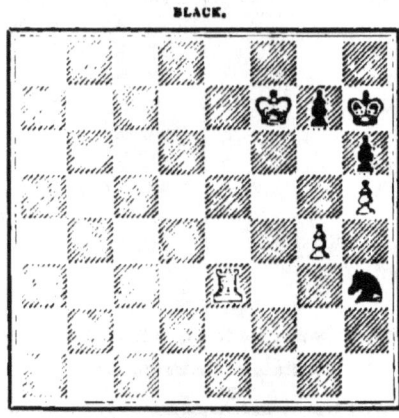

GAME 197.

The following two games were played during the meeting of the British Chess Association, at the St. James's Hall, by Lord Lyttelton against Mr. Chinnery.

HANDICAP TOURNEY.

First Game. (*Ruy Lopez Knight's Game.*)

White. (Lord Lyttelton.)	Black. (Mr. Chinnery.)
1. P. to K. fourth	1. P. to K. fourth
2. Kt. to K. B. third	2. Kt. to Q. B. third
3. B. to Kt. fifth	3. P. to Q. R. third
4. B. to R. fourth	4. Kt. to B. third
5. Kt. to Q. B. third	5. P. to Q. third

6. P. to K. R. third	6. B. to K. second
7. Castles	7. Castles
8. P. to Q. third	8. P. to K. R. third
9. B. to K. third	9. Kt. to R. second
10. B. to Kt. third	10. B. to K. third
11. B. takes B.	11. P. takes B.
12. Kt. to R. second	12. Q. to K. square
13. Q. to Kt. fourth	13. R. to B. third
14. P. to B. fourth	14. R. to Kt. third
15. Q. to K. second	15. P. takes P.
16. R. takes P.	16. B. to Kt. fourth
17. R. to B. third	17. Kt. to K. fourth
18. K. R. to B. square (a)	18. Q. to K. second
19. B. takes B.	19. Kt. takes B.
20. K. to R. square	20. Kt. to Q. second
21. R. to B. fourth	21. P. to Q. B. third
22. Q. R. to K. B. square	22. P. to K. fourth
23. R. to B. fifth	23. Kt. to B. third
24. P. to K. R. fourth	24. Kt. to K. third
25. Q. to B. second	25. Kt. to B. fifth
26. P. to K. Kt. third	26. Kt. from B. third to R. fourth
27. P. to K Kt. fourth	27. Kt. to R. sixth
28. Q. to B. third (b)	28. Kt. from R. fourth to B. fifth
29. P. to R. fifth	29. R. to Kt. fourth
30. R. takes R.	30. Q. takes R.
31. Q. to Kt. third	31. K. to R. second
32. Kt. to B. third	32. Q. to K. second
33. Kt. to R. fourth	33. R. to K. Kt. square
34. Kt. to Kt. sixth	34. Q. to Kt. fourth
35. Kt. to K. second	35. Kt. takes Q. Kt.
36. Q. takes Kt.	36. Kt. to B. fifth
37. Kt. takes Kt.	37. P. takes Kt.
38. R. to B. third	38. P. to K. Kt. third
39. P. takes P. (check)	39. R. takes P.
40. K. to R. second	40. P. to R. fourth (c)
41. R. to B. square	41. R. to R. third
42. K. to Kt. square	42. P. takes P.
43. Q. to Kt. second	43. Q. to B. fourth (check)
44. Q. to B. second	44. Q. takes Q. (check)
45. R. takes Q.	45. P. to B. sixth
46. R. to B. square	46. K. to Kt. third
47. K. to B. second	47. K. to Kt. fourth

48. K. to K. third	48. R. to R. seventh
49. R. to B. second	49. R. takes R.
50. K. takes R.	50. K. to B. fifth, and wins.

NOTES.

(*a*) White loses a little time with this Rook; nevertheless his game is not a bad one.

Position after Black's 27th move.

BLACK.

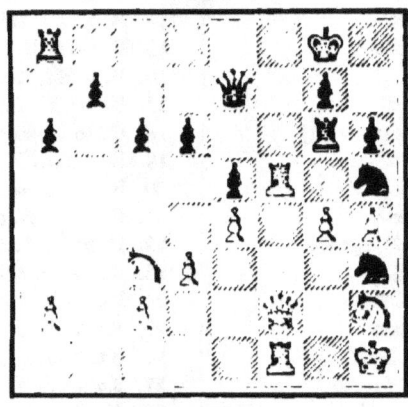

WHITE.

(*b*) Some of the first player's previous moves look hazardous, but they are not so in reality. Had he now followed up his skilful conception by moving his Q. to K. third, Black's game would have been untenable. Suppose

28. Q. to K. third.	28. Kt. from R. fourth to K. B. fifth.

There is no better move to save a piece.

29. R. to K. B. third	29 Q. takes P.

The only feasible move.

30. R. to K. R. fifth	30. Q. takes R.
31. P. takes Q.	31. R to Kt. eighth (check)
32. Q. takes R., winning a piece.	

(*c*) The best mode of bringing the game to a speedy termination.

GAME 198.

Second Game.   (*Petroff's Defence.*)

White. (LORD LYTTELTON.)	*Black.* (MR. CHINNERY.)
1. P. to K. fourth	1. P. to K. fourth
2. Kt. to K. B. third	2. Kt. to K. B. third
3. Kt. to Q. B. third	3. Kt. to Q. B. third
4. B. to B. fourth	4. B. to B. fourth

5. Castles	5. P. to Q. third
6. P. to K. R. third	6. Castles
7. P. to Q. third	7. Kt. to K. second
8. Q. B. to Kt. fifth	8. P. to Q. B. third
9. B. takes Kt.	9. P. takes B.
10. Q. to Q. second (*a*)	10. Kt. to Kt. third
11. P. to Q. fourth (*b*)	11. P. takes P.
12. Kt. takes P.	12. Kt. to K. fourth
13. B. to Kt. third	13. B. takes R. P.
14. P. to K. B. fourth (*c*)	14. K. to R. square (*d*)
15. P. takes Kt. (*e*)	15. R. to K. Kt. square
16. R. to B. second	16. Q. P. takes P.
17. Q. to R. sixth	17. B. takes P.
18. R. takes B.	18. Q. takes Kt. (check)
19. K. to R. second	19. R. takes R. (check)
20. K. takes R.	20. Q. to B. seventh (check)
21. K. to R. third	21. R. to K. Kt. square
22. Kt. to K. second	22. Q. to Kt. seventh (check)
23. K. to R. fourth	23. Q. to Kt. fifth (mate)

NOTES.

(*a*) Kt. to K. R. fourth is a stronger move.

(*b*) Evidently an unsound combination.

Position after Black's 13th move.

BLACK.

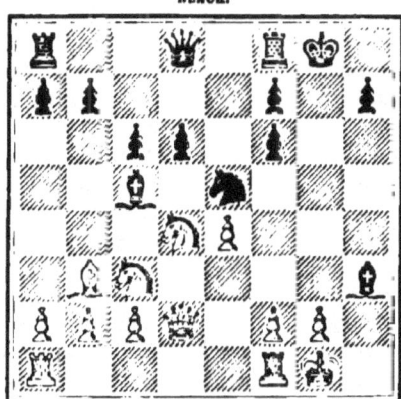

WHITE.

(*c*) White must lose a Pawn; for, had he taken the Bishop, Black would have captured the Knight with his remaining Bishop, and, if that piece were taken in turn, have won the Queen.

(d) Strange to say, Black here throws away his advantage, as the Bishop can be taken after this move. He should now have withdrawn that piece to a secure position.

(e) As we suggested in our previous note, it was the Bishop, not the Knight, which should now have been captured.

GAME 199.
(Sicilian Opening.)

White. (Herr H. Meyer.)   *Black.* (A Member of the St. George's Chess Club.)

White	Black
1. P. to K. fourth	1. P. to Q. B. fourth
2. K. B. to B. fourth	2. P. to K. third
3. K. Kt. to B. third	3. P. to Q. third
4. P. to Q. fourth	4. P. takes P.
5. Kt. takes P.	5. P. to Q. R. third
6. Castles.	6. Q. Kt. to B. third
7. P. to Q. B. third	7. P. to K. R. third
8. B. to K. third	8. K. Kt. to B. third
9. Q. Kt. to Q. second	9. B. to K. second.
10. P. to Q. Kt. fourth	10. Castles
11. Q. to K. B. third	11. P. to K. fourth
12. Kt. to K. B. fifth	12. B. to Q. second
13. Q. to Kt. third	13. B. takes Kt.
14. P. takes B.	14. K. to R. second
15. P. to K. B. fourth (a)	15. P. to Q. fourth
16. B. to Q. third	16. P. to K. fifth
17. K. B. to B. second	17. Q. to Q. B. square (b)
18. P. to Q. R. third	18. Q. takes P.
19. Kt. to B. third	19. Q. to Kt. fifth
20. Q. to B. second	20. K. to R. square
21. P. to K. R. third	21. Q. to K. third
22. Kt. to Q. fourth	22. Q. to Q. B. square
23. P. to K. Kt. fourth	23. Kt. takes Kt.
24. B. takes Kt.	24. P. to Q. Kt. fourth
25. Q. to K. R. fourth	25. Kt. to Kt. square
26. P. to K. Kt. fifth	26. Q. to K. B. fourth
27. K. R. to B. second	27. P. to K. B. third
28. Kt. P. takes R. P.	28. Kt. takes P.
29. R. to K. Kt. second	29. Q. R. to K. square
30. K. B. to Kt. third (c)	30. Q. R. to Q. square (d)
31. Q. R. to K. square (e)	31. B. to Q. third

32. Q. R. to K. B. square	32. B. to K. second
33. K. to R. square	33. K. R. to K. B. second
34. Q. R. to K. Kt. square	34. Q. to R. second
35. Q. to K. R. fifth	35. B. to K. B. square
36. K. R to Kt. sixth	36. Kt. to Kt. square
37. Q. to Kt. fourth	37. Kt. to K. second
38. P. to K. B. fifth	38. Kt. to Kt. square
39. B. to K third	39. K. R. to Q. B. second
40. B. to Q. fourth (*f*)	40. Kt. to K second
41. Q. R. to Kt. third	41. Kt. takes R. (*g*)
42. P. takes Kt.	42. Q. to R. third
43. B. to K. third	43. P. to K. B. fourth
44. Q. takes B. P.	44. Q. to R. fifth
45. R. to Kt. fifth	45. Q. to K. eighth (check)
46. B. to Kt. square	46. R. to K. second

White mates in four moves.

NOTES.

(*a*) Q. B. takes R. P. looks promising, but would not lead to any advantage, *e g.*:—

15. Q. B. takes R. P.	15. K. takes B.
16. B. takes B. P.	16. P. to K. Kt. fourth
17. P. takes P. *en passant*	17. K. to Kt. second

With a good game.

(*b*) This secures the gain of a Pawn, as Black threatens Kt. takes Kt. P., &c.

Position after White's 30th move.

BLACK.

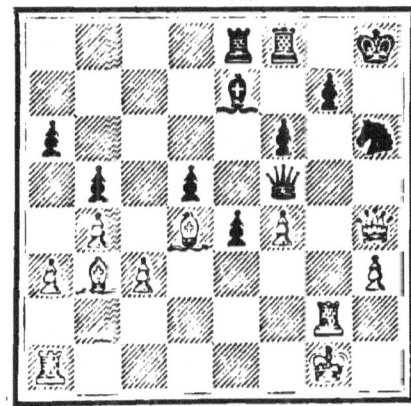

WHITE.

(*c*) An excellent move, having in view

31. R. to Kt. fifth	31. P. takes R.
32. Q. takes Kt. (check)	32. Q. to R. second

33. B. takes P. (check)   33. K. to Kt. square
34. B. takes P. (check)   34. R. to B. second
35. B. takes R. (check), winning the Queen.

(*d*) This is undoubtedly Black's best reply.

(*e*) Losing time. White should at once have played 31. K. to R. square.

(*f*) Much better than B. to Q. Kt. sixth, as the following variation will show:—

40. B. to Q. Kt. sixth   40. R. takes B. P.
41. B. takes R.   41. R. takes P. (check)
42. K. to Kt. second   42. R. takes B.

And White's King is somewhat exposed.

(*g*) Fatal, as will presently be seen.

GAME 200.

GRAND CHALLENGE CUP TOURNEY.

The following game was played by the Rev. G. A. MacDonnell against Mr. De Vere.

(*Scotch Gambit.*)

White. (MR. MACDONNELL.)	Black. (MR. DE VERE.)
1. P. to K. fourth	1. P. to K. fourth
2. Kt. to K. B. third	2. Kt. to Q. B. third
3. P. to Q. fourth	3. P. takes P.
4. B. to Q. B. fourth	4. B. to Q. B. fourth
5. P. to Q. B. third	5. Kt. to K. B. third
6. P. to K. fifth	6. P. to Q. fourth
7. B. to Q. Kt. fifth	7. K. Kt. to K. fifth
8. P. takes P.	8. B. to Q. Kt. third
9. Castles	9. Castles
10. B. takes Kt.	10. P. takes B.
11. Kt. to Q. B. third	11. P. to K. B. fourth
12. P. takes P. *en passant* (*a*)	12. Q. takes P.
13. Kt. takes Kt.	13. P. takes Kt.
14. Kt. to K. fifth	14. R. to Q. square
15. Q. to Kt. third (check) (*b*)	15. B. to K. third
16. B. to K. Kt. fifth	16. B. takes Q.
17. B. takes Q.	17. P. takes B.
18. Kt. takes P.	18. B. to Q. fourth
19. Kt. takes R.	19. B. takes Q. P.

And White resigns.

NOTES.

(*a*) The capture of the Pawn in passing is extremely hazardous, as it brings the hostile Queen into co-operation with the rest of her forces, and renders White's centre Pawn an object of immediate attack.

(*b*) The first player cannot be said to have any good move at his command, but the one adopted clearly makes matters worse.

CHESS INTELLIGENCE.

HANDICAP TOURNAMENT OF THE BRITISH CHESS ASSOCIATION.

In our last report of this interesting contest we reached only the pairing-off for the second round. The winners of that turned out to be Herr Steinitz, Messrs. S. J. Green, Mocatta, and Mongredien, jun. These gentlemen were paired off; Herr Steinitz to give the Pawn and move to Mr. Mocatta, and Mr. Green the Pawn and two moves to Mr. Mongredien. In each case the giver of the odds won. Herr Steinitz then contended successfully against Mr. Green, who received the Pawn and two moves. The first two prizes being thus disposed of, the third and fourth prizes were decided by Mr. Mocatta's winning against Mr. Mongredien, although he gave the large odds of the Pawn and two moves. This handicap was remarkable for the fact that several players, who had not up to this time obtained any considerable reputation, showed great aptitude for the game. It would be invidious to particularise names, and the more so as we suspect that some of the amateurs to whom we have alluded generally will soon force their way to a better recognised position.

WESTMINSTER CHESS CLUB.—This club has removed to Haxel's Hotel in the Strand, where they occupy spacious apartments. An interesting match is now in progress there between Herr Steinitz (the victor in the late match with Anderssen) and Mr. Bird, well known for his brilliant style of play. This club being frequented by distinguished amateurs, such as Messrs. Bird, Barnes, Burden, Hewitt, Duffy, Browne, and by the veterans Staunton and Boden, and by Herr Steinitz, is a very attractive resort for Chess-players, and may be esteemed as ranking with the very first metropolitan Chess *cercles*.

OBITUARY.—We extremely regret to announce that the son of Count Pongracz was slain in the battle of Königsgräz. He was a lieutenant in the Austrian army. He had already shown aptitude in Chess-problem composing, a branch of the game in which his father enjoys a deservedly high reputation.

Problem No. 101. By Dr. Conrad Bayer.

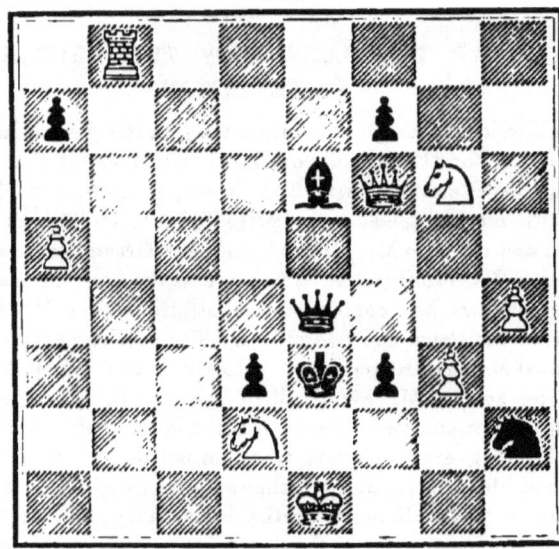

White to play, and mate in three moves.

Problem No. 102. By Herr Lieutenant Ph. Klett, of Stuttgart.

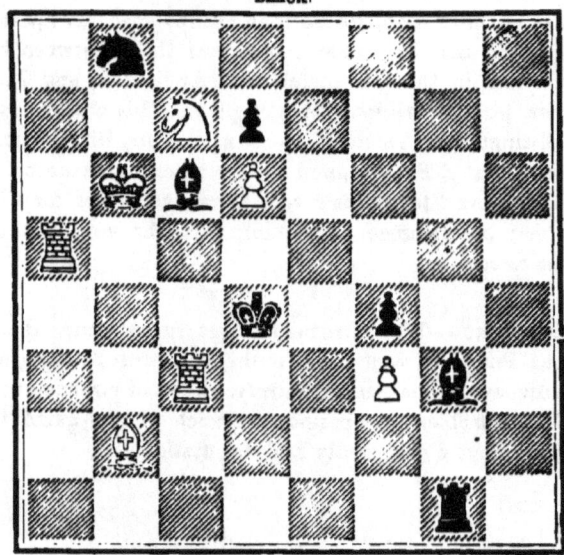

White to play, and mate in five moves.

Problem No. 103. By Herr H. Meyer, late of Hanover.

BLACK.

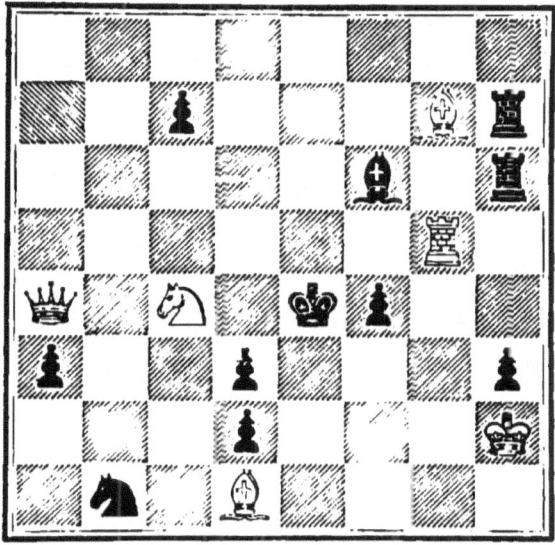

WHITE.

White to play, and mate in three moves.

Problem No. 104. By Herr Charles Kockelkorn, of Cologne.

BLACK.

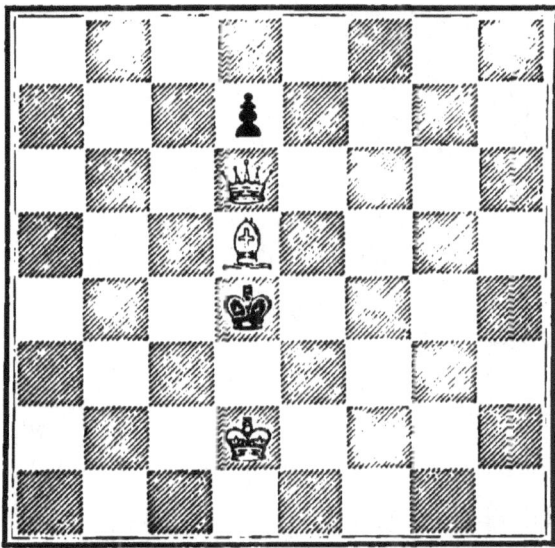

WHITE.

White to play, and mate in three moves.

Problem No. 105. By Th. Smith, Esq.

White to play, and mate in four moves.

Problem No. 106. By Herr Kontz. (From the *Schachzeitung*, Leipzig.)

White to play, and mate in three moves.

Chess Study No. 25. By W. T. Pierce, Esq.

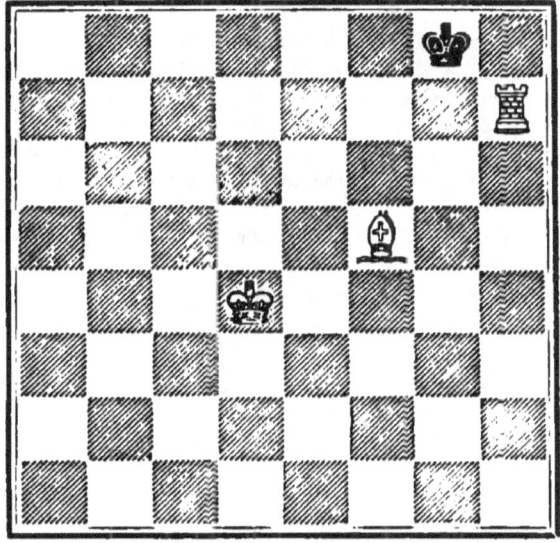

White to play, and mate in ten moves, only moving his King once.

Chess Study No. 26. By Herr H. Meyer, late of Hanover.

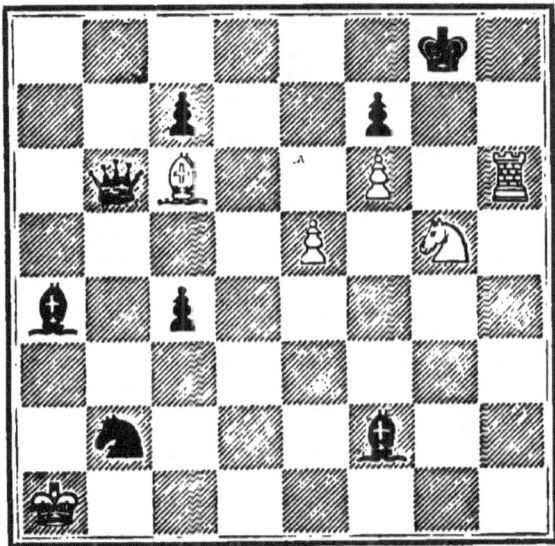

White to move and win.

CHESS STUDY.

BY "EUCLID."

An ingenious correspondent has favoured us with the following analysis of the position in the interesting end-game of the Rook and Bishop against Rook. Many of our greatest writers have analysed the various phases in this remarkable study, and have attempted to demonstrate the results to which they have arrived; but we have never yet seen so satisfactory a solution as this. We strongly recommend our readers to examine it carefully. The enormous amount of patient industry and skill which the author must have bestowed upon this labour entitle him to our highest praise.

Rook and Bishop against Rook.

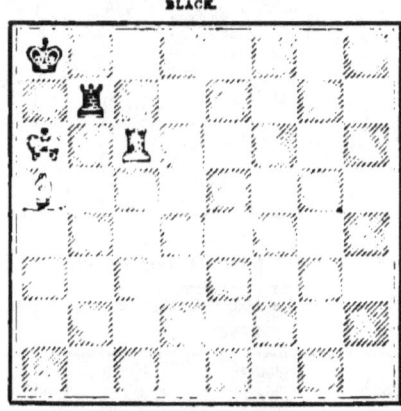

White to play and win.

A correct solution of this position has never yet been published. The moves given in Mr. Staunton's *Handbook* (page 464), as translated from *Le Palamède*, are—

1. R. to Q. B. eighth (check)
2. R. to Q. B. fourth
3. R. to K. R. fourth
4. B. to Q. Kt. fourth

1. R. to Q. Kt. square
2. R. to Q. Kt. seventh
3. R. to Q. Kt. eighth

But this line of play is evidently ineffectual, because Black can at once draw the game by taking the Bishop with Rook. Also, neither the *Handbook* nor *Le Palamède* contain directions for winning if Black, instead of playing Rook along Q. Kt. file, persists in keeping it on that occupied by his King, and it will be seen that this is by far the most difficult part of the problem.

The solution here given is divided into two parts, the first containing the variations which arise from Black playing his Rook along Q. Kt. file, and the second showing how the game is to be won when the Rook remains on his first line.

Part I.

1. R. to Q. B. eighth (check)   1. R. to Q. Kt. square
2. R. to Q. B. fourth   2. R. to Q. Kt. sixth, seventh,
                                        or eighth

If 2. R. to Q. Kt. second—
3. R. to K. fourth, as at move 4 below.
If R. to K., K. B., K. Kt., or K. R. squares, see Part II.
3. R. to K. fourth

From this point it is immaterial whether White's Rook occupies K., K.B., K. Kt., or K. R. files.

                      3. R. to Q. Kt. second

If 3. R. to Q. Kt. square, see Variation A.
If 3 R. to Q. Kt. sixth, seventh, or eighth—
4. R. to K. sixth, as at move 5 below.

White cannot now win either by 4. R. to K. sixth or 4. B. to Q. Kt. sixth, and the best plan is to make an indifferent move with Rook.

4. R. to K. R. fourth   4. R. to Q. Kt. sixth, seventh,
                                       or eighth

If 4. R. to Q. R. second (ch.), see Variation B.
If 4. R. to Q. Kt. square—
5. B. to Q. B. seventh, as at move 4, Variation A.
5. R. to K. R. sixth   5. R. to Q. Kt. sixth, seventh,
                                       or eighth

If 5. R. to Q. Kt. second, see Variation C.
If 5. R. to Q. Kt. square—
6. B. to Q. B. seventh wins, as in Variation A.
6. B. to Q. Kt. sixth   6. R. to Q. R. sixth, seventh,
                                       or eighth (check)
7. K. to Q. Kt. fifth   7. R. to Q. B. sixth, seventh,
                                       or eighth

If 7. K. to Q. Kt. second—
8. R. to K. R. seventh   8. K. to Q. B. square
9. K. to Q. B. sixth   9. R. to Q. B. seventh (check)
10. B. to Q. B. fifth makes the position as at move 10 below.
                    Or if 7. R. to Q. Kt. sixth (check)—
8. K. to Q. B. sixth   8. R. to Q. B. sixth (check)
9. B. to Q. B. fifth   9. R. to Q. Kt. sixth
10. R. to K. R. fourth, and mates in four moves.
                  Again, if 7. R. to K., K. B., K. Kt., or K. R. files—
8. K. to Q. B. sixth   8. R. to K., K. B., K. Kt., or
                                       K. R. squares
9. B. to Q. B. seventh, as at move 9, Variation C
8. B. to Q. B. fifth   8. K. to Q. Kt. second

If 8. R. to Q. Kt. sixth (check)—
9 K. to Q. B. sixth   9. R to Q. Kt. second or Q.
                                       Kt square
10. B. to Q. Kt. sixth and wins.

9. K. to Q. B. sixth	Or if 8. R. to Q., K., K. Kt., or K. R. files—
	9. R. to Q., K., K. Kt., or K. R. squares
10. D. to Q. sixth wins.	
9. R. to K. R. seventh (check)	9. K. to Q. B. square
	If 9. K. to Q. Kt or Q. R. square—
10. K. to Q. B. sixth wins easily.	
10. K. to Q. B. sixth	10. R. to Q. seventh
	If 10. R. to Q. eighth—
11. R. to Q. R. seventh, as at move 12 below.	
	Or if 10 R. to Q. sixth—
11. R. to Q. R. seventh	11. R to Q. Kt. sixth
12. R. to Q. B. seventh (check), as at move 16 below.	

It is now a variety of the celebrated "Philidor" position, solutions of which will be found on pages 449, 450, 451, and 465 of Mr. Staunton's *Handbook*, and the best mode of winning from here is given below.

11. R. to K. Kt. seventh	11. R. to Q. eighth
	If 11. R. to Q. sixth—
12. R. to Q. R. seventh	12. R. to Q. Kt. sixth
13. R. to Q. B. seventh (check), as at move 16 below.	
	Or if 11. R. to Q. square—
12. B. to K. seventh	12. R. to K. R. square
13. R. to K. Kt. fourth, and then 14. R. to Q. R. fourth wins easily.	
12. R. to Q. R. seventh	12. R. to Q. Kt. eighth
	If 12. K. to Q. Kt. square—
13. R. to Q. R. fourth	13. R. to Q. B. eighth
14. R. to K. fourth wins.	
13. B. to Q. R. third	13. R. to Q. Kt. sixth
	If 13. K. to Q. Kt. square—
14. R. to K. R. seventh	14. K. to Q. R. square
15. R. to K. R. fourth	15. R. to Q. Kt. second
16. R. to K. Kt. fourth, and mates in four moves.	
14. B. to Q. sixth	14. R. to Q. B. sixth (check)
15. B. to Q. B fifth	15. R. to Q. Kt. sixth
16. R. to Q. B. seventh (check)	16. K. to Q. Kt. square
If K. to Q square, 17. R. to K. B. seventh wins.	
17. R. to K. R. seventh	17. K. to Q. R. square
18. R. to K. R. fourth, and mates in four moves.	

Part II.

The following analysis shows how White wins the game when Black Rook remains on the same row as his King. It becomes necessary to force Black's King out of the corner square into a position where White's Rook can get to attack him from both sides, and the mode of accomplishing this is by no means obvious, and will repay a careful examination:—

1. R. to Q. B. eighth (check)	1. R. to Q. Kt. square
2. R. to Q. B. fourth	2. R. to K., K. B., K. Kt., or K. R. squares
	If 2. R. to Q. Kt. second, sixth, seventh, or eighth—
3. R. to K. fourth wins, as in Part I.	

3. R. to Q. B. sixth	3. R. to K. R., K. Kt., K. B., or K. square

    If 3. K. to Q. Kt. square, see Variation D.
    If 3. R. to Q. Kt. square, see Variation E.

4. B. to Q. B. third	4. R. to Q. Kt. square

    If 4. K. to Q. Kt. square—
5. B. to Q. Kt. fourth, as at move 4, Variation D.
    Or if 4. R. to Q., K., K. Kt., or K. B. squares—
5. B. to K. fifth wins easily.

5. R. to K. sixth	5. R. to Q. B. square

    If 5. R. to K. Kt. square, see Variation F.
    Or if 5. R. to K. B. or Q. square, 6. B. to K. fifth wins soon.
    Again, if R. to Q. Kt. second—

6. R. to K. eighth (check)	6. R. to Q. Kt. square

7. R. to K. second, as at move 9 below.
    And if R. to Q. Kt. sixth or eighth, 6. B. to Q. R. fifth makes the position at move 5, Part I.

White must now proceed to get this position with Black to play; the Bishop is therefore made to lose a move, but keeps on the diagonal, which prevents Black's Rook from going to any other square but Q. Kt. or Q. B. It is obvious that if White attempts to win at once by placing Bishop on K. fifth, either now or at moves 7 and 8, the game is drawn by R. to Q. Kt. third, or Q. B. third (check).

6. B. to Q. Kt. second	6. R. to Q. Kt. square

    If 6. K. to Q. Kt. square—

7. B. to K. fifth (check)	7. K. to Q. R. square

8. K. to Q. Kt. sixth wins easily.
    If R. to Q., K. B., or K. Kt. squares, 7. B. to K. fifth, as at move 6, Variation F.

7. B. to Q. fourth	7. R. to Q. B. square

    If 7. R. to Q. Kt. second, sixth, or eighth—
8. B. to Q. Kt. sixth, as at move 6, Part I.
    Or if 7. R. to Q. Kt. fifth—

8. B. to Q. Kt. sixth	8. R. to Q. R. fifth (check)

9. B. to Q. R. fifth wins.
    Again, if 7. R. to Q., K. B., or K. Kt. squares—
8. B. to K. fifth, as in Variation F.

8. B. to Q. B. third

It is now the position after move 5 above, but Black has to play here—
                               8. R. to Q. Kt. square
    If 8. R. to Q., K. B., or K. Kt. squares—
9. B. to K. fifth (check), as at move 6, Variation F.
    Or if 8. K. to Q. Kt. square—
9. B. to K. fifth (check) wins easily.

The pieces are now in the proper places for White to draw back his Rook, and Black will then be compelled either to lose, as in Part I., by playing Rook along Q. Kt. file, or at the following move to take his King away from the corner square.

9. R. to K. second	9. R. to Q. square

    If R. to Q. B. square, see Variation G.

If R. to K. B. square, see Variation H.
If R. to K. Kt. square, see Variation J.
If R. to Q. Kt. second, sixth, or eighth—
    10. B. to Q. R. fifth makes the position as at move 3, Part I.

10. K. to Q. Kt. sixth   10. K. to Q. Kt. square
                 If R. to Q. Kt. square (check)—
11. K. to Q. B. seventh   11. R. to Q. Kt. second (check)
12. K. to Q. B. sixth makes the position as at move 13, Variation G.
                 Or if 10. R. to K. Kt. square—
11. K. to Q. B. seventh, and mates in three moves.
                 Again, if 10. R. to K. B. square—
11. K. to Q. B. seventh, as at move 11, Variation G.
                 And if 10. R. to Q. third (check)—
11. K. to Q. B. seventh wins easily.

11. B. to Q. Kt. fourth   11. K. to Q. B square
    If 11. R. to K. Kt. or K. R. squares, see Variation K.

12. K. to Q. B. sixth   12. R. to Q. second
                 If 12. R. to Q. fifth—
13. R. to Q. sixth   13. R. to Q. B. fifth (check)
14. B. to Q. B. fifth   14. K. to Q. square
15. R. to Q. second (check)   15. K. to K. or Q. B. square
16. R. to K. B. second wins.
                 Or if 12. R. to Q. sixth—
13. B. to Q. R. fifth   13. K. to Q Kt. square
14. R. to K. eighth (check), and mates in three moves.
                 Or if 12. R. to Q. eighth—
13. B. to Q. second, and mates in three moves.
                 Or if 12. R. to K. Kt. or K R. square—
13. B. to Q. sixth makes the position as at move 13, Variation K.
                 Again, if 12. K. to Q. Kt. square—
13. B. to Q. sixth (check)   13. K. to Q. B. square
14. R. to Q. Kt. second wins.

13. R. to K. eighth (check)   13. R. to Q. square
14. R. to K. seventh   14. R. to K. Kt. square
                 If 14. R. to K. R. square—
15. B. to Q. sixth   15. K. to Q. square
16. R. to Q. R. seventh wins Rook.
                 Or if 14. R to Q. eighth—
15. B. to Q. sixth   15. R. to Q. B. eighth (check)
16. B. to Q. B. fifth   16. R. to Q. eighth
17. R. to Q. R. seventh, as at move 12, Part I.
                 Or if 14. R. to Q. sixth—
15. B. to Q. R. fifth wins easily.
                 And again, if 14. R. to Q. fifth—
15. B. to Q. sixth   15. R. to Q. B. fifth (check)
16. B. to Q. B. fifth   16. K. to Q. square
17. R. to K. third   17. R. to Q. B. seventh or eighth
18. R. to Q. R. third   18. K. to K. square
19. R. to K. B. third wins.

15. B. to Q. sixth   15. K. to Q. square
                 If 15. R. to K. R. square—
16. R. to Q. R. seventh wins.

16. R. to K. sixth   16. R. to K. R.
      If 16. K. to Q. B. square—
 17. R. to K. second makes the position at move 13, Variation K.
      Or if 16. R. to K. Kt. second—
 17. B. to K. fifth   17. R. to K. Kt.
 18. B. to K. B. sixth (check) as at move 19 below.
17. B. to K. fifth   17. R. to K. B.
      If 17. R. to K. Kt. square—
 18. B. to K. B. sixth (check) as at move 19 below.
18. B. to K. Kt. seventh   18. R. to K. Kt.
19. B. to K. B. sixth (check)   19. K. to Q. B.

The mode of play given below for White wins much more quickly than 20. R. to K. seventh.

20. R. to K. fourth   20. R. to K. B.
      If 20. K. to Q. Kt. square—
 21. R. to Q. Kt. fourth (check) and mates in 3.
21. B. to K. Kt. seventh   21. R. to K. Kt.
      If 21. R. to Q. square—
 22. R. to Q. R. fourth wins easily.
22. R. to Q. R. fourth   22. K. to Q.

White would lose much time by at once checking at Q. R. eighth, and then taking Rook, but can mate in nine moves by the following mode of play—

 23. R. to Q. R. seventh   23. K. to K.
 24. K. to Q. sixth   24. R. takes B.
 25. R. takes R.   25. K. to K. B.
 26. R. to Q. R. seventh, and mates in five moves.

(To be continued in our next.)

SOLUTIONS TO PROBLEMS.

No. 86.—By C. R. ALEXANDER, Esq.

White.   *Black.*
1. R. to K. B. square   1. Kt. takes R. (A)
2. Q. to Q. Kt. square (check) 2. Q. takes Q. (best)
3. Kt. to B. eighth, and mates next move.

(A)

          1. R. takes R. (B)
2. Q. takes R. (check)   2. B. to Q. fourth (best)
3. B. to Q. fourth, and Q. mates.

(B)

          1. R. to K. fourth
2. R. takes Kt.   2. B. to B. fifth
3. B. to Kt. fourth (check) 3. Kt. takes B.
4. R. takes B. (mate)

No. 87.—By T. Smith, Esq.

White.	Black.
1. Kt. to Q. Kt. fourth	1. B. takes R. (A)
2. Kt. to B. second (check)	2. K. to K. fifth
3. Kt. to R. square (discovered check)	3. K. to Q. fifth
4. Kt. to Kt. third (mate)	

(A)

	1. K. takes R.
2. R. takes Kt.	2. K. to B. fifth (B)
3. B. to Q. third (check)	3. K. to B. sixth
4. Kt. (discovering check) mates.	

(B)

	2. Any other move
3. Kt. to B. second (discovered check)	3. K. moves
4. Kt. to K. third (mate)	

No. 88.—By Herr Klett.

White.	Black.
1. Kt. to Q. B. second	1. R. to R. third (A)
2. Kt. to K. fourth	2. B. takes Kt. (a) (b)
3. Kt. to K. third	3. P. takes Kt.
4. P. mates.	

(a)
	2. K. takes Kt.
3. Q. to K. sixth (check)	3. Any move
4. Q. or Kt. mates.	

(b)
	2. P. to K. Kt. fourth
3. Q. to K. eighth (check)	3. K. moves
4. Kt. mates.	

(A)
	1. K. P. takes Kt. (B)
2. Q. to K. seventh (check)	2. K. to K. B. fourth
3. Kt. to Q. fourth (check)	3. K. to Kt. fourth
4. Q. to K. third (mate)	

(B)
	1. P. to K. Kt. fourth
2. Q. to K. seventh (check)	2. K. to B. fourth
3. Q. to K. eighth	3. Any move.
4. Kt. to Q. fourth (mate).	

No. 89.—By Herr Meyer.

White.	Black.
1. Q. to Q. B. third	1. Anything
2. Q. takes B. (check), and mates next move.	

No. 90.—By Lieutenant Ph. Klett.

White.	Black.
1. R. to K. Kt. second	1. P. takes R. (check)
2. K. takes P.	2. Kt. to Q. Kt. fifth (disc. check)
3. Kt. to Q. B. sixth	3. Q. takes Kt. (check)
4. R. to Q. fifth (check)	4. Q. takes B.
5. R. to Q. B. fifth (mate)	

No. 91.—By Herr Kockelkorn.

White.	Black.
1. Q. to Q. B. second	1. Q. takes Q.
2. R. to Q. Kt. third	2. Any move
3. Kt. mates.	

No. 92.—By Herr Mehrtens.

White.	Black.
1. Kt. to Q. Kt. seventh	1. K. to Q. fourth
2. Q. to Q. third	2. P. takes Q.
3. R. to Q. B. fifth (mate).	

No. 93.—By C. R. Alexander, Esq.

White.	Black.
1. R. to Q. B. fifth	1. B. takes R. (best) (A)
2. Q. to Q. Kt. square	2. Q. takes Q. P. (best)
3. Kt. takes B. (discovered check)	3. Q. covers
4. Q. takes Q. (mate)	

(A)

	1. Kt. to B. fifth
2. Q. to K. seventh	2. Kt. from B. square to K. third
3. Q. takes Kt. (check)	3. Kt. takes Q.
4. Kt. takes P. (mate)	

CHESS STUDY.

No. 21.—By T. Smith, Esq.

White.	Black.
1. B. to R. fifth (check)	1. K. to K. second
2. K. R. to K. sixth (check)	2. K. to Q. second
3. B. to K. eighth (check)	3. R. takes B.
4. R. to B. seventh (check)	4. K. takes R.
5. Kt. to Q. eighth (check)	5. R. takes Kt.
6. Q. to K. fifth (check)	6. K. takes Q.
7. R. to K. seventh (double check)	7. K. to Q. fifth
8. B. to K. fifth (check)	8. K. takes Kt.
9. B. to Q. B. third (dis. check)	9. K. to K. B. fifth
10. B. takes Kt. (check)	10. B. takes B.
11. K. B. P. takes P. (mate)	

First three moves as before—

4. Q. Kt. takes P. (check)	4. K. to Q. square
5. Kt. to Kt. seventh (check)	5. K. to Q. second
6. R. to B. seventh (check)	6. K. takes R.
7. Kt. to Q. eighth (check)	7. R. takes Kt.
8. Q. to K. fifth (check)	8. K. takes Q.
9. R. to K. seventh (double check)	9. K. to Q. fifth
10. B. to R. seventh (check)	10. Q. takes B.
11. Q. B. P. mates.	

NOTICES TO CORRESPONDENTS.

⁎ VEIT AND CO., Leipsic.—At your request we here state with pleasure that your excellent Chess journal is now entitled *Schachzeitung* (Leipsic), and not, as frequently stated by us, *Berliner Schachzeitung*. The change which you made in your title escaped our notice.

⁎ The Editor of the "Chess Directory" tenders his best thanks for the contributions he has already received from officials in England, Europe, America, and the Colonies.

ERRATA.

The solution of Mr. Watkins's Chess Study was, we regret to say, incorrectly printed. It should run thus:—

White.	Black
1. R. to Kt. 6 (check)	1. K. to K. R. 6
2. R. to K. Kt. square	2. P. takes R. (check)
3. K. takes Q	3. K. to Kt. 6
4. K. to B. square	4. K. to B. 6
5. K. to Kt. square, &c.	

A communication has been made to us by Herr Kling, to the effect that in Study No. 23 two Pawns were inadvertently omitted—viz., a Black Pawn at K. B. 2, and a White Pawn at K. B. 6.

Herr Meyer has pointed out to us that in Problem No. 89 the Black Pawn at K. R. 4 is superfluous.

S. W.—Not having been furnished till recently with the names of the seconds and umpire in the late match between Anderssen and Steinitz, we were unable to state that Messrs. Staunton and Hewitt acted as seconds for the former, and Messrs. Strode and Boden for the latter. Earl Dartry was the umpire.

C. R.—We quite agree with you that Herr Klett's problem (No. 88) is a masterpiece of stategy. White's second move is particularly ingenious, which, however, can only be properly appreciated by connoisseurs who, like yourself, are well versed in the subtleties of this branch of the game.

F. D.—Received with thanks. A private communication shall shortly be made to you.

W. H.—You are quite right. The Problem No. 4 is simply an imitation of Plachutta's competing problem which appeared in the book of the Chess Congress.

A. M.—True. It was suggested to us that a Black Pawn placed at K. 2 in Problem No. 87 would render the position correct; as it was printed, the author's intended solution is impracticable on account of Black's second move, B. to K. B. square.

C. W. H.—The observations in the publications to which you draw our attention cannot be meant to apply to Mr. Lowenthal. After a residence in this country of sixteen years, even if he were not, as he is, legally naturalised, he could not fairly be described as a "foreign professional."

J. W., Huddersfield.—Many thanks for your inclosure. Please acquaint J. H. T. that his position is incorrect: it admits of a second solution by 1. B. to R. 2, &c.

H. M.—A problem connoisseur sends us a second version of Chess Study No 21, in which mate is effected in ten moves instead of eleven, as intimated by the author. We shall give the second solution in a future number; we withhold it for the present to enable our readers to make the discovery for themselves.

THE Chess Player's Magazine.

ILLEGAL MOVES.

[The following article upon "illegal moves" was contributed originally by the eminent Chess author and practical player Von H. der Lasa to the columns of our contemporary the *Schachzeitung* (Leipzig) At the same time that it treats specially of the disputed questions respecting the King's compulsory move in case of the occurrence of certain irregularities, it contains also abundance of interesting matter throwing light upon the general discussion concerning the laws of Chess. In presenting it to our readers in an English dress we have not scrupled to make a few verbal alterations where they seemed to make the meaning clearer, but have never, we believe, willingly or wittingly departed from the sense of the distinguished writer's text. It would, indeed, be a task of more than ordinary difficulty to attempt to publish in a condensed form any of the articles derived from such a source, since Von H. der Lasa is so strictly logical, and accurate that almost every expression of his is pregnant with force and reflection. We have ventured to embody many of the author's notes with his text for the double reason of avoiding too prolix a commentary and of interspersing with the discussion of a somewhat dry and intricate subject matter generally of a livelier character.]

The attention of a great number of Chess-players is at present directed to the necessity of revising the laws of Chess. The subject has been discussed by masters as well as novices and also in articles in the magazines. A solution of the different questions which have been thereby raised seems to us to be of less importance than it is generally considered, but with them, as with many other matters which might be allowed to drop altogether without any inconvenience, discussion once commenced is extended to every particular, however minute. Not long ago we were asked whether in the case of illegal, or so-called false, moves the punishment of compelling the King of the offending player to move was an ancient custom, or whether its origin was of a comparatively modern date.

The sources at our command allow us to compare the rules of Chess existing at different epochs in various countries, consequently we can answer the question addressed to us in the following manner:—Compelling the King to move in a certain case is a punishment of a very ancient date, but to the extent recognised in the present day, and according to our present regulations, it can be traced back only to the year 1777, and originated in England. We shall take leave to enter into this question fully, and also examine the more ancient rules connected therewith.

The compulsory move of the King now arises when a piece is touched, moved, or captured which cannot be moved or captured without contravening the existing rules, such as leaving the King exposed to check, or if there be no square unoccupied where the piece could be placed, &c.* These oversights presuppose considerable inattention, still they occur, as experience teaches, in hastily-played games and sometimes even in serious matches. If, however, the blunder is not immediately taken notice of, the false move stands good as if it had been a proper one.

The move of the King can, besides, be insisted on if any unlawful move whatever has been made—for instance, if the Bishop has been moved like a Knight, or the opponent's piece has been played by mistake, and the blunder has been immediately noticed. As these irregularities happen more rarely even than the former ones, there may be a disposition not to assign a punishment at all to what are really mistakes, but after replacing the piece on the square from which it was removed, to consider the move not to have been made. Upon closer inspection some difficulty may be found in the application of this principle, but for ourselves we should certainly not hesitate to play on these terms, even if the seemingly just condition was added to it that the touching of pieces which cannot be legally moved or taken should be of no further consequence. In practical play such a rule would always suffice, if both players were equally intent upon rectifying their own mistakes and those of their adversaries. It would, however, enjoy but a very limited recognition, as in France as well as in England players seem to adhere to the punishment of moving the King, and as a universal adoption of common rules should be the aim, it would not be advisable to propose it. We do not, however, intend to point out either the best possible rule or to explain why this or that proposition has no partisans, but simply to enumerate the different modes of punish-

---

* A complete list of these irregularities may be seen in the work published by Von Jänisch in 1855, entitled, *Nouveau Réglement des Echecs adopté par les amateurs de ce jeu à St. Pétersbourg*. We must, however, observe that these rules have not been adopted anywhere out of Russia.

ment which have been in use in various countries since the beginning of modern Chess down to the predominant adoption of the King's penal move in regard to unlawful moves.

The first mention we find in Lucena, whose work was dedicated to a prince who died in 1497, and therefore still belongs to the mediæval period. He says in the preface (*Berliner Erinnerungen*, 1859, page 176), "Even if you play without a stake, you must play the piece you touched, except when it covers the King. In that case you must play the King."

From Lucena's rule, which is given rather as advice than as a law, it will be seen that the move of the King as a penalty is of very ancient date in certain cases, but its application was far more restricted. To come to its present extended use the reader will be obliged to follow us through three centuries of Chess regulations. If it be, however, supposed that the rules grew stricter and more severe in the course of time, we must at once observe that this is an error. It is true that they have become more severe in particular instances, but in general they have become only more logical or rational. In some respects the more modern practice, even as to false moves, has been less severe, as we shall perceive when speaking about the Modenese. But we can even give an example of mitigated penal laws from the very book of the old Spaniard quoted. Therein a piece when played ought to be left upon the square it had once touched. Lopez, Salvio, and with him Greco did not accept this "dictum," whilst Carrera and the Modenese authors accepted it, and thus the law still exists in Italy, but with the addition (Ponziani Ed. Venezia, 1861, p. 23) that the piece may be moved beyond the square it had touched, but could not be left on any of the intermediate squares. With us a piece may be played to any square whatever until the hand is taken off it. "Touch man and goe, out of hand and stand," is the rule in Saul's *Famous Game of Chesse-Play*, 1640. We are therefore less severe in this respect.

Damiano, in 1512, supplies no rules or regulations, but we find some in Lopez (1561), and very explicit ones as regards illegal moves, in Salvio and Carrera. It seems that it was then the general custom to play for stakes and to move quickly. Blunders may therefore have occurred, and, as they might have been intentional after all, ought to have been properly punished.

Lopez, in his fifth law, concurs with Lucena in thinking that the King, having been exposed to check, ought to move; and this opinion was formed quite independently of that of his predecessor, with whose work he was unacquainted. He says, "El Rey es obligado a satisfaser la pena. Questa es mi opinion en esto." "The King is obliged to undergo the penalty, and this is my opinion thereon." It appears from this that, at the time, the law was not altogether fixed. Gianutio and Salvio (Ed. 1723, p. 73) are in favour of the compulsory move; but these regulations disappeared afterwards in Italy, giving way to a fresh theory upon false moves in general. In the "Réglement" of the French Amateurs (1775, p. 403) we find the case again, with the penalty attached to it that the King must move if he can. We have had here in juxtaposition the most important notices of Lucena's example, and will now pass on to a more special examination of the several regulations.

The author who first employed the expression, so common afterwards, *false move*—which, however, would better be termed *illegal*—was Lopez. His laws begin with the rule, that, after a false move (*trecha falsa*), the adversary has the option, in order to punish the irregularity, of either allowing the illegal move to stand, or of requiring the piece moved to be played properly. In the following laws, other cases of illegal moves are discussed, such as the capture of a player's own piece, or of an adversary's when made illegally, but still the penalty of moving the King is only spoken of as in the above-mentioned case by Lucena. Thus, Gianutio (Turino, 1597) only gives the penalty of the King's move when check has been uncovered.

More general, but probably only in appearance more extended, is the rule of Salvio (Neapol., 1604, p. 22); and, in a French translation of Lopez (1615), in which, instead of that author's laws, those of Salvio are adopted, it is said, "The King must be played when a piece or Pawn is touched which cannot be moved." Similar is the rule of Greco (Ed. 1821), (*Berliner Erinnerungen*, 1859, page 128), who took it, with the other laws, almost verbatim from Salvio. By the way in which this law is given, it may almost seem that, in cases also where a piece cannot be played at all and has been touched, the move of the King is indicated as a penalty; but we are of opinion that Salvio, and those who repeat his rules, only mean the case of uncovering a check, or else they would have spoken of it more *in extenso*.

In 1634, Salvio, in distinguishing several sorts of illegal moves, discussed the question how far the offending party, when the game was played for a stake, and in case the illegal move, not having been rectified during the game, had occasioned the victory, owed redress to his opponent. These inquiries of the Neapolitan lawyer, which we mention for their curiosity, have for us no further interest. We must observe, also, that various categories of mistakes mentioned by Salvio are neither complete, nor are they in principle logically separate. There is, however, no mention of moving the King as a penalty.

(*To be concluded in our next.*)

CHESS INTELLIGENCE.

BRISTOL ATHENÆUM CHESS CLUB.

(*From a Special Correspondent.*)

The annual meeting of this club was held on Thursday evening, September 6th, Mr. W. P. Meeker, vice-president, in the chair. Present—Messrs. Corfe, J. Burt, C. Boorne, J. Boucher, J. Burcher, W. Hibbins, W. S. Pryor, H. J. Haycraft, H. Isaacs, R. T. Stoate, J. S. Tilly, and W. Berry (hon. secretary).

The chairman called upon the secretary to read the minutes of the last meeting, and the treasurer to read a statement of accounts, which showed a balance in favour of the club.

The secretary next read a letter from Captain Kennedy, in which he expressed his desire to resign the office of president to the club. For some time he had, to his regret, been prevented from attending any of their meetings, and he did not think there was any prospect of his being able to make more than a rare appearance there in the future, and he thought the growing importance both in numbers and strength of players required something more than a nominal president. He expressed his cordial thanks to all the members for the invariable support and assistance he had received during the time he had been president of the club, in the continued prosperity of which he would always feel a very warm interest.

A letter from Mr. Cleland to the secretary was next read, in which he expressed his intention of returning to Bristol for the winter and uniting himself with the club as usual.

A discussion then ensued relative to the desirability of retaining Captain Kennedy as their president, notwithstanding the fact of his living at such a distance as Dover. Most of the members thought his name was a tower of strength to the club, and therefore, although he might not be able to attend often at their meetings, it would be advantageous to still retain him at their head. Ultimately the following resolution was carried unanimously (proposed by Mr. C. Boorne, seconded by Mr. Stoate, and supported by Mr. Corfe):—
"That this meeting learns with unfeigned regret of the wish on the part of Captain Kennedy to resign the office of president to the Bristol Chess Club. That whilst gratefully acknowledging the many valuable services rendered by him to the club (extending over a period of seven years), the vast improvement that has taken place, both in numbers and strength of players, the proud position the club has attained in the country owing chiefly to his skilful management and great reputation, and bearing in mind the fact that they possess two able and efficient local vice-presidents, thus rendering his constant presence unnecessary except when perfectly convenient to himself, they cannot but unanimously desire that he should reconsider his decision, and kindly consent to retain that position from which his retirement would prove an irreparable loss to the club."

It was then agreed that the usual *soirée* should be held at the opening of the season, and on the motion of Mr. Boucher the following members were appointed as a committee for carrying out the same:—Messrs. Corfe, Cleland, Meeker, Boorne, Stoate, H. Isaacs, Badcock, and W. Berry. Mr. Tilly having expressed his desire to resign the office of treasurer, and the meeting being unable to prevail upon him to continue the same, Mr. Burt proposed and Mr. Badcock seconded the nomination of Mr. R. T. Stoate (a member of the committee), which being put to the meeting was carried unanimously. Mr. Badcock proposed and Mr. H. Isaacs seconded, "That a tournament on the handicap principle be formed, open to the members of the Bath and Bristol Chess Clubs, but all games to be played at the Bristol Club-room, and that the committee of management be requested to carry out the necessary arrangements. Entrance fee about 2s. 6d." Mr. Isaacs proposed and Mr. J. D. Corfe seconded, "That the best thanks of this meeting be given to Messrs. W. Thomson, W. P. Meeker, J. S. Tilly, and W. Berry for their kind services as vice-presidents, treasurer, and hon. secretary during the past year, and that they be requested to continue the same for the ensuing year." Carried *nem. con.*

Mr. Boucher proposed and Mr. W. Hibbins seconded, "That the best thanks of this meeting be given to the committee, Messrs. J. D. Corfe, A. Smyth Pigott, C. Boorne, J. S. Cleland, J. S. Sanders, R. T. Stoate, and J. Burt, for their great attention to the interests of the club during the past year, and that they be requested to allow themselves to be re-elected." Carried. Mr. W. Hibbins and Mr. H. Isaacs were appointed auditors of accounts for the year.

Votes of thanks having been passed to the late treasurer, Mr. Tilly (who was appointed on the committee), for his past services, and to Mr. Meeker for his able conduct in the chair, the meeting was declared adjourned for a fortnight to afford the secretary time to communicate with Captain Kennedy respecting his resignation, and also to receive his reply.

September 20th, the adjourned annual meeting was held, Mr. Stoate, treasurer, in the chair. The secretary read a long and interesting letter from Captain Kennedy, in which he very cordially thanked the members for the flattering resolution they were good enough to pass respecting his resignation, and also for their kindness in promising to overlook any shortcomings on his part in the performance of the duties of president, but after careful reconsideration, and with every desire to carry out the kind wishes of its members, he was compelled to abide by the resolution contained in his former communication, as the non-performance of the duties had been, and still would continue to be, a source of disquiet to him.

The meeting was therefore very reluctantly compelled to accept of the resignation of their much-respected president, and the following resolution was unanimously agreed to (proposed by Mr. W. Berry and seconded by Mr. J. Barber):—" That this meeting deeply regrets the loss they are about to sustain by the retirement from office of their much-esteemed and highly-respected president Captain H. A. Kennedy, who for more than seven years held that post with such unmixed satisfaction to the whole body of members and advantage to the club itself, and wish hereby to record their high appreciation of the valued services rendered by his frequent presence at their meetings, and of the unabated interest and liberality which he at all times manifested for the welfare and prosperity of the club, and that he be elected an honorary member."

It was then proposed by Mr. Stoate and seconded by Mr. Ferrier, and carried unanimously, "That Edmund Thorold, Esq., be requested to accept the office of president to the club." A vote of thanks to the chairman closed the business of the evening.

[*** Since the above report was received by us we learn that Mr. Thorold has accepted the presidency, and we congratulate the club upon having secured the co-operation of a gentleman under whose supervision the Sheffield Chess Club attained great prosperity. So excellent an appointment is the only consolation which the members can have for the loss of the truly admirable services of Captain Kennedy, whose retirement everybody deeply regrets. We can reasonably hope, however, that the club may continue to flourish under Mr. Thorold's auspices, and may increase in strength as time advances.—ED.]

SHEFFIELD ATHENÆUM CHESS CLUB.
(Communicated.)

The annual *soirée* of this club was held on the 18th September. There were about forty gentlemen present, including the distinguished amateur Dr. Wilson, of Clay-cross, whose attendance afforded the members much gratification. Another tournament on the principle of that which was held in the early part of the year has been arranged. The play commenced on the 21st September, and is to be concluded on the 18th December. The members hope by diligent and well-studied practice to improve the playing strength of the club.

EVERTON CHESS CLUB, LIVERPOOL.

We have received from the secretary of this club, Mr. Redfern, an interesting and carefully-prepared tabular statement of the games played there during the year by each member and the results, showing which were won, lost, and drawn. From the *résumé* we perceive that the number of the games played was 2,767 between thirty members. We consider that such a record as that before us should be kept in every Chess Club, showing as it does at a glance the relative strength of the members, the regularity of their attendance, and serving as a memorial of the progress of the society. We would willingly give insertion to this document, but are prevented doing so by press of other matter. The respected president of this club, Mr. Hopwood, has kindly favoured us with some contributions, which we shall duly lay before our readers.

BRIGHTON CHESS CLUB.

This club has recently been the scene of some interesting contests. Several members of the St James's Chess Club, including Mr. Spencer Perceval and Mr. H. T. Young, have occasionally been playing here. In a series of games between Mr. Mayall, jun., the celebrated photographer of London, and Mr. Paul Foskett, of Brighton, the former was successful, winning four to two.

HUDDERSFIELD CHESS CLUB.

The annual meeting of this club took place on Saturday, October 20th, in the Club-room, Queen-street, Mr. D. Marsden, the president, in the chair. Some interesting play took place in the course of the afternoon, and at half-past six a very excellent knife and fork tea was partaken of by those present. After tea the usual business was transacted. On the motion of Mr. J. Watkinson, Mr. Marsden was re-elected to the presidency. Mr. J. R. Robinson proposed, and Mr. Mellor seconded, the appointment of Dr. Scott to the vice-presidency. The chairman remarked that he thought there would be nothing to say about re-electing Mr. Watkinson to the secretaryship; he made a most efficient secretary, and, in fact, kept the club alive, Mr. Watkinson representing, however, that he would be glad to be relieved of his duties, or at least to share them with some other gentleman, Mr. Freeman proposed and Mr. Robinson seconded that Messrs. Watkinson and Finlinson be joint secretaries for the ensuing year. Mr. Watkinson proposed, and Mr. Tindall seconded, that Mr. G. Brook, Mr. J. Eastwood, Mr. D. A. Cooper, and Mr. J. R. Robinson be the committee for the ensuing year. This, with a brief statement from the secretary, showing that the club was, as far as finances went, in a very satisfactory condition, concluded the business. The rest of the evening was very enjoyably spent in some interesting contests.

SCORE OF THE TOURNAMENT NOW IN PROGRESS AT THE BIRMINGHAM CHESS CLUB

For the Champion Chess Men and First Prize.

	Wins.	Draws.		Wins.	Draws.
Mr. A. Badams	3		Mr. J. L. Smith	2	2
Mr. H. Fry	4		Mr. T. F. Best	1 Resigned	
Mr. S. G. Kempson	4	1	Mr. W. Buncher	1	
Mr. J. B. Stone	2		Mr. G. F. Sutton	4	
Mr. C. T. Saunders	Resigned		Mr. H. Haselden	4	1
Mr. J. Halford			Mr. E. P. Warren	2	
Mr. F. S. Hill	3	1	Mr. H. Badams	2	
Dr. Lloyd	4		Mr. H. S. Hill	4	
Rev. S. W. Earnshaw	4	1	Mr. Balden	0	
Mr. F. H. Warner	0		Dr. Freeman	4	

This first round was commenced on the 12th of last April, the players being paired by lot, and eight weeks allowed for finishing each round.

Second Round.
Begun on 14th June, 1866.

	Wins.			Wins.
Rev. S. W. Earnshaw	Resigned		Mr. J. Halford	4
Mr. G. F. Sutton			Mr. J. L. Smith	1
Mr. H. Fry	2		Mr. Haselden	3
Dr. Lloyd	4		Mr. S. G. Kempson	4
Dr. Freeman	4			
Mr. H. S. Hill	1			

Third Round.
Begun 10th September.

	Wins.	
Rev. S. W. Earnshaw	1	Mr. S. G. Kempson is drawn a
Mr. J. Halford	1	winner in this round.
Dr. Freeman		
Dr. Lloyd		

The following gentlemen who were so unfortunate as to be thrown out in the first and second rounds of this Tournament, have been paired together to play for the prize in the Consolation Tournay, as follows:—

Mr. Balden } Mr. Sutton }	Mr. Warren } Mr. Stone }
Mr. Haselden } Mr. Smith }	Mr. H. Badams } Mr. H. Fry }
Mr. H. Hill } Mr. Best, resigned }	Mr. Warren } Mr. Saunders, resigned }
Mr. A. Badams } Mr. Buncher }	Mr. F. Hill, drawn a winner in this first round.

THE LATE REDCAR MEETING.

We have received the two following letters in vindication of the management, and in reply to certain disparaging remarks which have been made respecting this meeting. It is far from our custom to enter upon any controversial matter in these columns, which we wish to use solely for the instruction and information of our readers. In the present instance, however, we depart somewhat from strict rule, because we think it but fair to the writers of the subjoined letters to allow them to make a reply to the statements which have been elsewhere made public:—

TO THE EDITOR OF "THE CHESS PLAYER'S MAGAZINE."
North Yorkshire and Durham Chess Association.
Redcar, Oct. 22nd, 1866.

DEAR SIR,—Will you kindly allow us, through the CHESS PLAYER'S MAGAZINE, to answer, as briefly as possible, the illiberal remarks which have been made with regard to the Chess Meeting which was held here last August? We ask this favour of you, not that we care to defend ourselves, but that we may keep up and further the interests of Chess in the North. The accusations comprised in these illiberal remarks seem to be five in number. (1) Patrons conspicuous for their absence. (2) No hospitality. (3) No tables d'hôte. (4) No excursions excepting (5) Saltburn. We answer them seriatim. (1) The patrons were not generally Chess Players at all, and the busy week in York, the occasion of the visit of the Prince and Princess of Wales, clashing, as it unfortunately did, with the Chess week, and fixed far too late for the Chess week to be altered, prevented very many of them being present. (2) Very few Chess Players reside in Redcar, and those who do are not in a position to keep open house. Besides, we have attended other Chess meetings where the arrangements were the same—each person paying for what he himself required. We are by no means complaining—only asking not to be complained of. (3) The members generally were consulted as to the tables d'hôte, and the majority preferred to order their own dinner; the tables d'hôte were in consequence abandoned. (4) The weather was too unfavourable to attempt any excursions excepting the one to (5) Saltburn. There, at a first-class hotel, the waiting was shocking. While we feel sorry for and confess this shortcoming, we must beg to exonerate ourselves. The fault was with the landlord of the hotel, and let those who wish to punish him avoid the Zetland Hotel whenever they visit Saltburn. We have had, moreover, sir, several letters from amateurs who were present, expressing their own entire satisfaction, and belief in a general satisfaction, as to the whole week's arrangements. In our innocence, perhaps, we only suspect one of being discontented, and whatever be his position he still counts but one.

However severely or illiberally we may hereafter be criticised, we shall not again ask for your valuable space for valueless matter, for valueless must be further correspondence on this subject. Thanking you in the name of British Chess Players for the favour you have shown us,

We are, dear sir, your faithful servants,

J. H. BENNETT, } Hon. Secs.
G. F. BODINGTON, }
B. N. R. BATTY, Treasurer.
A. B. SKIPWORTH, one of the Managing Committee.

TO THE EDITOR OF "THE CHESS PLAYER'S MAGAZINE."

MY DEAR SIR,—After the full and very correct report of the proceedings of the late Chess Congress at Redcar which appeared in the September number of your Magazine, it may seem superfluous to add any comment on the subject. But I cannot forbear to offer my testimony as an eye-witness of its success, especially since the publication of what I am compelled to designate as a very ungenerous report of the meeting which appeared in the pages of the *Chess World*, and has subsequently been confirmed by quotation, in the Chess column of the *Illustrated London News*. The mere list of names of the gentlemen who attended and took part in the congress is in itself more than sufficient to rebut the charge of *failure*, and the fact that *all* the arrangements contemplated in the programme were not carried out is surely insufficient to warrant the unconditional application of the epithet "delusive." Everybody conversant with these meetings is well aware of the trouble, expense, and preparations requisite for their being successfully carried out, and when it is remembered that the recent congress was almost of a tentative character, and the first assemblage of the kind convened in a remote corner of England, I think the dominant impression cannot but be that of surprise at the large number of strong players actually attracted to the scene. For my own part I think that the promoters of the congress are entitled to our warmest thanks for the pleasant week of Chess enjoyed by their exertions, and from personal acquaintance with the majority of those present, I can testify as well to the general feeling of satisfaction which pervaded the meeting as to the good fellowship and harmony that prevailed. The competitors certainly comprised a very fair number of good *English* players (the record of whose games, by-the-bye, was an avowed aim of the establishment of the *Chess World*), and professional rapacity was discouraged by the absence of any large money-prizes, Therefore, whatever impression the Chess editor of the *Illustrated London News* may seek to convey to his Yorkshire correspondents (are they at all analogous to the *chateaux en Espagne?*), those who were unbiassed spectators will retain their own opinions as to its undoubted success, and I venture to think *his* will be the only dissentient voice. Because, though present, he was not enshrined as the exclusive idol of an admiring group, is it fair that he should dip his pen in the *succus loliginis*, and ruthlessly asperse the scheme as a delusion and a failure?

I remain, Sir, your obedient servant,

October 6th, 1866.   A CONTENTED VISITOR.

SHEFFIELD ATHENÆUM CHESS CLUB.

TO THE EDITOR OF "THE CHESS PLAYER'S MAGAZINE."

Oct. 17th, 1866.

DEAR SIR,—By request of the Committee of the above-mentioned club, I write to ask you to be kind enough to make known in your esteemed Magazine that, having challenged the Huddersfield and the Bradford Chess Clubs, both of which have declined to play, this club is now prepared to play the club of any other town in the West Riding of Yorkshire a match for a prize of the value of £3 3s. or £5 5s. We should prefer to play not fewer than ten members—of course Huddersfield and Bradford are not included in this challenge.—I am, dear sir, yours faithfully,

J. J. CHAMPION, Hon. Sec.

GAMES.

GAME 201.

The two following games were played some time ago by the Rev. W. Wayte and the Rev. C. E. Ranken. We think them sufficiently interesting to entitle them to insertion.

First Game. (*Evans's Gambit.*)

White. (Mr. WAYTE.)	Black. (Mr. RANKEN.)
1. P. to K. fourth	1. P. to K. fourth
2. K. Kt. to B. third	2. Q. Kt. to B. third
3. K. B. to Q. B. fourth	3. K. B. to Q. B. fourth
4. P. to Q. Kt. fourth	4. B. takes Q. Kt. P.
5. P. to Q. B. third	5. B. to Q. B. fourth
6. Castles	6. P. to Q. third
7. P. to Q. fourth	7. P. takes P.
8. P. takes P.	8. B. to Q. Kt. third
9. P. to Q. fifth	9. Kt. to Q. R. fourth
10. B. to Q. Kt. second	10. Kt. to K. second
11. B. to Q. third	11. Castles
12. Q. Kt. to B. third	12. K. Kt. to Kt. third
13. Q. Kt. to K. second	13. P. to Q. B. fourth
14. K. to R. square	14. P. to K. B. third

15. Q. R. to Q. B. square	15. Kt. to K. fourth (a)
16. Kt. takes Kt.	16. K. B. P. takes Kt.
17. P. to K. B. fourth	17. P. takes P.
18. Kt. takes P.	18. Q. to K. Kt. fourth (b)
19. P. to K. Kt. third (c)	19. Q. B. to K. Kt. fifth
20. Q. to Q. R. fourth (d)	20. P. to Q. B. fifth (e)
21. K. B. takes P.	21. Kt. takes B.
22. Q. takes Kt.	22. B. to K. sixth
23. Kt. to K. sixth	23. Q. to K. R. fourth
24. P. to K. R. fourth	24. B. to K. B. seventh (f)
25. R. takes B. (g)	25. R. takes R.
26. Q. to Q. B. eighth (check)	26. R. to K. B. square (h)
27. R. to Q. B. seventh	27. Q. to K. Kt. third
28. Q. takes K. R. (check)	28. R. takes Q.
29. R. takes K. Kt. P. (check)	29. Q. takes R.
30. Kt. takes Q.	30. R. to K. B. seventh, and wins

NOTES.

(a) Perhaps it is better to play B. to Q. second at this point, keeping the move in the text in reserve until the first player's Knight has occupied King's square.

(b) This is somewhat hazardous, as will be shown in our next note.

(c) 19. Q. to K. R. fifth would have given him an immediate advantage. If Black, in reply, were to capture the Queen, White by retaking with Kt. would have at once gained a very powerful position. It would be useless for Black in his dilemma to advance his Queen to K. Kt. fifth, as she could be attacked on the instant by the Rook's Pawn. Therefore the following variation may seem to demand more serious attention. Suppose—

19. Q. to K. R. fifth	19. Q. to K. second
20. P. to K. fifth	20. P. to K. Kt. third

There can be no better move.

21. B. takes P.	21. R. takes Kt.

He might also play P. takes B., or B. to K. Kt. fifth. In the first case, White would win easily by Kt. takes P.; and in the second by B. takes P. (check), followed by Q. takes B. (check).

22. R. takes R.	22. P. takes B.
23. Q. takes P. (check)	

And the second player has no resource.

(d) B. to K. second would certainly have been stronger.

(e) The beginning of a beautifully-conceived combination.

(f) B. to K. seventh would have led to some really fine positions, and is, we believe, at least as good as the move in the text.

(g) To show the excellence of Black's 24th move, let us look at one or two of White's other possible replies at the present moment. In the first place—

25. Q. to Q. B. seventh	25. B. to K. B. sixth (check), or (B)

The only train of play to win, and, curiously enough, also to save the game.
For the result of R. to K B. second, see variation B.

26. K. to K. R. second	26. B. takes P. (check)

Again the only mode of winning the game, as a careful glance at variation A will also demonstrate.

27. K. to Kt. square, or (A)   27. B. to K. fourth
28. B. takes B.

Position after Black's 24th move.

BLACK.

WHITE.

If he refuse to take the Bishop, Black will win by a method analogous to that traced out in this note, with the additional advantage of having another piece still on the board.

	28. Q. to K. Kt. fifth (check)
29. K. to K. B. second	29. Q. to K. Kt. seventh (check)
30. K. to K. third (best)	30. Q. to K. seventh (check)
31. K. to Q. fourth	31. Q. takes K. P. (check)
32. K. moves	32. K. R. to Q. B. square (check)

And wins.

(A)

| 27. K. takes B. | 27. Q. to K. Kt. fifth (check) |
| 28. K. to K. B. second | 28. Q. to K. Kt. seventh (check) |

And wins on the system adopted in the previous variation, the different position of White's Bishop not affecting the result. Let us now return to the first move of the main variation.

(B)

	25. R. to K. B. second (bad)
26. R. takes B.	26. R. takes Q.
27. R. takes R.	

And, whatever Black plays, White must win the game.

In the second place—

| 25. Kt. takes R. | 25. B. to K. seventh |
| 26. Q. to Q. B. third | |

Apparently his best move.

	26. B. to K. B. sixth (check)
27. K. to K. R. second	27. B. takes Kt. P. (check)
28. K. to Kt. square	

If he were to take the Bishop he would lose the game off-hand.

28. B. to K. R. seventh (check)

29. K. to B. second

The capture of the Bishop would involve mate in two moves.

29. B. to K. fourth.

Q. takes R. P. (check) looks a plausible move at this point; but White can then take the Bishop with his King, and, whether Black pursue the attack by capturing Knight with Rook (check), or playing B. to K. fourth, the advantage would, we imagine, rest with White, as, in the first supposed case, he would bring back his King in safety to Kt. second, and in the other, sacrifice his Queen.

30. Q. takes Q. B.

If she take the King's Bishop, with the view of playing the Kt. afterwards to K. sixth, Black would, in all probability, win by moving B. to K. Kt. fifth in answer to the retreat of the Knight.

30. R. takes Kt.

31. Q. takes R. (check) 31. K. takes Q.
32. K. to K. third (disc. check)

And White has certainly the advantage of two Rooks against the Queen. Nevertheless, Black's game is not without resource.

(*h*) Had he taken the Queen, White could have drawn the game by perpetual check.

GAME 202.

Second Game. (*Evans's Gambit.*)

White. (Mr. Ranken.)	Black. (Mr. Watte.)
1. P. to K. fourth	1. P. to K. fourth
2. K. Kt. to B. third	2. Q. Kt. to B. third
3. K. B. to Q. B. fourth	3. K. B. to Q. B. fourth
4. P. to Q. Kt. fourth	4. B. takes Q. Kt. P.
5. P. to Q. B. third	5. B. to Q. B. fourth
6. Castles	6. P. to Q. third
7. P. to Q. fourth	7. P. takes P.
8. P. takes P.	8. B. to Q. Kt. third
9. Q. Kt. to B. third	9. Kt. to Q. R. fourth
10. B. to Q. third	10. Kt. to K. second
11. B. to Q. Kt. second	11. Castles
12. Q. Kt. to K. second	12. P. to Q. fourth
13. Q. to Q. B. second	13. P. to K. R. third
14. B. to Q. R. third	14. P. takes P.
15. B. takes P.	15. P. to K. B. fourth
16. B. to Q. third	16. R. to K. B. third
17. B. takes Kt.	17. Q. takes B.
18. Kt. to K. B. fourth	18. B. to K. third (*a*)
19. K. R. to K. square	19. Q. to Q. third
20. Kt. takes B.	20. R. takes Kt.
21. R. takes R.	21. Q. takes R.

22. B. takes P.	22. Q. to Q. third
23. B. to K. R. seventh (check)	23. K. to R. square
24. Kt. to K. fifth	24. Q. to K. B. third
25. R. to K. square (b)	25. B. takes P.
26. Kt. to K. Kt. fourth	26. Q. to Q. B. third
27. Q. to K. B. fifth	27. R. to K. square
28. R. to Q. square	28. Q. to Q. R. fifth
29. R. to Q. B. square	29. Q. to Q. Kt. fifth
30. P. to K. Kt. third	30. R. to K. B. square
31. Q. to Q. third	31. Q. to Q. Kt. seventh
32. R to Q. B. second	32. Q. to Kt. eighth (check)
33. K. to Kt. second	33. Kt. to Q. B. third
34. B. to K. fourth	34. Kt. to Q. Kt. fifth
35. Q. takes B.	35. Kt. takes R.
36. Q. to K. fifth (c)	36. Q. to Q. eighth
37. Kt. takes K. R. P.	37. Kt. to K. sixth (check) (d)
38. K. to R. third	38. Q. to K. B. eighth (check)
39. K. to R. fourth	39. Q. takes P.
40. Kt. to K. Kt. fourth	40. Kt. takes Kt.
41. K. takes Kt.	41. Q. to K. seventh (check)
42. K. to R. third	42. P. to Q. B. third
43. Q. to K. seventh	43. Q. to K. B. eighth (check)
44. K. to Kt. fourth	44. Q. to K. B. third
45. Q. to Q. B. fifth	45. Q. to K. third (check)
46. B. to K. B. fifth	46. Q. takes B. (check)

And White resigns.

NOTES.

(a) This hasty move loses at least a Pawn.

(b) White here, in his turn, loses a Pawn by inadvertence.

(c) Mr. Ranken, before making this move, pointed out that he could draw the game by the following mode of play:—

36. Q. to Q. B fifth	36. Kt. to K. eighth (check) (best)
37. K. to R. third	37. Q. takes B.
38. Q. takes R. (check)	38. K. to R. second
39. Kt. to K. B. sixth (check)	

And as Black must take this Knight, the game will be drawn by perpetual check.

(d) This counter-stroke renders all the first player's ingenious manœuvres unavailing.

GAME 203.

The ensuing two games were played at the late Redcar Meeting, the first being a Ruy Lopez Knight's game, played by the Rev. Mr. Skipworth against the Rev. Mr. Owen, and the second an Evans's Gambit, played by the Rev. F. R. Drew against Mr. Hamel.

(*Ruy Lopez Knight's Game.*)

White. (Rev. A. B. Skipworth.)	Black. (Rev. John Owen.)
1. P. to K. fourth	1. P. to K. fourth
2. K. Kt. to B. third	2. Q. Kt. to B. third
3. B. to Q. Kt. fifth	3. P. to Q. R. third
4. B. to Q. R. fourth	4. Kt. to K. B. third
5. Castles	5. B. to K. second
6. P. to Q. fourth	6. P. to Q. Kt. fourth
7. B. to Q. Kt. third	7. P. to Q. third
8. P. takes K. P.	8. Q. Kt. takes P.
9. Kt. takes Kt.	9. P. takes Kt.
10. Q. takes Q. (check) (*a*)	10. B. takes Q.
11. B. to K. third	11. P. to Q. B. third
12. Kt. to Q. second	12. Castles
13. Q. R. to Q. square	13. B. to K. second
14. Q. Kt. to K. B. third	14. B. to K. Kt. fifth
15. P. to K. R. third	15. B. takes Kt.
16. P. takes B.	16. P. to K. R. third
17. P. to Q. B. third	17. Q. R. to Q. square
18. K. to R. second	18. R. takes R.
19. B. takes R.	19. R. to Q. square
20. B. to Q. B. second	20. Kt. to K. R. fourth
21. P. to Q. R. fourth	21. P. to Q. Kt. fifth (*b*)
22. P. to Q. R. fifth	22. Kt. to K. B. fifth
23. R. to Q. square	23. R. takes R.
24. B. takes R.	24. P. takes P.
25. P. takes P.	25. Kt. to K. third
26. B. to Q. Kt. sixth	26. Kt. to Q. B. fourth (*c*)
27. K. to Kt. third	27. K. to B. square
28. B. takes Kt.	28. B. takes B.
29. B. to Q. R. fourth	29. B. to Q. third
30. B. takes P.	30. B. to Q. B. second
31. B. to Q. Kt. seventh	31. B. takes R. P.
32. P. to Q. B. fourth	32. B. to Q. Kt. third
33. B. takes R. P.	33. K. to his second

And the game was given up as drawn.

NOTES.

(*a*) One-game Tournaments, with all their numerous benefits, are liable, it must be owned, to the disadvantage that both players being obliged to exhibit the utmost accuracy, something like caution bordering upon timidity is apt to become the order of the day.

(*b*) B. to K. Kt. fourth would have been a stronger move, as, if the first player had then exchanged Bishops, Black would have remained with a Knight against a Bishop, the former piece being a little superior in end-games of this description; and if White had declined to make the exchange, the Bishop could afterwards have been advanced to his own fifth, with command of the position.

(c) As we have suggested in our previous note, a Knight should not be lightly exchanged for a Bishop in such games.

GAME 204.
(Evans's Gambit.)

White. (Rev. F. R. Drew.)	Black. (Mr. Hamel.)
1. P. to K. fourth	1. P. to K. fourth
2. Kt. to K. B. third	2. Kt. to Q. B. third
3. B. to Q. B. fourth	3. B. to Q. B. fourth
4. P. to Q. Kt. fourth	4. B. takes Kt. P.
5. P. to Q. B. third	5. B. to Q. B. fourth
6. P. to Q. fourth	6. P. takes P.
7. P. to K. fifth	7. P. to Q. fourth
8. P. takes P. (en passant)	8. B. takes P.
9. Castles	9. Kt. to K. B. third
10. R. to K. square (check)	10. B. to K. second
11. B. to Q. R. third	11. Castles
12. B. takes B.	12. Kt. takes B.
13. Kt. to K. fifth	13. B. to K. third (a)
14. B. takes B.	14. P. takes B.
15. P. takes P.	15. Q. Kt. to Q. fourth
16. P. to K. Kt. third	16. Q. to Q. third
17. Kt. to Q. second	17. P. to Q. Kt. fourth
18. R. to Q. B. square	18. Kt. to Q. Kt. fifth (b)
19. P. to Q. R. third	19. Kt. to Q. R. seventh
20. R. to Q. B. sixth (c)	20. Q. takes Q. P. (d)
21. Q. to Q. B. second	21. Kt. to Q. second
22. Kt. to Q. Kt. third	22. Q. to Q. fourth
23. Kt. takes Kt.	23. Q. takes Kt.
24. R. takes Q. B. P.	24. Q. to Q. third
25. K. R. to Q. square	25. Q. takes Q. R. P.
26. K. R. to Q. seventh	26. R. to K. B. fourth
27. R. takes K. Kt. P. (check)	27. K. to K. R. square
28. R. takes K. R. P. (check)	28. K. to K. Kt. square
29. P. to K. Kt. fourth (e)	29. R. to K. Kt. fourth
30. R. to R. eighth (check)	30. K. takes R.
31. Q. mates	

NOTES.

(a) An exceptionable move, as the isolation of the Pawn now brought to the centre will always expose Black to more or less attack.

(b) Kt. to K. second would have been much safer.

(c) R. to Q. B. second, threatening Q. to Q. R. square, whether White take the Q. R. Pawn or move his Queen to her fourth, seems to be a simple way to secure the gain of a piece.

(d) Having got into a dilemma, Black would, perhaps, have found more resource in the capture of the other Pawn by the Queen.

(e) Leading to a neat termination.

GAME 205.

The following games were played in the Handicap Tournament at the late London Congress by Herr Steinitz against Mr. MacDonnell and Mr. Mocatta. Considering the odds given in the one instance and the skill of his adversary in the other, we think that Herr Steinitz has by his success in these games furnished additional proof of his high powers.

(Philidor's Defence.)

White. (Mr. MacDonnell.)	Black. (Mr. Steinitz.)
1. P. to K. fourth	1. P. to K. fourth
2. K. Kt. to B. third	2. P. to Q. third
3. P. to Q. fourth	3. P. takes P.
4. K. B. to B. fourth	4. Kt. to K. B. third
5. Castles	5. B. to K. second
6. Q. B. to K. Kt. fifth	6. P. to Q. B. fourth
7. P. to Q. B. third (a)	7. P. takes P.
8. Kt. takes P.	8. Castles
9. Q. to K. second	9. Q. Kt. to Q. B. third
10. P. to K. R. third	10. B. to K. third
11. K. B. to Q. third	11. P. to Q. R. third
12. Q. R. to Q. square	12. Q. to Q. B. second
13. B. takes Kt.	13. B. takes B.
14. Kt. to Q. fifth	14. Q. to Q. square
15. B. to Kt. square	15. K. B. to Q. fifth
16. P. to K. Kt. fourth (b)	16. P. to K. R. fourth (c)
17. Kt. takes B.	17. Kt. takes Kt.
18. R. takes Kt.	18. P. takes R.
19. Q. to Q. third	19. P. takes P.
20. P. to K. fifth	20. Q. to R. fifth
21. Kt. to K. seventh (check)	21. K. to R. square
22. P. takes Q. P.	22. P. takes R. P.
23. P. to K. B. fourth	23. B. to Q. B. fifth
24. Q. to K. B. third	24. B. takes R.
25. K. takes B.	25. P. to R. seventh
26. B. to K. fourth	26. Q. R. to Q. square
27. Kt. to K. B. fifth	27. P. to R. eighth (Qn.'s) (check)

28. Q. takes Q.	28. Q. takes Q. (check)
29. B. takes Q	29. P. to Q. sixth
30. B. takes Q. Kt. P.	30. P. to K. Kt. third
31. B. takes P.	31. P. takes Kt.
32. B. takes P.	32. R. takes P.
33. B. to Q. B. fourth	33. R. to Q. seventh

And White resigns.

NOTES.

(a) This move is not so effective in the present variation of the Philidor Defence as it is in the regular Scotch Gambit. We should have preferred P. to K. fifth.

(b) A hazardous exposure of the King to attack.

(c) The advance of this Pawn appears to be a perfectly safe, and perhaps the best manner of taking immediate advantage of White's dangerous move.

GAME 206.

First Game. (Remove Black's King's Bishop's Pawn.)

White. (Mr. MOCATTA.)	*Black.* (Mr. STEINITZ.)
1. P. to K. fourth	1. P. to Q. third
2. P. to Q. fourth	2. K. Kt. to B. third
3. B. to Q. third (a)	3. Q. Kt. to B. third
4. P. to Q. B. third	4. P. to K. fourth
5. K. Kt. to B. third	5. B. to K. Kt. fifth
6. B. to K. third	6. Q. to Q. second
7. Q. Kt. to Q. second	7. B. to K. second
8. Q. to Q. Kt. third.	8. P. takes P.
9. P. takes P.	9. Kt. to Q. square
10. Castles (K.'s R.)	10. P. to Q. B. third
11. Q. R. to Q. B. square	11. B. to K. third
12. P. to Q. fifth	12. Q. B. to K. B. second
13. B. to Q. B. fourth	13. Castles
14. Kt. to K. Kt. fifth	14. P. to Q. R. third
15. Kt. takes B.	15. Kt. takes Kt.
16. P. to K. B. fourth (b)	16. P. to Q. Kt. fourth (c)
17. B to K. second	17. P. takes P.
18. P. takes P.	18. B. to Q. square
19. B. to K. B. third	19. K. R. to K. square
20. B. to Q. fourth	20. B. to Q. R. fourth
21. Q. to Q. square	21. Q to K. B. fourth
22. B. takes Kt.	22. Q. takes B.
23. R. to Q. B. second	23. Q. takes B. P.
24. K. to R. square	24. Q. to Q. fifth
25. Kt. to Q. Kt. third	25. Q. takes Q.

26. B. takes Q.	26. B. to Q. Kt. third
27. R. to Q. B. sixth	27. B. to K. sixth
28. B. to K. Kt. fourth (d)	28. Kt. to K. fourth
29. P. to K. R. third	29. Kt. takes B.
30. P. takes Kt.	30. B. to Kt. third
31. Kt. to Q. B. square	31. R. to K. sixth
32. R. to Q. square	32. Q. R. to K. square
33. Kt. to Q. third	33. Q. R. to K. fifth
34. P. to Q. R. third	34. Q. R. to Q. fifth
35. Kt. to K. B. second	35. R. takes R. (check)
36. Kt. takes R.	36. R. to K. eighth (check)
37. K. to R. second	37. P. to K. Kt. third
38. Kt. to B. third	38. R. to Q. B. eighth
39. K. to Kt. third	39. K. to B. square
40. B. to B. third	40. K. to K. square
41. K. to B. fourth	41. K. to Q. square
42. B. to K. fourth	42. B. to Q. fifth
43. Kt. to K. second	43. R. to B. eighth (check)
44. K. to Kt. fifth	44. B. takes P.
45. K. to R. sixth	45. R. to B. second
46. B. to Q. fifth	46. R. to K. second
47. B. to B. third	47. B. takes P
48. P. to Kt. fourth	48. R. to K. sixth
49. Kt. to Q. fourth	49. B. to Kt. seventh, and wins.

NOTES.

(a) Kt. to Q. B. third is perhaps the strongest move at this point.

(b) Up to this point, White seems to have opened the game with great care and skill. Here, however, we believe that he could have strengthened his attack by taking Pawn with Pawn, and then moving his Bishop to K. sixth, a position from which he could not easily have been dislodged.

(c) This secures Black's game from the danger with which he was menaced.

(d) B. to Q. B. second would probably have led to a more enduring attack. The move in the text, we presume, is a blunder.

GAME 207.

Second Game. (Remove Black's King's Bishop's Pawn.)

White. (Mr. MOCATTA.)	*Black.* (Mr. STEINITZ.)
1. P. to K. fourth	1. P. to K. third
2. P. to Q. fourth	2. Q. Kt. to B. third
3. K. Kt. to B. third	3. P. to Q. Kt. third
4. P. to Q. B. fourth	4. B. to Kt. second
5. B. to Q. third	5. K. Kt. to R. third
6. Q. Kt. to B. third (a)	6. K. Kt. to B. second

7. Castles	7. P. to K. Kt. third
8. B. to K. third	8. B. to Kt. second
9. Q. to Q. second	9. Castles
10. P. to K. fifth	10. R. to Q. B. square
11. Q. Kt. to K. fourth	11. Kt. to K. second
12. K. Kt. to Kt. fifth	12. Kt. takes Kt.
13. B. takes Kt.	13. Q. B. takes Kt.
14. B. takes B.	14. Q. to K. square
15. P. to K. Kt. fourth	15. P. to Q. B. fourth
16. Q. R. to Q. B. square	16. P. takes P.
17. Q. takes P.	17. Kt. to B. third
18. B. takes Kt.	18. R. takes B.
19. B. to B. sixth	19. B. takes B.
20. P. takes B.	20. P. to K. fourth (*b*)
21. Q. to Q. fifth (check)	21. K. to R. square
22. P. to K. Kt. fifth	22. Q. R. to B. fourth
23. Q. to K. fourth	23. Q. to K. third
24. P. to Q. Kt. fourth	24. Q. R. to Q. B. second
25. R. to Q. B. third	25. K. R. to Q. B. square
26. K. R. to Q. B. square	26. K. to Kt. square
27. P. to Q. R. third	27. P. to Q. third
28. P. to Q. R. fourth (*c*)	28. K. to B. square
29. K. to B. square	29. P. to Q. R. fourth
30. P. to Q. Kt. fifth	30. K. to K. square
31. P. to K. R. fourth	31. K. to B. square
32. K. to K. second	32. K. to K. square
33. K. to Q. second	33. Q. to K. B. fourth
34. Q. takes Q.	34. P. takes Q.
35. K. to Q. third	35. K. to B. second
36. K. R. to Q. square	36. P. to Q. fourth
37. K. R. to Q. B. square	37. P. to Q. fifth
38. K. R. to Q. B. second	38. R. to B. fourth
39. P. to K. B. fourth	39. P. to K. fifth (check)
40. K. takes Q. P.	40. R. to Q. square (check)
41. K. to K. third	41. R. to Q. sixth (check)
42. K. to K. second	42. R. to K. R. sixth
43. Q. R. to Q. second	43. R. to R. seventh (check)
44. K. to K. third	44. R. to R. sixth (check)

Abandoned as drawn.

NOTES.

(*a*) B. takes Kt. is much stronger, although it gives an open file to the hostile Rook.

(b) Had Black now played R. to Q. B. fourth, threatening the move in the text, he might perhaps have improved his game.
(c) As it was evidently White's intention to advance this Pawn to the fourth square, he should have done so last move, and thereby have gained time.

GAME 208.

Third Game. (Remove Black's King's Bishop's Pawn.)

White. (Mr. MOCATTA.)	*Black.* (Mr. STEINITZ.)
1. P. to K. fourth	1. P. to K. third
2. P. to Q. fourth	2. P. to Q. fourth
3. Q. to R. fifth (check)	3. P. to K. Kt. third
4. Q. to K. fifth	4. K. Kt. to B. third
5. Q. B. to K. Kt. fifth	5. K. B. to K. second
6. P. takes P. (a)	6. Castles
7. P. takes P.	7. Kt. to Kt. fifth (b)
8. B. takes B.	8. Q. takes B.
9. Q. to K. second	9. Kt. takes B. P.
10. K. Kt. to B. third	10. Kt. takes R.
11. P. to Q. fifth	11. Q. Kt. to Q. R. third
12. Q. Kt. to B. third	12. P. to Q. B. third
13. P. takes P.	13. P. takes P.
14. Castles	14. Q. Kt. to B. fourth (c)
15. Q. to K. third	15. B. takes P.
16. B. to B. fourth	16. Q. R. to K. square
17. B. takes B. (check)	17. Kt. takes B.
18. R. takes Kt.	18. Kt. to B. fifth (d)
19. Q. to B. second	19. Kt. takes Kt. P.
20. Q. takes Kt.	20. Q. to K. sixth (check)
21. Kt. to Q. second	21. R. to B. seventh
22. Q. takes R.	22. Q. takes Q.
23. Q. Kt. to K. fourth	23. Q. to Kt. seventh
24. Kt. to B. sixth (check)	24. K. to R. square
25. R. to K. B. square	25. R. to K. B. square
26. P. to Q. Kt. third	26. Q. to K. Kt. fourth

And White resigns the game and the match.

NOTES.

(a) For the result of B. to Q. Kt. fifth (check) which appears to us the best move, see "Morphy's Games" (Bohn's edition), p. 130, first note.
(b) It has been proved, in a weekly paper, that Q. Kt. to Q. B. third at this juncture gives Black a powerful attack. The move in the text also seems to be good.
(c) In order to be able to take the Pawn with safety.
(d) This is well conceived, as the subsequent capture of the K. K P will win the game without trouble.

Problem No. 107. By Herr A. Beck.

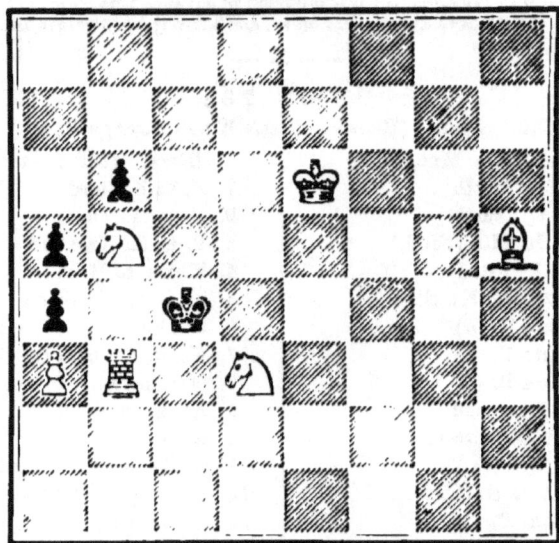

White to play, and mate in three moves.

Problem No. 108. By Dr. H. A. Stavenuter, of Hamburg.

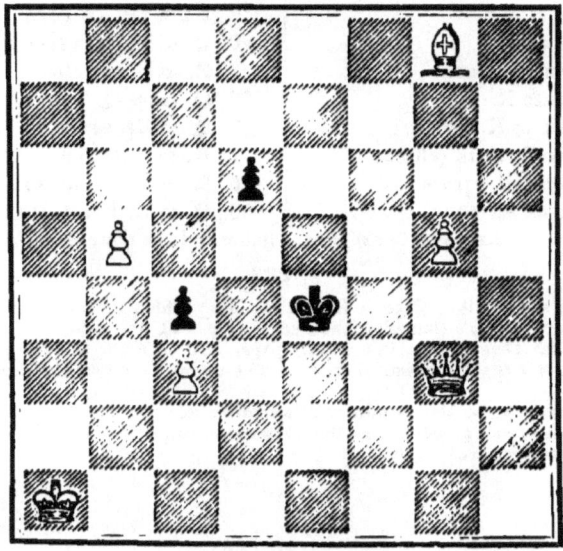

White to play, and mate in three moves.

Problem No. 109. By Dr. Conrad Bayer.

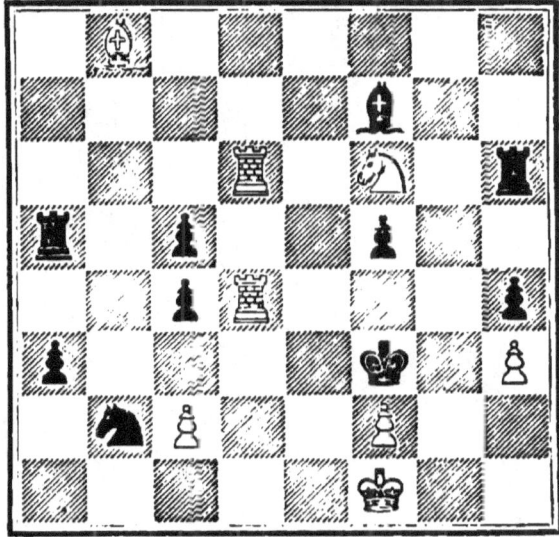

White to play, and mate in four moves.

Problem No. 110. By Herr W. Martini, of Hanover.

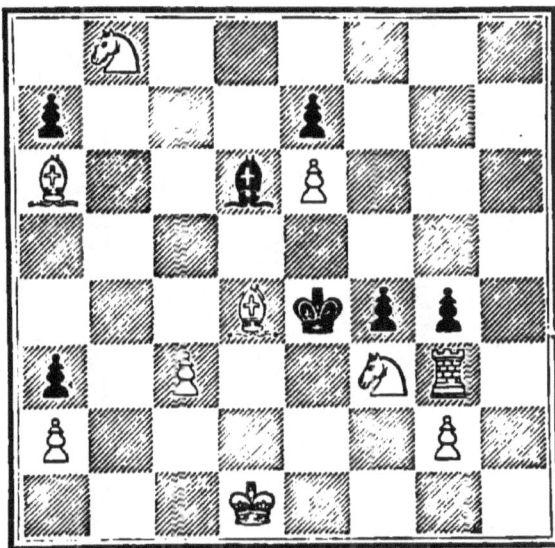

White to play, and mate in four moves.

Problem No. 111. By Herr G. Mehrtens, of Bremen.

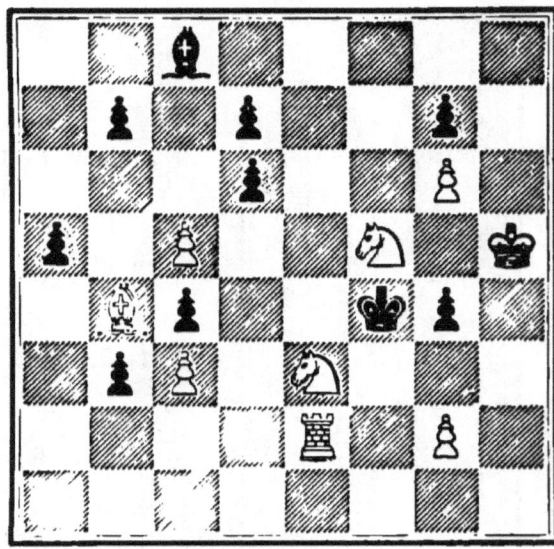

White to play, and mate in four moves.

Problem No. 112. By Herr H. Meyer, late of Hanover.

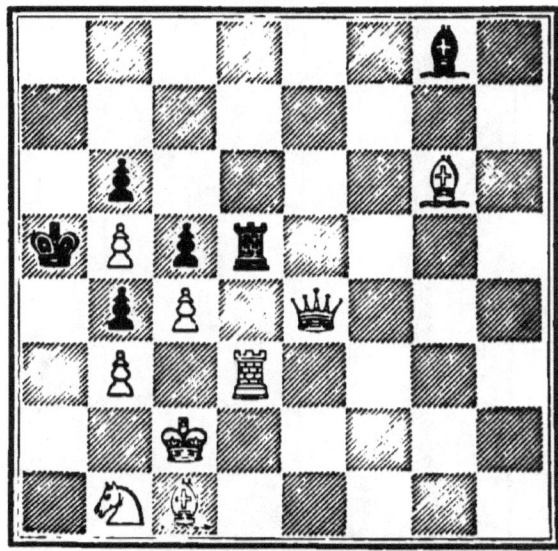

White to play, and mate in three moves.

Chess Study No. 27. By T. Smith, Esq.

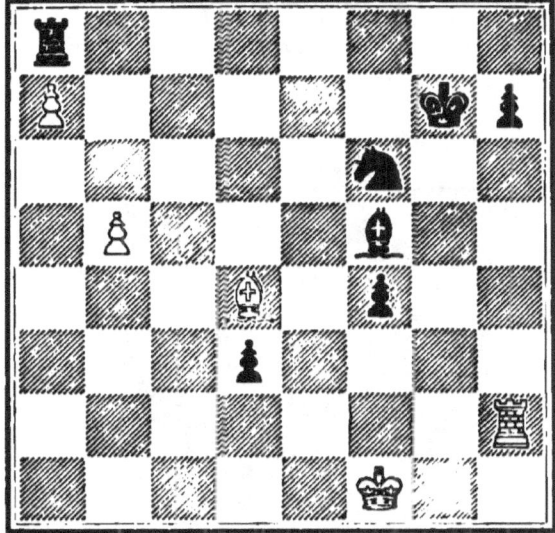

WHITE.
Black to move and win.

Chess Study No. 28. By Herr Horwitz.

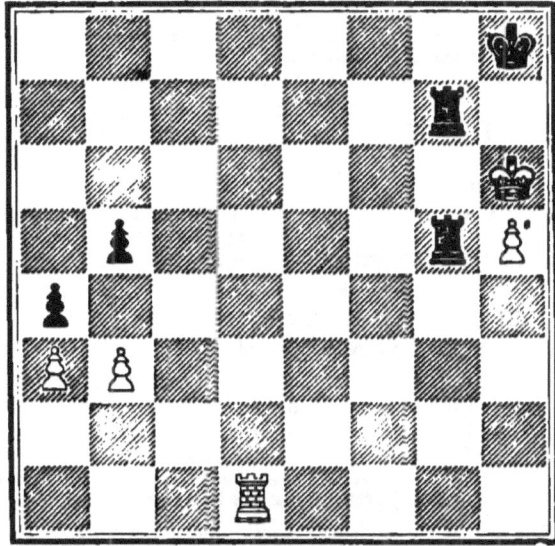

WHITE.
White to move and draw.

CHESS STUDY.
BY "EUCLID."
(Continued from Page 317.)

VARIATION A.
At Black's third move of Part I.

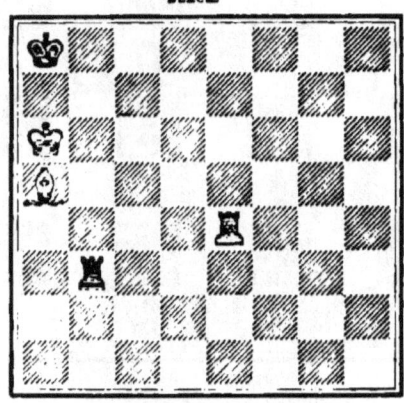

White.	Black.
	3. R. to Q. Kt. square
4. B. to Q. B. seventh	4. R. to K. B., K. Kt., or K. R. square

If 4. R. to Q. B. square—
5. K. to Q. Kt. sixth, and mates in two moves.

White.	Black.
5. B. to Q. sixth	5. R. to Q. square

If 5. R. to Q. B. square—
6. K. to Q. Kt. sixth wins

White.	Black.
6. R. to K. sixth	6. R. to Q. B. square
7. K. to Q. Kt. sixth	7. R. to Q. square
8. R. to K. B. sixth	8. R. to Q. B., K., K. Kt., or K. R. square
9. R. to K. B. fourth, and mates in two moves.	

VARIATION B.
At Black's fourth move of Part I.

White.	Black.
	4. R. to Q. R. second (check)
5. K. to Q. Kt. sixth	5. R. to Q. Kt. second (check)
6. K. to Q. B. sixth	6. R. to Q. Kt. sixth, seventh, or eighth

If 6. R. to K. B. second, or K. to Kt. second—
7. R. to K. R. eighth (check), and mates in four moves.

	Or if 6. K. to Q. Kt. square—
7. B. to Q. Kt. sixth	7. K. to Q. R. square
8. B. to Q. B. seventh, and mates in two moves.	
	And if 6. K. to Q. R. second—
7. B. to Q. B. seventh	7. K. to Q. R. square
8. B. to Q. Kt. sixth, and mates in two moves.	
7. B. to Q. Kt. sixth	7. R. to Q. B. sixth, seventh, or eighth (check)
8. B. to Q. B. fifth, an easily won position.	

Variation C.
At Black's fifth move of Part I.

	5. R. to Q. Kt. second
6. B. to Q. Kt. sixth	6. R. to Q. R. second (check)
	If 6. R. to Q. Kt. square—
7. B. to Q. B. seventh wins as in Variation A.	
7. K. to Q. Kt. fifth	7. R. to K. second, K. B. second, or K. Kt. second
	If 7. R. to Q. R. sixth, seventh, or eighth—
8. K. to Q. B. sixth	8. R. to Q. B. sixth (check)
9. B. to Q. B. fifth wins easily.	
	Or if 7. R. to Q. Kt. second—
8. K. to Q. B. sixth	8. R. to Q. Kt. square
9. R. to K. R. fourth	9. R. to Q. Kt. second
10. R. to K. Kt. fourth, and mates in two moves.	
8. K. to Q. B. sixth	8. R. to K., K. B., or K. Kt. square
9. B. to Q. B. seventh	9. K. to Q. R. second
10. R. to K. R. fourth	10. R. to K. third, K. B. third, or K. Kt. third (check).
11. B. to Q. sixth wins easily.	

Variation D.
At Black's third move of Part II.

	3. K. to Q. Kt. square
4. B. to Q. Kt. fourth	4. K. to Q. R. square
	If 4. R. to K., K. Kt., or K. R. square—
5. B. to Q. sixth (check)	5. K. to Q. R. square
6. R. to Q. B. seventh, as at move 6 below.	
	Or if 4. R. to Q. square—
5. B. to Q. sixth (check)	5. K. to Q. R. square
6. K. to Q. Kt. sixth wins.	
5. B. to Q. sixth	5. R. to K., K. Kt., or K. R. square
	If 5. R. to Q. square—
6. K. to Q. Kt. sixth	6. R. to K., K. Kt., or K. R. square
7. R. to Q. B. fourth, and mates in three moves.	
6. R. to Q. B. seventh	6. K. to Q. Kt. square
7. R. to Q. B. fourth (dis. check)	7. K. to Q. R. square
8. K. to Q. Kt. sixth, and mates in three moves.	

Variation E.

At Black's third move of Part II.

                      3. R. to Q. Kt. square
4. B. to Q. Kt. sixth   4. R. to K., K. B., K. Kt., or K. R. square

              If 4. R. to Q. Kt. second—
   5. R. to K. R. sixth makes the position as at move 6, Variation C.

5. B. to Q. fourth   5. R. to Q. Kt. square

           If 5. R. to Q., K. B., K. Kt., or K. square—
6. B. to K. fifth wins as in Variation D.

              If 5. K. to Q. Kt. square—
   6. B. to Q. B. fifth makes the position as at move 4, Variation D.

6. R. to K. sixth makes the position as at move seventh of Part II.

Variation F.

At Black's fifth move of Part II.

                      5. R. to K. Kt. square
6. B. to K. fifth   6. R. to K. Kt. third

              If 6. R. to Q. B. square—
7. K. to Q. Kt. sixth   7. R. to Q. square
8. B. to Q. sixth makes the position as at move 8, Variation A.

             Or if 6. R. to Q. square—
7. B. to Q. sixth   7. R. to Q. B. square
8. K. to Q. Kt. sixth makes the position as at move 7, Variation A.

             And again if 6. R. to K. B. square—
   7. R. to K. seventh wins easily.

7. B. to K. B. sixth   7. K. to Q. Kt. square

              If 7. R. to K. Kt. square—
8. R. to K. seventh   8. K. to Q. Kt. square
9. K. to Q. Kt. sixth makes the position as at move 9 below.

8. K. to Q. Kt. sixth   8. R. to K. Kt. square

              If 8. K. to Q. B. square—
9. K. to Q. B. sixth   9. R. to K. Kt. square
10. R. to K. fourth, as at move 20, Part II.

9. R. to K. seventh   9. R. to K. B. square

             If 9. K. to Q. B. square—
10. R. to Q. B. seventh (check)   10. K. to Q. Kt. square
11. B. to K. fifth   11. R. to K. Kt. third (check)
12. R to Q. B. sixth (dis. check)   12. K. to Q. R. square
13. B. to Q. sixth wins.

            Or if 9. K. to Q. R. square—
10. R. to Q. R. seventh (check)   10. K. to Q. Kt. square
11. B. to K. fifth (check) wins Rook.

10. R. to Q. Kt. seventh (check)   10. K. to Q. R. square

            If 10. K. to Q. B. square—
11. R. to Q. B. seventh (check)   11. K. to Q. Kt. square
12. B. to K. fifth wins.

11. R. to Q. R. seventh (check)   11. K. to Q. Kt. square
12. B. to K. fifth (check), and wins Rook.

(To be concluded in our next.)

SOLUTIONS TO PROBLEMS.

No. 94.—By Herr Keller.

1. Kt. to Q. Kt. fifth
2. R. to Q. fourth
3. R. to Q. B. fourth (check)
4. Q. to Q. B. third (mate)

1. R. takes Kt. (A)
2. R. to Q. fourth
3. K. takes R.

(A)

2. Q. to K. B. fifth (check)
3. R. to Q. B. fourth
4. R. takes Kt. (mate)

1. R. to K. Kt. third
2. K. moves
3. Kt. covers

No. 95.—By Herr Braune.

White.

1. P. to Kt. sixth
2. Kt. to Q. B. sixth
3. R. to Q. eighth
4. B. to Kt. seventh (check)
5. R. to Kt. eighth (mate)

Black.

1. Kt. takes B.
2. P. takes Kt. (best)
3. Kt. to K. B. second
4. K. takes B.

No. 96.—By Herr Vorwerk.

White.

1. B. to Kt. fourth
2. Q. takes P. (check)
3. Q. to Q. square (mate)

Black.

1. K. to Q. sixth (A)
2. K. to B. seventh

(A)

2. B. to B. fifth, and mate follows

1. P. to K. sixth (B)

(B)

2. Q. to Kt. third, and mates next move.

1. R. to Kt. third, or P. to Q. Kt. fourth

No. 97.—By J. J. Watts, Esq.

In five moves.

White.

1. R. takes B. (check)
2. B. takes P.
3. K. to R. seventh
4. K. to R. sixth
5. P. mates.

Black.

1. P. takes R.
2. P. to Kt. fourth
3. P. takes B.
4. P. moves

In four moves.

1. R. to K. B. square
2. B. to K. B. second
3. B. takes R. P.
4. R. takes B. (mate)

1. P. moves
2. B. to Q. third
3. B. covers

No. 98.—By E. Heath, Esq.

White.

1. R. takes Kt.
2. Kt. to K. third (check)
3. P. mates

Black.

1. B. takes R. (A)
2. K. to B. fourth

(A)

2. Kt. to K. third (check)
3. Kt. to Q. B. square (mate)

1. K. takes R.
2. K. to Q. sixth

No. 99.—By T. SMITH, Esq.

White.
1. B. to Q. R. fourth
2. R. to R. fifth (check)
3. B. mates accordingly.

Black.
1. K. takes P.
2. K. moves anywhere

No. 100.—By Herr H. MEYER.

White.
1. Q. takes R. P.
2. Kt. to K. fourth
3. R. to Q. B. third (mate).

Black.
1. Kt. takes Q. (or A, B)
2. K. takes Kt.

(A)

2. R. to Q. sixth (double check)
3. Q. to Q. B. sixth (mate).

1. P. takes Kt.
2. K. takes R.

(B)

2. R. takes Kt. (double check)
3. R. to Q. fifth, or Kt. to K. fourth (mate).

1. Kt. to Q. fifth
2. K. moves, or takes R.

CHESS STUDIES.

No. 22.—By W. T. PIERCE, Esq.

White.
1. P. to K. B. seventh
2. R. to Q. eighth
3. R. takes R. at Kt. square
4. R. to K. eighth

Black.
1. R. to K. B. square
2. R. to Q. Kt. square (best)
3. B. takes R.
4. B. to Q. third

Drawn game.

No. 23.—By Herr KLING.

White.
1. Q. to K. second
2. Q. to K. square (check)
3. Q. takes P. (check)
4. Q. to Q. fifth
5. Q. takes Q.

Black.
1. Q. to Q. B. seventh
2. Q. to Kt. eighth
3. P. to Kt. seventh
4. Q. to Q. sixth (check)
5. P. to Kt. eighth, becoming a Knight (check)

White mates in three moves.

THE BLACKHEATH CHESS CLUB.—The contemplated *soirée* which was arranged to take place, under the auspices of the above club, on Tuesday, the 6th inst., has, in consequence of an unfortunate accident to the Treasurer, Mr. G. Barber, been postponed to December.

NOTICE TO CORRESPONDENTS.

We are sorry that demands upon our space compel us to defer replying to several correspondents until next month.

ILLEGAL MOVES.

(*Concluded from page* 325.)

Carrera (1617), in his first rule, lays down, " We say, further, that, if the piece that has been touched covers the King, and therefore cannot be moved, he who has touched it is not thereby obliged to move the King, as some pretend wrongly; nor is he obliged to move the King if the piece touched has no square left to go to and cannot take an adverse piece."

As the reader may not clearly understand this law, and especially the latter portion of it, we must remark that it is often difficult to understand ancient writers, and to find a clear meaning in sentences frequently based upon indistinct ideas and interspersed with obsolete words. In our opinion, Carrera disallows the forced move of the King in two cases, viz., when the piece touched covers the King from a check, and when it has no other square to go to; and we also conclude from it that, about the year 1617, it was customary with certain players to punish every attempt at irregularity with the penalty of moving the King; but we do not yet find this rule a fixed law.

As to the mistakes which Carrera (p. 246) calls "*ministratti*," he is very prolix, for he divides these blunders into proper and improper ones, with no fewer than nine subdivisions; but he was evidently not clear-headed, and is very incomplete in his theory. The result of his decisions is, that a wrongly-moved piece, if the opponent take immediate notice of the move, ought to be taken off the board, which would generally be a worse punishment than the forced move of the King. He does not mention whether the party is allowed to make a proper move after the loss of the piece. If the King, however, make an illegal move, he is to be replaced, and the move lost to the player. If the mistake be found out after only a few moves, those moves are to be replaced on both sides, and the false one amended; but, if the position cannot be amended, the game is to begin anew, which the later Italians called *giuoco à monte*. Carrera, however, did not yet make use of that expression for a void game. The laws, not mentioned, given by Carrera in the third and sixth of his rules, are, in many respects very doubtful. The idea, first started by him, of the loss of the wrongly-played piece, and the wish that a mistake should never be legalised, may be found in later regulations, such as Allgaier's (1819, p. 15), and those of Jänisch (1858). The ninth law of Allgaier runs—" Whoever makes a false move, that is, moves his piece not according to the laws of the game, must replace the piece, with the loss of the move. The opponent, however, has also the choice of letting the false move stand as played." This law remained in the same words in the later editions of Allgaier; but, in the earlier ones of 1811, 1802, 1795, the words "with the loss of the move" are not inserted, so that in these there is no penalty fixed. But these new attempts to propagate the Italian rules have no chance of general success. Carrera, like Salvio, makes several observations as to the stakes, if won in consequence of false moves. We cannot enter into such digressions, still, we may mention that, according to Carrera, when a game with a stake upon it was won through an intentional false move, the opponent's stakes ought to be returned, and those of the guilty party forfeited in addition—that is, if the offender had a bad game when he committed his fault. If the mistake, however, was only accidental, the player should not incur any such obligations. An intended false move, even if not executed, is, in Carrera's judgment (p. 541), always a sin, which may be forgiven or not, according to the importance of the stakes. This last observation we owe rather to the Sicilian monk than to the practical Chess author.

The works published at and after the time of Salvio and Carrera, such as those of Selenus (1616 and 1617), "Traité d'Lausanne" (1698), Bertin (1735), Stamma (1745), and Philidor's first edition (1749), contain no rules, or at least none to serve our present purpose. The same may be said of A. Saul's little work, published in 1614 by Barbiere, in London, and of which we have an edition in our possession published in 1640, with a complete code of rules.

It does not mention the forced move of the King, but is worthy of notice as first noticing the abnormal rule which was for a long time observed in England, that the player who stalemated the other lost the game—that is to say if A played and B was stalemated, A lost the game.* As a motive for this rule Saul gives the reason that the player who sets the other stalemate terminates the game in an abrupt way, which according to its spirit should only end with a checkmate.

. It is impossible for us to enter into all the details of the various regulations, many of which are curious in themselves. Amongst the latter we may place Saul's law, that the opponent's piece though touched may be replaced, if the offender kisses it, and at the same time ask the opponent's pardon, otherwise the game is lost. The original words are, "If you take up your adversarie's man, and, before you set your piece in place thereof, thinke best to let it stand untaken, you must kisse the foot thereof, and cry him mercy, or lose the game; because you deserve to pay for the surgery if you breake a man's head, and will not give him a plaister, which is but small amends." We do not know whether these rules are to be found in the edition of Saul of 1614. The reader may see, however, by such an example, how the presumption of authors leads them to try to establish most extraordinary rules.

We now come to the three great Italians, Rio (1750) Lolli (1763), and Ponziani (1769); even they do not mention the penalty of moving the King in their rules. When speaking of illegal moves, they punish the offender with the loss of the piece and the move, and in certain cases, as when the King had remained in check, when a player had two Bishops of the same colour, or when the pieces had been wrongly placed at the outset, the opponent or both players may ask the game to be recommenced. Lolli (p. 11), following the erroneous view of an anonymous writer at the end of Salvio (Ed. 1723), thinks that these rules were only repetitions of Carrera's laws, but there is the very essential difference that Rio, on whose regulations Lolli comments, always has the game begun

---

* Philidor (Ed. 1777) on the last page asserts that the rule is mentioned in a London edition of Greco, of 1656, but Sarratt says (1821, p. 55) that he has no recollection of having seen it there. But in point of fact it is to be found at p. 13, and was for a long time the law in E

afresh,* whilst Carrera only retraces the game to the wrong move, and never has it played anew, unless the players are unable so to retrace the moves. The three Modenese authors concede to the player at any time in the game the "giuoco à monte," in case the board was wrongly placed, whilst Carrera scarcely pays any attention to the misplacement of the board, considering (p. 513) the position of the board with the black square on the right hand side as a common case in which the King should still be at the right of the Queen.†

Ponziani does not mention any penalty for touching a piece which covers the King, or which cannot be moved to another square. His rules will also be found in the "Lettere di Verzi" (Venezia, 1778, p. 109), and still continue to be the normal laws all over Italy. During the epoch of the three Modenese writers there was published in Turin (1766) the "Giuoco degli Scacchi," by Count Carlo Cozio. As he follows the rest of the Italians in his rules, which contain twenty-four paragraphs, it would be useless to give them further analysis.

We arrive next at the work of the French Amateurs, which was published in 1775, two years before the second edition of Philidor, and concludes with a code of laws, based no doubt upon the regulations then in use amongst the visitors at the Café de la Regence, already famous as a place of meeting for French Chess players. On account of this, as well as of its superiority to all former collections of Chess laws, both in completeness and clearness

---

* The technical expression is, as we have already mentioned, *giuoco à monte*. Sarratt (1821, I. p. 27) misunderstands its meaning, thinking that, though the game must be played anew, the moves previous to the occurrence of the blunder must be the same as in the annulled game. The mistake has probably happened through misinterpretation of Lolli's words, at p. 11, where he explains, *giuoco à monte* by "vale a dire di doverto ricominciare sotto le medesime convenzioni," which means on the same conditions, the player having the move, &c. Compare also the "Miscellanea" (1861, p. 572), where, as in Lolli, the distinction is pointed out between *giuoco patto* and *giuoco à monte*.

† The custom of placing the board with the white square on the right hand is ancient, but we cannot fix the date of its commencement. Cessolis, about 1300, does not mention it explicitly, but seems to follow it. Carrera (p. 109) quotes a Latin epigram, but without assigning any date—

"Quod niveo in solio turris sit dextera, in atro
    Sit laeva, antiqui sic voluere patres."

of style, the treatise of the Amateurs merits our fullest attention. But their rules give no information respecting either the forced move of the King, the date of its origin, or the variety of its application. Instead of it we find that a player, if he touch a piece of his opponent which he cannot take, incurs no penalty but may play as he likes. Even if a player has taken his own piece, he has a right to replace it upon the board, provided that he do so before his opponent has made his next move, but he is compelled, according to the choice of his adversary, to play either the piece which he took or that with which he made the capture. The penal move of the King is only mentioned for the case in which a piece which covers the King from check has been touched. The Italian "giuoco à monte" does not appear amongst the regulations of the Amateurs, although they were acquainted with the writings of the Modenese. The laws of 1775 would no doubt have spread rapidly had not Philidor's Analysis, with the English rules, been published soon afterwards. In one point the Amateurs have found general recognition in the course of time. We refer to the now commonly received rule that if the board or the pieces have been wrongly placed, the mistake may be rectified during the first four moves. In an essay in the Schachzeitung for 1852 (p, 62) we tried to have the number of moves extended to six, but, our proposition not having been approved of, have made no further mention of our plan, which we intended to have served as a basis for a projected general code of laws.*

Our inquiry has now reached a stage at which we shall be able to solve the problem proposed, and to supply the desired information from the rules of Philidor. In these regulations, which, according to Philidor, are the same as those of a London Chess club meeting at the time in St. James'-street, the original copy of which, however, has never been printed, we find, in Articles VI. and VIII., that the King ought to be moved as a penalty when a player has touched an adverse piece which cannot be taken, or has made an illegal move It is remarkable that the addition which evidently belongs to these rules is omitted, that the King ought also to be moved when a piece

* In Bilguer's "Handbuch," and in our "Leitfaden," we have, in all the editions since 1843, and therefore before a revision of the Chess laws was spoken of, always given these same rules without variation.

which cannot be played without exposing the King to check has been touched. The general meaning of these laws requires that addition, which was made in Lewis's work (1842). See his rules at section 17, in a separate form.

The extensive recognition accorded to Philidor's work, as well as the consequent authority with which his rules were invested, must be well known to our readers. The spirit of his laws, indeed, continues to prevail to such a degree everywhere, excepting Italy, that other views would obtain access with great difficulty.

We believe that we have answered the question respecting the forced move of the King by referring to the rules of Philidor, originating in England (1777). We cannot, however, conclude without mentioning a thought which forced itself upon us with regard to the laws of Philidor and those of the "Traité des Amateurs." In what relationship do they stand to one another? Was the great master acquainted with the other treatise? Truly, it can scarcely be credited that, in 1777, the work of Philidor's countrymen, which was sold in the Café de la Régence, was not known to him. Still, he does not mention the "Traité Théorique et Pratique" even in those passages where he ought to have defended himself against their criticism upon his "Analysis" of 1749. Further than this, he says, in the edition of 1777, that he believes himself to be the first of his nation who has presented in their proper light the theory and practice of the game; whilst the Amateurs, in the first lines of their treatise, claim this very advantage for themselves. We might thus be tempted to conclude that either Philidor was unacquainted with the "Traité," or would not know it, and, at any rate, had not read it, the reason for which may have been that the "Traité" adopted Stamma's notation, the moves being marked by letters and numbers, and with which Philidor was not familiar. Against these reflections, however, militates the fact that Art. V. in the laws of Philidor so much resembles Art. VIII.* of the Amateurs that it is difficult to conceive that Philidor, or, at all events, he who corrected the literary portion

---

* The beginning of the article is the same in both sets of rules, and continues in Philidor thus:—"Quand on a touché une pièce, on est obligé de la jouer, à moins de dire 'j'adoube' en la touchant." "The "Traité" says, "à moins qu'on n'ait dit 'j'adoube' en la touchant." The difference is only that of tense.

of his work, had not seen the text of the Amateurs. Be it as it may, we will not inquire further into the subject by vain suppositions, but rest satisfied with having simply pointed out the remarkable relationship between the two works in that respect.

CHESS STUDY.
BY "EUCLID."
(Concluded from page 350.)

VARIATION G.
At Black's 9th move of Part II.

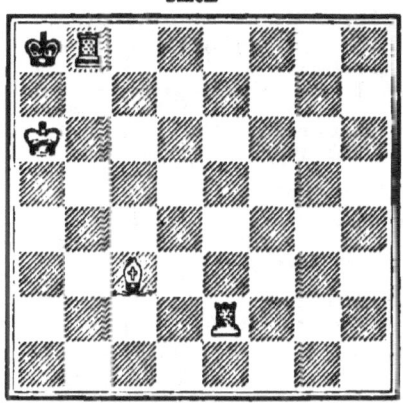

White.	Black.
	9. R. to Q. B. square
10. K. to Q. Kt. sixth	10. R. to K. B. square

If 10. R. to Q. Kt. (check)—
11. K. to Q. B. seventh   11. R. to Q. Kt. second (check)
12. K. to Q. B. sixth makes the position as at move 18 below.
Or if 10. R. to Q. square—
11. R. to Q. R. second (check)   11. K. to Q. Kt. square
12. B. to K. fifth (check)   12. K. to Q. B. square
13. K. to Q. B. sixth, and mates in 2 moves.
And if 10. R. to K. Kt. square—
11. K. to Q. B. seventh wins easily.
Again, if 10. K. to Q. Kt. square—
11. B. to K. fifth (check) wins Rook.

If White now tries 11. B. to K. fifth, Black draws the game by 11. R. to K. B. seventh.

11. K. to Q. B. seventh	11. R. to K. B. second (check)
12. K. to Q. B. sixth	12. R. to Q. Kt. second

White must now make an idle move with Rook, or play 13. B. to K. B. sixth; if he tries 13. B. to Q. fourth or K. fifth, Black gets a drawn position by 13. R. to Q. B. second, or Q. Kt. third (check).

13. R. to K. R. second	13. R. to K. second, or K. B. second

If 13. K. moves—
14. R. checks and mates in three moves.

14. R. to K. R. eighth (check), and mates in three moves.

VARIATION H.

At Black's ninth move of Part II.

	9. R. to K. B. square
10. K. to Q. Kt. sixth	10. K. to Q. Kt. square

If 10. R. to Q. Kt. (check)—

11. K. to Q. B. seventh	11. R. to Q. Kt. second (check)

12. K. to Q. B. sixth makes the position as at move 13, Variation G.

Or if 10. R. to Q. square—

11. R. to Q. R. second (check)	11. K. to Q. Kt. square

12. B. to K. fifth (check), and mates in three moves

And if 10. R. to K. Kt. square—
11. K. to Q. B. seventh wins.

11. R. to K. seventh	11. K. to Q. B. square

If 11. R. to K. Kt. square—
12. B. to K. fifth (check), as at move 18 below.

Or if 11. R. to Q. square—

12. B. to K. fifth (check)	12. K. to Q. B. square

13. R. to Q. B. seventh (check) wins easily.

12. K. to Q. B. sixth	12. R. to K. Kt. square

If 12. R. to Q. square—
13. B. to Q. Kt. fourth makes the position as at move 14, Part II.

Or if 12. K. to Q. square—

13. R. to K. fourth	13. R. to K. B. fourth
14. B. to Q. fourth	14. R. to K. B. square
15. R. to K. second	15. K. to Q. B. square

16. B. to K. Kt. seventh, as at move 21, Part 2.

And if 12. K. to Q. Kt. square—

13. B. to K. fifth (check)	13. K. to Q. B. square

14. R. to Q. R. seventh wins Rook.

13. B. to K. B. sixth	13. R. to K. B. square

If 13. K. to Q. Kt. square—

14. B. to K. fifth (check)	14. K. to Q. B. square

15. R. to Q. R. seventh wins Rook.

14. B. to K. Kt. fifth	14 R. to K. Kt. square

If 14. R. to K. R. square—

15. B. to K. B. fourth	15. K. to Q. square
16. R. to K. fourth	16. R. to K. Kt. square
17. B. to Q. B. seventh (check)	17. K. to Q. B. square
18. R. to Q. Kt. fourth wins.	

	Or if 14. K. to Q. Kt. square—
15. K. to Q. Kt. sixth	15. R. to K. Kt. square
16. R. to Q. Kt. seventh (check)	16. K. to Q. R. square
17. R. to Q. R. seventh (check)	17. K. to Q. Kt. square
18. B. to K. B. fourth (check) wins Rook.	
15. R. to K. B. seventh	15. R. to K. Kt. third (check)

If 15. R. to K. or K. R. square—
16. B. to K. seventh, followed by
17. B. to Q. sixth, winning speedily.
                  Or if 15. K. to Q. Kt. square—
16. B. to K. B. fourth (check)   16. K. to Q. B. square
17. R. to Q. R. seventh wins Rook.

16. B. to K. B. sixth	16. K. to Q. Kt. square

If 16. R. to K. Kt. square—
17. B. to K. seventh wins easily.

17. K. to Q. Kt. sixth	17. R. to K. Kt. square

If 17. K. to Q. B. square—
18. R. to Q. B. seventh (check)   18. K. to Q. Kt. square
19. R. to Q. B. sixth   19. R. to K. Kt. square
20. B. to K. fifth (check)   20. K. to Q. R. square
21. K. to Q. B. seventh wins.

18. B. to K. fifth (check)	18. K. to Q. B. square
19. R. to Q. B. seventh (check)	19. K. to Q. square
20. B. to K. Kt. seventh wins as after move 23 of Part II.	

Variation J.

At Black's ninth move of Part II.

	9. R. to K. Kt. square
10. K. to Q. Kt. sixth	10. K. to Q. Kt. square

If 10. R. to Q. Kt. square (check)—
11. K. to Q. B. seventh   11. R. to Q. Kt. second (check)
12. K. to Q. B. sixth makes the position as at move 13, Variation G.
                Or if 10. R. to Q. square—
11. R. to Q. R. second (check)   11. K. to Q. Kt. square
12. B. to K. 5th (check), and mates in three moves.
              Again, if 10. R. to K. B. square—
11. K. to Q. B. seventh, as at move 11, Variation G.
              And if 10. R. to K. Kt. third (check)—
11. K. to Q. B. seventh   11. R. to Q. R. third
12. R. to K. eighth (check) wins easily.

11. B. to K. B. sixth	11. R. to K. B. square

If 11. K. to Q. B. square—
12. K. to Q. B. sixth makes the position as at move 20, Part II.

12. B. to K. seventh	12. R. to K. B. sixth or eighth

If 12. R. to K. Kt. or K. R. square—
13. B. to Q. sixth (check), as at move 12, Variation K.
              Or if 12. R. to K. B. second—
13. R. to Q. second, and mates in three moves.

13. R. to K. R. second	13. K. to Q. B. square

If 13. R. to Q. Kt. sixth or eighth (check)—
14. K. to Q. B. sixth wins easily.

14. K. to Q. B. sixth	14. R. to Q. B. sixth or eighth (check).
15. B. to Q. B. fifth	15. R. to Q. sixth or eighth

It is now similar to the position after move 10 of Part I., and White proceeds as there shown by—

16. R. to K. R. seventh	16. R. to Q. seventh (best)
17. R. to K. Kt. seventh, &c.	

VARIATION K.
At Black's 11th move of Part II.

	11. R. to K. Kt. or K. R. square
12. B. to Q. sixth (check)	12. K. to Q. B. square
13. K. to Q. B. sixth	13. K. to Q. square

If 13. R. moves—
14. R. to Q. Kt. second wins.

14. B. to Q. B. seventh (check).	14. K. to Q. B. square
15. R. to Q. Kt. second, winning easily.	

We have several letters eulogising the skill and patience displayed by the author of this remarkable study, which we believe will ever remain on record as one of the most instructive examples of analytical power in this branch of the game.

GAMES.

GAME 209.

The following two games were played in the Handicap Tourney of the late Congress between Herr Steinitz and Mr. S. J. Green, the former giving the odds of the Pawn and two moves.

First Game. (Remove Black's King's Bishop's Pawn.)

White. (Mr. S. J. Green.)	Black. (Herr Steinitz.)
1. P. to K. fourth	
2. P. to Q. fourth	2. P. to K. third
3. K. B. to Q. third	3. P. to B. fourth
4. P. to Q. B. third	4. P. to K. Kt. third
5. P. to K. fifth	5. Q. Kt. to Q. B. third
6. K. Kt. to K. B. third	6. P. to Q. third
7. K. B. to Q. Kt. fifth (a)	7. P. to Q. fourth
8. P. to K. R. fourth	8. P. takes P.
9. P. takes P.	9. Q. to R. fourth (check)
10. Kt. to Q. B. third	10. K. B. to Q. Kt. fifth
11. B. takes Kt. (check)	11. P. takes B.
12. B. to Q. second	12. Q. B. to R. third
13. Kt. to K. Kt. fifth	13. K. to Q. second (b)

14. Kt. to B. seventh	14. Kt. to K. second
15. Kt. takes R.	15. R. takes Kt.
16. P. to Q. R. third	16. B. takes Kt.
17. B. takes B.	17. Q. to Kt. fourth
18. P. to Q. R. fourth (c)	18. Q. to B. fifth
19. P. to Q. R. fifth	19. Q. to Kt. fourth
20. Q. R. to R. fourth	20. P. to B. fourth
21. P. takes P.	21. Kt. to B. third
22. K. R. to K. R. third (d)	22. K. to B. square
23. K. R. to K. B. third	23. P. to Q. fifth
24. B. takes P.	24. R. to Q. square
25. R. to K. third	25. Kt. takes B.
26. R. takes Kt.	26. Q. to B. eighth (check)

And White resigns.

NOTES.

(*a*) This enables Black to advance at once his Pawn to Q. fourth, always a great defensive move in this opening. We should have preferred P. takes Q. P.

(*b*) We suppose that this was played to bring the Knight into the field. Nevertheless, the loss of the exchange ought to have been fatal. Black's previous move of B. to Q. R. third was not nearly so good as it looks.

(*c*) The move in the text seems to be inferior to three other modes of play— P. to K. Kt. fourth, Q. to Q. B. second, and Q. to Q. second—any one of which would have effectually maintained White's attack.

(*d*) After this, and the next move of his Rook, the first player cannot save the game.

GAME 210.

Second Game. (Remove Black's King's Bishop's Pawn.)

White. (Mr. S. J. GREEN.)	*Black.* (Herr STEINITZ.)
1. P. to K. fourth	
2. P. to Q. fourth	2. Q. Kt. to B. third
3. P. to Q. fifth	3. Kt. to K. fourth
4. P. to K. B. fourth	4. Kt. to B. second
5. P. to K. fifth	5. K. Kt. to R. third
6. P. to Q. B. fourth	6. P. to K. Kt. third
7. K. Kt. to B. third	7. K. B. to Kt. second
8. P. to Q. B. fifth (a)	8. P. to Q. B. third
9. Q. Kt. to B. third	9. Castles
10. K. B. to Q. B. fourth	10. P. takes P.
11. Q. takes P.	11. P. to K. third
12. Q. to K. fourth	12. Q. to Q. B. second
13. B. to K. third	13. K. Kt. to B. fourth

14. B. to B. second	14. Q. R. to Q. Kt square
15. P. to Q. Kt. fourth (b)	15. P. to Q. fourth
16. B. P. takes P. *en passant* (c)	16. Q Kt. takes Q. P.
17. P. takes Kt.	17. B. takes Kt. (check)
18. K. to K. second	18. Kt. takes P.
19. B. takes P. (check)	19. B. takes B.
20. Q. takes B. (check)	20. K. to R. square
21. B. to K. third	21. Q. R. to K. square
22. Q. to Q. fifth	22. B. takes R.
23. R. takes B.	23. R. takes B. (check)
24. K. takes R.	24. Q. to Q. B. sixth (check)
25. K. to B. second	25. Q. to Q. Kt. seventh (check)
26. K. to K. Kt. third	26. Kt. to K. B. fourth (check)
27. K. to R. third	27. Q. takes R.
28. Q. takes Kt. P.	28. Q. takes Q. R. P.
29. Kt. to Kt. fifth	29. Kt. to Kt. second
30. Q. to K. fourth	30. P. to K. R. third
31. Kt. to B. third	31. Q. to K. third (check)

And White resigns the game and the match.

NOTES.

(a) Although this array of Pawns looks formidable, experience proves that it is difficult to maintain them without sacrifice of position.

(b) Clearly an oversight.

(c) Having made the previous blunder, White should have made the best of a bad bargain, and have boldly captured the Pawn with the Bishop.

GAME 211.

GRAND CHALLENGE CUP TOURNEY.

Game played during the meeting of the Chess Association between Mr. Minchin and Mr. De Vere.

First Game. (*Evans's Gambit Declined.*)

White. (Mr. MINCHIN.)	Black. (Mr. DE VERE.)
1. P. to K. fourth	1. P. to K. fourth
2. Kt. to K. B. third	2. Kt. to Q. B. third
3. B. to B. fourth	3. B. to B. fourth
4. P. to Q. Kt. fourth	4. B. to Kt. third
5. P. to Q R. fourth	5. P. to Q. R. third
6. Castles	6. P. to Q. third
7. P. to Q. R. fifth	7. B. to Q. R. second
8. P. to Q. B. third	8. K. Kt. to B. third

9. P. to Q. third	9. P. to K. R. third
10. B. to K. third	10. Castles
11. Q. to Q. Kt. third	11. Q. Kt. to K. second
12. Q. Kt. to Q. second	12. P. to Q. B. third
13. Q. to Q. B. second	13. P. to Q. fourth
14. B. to Q. R. second	14. Q. Kt. to K. Kt. third
15. Q. R. to K. square	15. K. R. to K. square
16. B. to Q. Kt. square	16. Q. P. takes P.
17. P. takes P.	17. Q. to Q. second (*a*)
18. B. takes B.	18. R. takes B.
19. Q. Kt. to Q. B. fourth	19. Q. to K. Kt. fifth
20. Q. Kt. to K. third (*b*)	20. Q. to K. R. fourth
21. Q. Kt. to K. B. fifth	21. Q. Kt. to K. B. fifth
22. Kt. to K. Kt. third	22. Q. to Kt. third
23. Kt. to R. fourth	23. Q. to Kt. fifth
24. K. Kt. to B. fifth	24. B. takes Kt.
25. P. takes B.	25. P. to R. fourth
26. P. to K. B. third	26. Q. to Kt. fourth
27. K. to R. square	27. P. to K. R. fifth
28. Kt. to K. fourth	28. Kt. takes Kt.
29. R. takes Kt	29. Q. takes P.
30. Q. to K. B. second	30. Q. R. to R. square
31. Q. takes P.	31. Kt. to K. Kt. third
32. Q. to K. B. second	32. Q. to B. third
33. P. to Kt. third	33. Q. R. to Q. square
34. K. R. to K. square	34. K. to B. square
35. P. to K. R. fourth (*c*)	35. Q. to Q. third
36. P. to K. R. fifth	36. Kt. to R. square
37. Q. to K. third	37. Q. to Q. seventh
38. Q. to Q. B. fifth (check)	38. Q. to Q. third
39. Q. takes Q. (check) (*d*)	39. R. takes Q.
40. P. to K. B. fourth	40. P. to K. B. third
41. B. to R. second (*e*)	41. R. to Q. sixth
42. P. takes P	42. R. takes K. P.
43. R. takes R.	43. P. takes R.
44. B. to K. sixth	44. R. takes B. P.
45. R. takes P.	45. R. takes P.
46. B. to Q. seventh	46. R. to Q. sixth
47. R. to K. eighth (check) (*f*)	47. K. to B. second
48. B. takes P.	48. P. takes B.
49. R. takes Kt.	49. R. to Q. Kt. sixth
50. R. to Q. R. eighth (*g*)	50. R. takes P.

51. R. takes P.	51. R. to Q. Kt. fourth
52. R. to Q. R. seventh (check)	52. K. to K. third
53. P. to Q. R. sixth	53. R. takes P. (check)
54. K. to Kt. second	54. R. to Q. R. fourth
55. R. to R. eighth	55. K. to Q. third
56. P. to R. seventh	56. K. to Q. B. fourth (h)
57. K. to B. third	57. K. to Kt. third
58. R. to Kt. eighth (check)	58. K. takes P.
59. R. to Q. Kt. third	59. R. to Q. Kt. fourth

And after a few more moves White resigns.

NOTES.

(a) This changes the aspect of the game, as he is evidently about to operate on his left, but White's position is perfectly secure.

(b) The move in the text is a good one. He might also have matured the attack which he subsequently obtains, by taking possession of the Queen's file with his Rook.

(c) "P. to K. B. fourth" would perhaps after all have been preferable.

(d) In such a position we should have been reluctant to have exchanged Queens.

(e) Perhaps the Bishop should not have quitted the Q. Kt. square at this moment, still his new post is a great one to maintain, as will be seen presently.

Position after Black's 46th move.

WHITE.

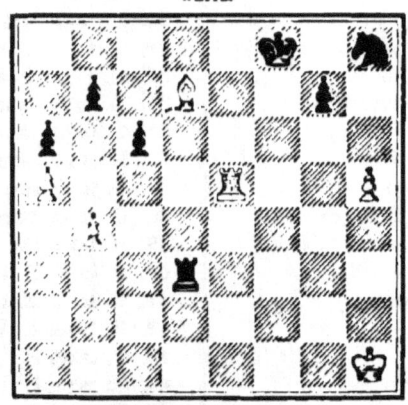

BLACK.

(f) We believe that White might have adopted a different line of play with striking advantage. Suppose—

White.	Black.
46. B. to Q. B. eighth	46. Kt. to K. B. second (or A)
47. R. to K. B. fifth	47. K. to K. second
48. B. takes P.	48. Kt. to Q. third

49. B. takes R. P.
50. R. to K. B. square, with the superiority.

49. R. to Q. eighth (check) best

(A)

47. K. to K. Kt. second
48. R. to K. B. fifth
49. B. takes P.
50. R. to K. Kt. fifth
51. R. to K. Kt. sixth (check), winning another Pawn.

46. R. to Q. eighth (check)
47. Kt. to K. B. second
48. K. to K. second
49. Kt. to Q. third
50. K. to B. third

(g) "R. to Q. B. eighth" is the simplest mode of play. When he had subsequently the opportunity of taking the Q. B. Pawn, he should have done so without delay.

(h) The ability to play the King to this square, under cover of the Pawn, wins the game.

GAME 212.

Lively skirmish between the Revs. W. Wayte and E. D. Rhodes.

(Allgaier Gambit.)

White. (Rev. W. WAYTE.)	Black. (Rev. E. D. RHODES).
1. P. to K. fourth	1. P. to K. fourth
2. P. to K. B. fourth	2. P. takes P.
3. K. Kt. to B. third	3. P. to K. Kt. fourth
4. P. to K. R. fourth	4. P. to K. Kt. fifth
5. Kt. to K. fifth	5. K. Kt. to B. third
6. B. to Q. B. fourth	6. P. to Q. fourth
7. P. takes P.	7. B. to Q. third
8. P. to Q. fourth	8. Kt. to K. R. fourth
9. Q. Kt. to B. third	9. Kt. to K. Kt. sixth
10. Q. B. takes P.	10. Kt. takes R. (a)
11. Q. Kt. to K. fourth	11. Q. takes K. R. P. (check)
12. P. to K. Kt. third	12. Q. to K. R. seventh
13. Q. to her third	13. Q to K. Kt. eighth (check)
14. K. to Q. second	14. Q. to K. Kt. seventh (ch.) (b)
15. K. to Q. B. third	15. Kt. to K. B. seventh
16. Q. Kt. to K. B. sixth (ch.) (c)	16. K. to B. square (d)
17. B. to K. R. sixth (check)	17. K. to K. second
18. Q. to K. third	18. Kt. to K. fifth (check)
19. Q. Kt. takes Kt.	19. B. takes K. Kt. (e)

NOTES.

(a) An analysis of this position appeared in THE CHESS PLAYER'S MAGAZINE for 1864, p. 167.

(b) Black may take the second Rook if he pleases, but White's remaining pieces being in full co-operation against the King would insure him a speedy victory.

(c) Mr. Wayte thinks this move more conclusive than Kt. takes Kt., followed by R. to K. B. square, the mode of play indicated in THE CHESS PLAYER'S MAGAZINE.

(*d*) If K. to K. second, White replies with Q. to K. third.

(*e*) As the position is instructive we have given it in a diagram in order that our readers may trace for themselves Mr. Wayte's method of terminating the game.

BLACK.

WHITE.

White to play, and mate in six moves.

GAME 213.

Interesting game recently played by Mr. E. Thorold against the Rev. W. Wayte.

(King's Gambit refused.)

White. (Mr. THOROLD.)	*Black.* (Mr. WAYTE.)
1. P. to K. fourth	1. P. to K. fourth
2. P. to K. B. fourth	2. K. B. to Q. B. fourth
3. K. Kt. to B. third	3. P. to Q. third
4. P. to Q. B. third	4. Q. B. to K. Kt. fifth
5. P. to Q. fourth (*a*)	5. P. takes Q. P.
6. P. takes P.	6. B. takes Kt.
7. P. takes B.	7. Q. to K. R. fifth (check)
8. K. to K. second	8. B. to Q. Kt. third
9. K. R. to Kt. square	9. Q. Kt. to B. third (*b*)
10. B. to K. third	10. K. Kt. to B. third
11. Q. Kt. to B. third	11. K. Kt. to R. fourth
12. Kt. to Q. fifth	12. Kt. to K. B. third

13. Kt. takes B.	13. R. P. takes Kt.
14. P. to Q. fifth	14. Q. Kt. to K. second
15. B. to K. B. second	15. Q. to K. R. third
16. B. to K. third	16. Castles Q. R. (c)
17. Q. R. to Q. B. square	17. K. R. to K. square
18. B. takes P.	18. Q. Kt. takes Q. P.
19. Q. to Q. Kt. third	19. K. Kt. takes K. P. (d)
20. K. to Q. square	20. K. Kt. to B. third
21. R. to K. Kt. fifth	21. K. to Kt. square
22. B. to Q. fourth	22. P. to Q. B. fourth (e)
23. K. B. to Q. R. sixth (f)	23. Q. Kt. to Kt. fifth
24. B. to Q. Kt. fifth	24. Q. takes K. R. P.
25. B. takes R.	25. R. takes B.
26. B. to K. third	26. Q. to K. R. eighth (check)
27. B. to K. Kt. square	27. K. Kt. to Q. fourth
28. K. to Q. second	28. K. Kt. takes P.
29. Q. R. to Q. square	29. Q. to K. R. third
30. R. to K. B. fifth	30. R. to K. seventh (check)
31. K. to Q. B. square	31. K. Kt. to Q. sixth (double ch.)
32. K. to Kt. square	32. Q. to K. Kt. third (g)
33. R. takes K. B. P.	33. Q. takes R.

And White resigns.

NOTES.

(a) White submits to the displacement of his King in order to establish his Pawns in the centre. The *Handbuch* pronounces the game an even one.

(b) B. to K. third at once, we believe, leads to a sound development of the first player's attack.

(c) If he were to take the offered K. R. Pawn he would lose much valuable time.

(d) A perfectly safe stroke of play.

(e) Not only attacking the Queen's Bishop, but threatening, if the other Bishop move to Q. R. sixth, to play Kt. to Q. Kt. fifth with great advantage.

(f) This portion of the game is capitally managed by the second player.

(g) Both a higher order of move and also more conclusive than R. takes Q. Kt. P. (check).

TERMINATION OF THE MATCH BETWEEN MESSRS. BIRD AND STEINITZ.

We are sorry to say that this match, which was looked forward to with so much interest, after all never received a legitimate termination. Mr. Bird had won five games and his opponent six, when circumstances beyond the control of the former compelled him to resign the match.

CHESS INTELLIGENCE.

BRISTOL ATHENÆUM CHESS CLUB.

A highly-interesting *soirée* was held at this Club on the 7th November, which was numerously attended by amateurs, not only of Bristol and its vicinity, but from remote localities. The lecture-hall, in which the assembly took place, was decorated with flags and pictures lent for the purpose, and was provided with microscopes, stereoscopes, and other means of amusement for general visitors, for whom also ample accommodation was provided in the shape of refreshment. Chess was, however, the paramount attraction, and was engaged in by both ladies and gentlemen. Among those present we may mention Mr. E. Thorold (President of the Club), the Rev. A. C. Rowley, the Rev. C. Holt (Bath), Messrs. Stephens (Bath), T. Jolly (Bath), Horner (Bath), Cooper (Bath), Nelson Fedden (Cardiff), Wakeford (Cardiff), Vatchell (Cardiff), W. Riley (Cardiff), M. Thorold (Bath), Fenton (Bath), W. P. Meeker and W. Thomson (Vice-Presidents of the Club), D. Vines, R. T. Stoate (Treasurer), W. Berry (Secretary), Badcock, J. D. Corfe, W. Hibbins, J. Haycroft, Fairbourn, J. Banfield, J. Sanders, F. A. King, H. Isaacs, jun., C. Boorne (Honorary Secretary of the Cotham Social Club), J. Burt (Chew Magna), J. C. Blackmore, J. Franklin, Worth, Whitwill, S. Fryer, E. Gammon, J. A. Hill, J. H. Perrin, Jeanes (Banfield), Cleland, Dr. Hill, Dr. Benham, Colonel Le Hardy, &c. Mr. Thorold (the President) played eight games even simultaneously—viz., with Messrs. Cleland, A. Billings, Stephens, jun., Welchwk, Benham, jun., K. Thomas, W. Hibbins, and J. H. Perrin. Mr. Thorold won all the games. The Rev. A. C. Rowley played even against Messrs. Worth, Banfield, and Jeanes, and he proved victor over the three. Mr. Thorold also played four simultaneous games against stronger players—viz., Messrs. Fedden (Cardiff), Fenton (Bath), Gammon and Isaacs (Bristol). Mr. Fedden lost, Mr. Fenton's game was drawn, Mr. Gammon lost, and Mr. Isaacs won. There was also played a new double game of Chess, introduced by the Rev. A. C. Rowley, that proved very interesting.

CROYDON WORKMEN'S CLUB.

Our readers are aware that there was formed some time ago a Chess Club in connection with this institution, and we are happy to say it has proved of great advantage to the Workmen's Club, as well as a source of much gratification to its members. A Tournament has lately been concluded which was some time in progress amongst them, and excited considerable interest. There were eight competitors, each playing against all the others. The prize was a handsome set of Chessmen (presented by Mr. E. Huntley) and a table and board (presented by Mr. G. Smith). After a prolonged struggle the victory was won by Mr. Coldwells, the General Secretary of the institution, who thus became its champion player. At a *soirée*, held on Tuesday, the 24th October, the prize was formally handed over to the successful competitor by Mr. G. W. Medley, the President of the Croydon Workmen's Chess Club, who congratulated the winner upon his success, and the members of the Club upon the great interest which had been exhibited by them in the study of this intellectual game.

LONDON CHESS CLUB.

The annual general meeting of the members of this Club was held on Saturday, October 27th, A. Mongredien, Esq., in the chair. The report, read by Mr. G. W. Medley, the Hon rary Secretary, showed the Club to be in a highly-prosperous condition, and was unanimously adopted. The meeting subsequently resolved that it was advisable the Club should obtain more convenient premises, and appointed Messrs. Medley and Lowenthal as a committee to make inquiries for the purpose, and to report to the next meeting.

WOLVERHAMPTON AND STOURBRIDGE CLUBS.

From the "Birmingham Daily Post," November 13, 1866.

A match was played between these clubs on Saturday, the 10th instant, at the residence of the president of the former club. It was arranged that the six players selected by each club should be paired by ballot, and that, it time allowed, the play should continue till three games had been scored by an antagonist at each of the six tables. The match resulted in a victory for the Wolverhampton Club. The following will show the pairing of the players, and the results of individual play:—

Antagonists.	Games won by Stourbridge.	Won by Wolverhampton.	Drawn Games.
Lord Lyttleton *v.* A. Scott	1	2	2
H. O. Firmstone (President) *v.* W. C. Umbers (Hon. Sec.)	0	3	—
T. M. Harding *v.* T. Chittenden	0	1	2
H. Freer *v.* S. Faulkes.	0	3	1
W. A. Baxter (Hon. Sec.) *v.* Wm. Lees.	1	1	1
Mr. Doughty *v.* John Neeve (President)	1	2	—
	3	12	

CORRESPONDENCE.

TO THE EDITOR OF "THE CHESS PLAYER'S MAGAZINE."

Huddersfield Chess Club,
November 15th, 1866.

DEAR SIR,—With reference to the letter from the Sheffield Chess Club, which appeared in the last number of your Magazine, I wish simply to refer your readers to a correspondence between the two Clubs in your April and May numbers, and to state that since that time no challenge has been received, and consequently none declined, by the Huddersfield Club. The terms then indicated by me are still open for acceptance either by the Sheffield Club or any other Club in the West Riding of Yorkshire. I remain, dear sir, yours very truly,

JOHN WATKINSON.

Problem No. 113. By Herr L. VOLANGE, of Hanover.

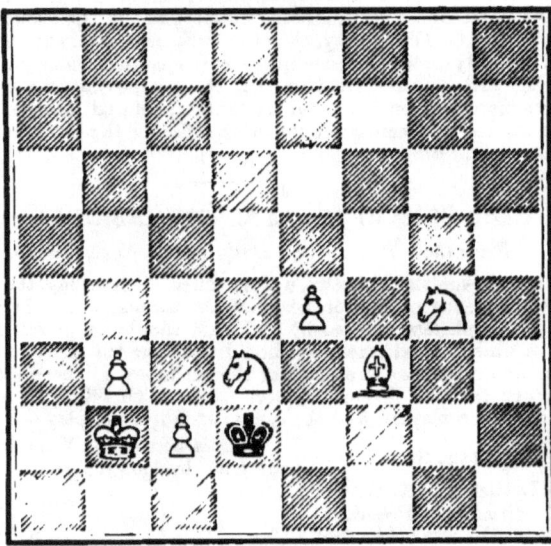

White to play, and mate in five moves.

Problem No. 114. By Dr. CONRAD BAYER.

White to play, and mate in four moves.

Problem No. 115. By Herr J. Minckwitz, of Leipsic.

BLACK.

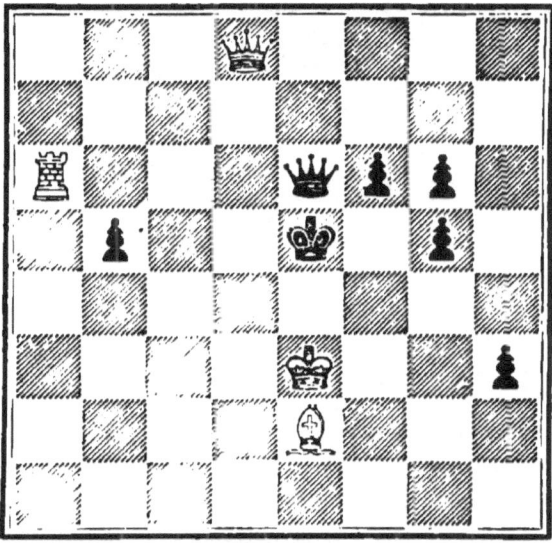

WHITE.

White to play, and mate in three moves.

Problem No. 116. By Herr J. Kohtz, of Cologne.

BLACK.

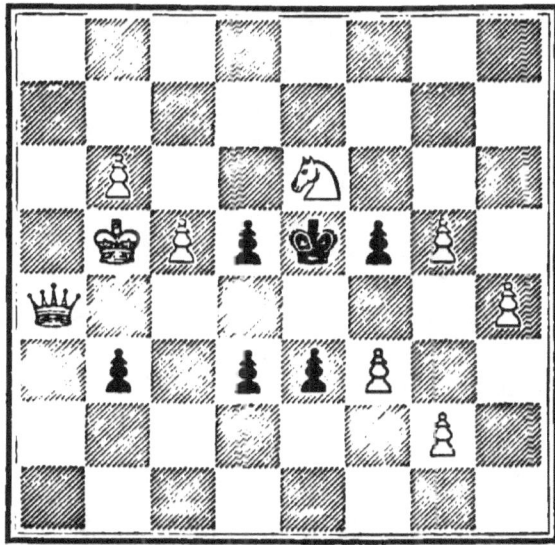

WHITE.

White to play, and mate in three moves.

Problem No. 117. By Herr H. Meyer, late of Hanover.

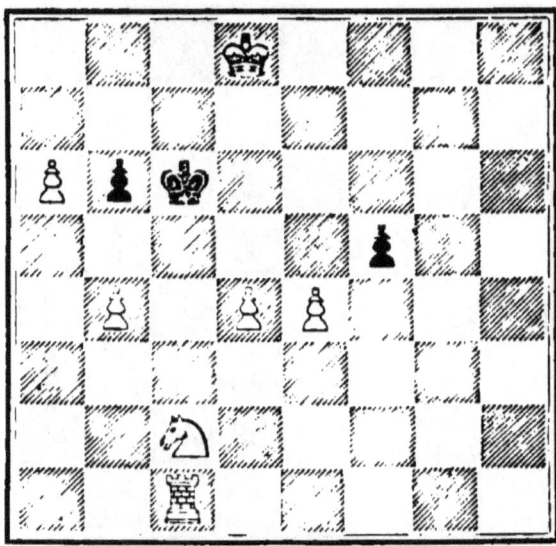

White to play, and mate in four moves.

Problem No. 118. By Dr. H. A. Stavenuter, of Hamburg.
(From the *Illustrirte Zeitung*.)

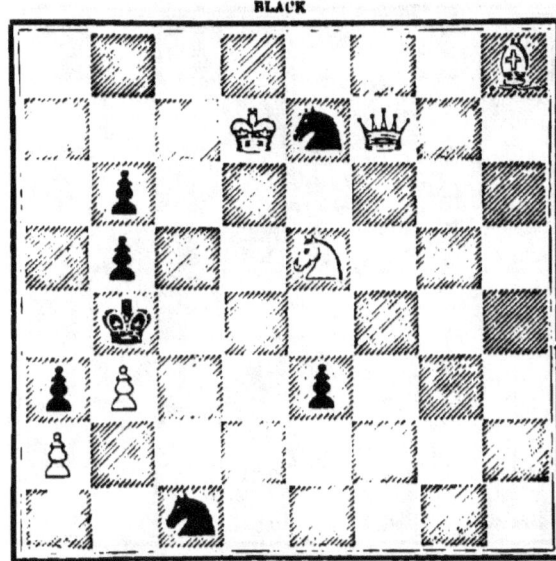

White to play, and mate in three moves.

SOLUTIONS TO PROBLEMS.

No. 101.—By Dr. Conrad Bayer.

White.	Black.
1. R. to K. eighth	1. P. to Q. R. third (A) (B)
2. Kt. to K. seventh	2. Any move
3. Either Kt. or Q. mates.	

(A)

	1. Q. to K. B. fourth
2. Q. takes Q.	2. Anything.
3. Q. mates accordingly.	

(B)

	1. P. takes Kt. (C)
2. R. takes B.	2. Anything.
3. Q. mates.	

(C)

	1. B. to Q. fourth (D)
2. R. takes Q. (check)	2. B. takes R.
3. Kt. to Q. B. fourth (mate)	

(D)

| | 1. Q. takes P. |
| 2. Q. to K. fifth (check), and mates next move. | |

No. 102.—By Lieutenant Ph. Klett.

White.	Black.
1. R. from R. fifth to R. third	1. K. to K. fourth (best)
2. R. to B. fifth (check)	2. K. takes P.
3. R. to K. third	3. P. takes R.
4. R. to K. fifth	4. Any move
5. Kt. or B. mates accordingly.	

No. 103.—By Herr Meyer.

White.	Black.
1. Q. to Q. Kt. fourth	1. R. takes B. (A)
2. Kt. to K. fifth (discovered check)	2. K. moves
3. Kt. or B. mates accordingly.	

(A)

	1. B. to Q. fifth (B)
2. Kt. to Q. sixth (check)	2. R. or P. takes Kt.
3. R. or Q. mates accordingly.	

(B)

	1. R. to R. fifth (C)
2. Q. to B. fifth	2. Anything
3. Kt. or Q. mates accordingly.	

(C)

	1. B. takes R.
2. Kt. to K. third (discovered check)	2. K. takes Kt.
3. Q. to Q. fourth (mate).	

No. 104.—By Herr Kockelkorn.

White.	Black.
1. K. to Q. square	1. K. to K. sixth, B. sixth, or Q. sixth
2. Q. to Kt. fourth or Q. B. fourth accordingly	2. K. or P. moves
3. Q. mates accordingly.	

No. 105.—By T. Smith, Esq.

White.
1. Q. to B. third
2. Q. Kt. to K. third
3. Kt. to K. B. fourth (check)
4. Kt. to B. fifth (mate)

Black.
1. P. takes Q. (A)
2. K. Kt. to K. fourth or (B)
3. K. moves

(A)

2. Q. to K. B. fifth
3. Kt. to B. fourth (check)
4. Q. to B. second (mate)

1. Q. Kt. to K. fourth
2. Any move
3. K. moves

(B)

3. R. to R. fourth (check)
4. Kt. to B. fourth (mate)

2. Q. Kt. to K. fourth or (C)
3. Kt. takes R.

(C)

3. R. to R. fourth (check)
4. Kt. to B. fourth (mate)

2. Kt. takes Kt.
3. Kt. takes R.

No. 106.—By Herr Kohtz.

White.
1. Q. to K. sixth
2. Kt. to K. eighth
3. Kt. mates

Black.
1. B. takes Q, or B. to Kt. second, or P. to K. B. fifth
2. Any move

No. 107.—By Herr A. Beck.

White.
1. Kt. to Q. B. fifth
2. B. to Q. square
3. B. mates.

Black.
1. P. takes Kt. (A) (B)
2. P. takes R.

(A)

2. K. to Q. sixth
3. B. mates.

1. P. takes R.
2. Any move

(B)

2. R. to B. third (check)
3. B. mates.

1. K. takes Kt.
2. K. takes Kt.

No. 108.—By Dr. Stavenüter.

White.
1. Q. to B. second
2. B. to Q. fifth
3. Q. to K. B. fifth (mate).

Black.
1. K. to K. fourth (A) (B)
2. K. takes B.

(A)

2. B. to R. seventh (check)
3. Q. to Q. Kt. second (mate).

1. K. to Q. sixth
2. K. takes P.

(B)

2. B. to R. seventh (check)
3. Q. to K. B. sixth (mate).

1. P. to Q. fourth
2. K. to K. fourth

No. 109.—By Dr. Bayer.

White.
1. Kt. to K. R. fifth
2. R. to B. fourth (check)
3. R. to K. sixth (dis. check)
4. P. or R. mates.

Black.
1. R. or B. takes Kt. (A)
2. K. takes R.
3. K. moves

(A)

1. P. takes R.
2. Kt. to Q. sixth
3. Any move

2. R. takes P.
3. P. takes Kt.
4. R. mates.

No. 110.—By Herr Martini.

White.
1. B. to Q. third (check)
2. Kt. to Q. second (dis. check)
3. Kt. to R. sixth
4. Kt. mates.

Black.
1. K. takes B. (A)
2. P. takes R. (best)
3. B. moves

(A)

1. K. to Q. fourth
2. K. takes K. P.

2. P. to B. fourth (check)
3. Kt. to Kt. fifth (mate).

No. 111.—By Herr Mehrtens.

White.
1. Kt. from K. third takes Kt. P.
2. Kt. from Kt. fourth to K. third
3. Kt. to Q. fifth (dis. check)
4. Kt. or P. mates.

Black.
1. P. to Q. Kt. seventh (A)(B)(C)
2. K. to K. fifth
3. K. moves

(A)

1. K. takes Kt.
2. P. takes B.
3. Any move

2. P. to Kt. third
3. P. takes Q. P.
4. R. mates.

(B)

1. P. takes B.
2. K. to Kt. sixth
3. Any move

2. Kt. takes Q. P.
3. R. to K. B. second
4. Kt. mates.

(C)

1. P. to Kt. third
2. B. to Kt. second
3. Any move

2. Kt. takes Q. P.
3. R. to K. B. second (check)
4. R. or Kt. mates.

No. 112.—By Herr Meyer.

White.
1. Q. to Q. R. square
2. Q. to Q. R. eighth
3. Q. mates accordingly.

Black.
1. B. to K. third (A)
2. Any move

(A)

1. R. to Q. square
2. Any move

2. Q. to K. Kt. seventh
3. Q. mates.

CHESS STUDIES.

No. 24.—By Herr Horwitz.

White.	Black.
1. K. to B. eighth (a)	1. B. takes Kt. (check)
2. K. to Q. eighth	2. K. to Q. Kt. second
3. R. to Kt. eighth (check)	3. K. takes P.
4. K. to Q. B. seventh	4. B. to Q. R. fifth
5. R. to Q. Kt. sixth	5. B. to K. square
6. R. to K. sixth	6. B. to Q. R. fifth
7. R. to K. fourth	7. B. to Q. Kt. fourth
8. R. to K. square, and wins.	

(a) The only move to win.

No. 25.—By W. T. Pierce.

White.	Black.
1. B. to Q. third	King moves
2. B. to B. fourth	
3. R. to K. B. seventh	
4. B. to Kt. fifth	
5. R. to Q. seventh	
6. B. to K. sixth	
7. R. to Q. eighth (check)	
8. K. to B. fifth	
9. R. to Q. seventh	
10. R. mates	

No. 26.—By Herr H. Meyer.

White.	Black.
1. P. to K. sixth	1. P. takes P.
2. R. to Kt. sixth (check)	2. K. to R. square or B. square
3. Kt. to B. seventh, or Kt. to R. seventh (check)	3. K. to R. second or B. second
4. R. to Kt. seventh (mate)	

No. 27.—By J. Smith, Esq.

White.	Black.
1. R. to K. R. fourth (A)	1. B. to K. fifth
2. R. takes P.	2. R. to Q. square
3. K. to K. second	3. P. to Q. seventh
	4. R. takes B. and wins.

(A)

1. P. to Kt. sixth	
2. R. to Q. Kt. second (B)	2. R. to Q. square
	3. B. to Kt. second and wins.

(B)

2. B. to B. third	
3. B. to Q. second	3. R. to Q. B. square
	4. R. to B. seventh and wins.

London:
Printed by Jas. Wade, 18, Tavistock-street, Covent-garden.

INDEX.

GAMES.

Anderssen and Neumann, 53, 54, 89, 90
Anderssen and Steinitz, 235—244, 269
  —280, 294—300
Barry and Bolt, 54—56
Berry, Meeker, and Selkirk v. Fenton,
  Briggs, and Cooper, 145
Bolt and Barry, 54—56
Briggs, Fenton, and Cooper v. Berry,
  Meeker, and Selkirk, 145
Cambridge and Dublin, 83—85
Campbell and Falkbeer, 78, 79
Chinnery and Lord Lyttelton, 300—304
Cooper, Briggs, and Fenton v. Berry,
  Meeker, and Selkirk, 145
Cronhelm and Jones, 56, 57
De Rivière and Morphy, 74—76
De Vere and Bird, 252, 253
De Vere and MacDonnell, 207, 208, 306
De Vere and Minchin, 362
De Vere and Steinitz, 10—16, 37—48,
  71—73, 244—251
Drew, F. R. and Hamel, 338, 339
Dublin and Cambridge, 83—85
Dublin and London, 213, 214
Dubois and Kempe, 87—89
E——n and Weaver v. Moffatt and
  Williams, 86, 87
E. S. and Tomlinson, 85, 86
Falkbeer and Campbell, 78, 79
Falkbeer and Lowenthal, 57—59, 76—
  78
Fedden and Sir T. Metcalf, 142, 143,
  144
Fedden and Thorold, 186, 187, 268,
  269
Fenton, Briggs, and Cooper v. Berry,
  Meeker, and Selkirk, 145
Fenton and Wayte, 214, 215
Green, S. J., and Steinitz, 362, 363
"Gamma" and Staunton, 90—92
Hamel and Drew, 338, 339
Hampton, Steinitz, and Medley v.
  Kennedy, Ranken, and Lowenthal,
  208—210
Hannah and Lowe, 80—83
Jones and Cronhelm, 56, 57

Kempe and Dubois, 87—89
Kennedy, Ranken, and Lowenthal v.
  Hampton, Steinitz, and Medley,
  208—210
Kennedy and Wayte, 179—181
Kolisch and Schumoff, 21, 22
London and Dublin, 213, 214
Lord Lyttelton and Chinnery, 300—
  304
Lowe and Hannah, 80—83
Lowenthal and Falkbeer, 57—59, 76—
  78
Lowenthal, Kennedy, and Ranken v.
  Hampton, Steinitz, and Medley,
  208—210
Lowenthal and Owen, 185, 186
Lowenthal and Sich, 141, 142, 146,
  147
Lowenthal and Stewart v. Ranken and
  Wayte, 48, 49
Lowenthal and Wayte, 16—18, 50, 51,
  150, 151
MacDonnell and De Vere, 207, 208,
  306
MacDonnell and Minchin, 263—265
MacDonnell and Steinitz, 339, 340
Mackenzie and Reichhelm, 148, 150
Medley, Hampton, and Steinitz v.
  Kennedy, Ranken, and Lowenthal,
  208—210
Metcalf, Sir T., and Fedden, 142—144
Meyer and Mr. ———, 304—306
Minchin and De Vere, 362
Minchin and MacDonnell, 263—265
Minchin and Steinitz, 216—218
Mocatta and Steinitz, 340—343
Moffatt and William v. Weaver and
  E——n, 86, 87
Morphy and De Rivière, 74—76
Mortimer and Rosenthal, 211—213
Neumann and Anderssen, 53, 54, 89, 90
Owen and Lowenthal, 185, 186
Owen and Skipworth, 337, 338
Ranken, Kennedy, and Lowenthal v.
  Hampton, Steinitz, and Medley,
  208—210

Ranken and Wayte v. Lowenthal and Stewart, 48, 49
Ranken and Wayte, 18—20, 111, 115, 117, 332—336
Reichhelm and Mackenzie, 148—150
Rhodes and Wayte, 367, 368
Robey and Steinitz, 51, 52
Rosenthal and Mortimer, 211—213
Schamoff and Kolisch, 21, 22
Selkirk, Berry, and Meeker v. Fenton, Briggs, and Cooper, 115
Sich and Lowenthal, 141, 142, 146, 147
Skipworth and Owen, 237, 238
Skipworth and Wayte, 139—141, 266—268
Staunton and "Gamma," 90—92
Steinitz and Anderssen, 235—244, 269—280, 294—300
Steinitz and De Vere, 10—16, 37—48, 71—73, 244—251
Steinitz and Green, S. J., 362, 363
Steinitz and MacDonnell, 339, 340
Steinitz, Medley, and Hampton v. Kennedy, Ranken, and Lowenthal, 208—210
Steinitz and Minchin, 216—218

Steinitz and Mocatta, 340—343
Steinitz and Robey, 51, 52
Stewart and Lowenthal v. Ranken and Wayte, 48, 49
Stewart and Mr. ———, 113, 114
Taylor, G. H. and Watkinson, 142, 143
Thorold and Fedden, 186, 187, 268, 269
Thorold and Wayte, 181—184, 215, 216
Tomlinson and E. S., 85, 86
Watkinson and G. H. Taylor, 142, 143
Wayte and Fenton, 214, 215
Wayte and Kennedy, 179—181
Wayte and Lowenthal, 16—18, 50, 51, 150, 151
Wayte and Ranken, 18—20, 111, 115, 332—336
Wayte and Ranken v. Lowenthal and Stewart, 48, 49
Wayte and Rhodes, 367, 368
Wayte and Skipworth, 139—141, 266—268
Wayte and Thorold, 181—184, 215, 216
Weaver and E———n v. Williams and Moffatt, 86, 87
Williams and Moffatt v. Weaver and E———n, 86, 87

OPENINGS.

King's Knight's Game—
  Evans' Gambit, 19, 48, 51, 113, 116, 145, 149, 181, 186, 211, 213, 216, 235, 238, 243, 272, 275, 278, 332, 335, 338
  Evans' Gambit declined, 364
  Giuoco Piano, 21
  Petroff's Defence, 83, 142, 302
  Phillidor's Defence, 54, 84, 339
  Ruy Lopez Knight's Game, 53, 76, 78, 89, 139, 140, 148, 244, 248, 252, 265, 266, 267, 290, 300, 337
  Scotch Gambit, 306
  Two Knights' Defence, 16, 115
King's Bishop's Game—
  Bishop's Opening, 143

King's Gambit—
  Allgaier Gambit, 50, 183, 268, 367
  Knight's Gambit, 74, 237, 241, 27, 277
  King's Gambit declined, 208, 263, 297, 368
  King's Bishop's Gambit, 150, 215

Queen's Gambit—
  Queen's Gambit, 180
  Queen's Gambit declined, 179

French Opening, 57, 81, 86, 207, 247
Sicilian Opening, 56, 80, 269, 294, 304
Fianchetto, 185, 250
Hampe's Opening, 85
Queen's Bishop's Pawn Opening, 111

GAMES AT ODDS.

Pawn and Move, 10, 12, 14, 37, 39, 40, 43, 44, 45, 47, 71, 72, 88, 101, 102, 214, 340, 343
Pawn and Two Moves, 90, 141, 146, 362, 363

INDEX.

PROBLEMS.

Alexander, 121, 222, 255
Bayer, C., 94, 156, 308, 345, 372
Beck, A., 344
Brewster, E. W. S., 26, 60
Browne, 256
C. W., of Sunbury, 28, 61
E. B. C., of Hoboken, 189
Graves, J. A., 95
Heath F., 283
Keller, 256
Klett, 293, 254, 308
Kockelkorn, 26, 122, 254, 309

Kohtz, 310, 373
Landesmann, H. 189
Loyd, S., 188
Martini, W., 345
Mehrtens, G., 255, 346
Meyer, H., 223, 284, 309, 346, 374
Minckwitz, J., 373
Smith, T., 27, 60, 93, 121, 157, 188, 222, 283, 310
Stavenuiter, H. A., 344, 874
Volange, L., 372
Vorwerk, 282

SUICIDAL PROBLEMS.

Wayte, W., 62, 124

CHESS STUDIES.

"Euclid," 312—317, 348—350, 359, 362
Horwitz, 284, 347
Kling, 28, 96, 158, 224
Lowenthal and Ward, 123
Meyer, H., 311

Pierce, W. T., 95, 123, 159, 190, 224, 311
Rainger, G. F., 62
Smith, T., 190, 347
Ward and Lowenthal, 123
Watkinson, 124

MISCELLANEOUS.

A Collection of 200 Chess Problems, Composed by F. Healey, Esq., 133—138, 171—178
Annual General Meeting of the St. James's Chess Club, 23, 24
Bath and Bristol Chess Clubs, 92, 93, 118, 119
Birmingham and Edgbaston Chess Clubs, 63, 329
Blackheath Chess Club, 9, 153, 154
"Blackwood on Chess," 97
Brighton Chess Club, 328
Bristol Athenæum Chess Club, 320
Cardiff Chess Club, 156
Chess Association at Redcar, 25
Chess Directory, 151
Chess and Gymnastics, 257
Chess in Hungary, 120
"Chess in India," 84, 100
City of London Chess Club, 119
Croydon Workmen's Club, 220, 320
Dublin Chess Club, 22
Eastbourne Chess Club, 192
Everton Chess Club, 328
Healey's Problems, 96, 205
Hirschfeld and St. Bon, 192

Huddersfield Chess Club, 104, 105, 328, 371
Illegal Moves, 321—325, 353—359
Ipswich and Colchester Chess Clubs, 220
Letter from "Eva," 206
London Chess Club, 371
Match between Anderssen and Steinitz, 92, 156, 164, 234
Match between Birmingham and Worcester, 152
Match for Championship of the United States, 120
Match by Correspondence between New York and Kingstown, 114
Match between Glasgow and Dundee Chess Clubs, 191
Meeting of the North Yorkshire and Durham Association, 154
New York Chess Club, 93
   „   Tournament, 120
Norfolk Chess Association, 119, 131, 169
Playing for a Man's Head, 221
"Ponziani," by D. F., 231
Problem Tourney, 120

Retirement of Mr. Lowenthal from the *Era* Newspaper, 154
Review of 1865, 1
Saint James's Chess Club, 92
"Shakespeare's Silence about Chess," 193, 196
"Sociable Chess," 89
Telegraph Match between Dublin and London, 67
Termination of the Match between De Vere and Steinitz, 59
Termination of the Match between Bird and Steinitz, 369
"Theory and Practice," 65
"The British Chess Association," 161
The British Chess Association, 24, 68, 119, 171, 192, 196, 232, 307
Ditto General Meeting, 107, 109, 110, 111
Ditto, Problem Tournament, 138, 155, 192, 230
The Chess Congress of 1866, 105
The English Challenge Cup, 225

"The Limitation of Time," 129
"The Match between Anderssen and Steinitz," 289
"The New Scheme of Tabular Chess Notation," 4, 36
"The late Redcar Meeting," 330
"The Relative Value of the Chess Pieces," 165
The Return Match between the Worcester and Birmingham Chess Clubs, 221
The Sheffield Athenæum Chess Club, 92, 152, 218, 328, 332
"The Two Knights' Defence," 33, 202
Ditto, New Variation, 132
"War Chess," 293
Waters, N. R., 260
Westminster Chess Club, 234, 307
West Yorkshire Chess Association, 144, 170, 219
"Why not?" 228
Wolverhampton and Stourbridge Club, 371

SOLUTIONS TO PROBLEMS.

Nos.	page
61—63	64
64—73	125, 126
74—77	159, 160
78—85	285—287
86—93	317—319
94—100	351, 352
101—104	375
105—108	376
109—112	377

SOLUTIONS TO CHESS STUDIES.

Nos.	page	Nos.	page
11—14	126—128	21	319
15, 16	160	22, 23	352
17—20	287, 288	24—27	378

SOLUTIONS TO SUICIDAL PROBLEMS.

No. 8 . . page 129 | No. 9 . . page 288

. Extra sheet after page 32—Tabular notation.

LATEST INTELLIGENCE.

THE BATH CHESS CLUB.—The annual meeting of this Society was held a few weeks ago at the Literary Institution (Post Office), under the able presidency of Captain H. A. Kennedy. After the usual routine business, votes of thanks to the officers, &c., it was resolved that the original scale of subscription for members of the Institution and non-members should be continued. The following gentlemen were elected as officers of the club for the ensuing year:—Captain H. A. Kennedy, President; Thomas Jolly, Esq., F. Wilkinson, Esq., Edmund Thorold, Esq., M.A., President of the Bristol Chess Club, Vice-Presidents; Mr. Thomas Gosse, Hon. Treasurer and Secretary. A cordial vote of thanks to the President was unanimously agreed to. It is gratifying to state that the Bath Chess Club is in a healthy and prosperous condition. Fostered by the talent it is privileged to possess in the persons of its President and Vice-Presidents, a marked improvement has taken place in the general play, and several young members are developing into strong players, to their advantage, let us hope, at the next friendly tournament between Bath and Bristol.

CLERKENWELL WORKING MAN'S CHESS CLUB.—We are glad to hear that a Chess Club under the above title has just been founded at 46, Lower Rosoman-street, Clerkenwell. Being one of the most populous parishes in London, the foundation of this Club affords additional evidence of the interest now taken in Chess by all classes of society.

CHURCH OF ENGLAND YOUNG MEN'S SOCIETY, 169, FLEET-STREET, LONDON, E.C.—A Chess Club has just been formed in connection with this Society.

We regret to announce the demise of Herr George Schultz, of Hanover, a Chess-player of no ordinary ability. Some of Mr. Schultz's variations were embodied in Heydebrand's *Handbuch* (fourth edition). Mr. Schultz was a gentleman of great wealth and influence, and took great interest in all branches of science and art. He built an astronomical observatory at Hanover at his own expense, which bears the inscription, "George Schultz, wine merchant, botanist, natural philosopher, astronomer, African traveller, poet, and Chess-player." Mr. Schultz was the original promoter of the Hanover Zoological Gardens, opened in May of last year.

We regret to state that Captain James Cunningham, for many years known as an enthusiastic and also skilful amateur of our game, died suddenly at the Westminster Chess Club. In his early days the Captain obtained some reputation as the opponent of the late Mr. Williams.

TO CORRESPONDENTS.

CHESS DIRECTORY.—We beg to acknowledge with thanks contributions from the following gentlemen:—

Geo. Peake, Esq., Abergavenny; Hon. Sec., Glasgow Chess Club; Thos. Long, Esq., Dublin Chess Club; S. J. Kempson, Esq., Birmingham Chess Club; Hon. Sec., Abingdon Chess Club; J. Haselgrave, Esq., Leicester; William Hodges, Esq., Reading and Berkshire Chess Clubs; T. H. Hopwood, Esq., Everton Chess Club, Liverpool; William Berry, Esq., Bristol Athenæum; H. T. Swain, Esq., Penzance; J. J. Champion, Esq., Sheffield Athenæum; H. Household, Esq.,

King's Lynn; J. F. Gillam, Esq., Worcester; W. Hannay, Esq., Leamington; Nelson Fedden, Esq., Cardiff; Rev. S. W. Earnshaw, Birmingham; A. Bird, Esq., Stamford; George Macaskie, Esq., Berwick; T. J. Greenfield, Esq., Clifton; John Watkinson, Esq., Huddersfield; J. B. Fraser, Esq., Dundee; Chas. Bovern, Esq., Westgrove, Bristol; F. G. Rainger, Esq., Norfolk and Norwich Chess Club; Hon. Sec., London Chess Club; Hon. Sec., St. George's Chess Club; Hon. Sec., St. James's Chess Club; Hon. Sec., Blackheath Chess Club; M. German Rösing, Durango, Mexico; M. Jean Pretl, Paris; M. G. Schnitzler, Dusseldorf; M. Julius Asbeck, junr., Barmen, Germany; T. M. Sargent, Esq., Georgetown, Demerara; N. T. W., Baltimore, W.S.; E. D. D., Fassin, Liège, France; Signor José S. Fabregas, Tarragona, Spain; M. J. Berger, Graz; M. J. Noordberger, Amsterdam; M. A. v. Leitner, Tessin; M. E. Hammacher, Cologne; M. A. Stohr, Zittau; M. E. Dornstein, Nordhausen; M. Scheibler, Aachen; M. Fasching, Ansbach; M. H. Specht, Glogan; Dr. A. Schliemann, Schwerin; M. J. A. Petrenz, Insterburg; M. R. Pfau, Magdeburg; M. C. Schiemann, Memel; M. G. Kirschke, Görlitz; M. E. Hartwich, Hamburgh; M. C. Schultz, Hanover; M. Schmidt, Wittenberge; Sec., Rehrorter; the Editors of *Bell's Life*, *Evening Bulletin*, *New York Clipper*, *Neue Berliner Schachzeitung*, *Schachzeitung* (Leipzig), *La Sphinx*, *Illustrirte Zeitung*.

TO COMPETITORS OF THE PROBLEM TOURNAY, BRITISH CHESS ASSOCIATION.— You are reminded that in accordance with the programme of this Tournay, contributions should be sent in not later than the 1st January, 1867.

R. M. T. (Blackheath Chess Club).—Many thanks for your analysis, which fully corroborates the opinion that we gave at the thirteenth line of page 328 in our first volume. We regret that from pressure of business we were unable to answer your kind communication before this; your variation is, we fancy, conclusive.

C. B., Olmutz.—Has our communication reached you?

Hon. Secretary, Sheffield; E. T., Bath; G. W., London; N. R. W., Baltimore; J. C. R., Kingston, U.S.—We have received your contributions, and beg to tender you our grateful acknowledgments.

F. R. D., Malvern.—The games are exceedingly interesting, and shall be published as soon as possible.

T. H. H., Liverpool.—Delayed but not forgotten. You shall hear from us shortly.

G. S.—Your valuable budget has just reached us. Many thanks.

W. B., Bristol.—The matter shall receive our best consideration.

G. S., Düsseldorf.—We cannot adequately express our thanks for your valuable contribution. We look forward to receiving your next budget at your convenience, when perhaps you will kindly send the parcel by the book-post (*unter-kreutzband*) with the ends open, so as to avoid the heavy rate of letter-postage.

G. R. N.—We have received your *cartel*, published in the September number of the *Neue Berliner Schachzeitung*, but at the last moment; you may be sure that it shall receive the consideration which it deserves.

C. R. T., Herr K., G. W. M. (London Club), T. S.—The Problem by Mehrtens, which you so much commend, has already received the universal panegyric of good players. It is indeed a masterpiece of strategy.

www.ingramcontent.com/pod-product-compliance
Lightning Source LLC
Chambersburg PA
CBHW030347230426
43664CB00007BB/558